# EASTERN TOUR (Continued)

MIDDAUGH MANSION
(Notre Dame School) ________ 43.2
(E past Clay St. with Hinsdale Museum r ½ block, to Symonds, EN to Walnut, E to Oak, S to:

HINSDALE HOSPITAL ________ 44.9
(S to 3rd, W to Oak, S to 6th, past W. Robbins house at 425 E. 6th, on to County Line Rd., S to 59th and:

KATHERINE LEGGE LODGE ________ 46.8
(S to Plainfield Rd., W past International Harvester Agriculture Engineering Center, to Cass, S to North Frontage Rd.; W to:

MADDEN MANSION
(Aylesford Center) ________ 52.3
(E to Cass, S, past Waterfall Glen Forest Preserve, to:

ARGONNE NATIONAL LABORATORY
(Visitor's Center) ________ 54.6
(N to 75th at NW corner and:

LACE SCHOOL
(Darien Historical Museum) ________ 57.6
(N past 55th to Dallas St., E to Linden, N to 117 S. and:

WILLIAM L. GREGG HOUSE
(Westmont Historical Museum) ________ 60.4
(N to Richmond, W. to Cass, N to Burlington Ave., W to Fairview, N past Hummer Park, to Wilson, W to Douglas and:

ST MARY'S CHURCH
(OF GOSTYN) ________ 62.2
(S to Rogers, E to Maple, SW to 831 and:

BLODGETT HOUSE
(Downers Grove Historical Museum) ________ 63.1
(W, past old Lincoln School, to Main, N past Downers Grove cemetery at 63.5 to Prairie, W to Seeley, N to 4437 and:

St. Joseph Church at Franklin
James Breasted House at 4629 Highland

DOWNER HOUSE AND WELL ________ 64.9
(S to Grant, E to Linscott, S to Warren, E to:

Downers' Cemetery at 4524 Linscott
Prince Pond at Franklin

THE DICKE TOOL CO. ________ 66.0
(E to Forest, S to Gilbert, W to past Gilbert Park, to Cornell, S to Hitchcock, W to Belmont, N to Haddow, W past Puffer School to:

OLD CHICAGO GOLF CLUB
(Downers Grove Golf Course) ________ 68.2
(E to Belmont, N to Finley Rd., N to Butterfield Rd., W .7 to:

STRONG'S HILL
(Hidden Lake Preserve) ________ 72.0
(W to Park, N to 22nd, W to Lambert and:

C.O.D. ________ 74.7

# DuPage Roots

Richard A. Thompson
& Contributors

Published by the DuPage County Historical Society

Library of Congress
Catalog Card No. 84-070877

Printed in the U.S.A.
Second printing, 1985

# Contents

Richard A. Thompson has been a DuPage County resident since 1964, during which time he has served as pastor of the Southminster Presbyterian Church, Glen Ellyn. He also developed and taught the course in county history at the College of DuPage; wrote a chapter for the county's bicentennial volume *DuPage Discovery — 1776–1976;* and authored *Around the Arboretum* for the DuPage County Historical Society.

# PREFACE

The fiftieth anniversary of the founding of the DuPage Historical Society — the first board of directors was selected in 1935 — provides the occasion for this updated history of the county. Beyond marking this event, however, there is a need for a systematic survey which summarizes the early days and especially highlights the post–World War II era, when 75 percent of DuPage development has occurred. The last thorough treatment of this subject was *DuPage County Guide,* prepared through the Federal Writers' Project in the 1930s as part of the American Guides Series and published in 1948. This valuable volume, however, not only is out of print, but predates the major change.

*DuPage Discovery 1776–1976,* published by the county's bicentennial commission in 1977, did contain coverage of recent events. But at the time it was in preparation, a number of localities were sponsoring bicentennial research projects and publications which have been awaiting incorporation into a unified presentation.

*DuPage Roots* has been written to meet this need. The first part of the book presents a consecutive narrative in order to give the reader an overview of the past. The second part consists of local highlights, with contributions from twenty-six communities which have historical societies and which are located mostly in DuPage. Their cooperation in this project has made for a unique, unified effort, which serves both historical and community-building interests.

After editing the material presented by each of the contributors to coordinate both form and substance, I am appreciative of the time and care volunteered for this common enterprise. I am also grateful for their having gathered pictorial material from their areas, thus augmenting the graphic value of the volume.

The original art for the cover and chapter headings of Part One is the result of David S. Burnside's willingness to give of his professional expertise. From his mural studio in Bensenville, this county resident brought forth images to share with posterity out of a devotion to the DuPage heritage. Likewise, the drafting skills of Mark Ravanesi were made freely available in the series of four maps in the first chapters as well as in the motor tour map of the county. That visual aid supplements my written identification of the places that can be visited in a day's time, in order to give the history a concrete form.

The broad base of support, which has made this undertaking even more of a joint venture, includes Marilyn Claus, a native of Downers Grove, who has served as research assistant in many varied ways. Louise Spanke, of the DuPage Historical Museum staff, has most graciously read through the whole of the manuscript to offer suggestions, as has Joanne Dutcher Maxwell. To George Ware of the Morton Arboretum, Terry Allen and Frank Bellinger of the College of DuPage for their critique of different chapters in Part One I am grateful. Others who have provided commentary on the local highlights include Wayne Benson, Lee Hestermann, Joe McHaley, Leonne Schmidt, Virginia Stewart, Genevieve Towsley, Leon Werch, Rita Martin, and Becki Wilhelmi. Ann Dirks, Howard Lytle, Bernice Pond, and Jean Rathje have kindly proofread various parts of the text.

The full staff of the county museum, under Pat Wallace, has been most cooperative, as have those of the Forest Preserve District of DuPage County and the DuPage County Development Department. Without the financial underwriting of the DuPage Historical Society and the guidance of Joyce Usher in the publishing technicalities, this publication would not have been possible. Typist Dolores Kiesel has also provided indispensable service.

A final word is in order about the sources. The author trusts that this work will be useful in the classroom. Thus I have attempted to compile as comprehensive a bibliography as possible in a section which also includes audiovisual and oral materials. The listing of museums/societies is, likewise, intended to lead the inquirer to other materials.

Yet *DuPage Roots* is meant also for the general reader. My references and those of the contributors are contained in the sources section rather than through footnotes, thus facilitating narrative flow. Moreover, duplication has been avoided by listing primary sources only once, under the heading of general bibliography. Works by Richmond and Vallette, Blanchard, Bateman and Selby, Knoblauch, Maas and Weber have been used repeatedly in Part One and by most contributors in Part Two. Only the material used exclusively in a particular chapter or contribution is cited in connection with that portion of the book.

This volume comes to you with the hope that the citizens of each DuPage community may have a greater sense of the whole; that those outside the area may have a keener appreciation of the county's uniqueness; that present and future generations may have a keener understanding of their roots in the past.

Richard A. Thompson

# Part I

# Overview

BY RICHARD A. THOMPSON

*Prehistoric Scene.*

# CHAPTER 1 Earth Making

## NATURAL HISTORY

## to 10,000 B.C.

Roots — both of plants and people — depend on the soil. So the history of DuPage, like all accounts of origins, must begin with the making of the earth itself. The ground beneath tells its story in the rocks.

### ROCK BOTTOM

The deepest layer, over 4,000 feet deep and into billions of years past, is granite. The granite expanse of the Precambrian Age is called the Canadian Shield. It extends into the northern reaches of the North American continent. Geologists have concluded that this bedrock represents roots of mountains which arose and wore away over eons of time.

An account of subsequent rising and falling of the earth's surface, often lying below an inland sea and resulting in the sedimentary layers of the Cambrian-Ordovicion period, is beyond the scope of this narrative. But the overlying Niagara dolomite, curving as it does across the northern rim of the Great Lakes, requires special comment, for this limestone is popularly referred to as the bedrock. It is significant in both the geological and biological history of northern Illinois.

To delve 200 to 400 feet below the surface is simultaneously to rewind time some 400 million years. That was the era of the Silurian Sea, of a tropical climate, of crustacian forms, crinoids, and other sea creatures whose limey (calcium carbonate) remains sank to the bottom and over millions of years accumulated to a vast bulk. As other tropical debris, mud, and ferns weighed on top, limestone was formed from the compression.

The climate was tropical because of the land's location at that time toward the globe's equator, with all continents joined in the one great landmass called Pangea. What was to

*A post-glacial landscape. The receding wall of ice is followed by the taiga, a moist forest of spruce and fir.*
*Art by Wayne Lampa*
*Courtesy Forest Preserve District of DuPage County*

become northern Illinois once had all the layers of the later geological epochs, such as the Mississippian coal deposits of 270 million years ago. But why does southern Illinois retain these strata and not the land below DuPage?

The difference is due to Pangea's breaking up 200 million years ago, and the North American continent drifting in a northwesterly direction. The landmass was not only heading in that direction but also tilting upward at its northern end, while central and southern Illinois came to reside in a basin. As northern Illinois became more and more exposed above sea level, the elements eroded the surface, wearing it down to the limestone base and completely weathering away hundreds of millions of years of geological history piled on top of the dolomite.

This was the scene a relatively short one million years ago. The DuPage vicinity looked the way the Galena area does today, with its high limestone hills and cliffs. Only that "driftless" region escaped the bulldozing and valley-filling effects of the glaciers from the north.

## MOUNTAINS OF ICE

The Ice Age, technically called the Pleistocene Epoch, was one in which massive mountains of ice covered the region for several million years. Mile-deep ice generated seventy-five tons of pressure per square foot, creating a heat so intense that the underside of the glacier melted, causing it to slide to the south. All was leveled and flattened in its path; at the same time clay, sand, and gravel were transported in frozen form from lands to the north. Igneous and metamorphic rocks not native to the area are called erratics. The largest known erratic in the county is the granite boulder along Big Rock Trail on the east side of the Morton Arboretum. As tall as a person and twice as deep below the soil, it was a "fellow traveler" that came with the glacier. The glacial debris is unevenly distributed, varying from a few to two hundred feet deep. There are, however, limestone outcroppings at the surface in some parts of the county.

The last glacial lobe followed the natural depression carved by its predecessors, which later became Lake Michigan. Some 100,000 years ago this final glaciation started into the area. After moving laterally as far as today's West Chicago, the glacier began to melt, leaving a series of north-to-south ridges called moraines. This new mass consisted of clay, sand, and gravel. The moving ice acted like a conveyor belt, its flow and melt balanced, depositing drifts and building the ridges. Thus the topography of DuPage is defined by the terminal moraines from west to east, now called the West Chicago, Wheaton, Keeneyville, Roselle, Valparaiso, and Tinley respectively. As the Wisconsin glacier finally retreated beyond the county 12,000 years ago, it left a series of shorelines.

The more extensive precursor of today's Lake Michigan is known as Lake Chicago. The glacial deposit left DuPage County with an average elevation of 750 feet, which is 152 feet higher than Chicago's Loop, which is on the old lake bed.

Two other results of the glacial action were the formation of the rivers and pockmarking of the land's surface. The West and East Branches of the DuPage River and Salt Creek followed the depressed areas between the moraines, where the meltwater was of such torrential force as to scour out the valleys. The gravel, the looser debris, was left strewn on the shoulders and floors of each valley. Such distribution accounts for the fact that 85 percent of the county's immediate subsurface consists mostly of clay, with scattered patches of silt and sand on upland moraines, while 15 percent consists of gravel along rivers and streams.

This distribution also accounts for the quarries' locations in the river valleys. For example, the Elmhurst & Chicago Stone Company's operation in Elmhurst is along Salt Creek; the one in Green Valley, along the East Branch; and the one at Warrenville Road, along the West Branch. In places the gravel lies as much as one hundred feet deep.

Early maps also show a thousand swamps, marshes, and bogs distributed over the 338 square miles of DuPage, all products of the glacier's carving. Likewise, bowl-shaped kettles were brought about as buried giant-sized ice cubes melted, causing the surrounding

*A glacial boulder. Downers Grove resident Marilyn Claus inspects the granite "erratic" on Big Rock Trail at the Morton Arboretum.*

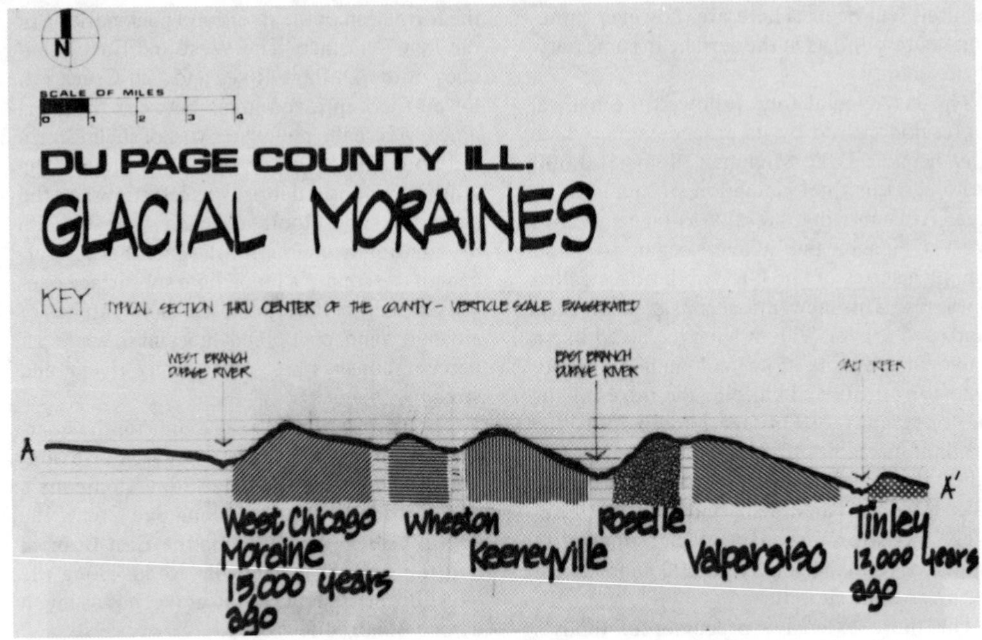


*Profile of DuPage Moraines. The moraines of the county are depicted in a cross-sectional view from west to east.*
*Art by Wayne Lampa*
*Courtesy Forest Preserve District of DuPage County*

gravel to cave in. A notable example may be found in the Maple Grove Forest Preserve in Downers Grove. The distinctive cavity (called the Sugar Bowl by local people) is about a hundred feet northwest of the footbridge over St. Joseph's Creek, off Gilbert Park.

No concluding word about the Pleistocene era would be complete without recognizing the massive, vital, and continuing effects of the glaciers on DuPage. Most water issues today are related to the primordial ice. The weight and pressure of the glacier was so great on the surface that it cracked the limestone layer beneath, thus creating the crevices which comprise much of the county's water-bearing strata called aquifers. The shallow dolomite wells provide 60 percent of the total water used today.

The glacial clay beneath the topsoil is generally impermeable. Saturation of the soil occurs easily and is followed by quick water runoff of rainfall and frequent flooding. However, in the river valleys the gravel substratum permits direct and continuing soaking into the aquifers, thereby replenishing the water supply. The implications of this landscape feature for current water-related issues will be discussed in the last chapter. But one recent incident has illustrated the continuing effect of the glacial outwash.

On the east side of the Morton Arboretum, Meadow Lake, which is situated in the gravels of the valley, began to recede mysteriously in the early 1980s. Its water had almost disappeared from view before an explanation was found. Across Route 53, in the Valley View subdivision, the utility company was constructing a lift-pump station. In order to install a concrete housing for the station, it was necessary to drop the water table by pumping. Because the stratum beneath the surface is gravel, the water table across the whole river valley dropped, thereby lowering the level of the lake dramatically, more than a thousand feet away. Cessation of pumping restored the lake's level.

Not the least of the glacial effects was the wind-blown loess, ground so fine as to give it

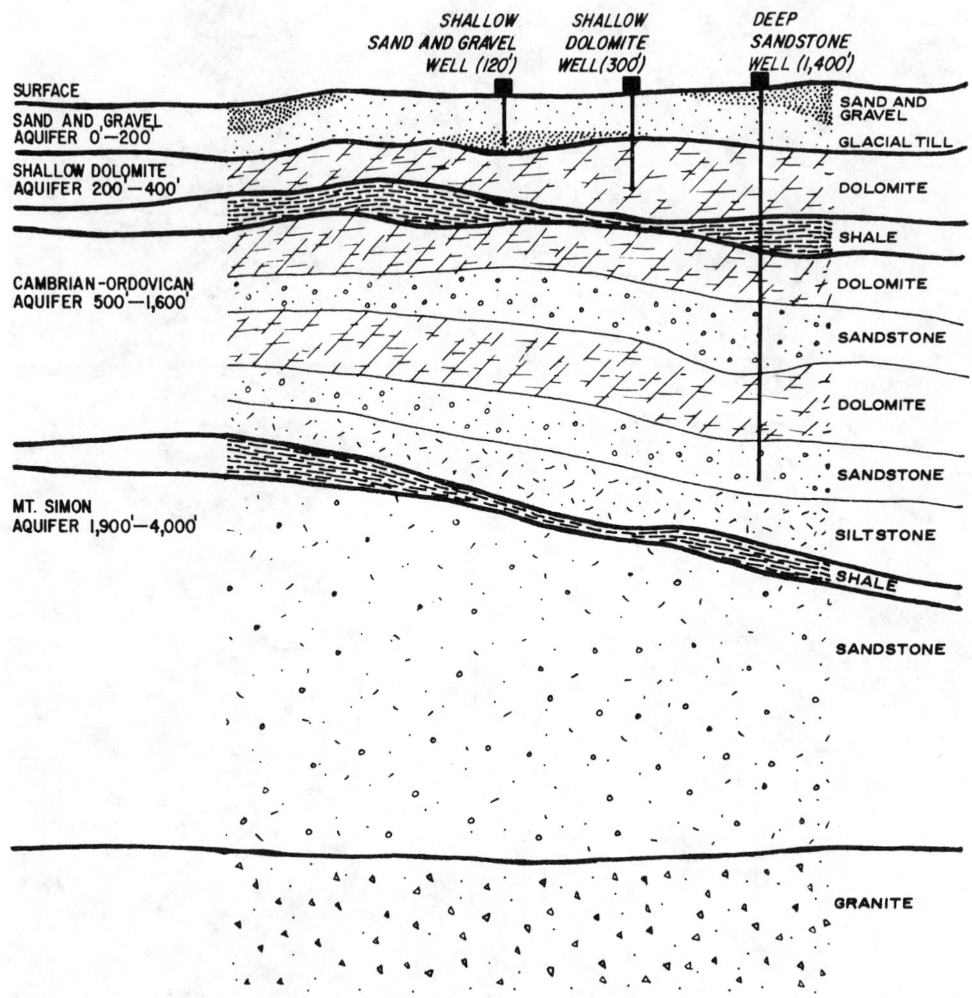


PRINCIPAL AQUIFERS (WATER-BEARING FORMATIONS) PROVIDING WATER SUPPLY IN DU PAGE COUNTY.
*Courtesy DuPage County Development Department*

nutrient value and distributed by the wind across the tundra and fir/spruce (taiga) forest which followed at the edge of the retreating ice sheet. But the richness of soil awaited the next and most distinctive process in Illinois earth making.

## HEAT AND GRASS

Ordinarily the hardwood trees would have succeeded the evergreens in this area, as elsewhere, as the climate warmed. But the climatic pendulum swung so far in that direction that DuPage became as dry as Nebraska is today. This hypsithermal period lasted for several thousand years, long enough to prevent the oaks, hickories, and maples from making their natural inroads north. This aridity provided the conditions necessary for prairie grass to spread from the west.

By 4000 B.C. the climate had become increasingly temperate, approaching its present characteristics, with an average of thirty-six inches of rain a year. The DuPage vicinity became part of the "Prairie Peninsula" in

*Torching a prairie. Wayne Lampa of the county forest preserve district begins the annual burn-off of a prairie restoration to eliminate European plants.*
*Courtesy Forest Preserve District of DuPage County*

*Perry Mastodon — on display at Wheaton College*
*Courtesy Wheaton College*

northern Illinois, for it is located on the edge of the prairie from the west and of the woodlands to the east, at the boundary of moisture streaming off the Gulf of Mexico and of the prevailing westerly winds. This intersection accounts for both the volatile weather and variety of plants.

The hardwoods resumed their northward march as moisture increased and would have displaced the prairie at this time, except for the introduction of a new factor — people. Newly arriving humans burned off the prairies to flush out game and make traveling easier. Only the heat-resistant burr oak on the uplands and protected groves along the rivers could survive the flames. About 85 percent of the county was prairie, and 15 percent oak and maple at the time of the first European settlement.

The topsoil of DuPage is so rich because of the organic matter from prairie plants. Their roots go as deep as fifteen feet, although the fertility develops primarily in the top two to three feet. The floodplain soil, which had run off from the ridges above, may have accumulated to a four-foot thickness, whereas on the hills it may average only six inches. Prairie ground is mollisol, a soft, black soil produced by the humus of thick grass roots, as distinct from the alfesols, characterized by high aluminum and iron content. These are the thinner, less fertile layers formed from the decomposing leaves of hardwood trees. It takes several thousand years to develop three feet of prairie topsoil but less than a day for it to be scraped off by a bulldozer. Native plants now are represented in only 1.5 percent of the county, having been replaced by European vegetation, which tends to be weedy.

An example of the fauna of prehistoric times is on display at Wheaton College's chemistry building. It is called the Perry Mastodon, because it was excavated in 1963 on the property of Judge Joseph Sam Perry in Glen Ellyn. Such creatures became extinct about 8,000 years ago.

Settlers found black bear, buffalo, cougars, timber wolves, soft shell turtles, and red squirrel. These animals are now extinct in a modern setting, having been replaced by rabbits and raccoons. Predatory birds have likewise increased, although 148 species of song birds may still be counted at Fullersburg Preserve. The Virginia white tail deer followed European migration from the east and are still to be found in the area's preserves.

Such was the place in which people were to come hunt, plant, and build — to put down roots of the community. That human story now commences.

*Blazing Lake Street.*

# CHAPTER 2 The Planting

## THE PIONEER EPOCH

## To 1850

The Indians, French trappers and traders, and nineteenth-century settlers from the eastern United States and trans-Atlantic countries comprised the cultural planting of DuPage County. The earliest Americans, originally from Asia, did the seeding on which the pioneers of European origin depended and to which they added. In fact, the influence of the Indians continues today in road patterns and in a landscape created by their fire practices.

### BLAZING TRAILS AND PRAIRIES

The periods of Indian habitation in the area may be summarized as follows:

Paleo—10,000–8000 B.C.
Archaic—8000–1000 B.C.
Woodland—1000 B.C.–A.D. 1673
Historic—A.D. 1673–1850

The story of the Paleo period begins when that of the glacier ends. As massive quantities of water were taken up into ice form, the ocean floor between Asia and North America lay exposed, forming a landbridge over which humans moved eastward. This connection across the Bering Straits, or Beringia as it is called, existed between 28,000 and 12,000 years ago.

These migrants were big game hunters. In the shadow of the melting ice mountains they pursued mammoths like the one unearthed at Roy C. Blackwell Forest Preserve in 1978. They hunted with Clovis or Fulsom points, first identified in New Mexico and dating from 12,000 B.C. Sanford Gates, in an *Illinois Archaeological Survey* article, identified thirty-two Indian sites in the DuPage River drainage, one of which—at the headwaters of the West Branch—was described as Paleo.

In 8,000 B.C., when the climate began to warm considerably, the Archaic period began.

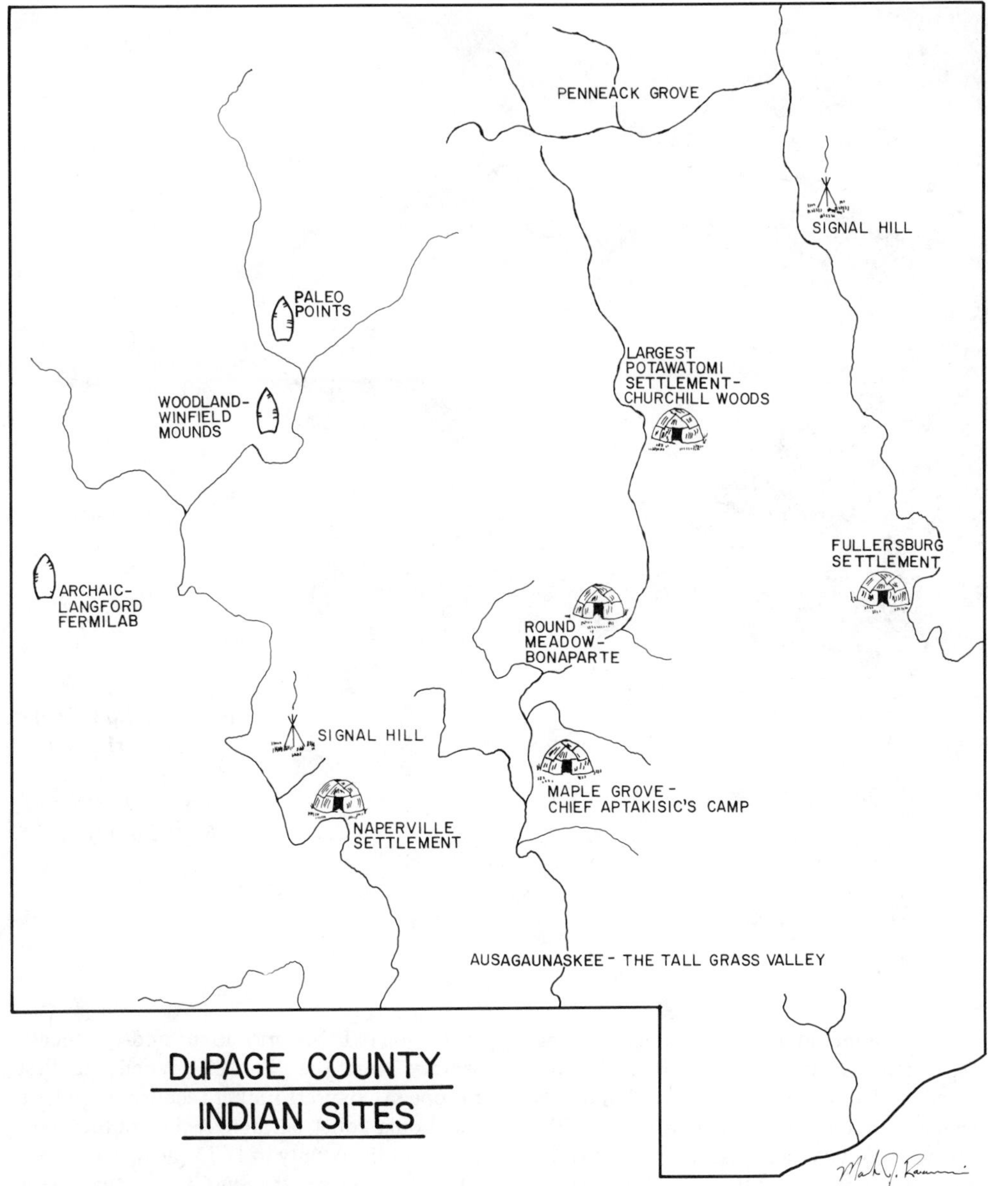


*Art by Mark Ravansei*

Life-style became less nomadic in river valleys to the south, and excursions into DuPage represented only temporary encampments, supporting the hunt for buffalo. As larger animals gave way to smaller game, new weapons evolved, such as spear throwers. An extensive dig on the grounds of the National Accelerator Laboratory in 1970 and 1971 revealed seventeen Archaic sites, dating from 6,500 B.C.. On the fifteenth floor of Fermilab is a public display of the finds.

The development of agriculture, pottery, and elaborate burial practices marked the change from the Archaic to the Woodland period. An archaeological excavation, which was under the auspices of Wheaton College

*Archaic Indian Scene. Art by Lori Schory Courtesy Forest Preserve District of DuPage County*

in 1975 in Winfield Township, unearthed the most extensive site of this period. In this project, called Du-33, three burial mounds were identified, covering the period from 300 B.C. to A.D. 700. Over a thousand artifacts and a variety of pottery represent this millennium of permanent settlement. Du-33 seems to have been the farthest north spillover of the Illinois River Valley civilization, which was in its most expansive stages at this time.

At the present site of Fermilab the Langford People, of the late Woodland period, resided on ten sites from the thirteenth to the early seventeenth century. Their globular-shaped pottery showed the advanced "state of the art," and their smaller triangular projectile points were shaped for bow-and-arrow use.

In the Historic era the predominant confederation of tribes prior to the mid-eighteenth century were the Iliniwek. When the first European explorers Father Jacques Marquette and Louis Joliet cut across the southeastern corner of the county in 1673, near the present site of St. James of the Sag Church, these were the "superior men" that they met.

It is ironic that in 1641, just a year after the French had initially heard of the Iliniwek, the first Potawatomi appeared at Sault St. Marie, the Jesuit-trader frontier outpost between Lake Superior and Lake Huron. The Potawatomi were of the Algonquian family, driven westward by the fierce Iroquois who were, in turn, yielding to the growing pressure of European settlement. The Potawatomi then moved south through Wisconsin, entered the Chicago area, and drove out the remnants of the Iliniwek.

*Artifacts spanning 8,200 years of Indian life — on display at Fermilab.*
*Courtesy of Fermi National Accelerator Lab*

*French fur trader. DuPage (the Anglicised form of DuPahze) traded at the forks of the two rivers subsequently named for him.*
*Art from* DuPage County Guide

By 1800 the Potawatomi had 6,000 people in fifty major villages, from Milwaukee around the bend of Lake Michigan to St. Joseph. In DuPage there were four major villages: one near Oak Brook on the Salt Creek, a second near Naperville on the West Branch, and others on the East Branch in the Morton Arboretum and in the Churchill Forest Preserve. The large settlement, just to the south of the Des Plaines River at the county's southeast border, was called Ausagaunaskee, "The Prairie," from which comes the term "The Sag." This was also the name of the spacious hunting grounds, which extended as far west as Churchill Woods.

The first European settlers in DuPage County found the Potawatomi a cooperative people who did not heed the call to join the Sauks during the 1832 Black Hawk War. Chief Black Hawk himself bore resentments as far back as 1803 because of the Treaty of St. Louis. Later, when the Indian Boundary Treaty had been established in 1816, tensions were further heightened. The boundary was a ten-mile-wide stretch of land, dedicated to a future canal, starting from the lake shore and extending southwest through the southeast section of Downers Grove Township and part of Lisle.

When word reached Naperville in May of 1832 that Black Hawk had launched an attack, the settlers fled to Fort Dearborn. Fort Payne was built by soldiers from Ottawa as protection for the settlers who returned after a month. The fort was located on the site of today's North Central College's athletic area.

By July General Winfield Scott had brought troops to Fort Dearborn. He led one contingent through Naperville on the way to Dixon, while most of his troops followed today's Lake Street and Army Trail Road. In August Black Hawk was defeated by Zachary Taylor at Bad Axe, Wisconsin. The Treaty of Chicago, of September 16, 1833, formalized the final removal of the Indians beyond the Mississippi River. Although there were still Potawatomis at the Round Meadow Village on the west side of today's Morton Arboretum in the 1840s, by the end of the pioneer era in 1850, virtually all of the natives were gone.

Their predecessors from time immemorial had blazed the trails which are still used today as Lake, St. Charles, Butterfield, Ogden, and Plainfield roads. The practice of setting the prairies ablaze to flush out game and improve traveling kept hardwood trees out and contributed to the soil's enrichment. The Potawatomi planted beans, peas, squash, and corn in the river valleys, near their domed bark, thatch, or hide-covered dwellings. They shared the fruits of their labor with the European pioneers in more than one way. That interaction will become apparent as the story of the county's name and earliest European settlers is told.

## THE FRENCH CONNECTION

The county took its name from the rivers, which were, in turn, named after a French fur trapper, DuPage. He established a trading post at the forks where the East and West Branch come together, four miles south of Naperville in today's Will County. A 1782 map, published in Steward's *Lost Maramech & Earliest Chicago,* identifies a "Lake DuPage" between the Fox River and Lake Michigan. Jean Baptiste Beaubien, who was trading in Illinois soon after the turn of the nineteenth century, recalled this old Frenchman who represented the

American Fur Trading Company of St. Louis for an indefinite time and whose departure was not recorded.

Jean Baptiste Beaubien and his brother Marc were to enter DuPage history again. But in the meantime these brothers of French-Canadian ancestry, whose family had moved to Detroit from Montreal in the eighteenth century, were to make a name for themselves in Chicago.

Jean Baptiste, after first coming to the newly built Fort Dearborn at the mouth of the Chicakajo River, had at one time been married to the sister of Potawatomi Chief Shabbona. After her death and by 1825, he had become the largest property owner in the hamlet at Fort Dearborn and successfully urged his brother to come from Detroit. In 1831 Marc opened the Sauganash Hotel, named after his friend Billy Caldwell, who was half Indian. It was there that Marc would not only entertain guests by playing the fiddle "like ze debble" but also that the election took place which made Chicago a village. During the Black Hawk War Jean Baptiste captained a company which did reconnaisance of the Naper settlement.

In 1840 Marc traded property at Lake and Wells streets for the 260-acre farm and tavern of William Sweet on the Lisle-Naperville border. In 1850 he operated a toll booth on the Southwestern Plank Road which ran in front of his establishment, a favorite spot for Indian visitors because the Beaubiens spoke their language. In 1858 Jean Baptiste moved to Naperville. Beaubiens were later buried in a family cemetery, located on the hill east of Yender Road and on the north side of Ogden Avenue.

The experience of this particular family typified the rapport that long had characterized French-Indian relations. The "coureurs de bois," as the traders/trappers were called, so assimilated with the Native Americans that, as one Quebec nun reportedly said, "It is

*Half Day's farewell. Potawatomi chief led early settlers to the safety of Fort Dearborn upon the outbreak of the Black Hawk War.*
*Art by Lester Schrader*
*Courtesy Naperville Heritage Society*

*Fort Payne — replica of the original, at the Naper Settlement restoration.*
*Courtesy Naperville Heritage Society*

*Beau Bien Tavern. Located by a toll gate on the Southwestern Plank Road.*
*Art by Lester Schrader*
*Courtesy Naperville Heritage Society*

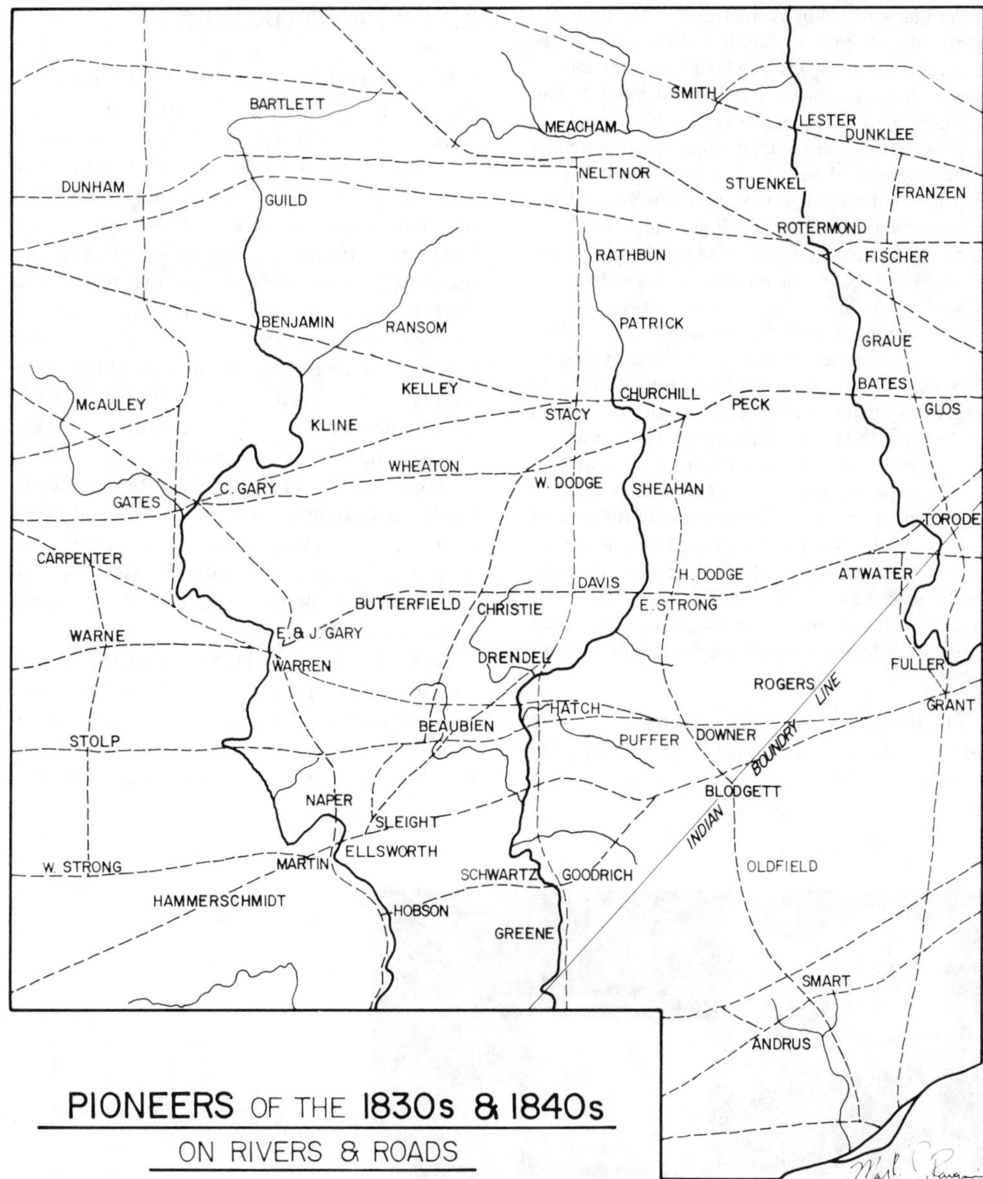


*Art by Mark Ravanesi*

easier for a Frenchman to learn to live like an Indian than for an Indian to live like a Frenchman."

Such friendship as that extended by Aptakisic, known also as Half Day, to the Yankee settlers in warning them of Black Hawk's impending attack and leading them to the safety of Fort Dearborn was all but forgotten in the rush to remove the Indians. Sixty years after the event, however, a distinguished Waukegan attorney, Henry Blodgett, son of DuPage pioneer Israel, would remember the kindness in a letter.

> About two o'clock in front of our cabin, on the morning of the 10th of May 1832, a loud shout or whoop was heard and on my father's opening the

door he was met by Aptakisic. He began to urge my father to take his family and start at once for the fort in Chicago. The whole family, of course, was aroused and with the aid of what Indian words we could muster we finally learned the cause of this solemn appearance—that there had been a council held that night at West Valley where Aurora now stands, between Black Hawk and a band of chiefs of the Potawatomi and Winnebago. They had been urged to join with Black Hawks's tribe in a general attack upon the white settlements in northern Illinois, but refused. As soon as the council broke up, he had mounted his horse and ridden as fast as he could by way of Naper Settlement to give the alarm so we might get away before the Sauks could get there.... In the fall of 1837, Aptakisic's band was removed to a reservation on the west side of the Missouri River near the mouth of the Platte and later were moved into what is now a portion of the state of Kansas, south of the Kansas River. I well remember the sad face of the old chief as he came to bid our family goodbye. . . . We all shed tears of genuine sorrow . . . his generous kindness to my parents has given me a higher idea of the red man's genuine worth.

The Blodgetts also came to symbolize those who would plant the seeds of conscience prior to the Civil War.

## RIVERS AND GROVES

When Israel Blodgett arrived at the fork of the DuPage River from Amherst, Massachusetts, in the early spring of 1831, he found the Stephen Scott family already settled. The Connecticut Yankees had in the 1820s been the first settlers to land and live at Grosse Point, now Evanston. But by 1830 they had made still another home by the rivers and groves where fur trapper DuPage had sojourned south of the present Will County border; thus he lost the distinction of being the county's first permanent European settler. That honor went to Bailey Hobson, a Quaker who set out armed only with a jacknife from Orange County, Indiana. He found shelter in the Scott settlement until he could build along what became Hobson Road in Naperville. With his Georgia-born wife Clarissa and five children he took up residence in the early spring of 1831.

By harvest of 1834 Hobson with the help of neighbors had erected on the West Branch of the DuPage River the only grist mill in northern Illinois. So long was the line of farmers waiting for their grain to be ground that Hobson's

*Joe Naper, Julius Warren, Warren Wheaton. These pioneers are among the notables featured in the DuPage Heritage Gallery at the DuPage Center.*

*Hobson's Mill. Only the grinding stones of Bailey Hobson's mill remain in Naperville's Pioneer Park; but the family home, far right, still stands.*
*Art by Lester Schrader*
*Courtesy of Naperville Heritage Society*

Greek Revival-style home doubled as a tavern.

One mile to the north the Naper settlement was well under way by that time. It was named for brothers Joseph and John who had sailed from Ashtabula, Ohio, on the *Telegraph,* a ship delivered to a purchaser in Chicago.

Among those who came as part of the Naper "colony" in July 1831 were Lyman Butterfield and Henry T. Wilson, who were to become Milton Township's first settlers in 1832; Robert Murray, who would later host Stephen Douglas in his 1841 home, now on display at the Naper Settlement restoration site; and William Strong, whose home on Eola and North Aurora Road would become a hideaway for runaway slaves prior to the Civil War. To the north of Strong, Frederick Stolp settled, after purportedly walking from Pultneyville, New York, to Illinois in 1834.

But it was Joseph Naper who proved to be the "Founding Father" of both his village and the county itself. He commanded the local militia, laid out the streets, and built a saw mill. Naperville was so thriving, with 180 settlers by the end of 1832, that it was the first town in Cook County to be chartered and was an even larger village than Chicago until 1836. By 1839 Naper was serving in the Illinois General Assembly, where he had formed a coalition with downstate legislators, including one Abraham Lincoln. As a result DuPage was among the counties detached from Cook, established on February 9, 1839, with Naperville as the county seat. But the northern half of Wheatland and DuPage townships remained part of Will County by one vote, for teetotalers there took offense at a voter from DuPage County who brought a bottle of whiskey to the polls.

The nearest neighbors to the Naper settlement upstream on the West Branch were the Warrens who, like the others who arrived early, claimed land in the groves where wood for building, fences, and fire was available. Father Daniel had taken possession of today's McDowell Woods in 1833; his son Julius established the village of Warrenville itself.

In 1834 Julius built a home which remains among the oldest still standing in the county. Across Batavia Road he erected a saw mill in 1835. In 1838 he constructed a tavern at the

*Gary's Mill.*
*Art by H. Gilbert Foote*

intersection of Warrenville and Winfield roads, which served as the connecting link between the Indiana and Wisconsin borders by way of St. Charles. Abel Carpenter had claimed the quarter section to the east of Winfield Road, married Julius Warren's sister Sarah, and eventually settled on a farm which is the site of today's Fermilab.

Brothers Erastus and Jude Gary preceded the Warrens by a year, traveling west in the most typical way, over the Erie Canal. Opened in 1825, this waterway provided the most direct route west from the northeastern states. Natives of Pomfret, Connecticut, where a road and school are still named after their forebears, the Garys staked claims to the east of Winfield Road and on both sides of Butterfield Road. Today's St. James Farm is situated on that homestead.

Another brother Charles, with other family members, arrived in 1837 and built a saw mill farther north on the West Branch. The vacated school, where sister Orinda had been the teacher, is all that remains of the Gary's Mill settlement, which was to be bypassed by the railroad. But before that happened Asel Gates and Mary Warne would be married in that school building, which doubled as a Methodist church. These offspring of pioneer families became the parents of the prominent industrialist John W. Gates.

George and Mary Miller McAuley were of Irish and Scottish descent; he had been educated as a Presbyterian minister. The school named after this family remains the only one-room school still in operation in DuPage County.

Another school, which is still in service, was named for Robert Benjamin, whose 1834 homestead was toward the headwaters of the West Branch in Wayne Township. But Wayne Center, the original village on the river, would by mid-century give way to Wayne Station, where the Galena & Chicago Union Railroad laid its tracks.

North of the headwaters of the East Branch, Vermonters Lyman, Harvey, Daniel, and Silas Meacham would locate in a grove to be named after them. Their nearest neighbor to the south was Lyman Butterfield, nine miles away. By 1842 Hiram B. Patrick, who previously had worked on the Erie Canal and as a lake captain, became a closer neighbor in the southern end of Bloomingdale Township. Two years later the Rowland Rathbuns took up residence at the dividing ridge between Lake Michigan and the Fox River. The Rathbun daughter gave birth to Cornelia, who eventually became Mrs. George Meacham. Much of Meacham's Grove is contained in today's Medinah Country Club.

Along the East Branch of the DuPage River, between the future sites of Glen Ellyn and Lombard, brothers Ralph and Morgan Babcock staked the first claim in 1833, an extensive enough claim for kinsmen and friends from Onondaga County, New York. Ralph's wife was a niece of Mrs. Deacon Winslow Churchill, who in turn was a sister of William Dodge.

Over the next two years these other families were to make homes in Babcock's Grove.

Churchill Woods Forest Preserve would be named after the 1834 arrivals, whose New York farm had been along the Erie Canal. The Churchills also had been neighbors of the Sheldon Pecks in Onondaga County. By 1837 the Pecks had built Lombard's oldest standing home at Grace and Parkside.

New Hampshire was represented by Luther and J. C. Hatch, who in 1832, after Bailey Hobson, were the next to settle in Lisle Township. They were located to the south of today's Morton Arboretum. Black Hawk War veterans Sherman King and Theron Parsons made a brief claim to those groves. After the former moved to Brush Hill and the latter to the Winfield area, these became woodlots for the incoming homesteaders.

Near the crossing of the East Branch with Hobson Road, the Goodrichs and Greenes were to live diagonally across from one another in what became Woodridge. Goodrich School continues at that intersection where Henry Goodrich had moved from Vermont in late 1832. Three years later Daniel Greene was to buy a quarter section in the Indian Boundary strip from the government. Thus, they did not have to await the validation of preemption claims as did of most pioneers in DuPage.

When Daniel's nephew William brought his new bride Harriet from Wallingford, Vermont, in 1845, she wrote a letter describing the trip on the Erie Canal. Her letter was recorded in *Greenes on the East Branch of the DuPage.* Her impressions were typical of the multitude who made their way west from Albany. During the week before reaching Buffalo, she was aboard with

> such a variety of characters as were assembled in the narrow limits of the boat... two grave Quaker ladies, a gouty old man, his difficult wife and daughter, two gay Frenchmen.... At Canal's end the dark, deep water of Erie lay before us.... The steamer then stopped at Cleveland, Detroit, arched over the Mackinac Straits, with Indian settlements visible along the eastern shore of Lake Michigan. Toward evening, we have a sight of the far famed Chicago to the West . . . calculated to make a Yankee feel not exactly at

*Babcock's Grove burial place. Forest Hill Cemetery contains the remains of families from the early days of the Glen Ellyn-Lombard area.*

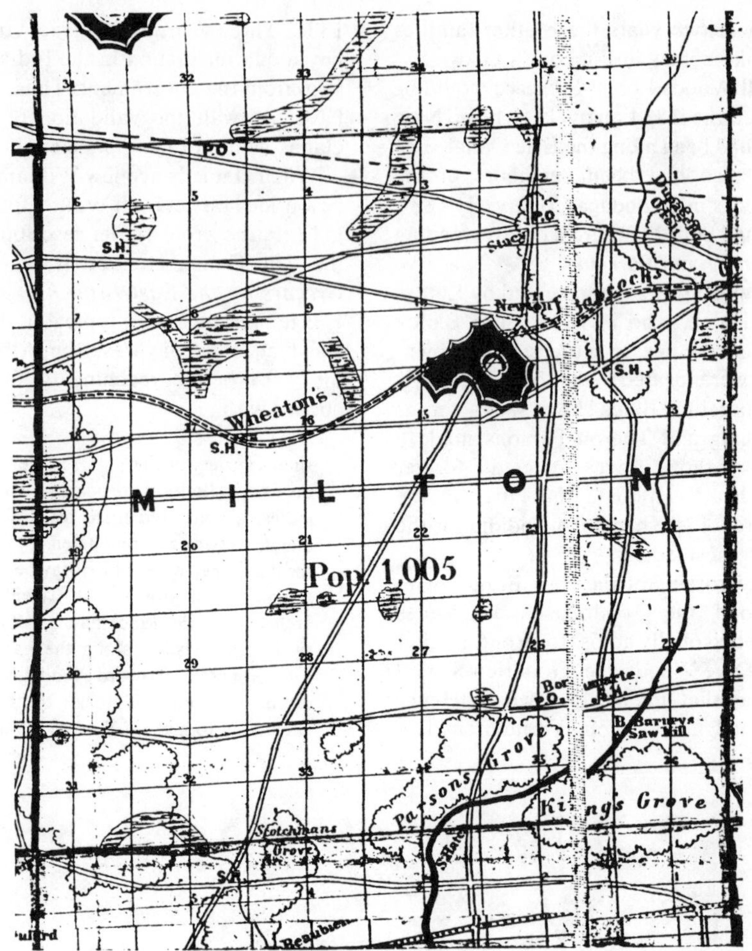


*Pioneers of the arboretum area. Rees' 1851 Map shows the settlements in and around today's Morton Arboretum.*
*Courtesy Chicago Historical Society*

home; a sandy plain . . . how unlike the East . . . twenty-six miles before us . . . we came to a rolling prairie . . . indeed pretty—saw a prairie hen, and a sandy crane. Had not the pleasure of encountering any wolves or snakes. 'Twas near dark and were glad to find ourselves in the last wood and soon turning from the main road to see a light at Uncle Daniel's. Met with a cordial reception, and . . . were glad . . . to indulge in the luxury of a featherbed.

No such luxury had awaited Sherman King in 1832 as he had returned to the site of the Potawatomi encampment to which Winfield Scott had sent him to scout, in what others of the militia would call Brush Hill. During the war King had helped evacuate the Naper settlers, including the Hobsons, to Fort Dearborn. But in the wake of the Treaty of Chicago, King established residence on the south end of Salt Creek before it veered eastward out of the county.

Soon after 1835 King collaborated with his new neighbor to the north, Nicholas Torode, in the construction of a saw mill. The latter's homestead, west of York's Roosevelt Road, was to be called Frenchman's Woods, because Torode was from the French-speaking Channel Island of Guernsey. He was the first in DuPage to quarry limestone. This building material King used in the construction of a saw mill on the Salt Creek. This was also the site of the future Graue grist mill.

The Frederick Graues of Hanover, Germany, arrived in the United States in 1833. After a year in Albany, New York, they moved farther west to claim land lying in both the future York and Addison townships and comprising a sizable portion of northern Elmhurst. Their son Ludwig, whose holdings along the east side of the Salt Creek included a quarry, would later sell that property to the Hammerschmidt family, who still own and operate the Elmhurst and Chicago Stone Company.

In 1838 another son Frederick moved to Brush Hill. After a fire destroyed the saw mill in 1847, he began erecting the Graue Mill. Completed in 1852, it was flourishing by 1858 and continued operation until the 1920s. To-

**DUNKLEE LOG CABIN**

*Art by Vivian Krentz*

*William Briggs and Harriet Elizabeth Meeker Greene — among the first to live in the Woodridge area.*
*from* The Greenes on the East Branch of the DuPage

day it is open to the public as a restored representation of that earlier era.

The heart of Addison Township contained the largest of the groves in the county, over three miles in length, and nearly a mile in width. It lay along the east bank of the Salt Creek, which received its name when a Hoosier team became stalled and the driver had to dump several barrels of salt to lighten the load. Like other early settlers who preferred the river bottoms where massive prairie grass did not have to be cut, Hezekiah Dunklee and Mason Smith were to stake claims there in 1833. In 1836 Dunklee, after whom the grove was named, planted three barrels of apples and thus started the first orchard in the county.

Others from New England soon to arrive included Edward Lester, who immediately built a fourteen- by-sixteen-foot board shanty. It required two weeks to prepare the rough white oak and a day to raise the home. There were no windows, only a hole in the wall, and a roof fashioned from prairie stalks. The fire in the hearth was used for heat, light, and cooking.

It was in a log house that daughter Julia was first to teach school in the township. In 1854 son Frederick married Ebenezer Dunklee's daughter Julia A., who had been the first white child born in the township.

German families came to predominate in Addison Township, and by 1870 more than half of the population were foreign-born. The Fischers and Franzens both came in 1837, the former to locate in the area called Churchville at the southern end of Dunklee's Grove. The Franzens settled farther north toward the later village of Bensenville. Henry Fischer would marry Maria Franzen. August Fischer married a daughter of the Glos', who had moved into the eastern end of the county along St. Charles Road in 1837. By this time the river bottoms were already claimed, and the latecomers had to settle for the higher prairie.

In that year, moreover, John Deere invented the self-scouring plow in his Grand Detour

*Graue Mill.*
*Art by H. Gilbert Foote*

blacksmith shop in western Illinois. He soon patented and mass produced this tool, which broke the prairie sod without the "gumbo," black clay soil, adhering to the blade as it did to a cast iron blade. Israel Blodgett, after moving his blacksmith's shop to Downers Grove in 1835, had also developed a similar plow to enable farmers to begin opening up the prairie in the 1840s, but he obtained no patent.

Also in the 1840s came initial institutional development. But the delineation of economic, political, and social change must await description of settlement along the county's early roadways.

## CROSSROADS

In Peck's *Traveler's Directory for Illinois for 1839* the earliest maps of settlements are shown. It is no accident that in DuPage these should be Brush Hill, Cass, Naperville, and Warrenville. In three of the four cases they were located where rivers and roads crossed. All the villages were along major road routes. Cass was the only one not on a main waterway, but it was located strategically on the Potawatomi thoroughfare, the "High Prairie Road," connecting Chicago to Ottawa. In 1831 the Cook County Board converted that Indian trail into a highway, calling it Plainfield Road: it later became U.S. Route 66.

The first stage coach operating west of Chicago, that of Dr. John L. Temple and soon purchased by Frink & Walker, made the initial run over this route in 1834. Thomas Andrus was quick to establish the Tremont Tavern at the place named Cass to serve the sixteen coaches a day. This native Vermonter had first come in 1833; he had helped to build the Tremont House in Chicago, from which he borrowed the name.

The other main route west entered DuPage near Salt Creek at Brush Hill, later Fullersburg. It followed the path which would become the Southwestern Plank Road and eventually Ogden Avenue. Naperville served as the connecting point of the routes that continue south

*Castle Inn.*
*Art by H. Gilbert Foote*

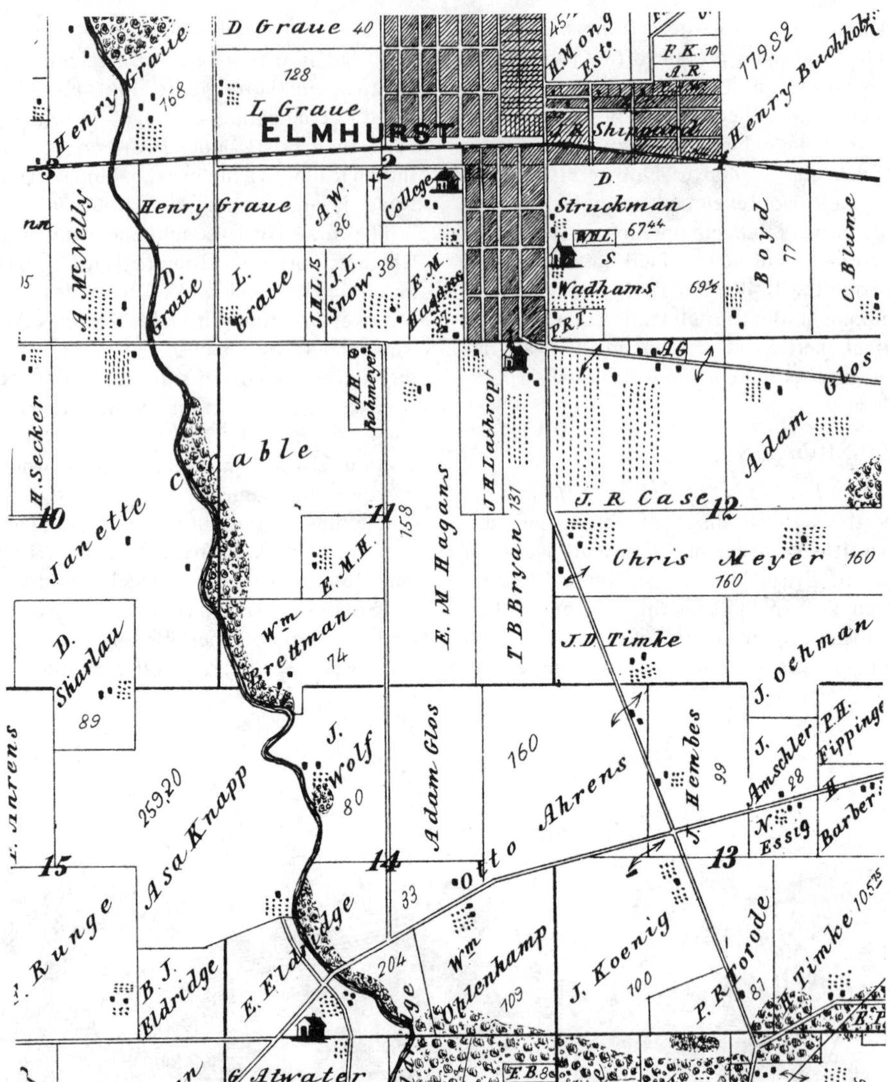


*Glos Claim in York Township.*
*from* 1874 Atlas & History of DuPage County, Illinois

to Oswego and north to Galena. At that juncture on the West Branch of the DuPage River stood the Pre-Emption House which, from 1834, was a renowned tavern serving up to fifty prairie schooners a night.

The Oswego road continued along the Fox River until it joined Plainfield Road east of Ottawa and on to Springfield and St. Louis. The road to the mining center of Galena was served by another stagecoach running through Warrenville just to the east of the river, where Julius Warren built his tavern.

As early as 1835 Orente and David Grant, distant relatives of Ulysses, built Castle Inn near today's intersection of York Road and Ogden Avenue. At the height of the plank road's activity, 500 teams of horses a day stopped to pay the toll before that tavern.

Meanwhile, in the northern part of the county, Meacham's first benefited from the 1836 state authorization that selected it as the starting point of a new road to Galena. On July 4th of that year, its citizens hauled a large log behind a team of oxen halfway to Elgin, which

*The Kline Farm.*
*Courtesy Forest Preserve District of DuPage County*

had a similar project moving eastward. Where they met, the two parties enjoyed "a grand Independence Day dinner." In the fall the Galena coach changed its run from Naperville to this route, entering the county at Grand Avenue where the Buckhorn Tavern was located at the York intersection. This "state road" would become the contemporary Lake Street (U.S. 20).

Today's St. Charles Road was laid out in the same year. By 1837 Moses Stacy built his first hostelry, which in 1846 gave way to the tavern still standing in Glen Ellyn at Five Corners. Fifty cents a night would provide supper, lodging, breakfast, and hay for two horses. On that same road in Elmhurst, Gerry Bates and his brother-in-law J. L. Hovey would build in 1843 the Hill Cottage Tavern, which would later serve several DuPage notables as a home.

North of Cottage Hill, as Elmhurst was first called, the Western Plank Road was built following the route of Irving Park Road. This construction of three-inch boards laid across a sixteen-foot-wide bed, with tolls every five miles, beginning with a 2½-cent fare for a single rider, was a phenomonon in DuPage County in the early 1850s. Like the stage coach, plank roads were rendered obsolete within a decade by the railroads.

## SPROUTING INSTITUTIONS

The career of tavern owner and railroad promoter Gerry Bates was not as typical as that of farmer John Glos, his neighbor to the east. The 1840 census showed 973 persons in agriculture, with only 105 in other occupations.

The manner by which the John Glos family located their acreage also followed a common pattern—one scouting the prospects before others were to follow. John, Jr., made the exploratory expedition. Leaving Bavaria in southern Germany in 1832, he first surveyed rocky New England before hearing of the stone-free Illinois country. The entire family arrived in Chicago in 1837. The older son, speaking English by this time, took his father and his brother Adam to the land office in Chicago. He asked to be shown farm sites, explaining that they had $600 with which to begin their enterprise. The land agent showed them property just west of the Chicago River, where the Northwestern Station now stands. It was swampy, and they declared it unfit for farming. "Let the frogs keep it," John, Sr., muttered. Then on horses furnished by the land agent, they rode west. It was not until they had forded the Des Plaines River and then found the elevation rising markedly, some 100 feet, that they were satisfied. They located on Section 12 in York Township.

According to the Northwest Ordinance of 1787, townships were divided into thirty-six sections. beginning at the northeast corner, they were numbered six across, one down and back, through the sixth row down. So Section 12 placed the Glosses at the county line, in the first small farmhouse north of St. Charles Road where Sandburg Junior High now stands.

The homestead of Caspar Kline, who first broke ground in 1835 in Winfield Township, has come into the possession of the forest preserve district, which operates it as a typical nineteenth-century farm. The original crops were wheat, barley, and oats. Corn became predominant later in the century as the center of wheat production moved farther west.

But agriculture was not limited to field crops. Daniel Kelly at the Bloomingdale/Milton border community of Gretna undertook the raising of Merino sheep. By 1870 Luther Bartlett, an 1842 pioneer at the DuPage/Cook County border in Wayne, was to pasture a flock of a thousand sheep. His attempt at growing pear trees, however, met an ill-fated end at the hands of northern Illinois winters.

Richmond and Vallette in the earliest of county histories (1857) described the wolf hunts that were held annually in Downers Grove Township to rid the farmers of these predators on their livestock. The farmers stationed themselves in a circle several miles in circumference. Upon a prearranged signal, they began their movement toward the center; thus they cornered the beasts for a kill of up to sixty a day. By 1846 wolves were extinct in the county.

Other enterprises during the pioneer period showed that DuPage was not as exclusively rural as other newly opened lands. Even the early prevalence of clapboard homes over log cabins reflected a less primitive circumstance.

Representing still another kind of economic interest was George Martin, originally a shipping merchant of Edinburgh, Scotland. He came to DuPage in 1832 with his wife Elizabeth and six-year-old son. Martin was soon followed by his brother-in-law John Christie. Martin's 1833 home of oak and walnut construction stood in Naperville until destroyed by fire in 1958. By 1883 George Martin II had erected the Victorian "Pine Craig" home which now houses the Martin-Mitchell Museum. In the meantime the family established the quarry where Centennial Beach is now located that supplied foundation material for the area.

On the site of Fort Payne, another Naperville notable, Lewis Ellsworth, organized the DuPage County Nurseries in 1849. The fifty acres embraced the most extensive assortment of fruit and ornamental trees, shrubs, and plants in northern Illinois. Thirty thousand evergreens and plants were imported from Europe in a single season. The transition from survival agriculture to refined horticulture had occurred within the first twenty years of European settlement.

At the other end of the county John Henry Franzen had the first linseed mill in Illinois in operation in 1847. By 1870 the mill was closed and flax crops along with wheat gave way to corn.

To the southeast of Franzens at Grant Avenue and the county line, Henry F. Fischer (no relation to the Fischers of Churchville) had by 1850 built the first windmill in the state. Five stories high, its capacity was forty barrels of grain a day. In 1925 the mill became the property of Mt. Emblem Cemetery, where it is still visible from the Tri-State Tollway.

Before mid-century two other events occurred that represented the economic wave of the future. The first took place in 1848 when the long awaited Illinois-Michigan Canal commenced service five miles south of Brush Hill. The influx of laborers, particularly from Ireland, temporarily kept Cass a viable community after the end of the stagecoach era. The 1834 Tremont post office, second oldest in the county, was finally discontinued in 1885.

The Irish also contributed to the second and even more significant development—the building of the Galena and Chicago Union Railroad in 1849. The "Sons of Erin" were involved not only in laying the track but in the trains' operations as well. Daniel Shehan at Babcock's Grove fired the first engine. The first permanent landmark of the Catholic church in the area is St. Mary's Cemetery on Finley Road, north of Butterfield. Here immi-

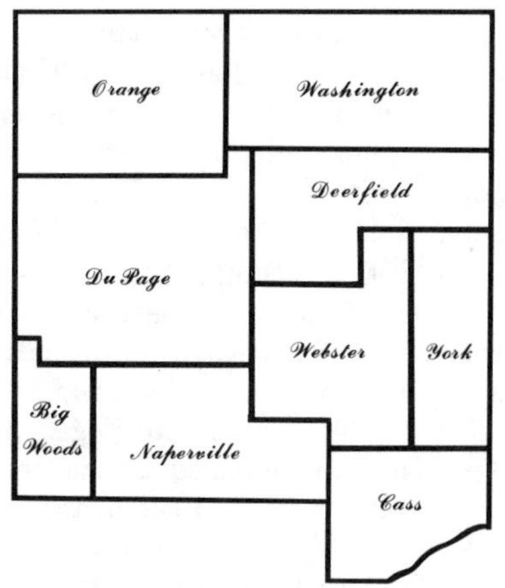


*Precincts of 1839.*
*from* The Life and Times of Warrenville
*Courtesy Leone Schmidt*

grants from Ireland were being buried as early as the 1840s. But before these wheels of progress are followed into the next era, other institutional growth must be noted.

The political development was represented in the person of Lyman Butterfield whose holdings in the vicinity of the present Arrowhead Golf Course were adjacent to neighbor Tullus, whose preemption was being challenged by "jumper" Harmond. When the latter pulled a gun, Butterfield and a Quaker friend placed themselves in front of the muzzle, challenging the interloper to kill "two birds with one stone," if he were to enforce his trespass. After a tense ten minutes Harmond left.

Likewise, Pierce Downer in 1832 had to confront Wells and Cooley who sought to "squat" on the land he had staked out. When he found them building a cabin there upon his return from a Chicago shopping expedition, his wrath simmered "like a pent sea over a burning volcano." The two not only withdrew, but Wells also left the area altogether, leaving a legitimately staked claim to Israel Blodgett. With neighbor Samuel Curtiss, Blodgett in 1838 cleared Maple Avenue with six oxen hitched to logs.

It was such pioneer cooperation that accounted for the emergence of claim-protecting societies which secured ownership until official surveys could be made by the federal government in 1842 and land patents issued. The first to be formed was that of Big Woods in 1836, a settlement along Eola Road east of the massive grove that extended from Batavia to Aurora.

This and the other societies corresponded to the precincts which were to define the county's subdivisions after its detachment from Cook. The others included Naperville, Webster, Deerfield, Washington, Orange, and DuPage. In the first election, held in 1839, the underdog Whigs' win surprised the opposition Democrats because in the Jacksonian era most on the frontier identified themselves with the latter party.

The governmental service first sought and received in every community was postal. Besides the post offices established along the main road routes already mentioned, such as Paw Paw station in Naperville (the oldest, established in 1834), there was Route 4311, which stopped at Samuel Curtiss's home on the new road, along which he and Blodgett had planted a row of sugar maple trees. Route 4312 from Cottage Hill west through Langdon (David Kelley's post office at Gretna) continued to the West DuPage Tavern of Giles Billings. Route 4325 ran on Butterfield Road, stopped at Jacob Fuller's place where Utopia and York Center communities later arose; continued on to Samuel Davies's house in the old Bonaparte community; and passed Julius Warren's house on the way to Big Woods and Aurora. Route 4313 extended through Addison and Bloomingdale until it was shifted to Itasca in 1873 because of the railroad's routing.

Although schools were not a governmental responsibility until 1856, there were already eighteen private subscription schools established by 1840. Lester Peet of Naperville was the earliest schoolmaster. In neighboring Lisle Thomas Jellies built the first frame school house in 1835.

In that same year the Benjamin Fullers moved to Brush Hill. This family came with the Atwaters, Austins, Eldridges, Knapps, Reeds, and Thurstons from Broome County, New York. Their settlement in the Oak Brook area was but the last stage of migration for most of this group because they had previously moved together to Broome from Washington County, New York. Atwater sisters, Olive, Anna, and Rachel were married to Benjamin Fuller, Robert Reed, and Edward Eldridge respec-

*Mary Fuller — an early teacher in the Fullersburg area.*
*Courtesy Hinsdale Historical Society*

tively. Fuller located on the Mayslake site, next to the remnants of an Indian village, where he taught the Indians how to shoe horses. Within twenty years he had purchased 800 acres, so that it was natural to call the community Fullersburg by the time he platted it in 1851.

In the meantime, his sister Mary was the first teacher in what became Salt Creek District 48. The schoolhouse was a cabin at the southwest corner of York and Roosevelt roads.

Sharing the educational function were the early churches, which brought the settlers not only the Good News but also the news on issues such as Abolition and Prohibition from outside the area. The earliest religious organizations divided less along Protestant and Catholic lines than they did between American and German church groups. Congregationalist, Methodist, and Baptists characterized the former; Evangelicals, Lutherans, and Roman Catholics the latter.

On July 13, 1833, the First Presbyterian Church of DuPage was organized near the forks of the East and West Branches under the leadership of the Rev. Jeremiah Porter. By August, 1834 the group was meeting in the Naper settlement; there it changed its name to the First Congregational Church of DuPage, since most of its members had been of that tradition. The move to Naperville was also motivated by what the Rev. Edwin R. Davis described at the church's fiftieth anniversary: "The place [Naperville] in the early days was notorious for its wickedness. Intemperance, profanity, Sabbath breaking and infidelity abounded in it. . . . Brother Clark desired to save the people from the calamity of becoming barbarians." Morris Sleight donated land upon which a building was erected in 1845.

By that date three other Congregationalist societies had been founded in the county: Downers Grove in 1837, Lisle in 1842, and Big Woods in 1844. The last of these reflected the rising Abolitionist sentiments, since it was led by Thomson Paxton, the Scotch-Irishman who had left Tennessee because of his opposition to slavery. He became disaffected with the Presbyterian church of Batavia, which he and other neighbors had helped form, because the national Presbyterian church had failed to take a strong stand on this issue in 1842. They withdrew to organize the Big Woods Congregational Church, whose building still stands on Eola Road.

By 1837 the Methodists were conducting class meetings in Cass, Gary's Mill, Stacy Corners, Orangeville (Wayne Center), Copenhagen (on Route 59 at the southern border of the county), and Big Woods. The mother church for Methodist churches in the southern end of the county was Cass, where Stephen R. Beggs rode the circuit in the 1830s. A 200-pound, six-foot-tall son of a Revolutionary War veteran, Beggs had such a voice that one pioneer averred that he could be heard a quarter of a mile away. To settlements as far flung as twelve miles south of Ottawa he traveled with stops at Downers Grove and Naperville in between. Blodgett relatives, the Horace Dodges and Eliphalet Strongs, hosted him at Strong's Hill on today's Hidden Lake Forest Preserve. He also wrote the book *Pages from the Early History of the West and Northwest.*

Gary's Mill was the focal point for other Methodist activity. It was in Gary's Mill School that Jesse Wheaton and Orinda Gary exchanged their wedding vows, concluding a romance which Rufus Blanchard describes in his 1882 *History of DuPage County, Illinois:* "Cupid is more unerring in his darts in new countries. . . ." These two Pomfret, Connecticut, families were also to be joined again as Warren Wheaton was to marry Harriet Rickard, daughter of a Gary sister. These were 1837 charter members of the church founded at the home of Charles Gary, who, in addition to operating the sawmill, serving as a county postmaster and justice of the peace, became an ordained lay preacher.

The Wheaton brothers moved east to the 600-acre preemption and plowed a furrow around it, and they took their Methodist convictions with them. In 1840 Jesse Wheaton voted for James G. Birney, the Abolitionist candidate for president. In 1843 the brothers were active in forming the Wesleyan Methodist church, which was organized in opposition to slavery, liquor, and Freemasonry.

The Baptists were also identified with the growing Abolitionist sentiment. The Baptist church in Warrenville was host to the Northwestern Baptist Anti-Slavery Convention in 1845. Among those attending were Baptist members from Bloomingdale, where services were first held in 1840, and where an 1849 building still serves as headquarters for the community's park district.

The German churches prior to 1850 were mostly Protestant. The earliest, Zion Evangelical in Naperville, whose 1840 building remains the oldest church structure in the county and serves as headquarters for the Naperville Heritage Society, began in 1837. The fifteen charter members were from Pennsylvania and were of the Evangelical and United Brethren denomination.

A year later a church composed of Lutheran and Reformed believers was organized at the southern end of Dunklee's Grove. Its extensive influence will be noted in the next chapter.

The Irish Roman Catholics were meeting at St. Patrick's in Cass in 1846. In that same year twenty-five German-speaking families from Alsace-Lorraine constructed St. Raphael's in Naperville, which by 1864, when it was named SS. Peter and Paul, had become the largest church in the county. Among these was Joseph Wherli, who also became the church's financial angel in 1848, when he assumed the indebtedness which threatened to put the building up for auction. One of Wherli's daughters, Mary, married Joseph F. Drendel whose grandfather had run a hotel in Chicago, where the federal building now stands, before buying 300 acres in Lisle Township.

*Big Woods Congregational Church*
*Art by A. Gilbert Foote*

From these Alsatian families, including Alois Schwartz, Xavier Reidy, and Joseph Yackley, came young men who joined hundreds from DuPage as Forty-Niners in the Gold Rush. Sheldon Peck's son Charles painted an eighteen-foot by nine-foot canvas *Panorama of California* which toured the nation. By the time some of these adventurers had returned home, they found that DuPage had passed beyond the pioneer era.

# CHAPTER 3 The Uprooting

## THE CIVIL WAR ERA

## 1850–1870

The Civil War period in DuPage County, as for the whole nation, was a time of uprooting. The extent of that upheaval is reflected in the fact that 10 percent of the population, some 1,500 young men, served in the War Between the States. The percentage of farmers to leave the land for battle was even higher.

The character of the turmoil was reflected, too, in the closing of the Warrenville Academy and the Bloomingdale Academy and the near-demise of the newly established Wheaton College, as their enrollments were depleted. Even the Naperville Brass Band, founded in 1859 and forerunner of that community's Municipal Band, suffered a loss of members.

Nevertheless, the same forces that caused disruption created new patterns of economic, political, and social life which transformed post–Civil War DuPage and America. While 10,000 field hands in Illinois were caught up in the conflict, the McCormick reaper more than offset that loss during the 1860s. Increasing productivity, in fact, made Illinois the center of the nation's agricultural activity. The coming of the railroads not only bound the northern states together, but also provided the economic framework for the county's development.

Prior to considering the war's local impact, it is necessary to recognize the social ferment that had preceded the decade of the 1860s.

### SOCIAL FERMENT

The Abolitionist movement was particularly strong in DuPage because virtually every church contributed to its strength. Among the Congregationalists, Israel and Avis Dodge Blodgett stand out as early promoters of the cause of Emancipation. Their blacksmith shop and home on Maple Avenue in Downers Grove, once established, became one of the early stops on the Underground Railroad. The Underground Railroad was the system of hiding runaway slaves in the North and helping transport them to the Canadian border, where they could make a permanent escape.

Blodgett had once served as a military blacksmith at Harper's Ferry and had, in that position, surreptitiously counseled blacks on how to escape by following the North Star and traveling only at night. Later in Illinois, when an owner who had captured two fugitives stopped and requested water for himself at the Blodgetts', Avis responded by holding the cup to the mouths of the slaves instead.

Likewise, Lucius Matlack, principal of the Illinois Institute, which had been founded in 1853, showed his Abolitionist conviction when he made his home available for runaways. The institute became Wheaton College in 1860 under the leadership of Jonathan Blanchard, a friend of the Beechers—Lyman, Edward, and Harriet Beecher Stowe. Previous connections with this prominent, activist family at Lane Seminary in Cincinatti and Knox College in Galesburg had prepared Blanchard for strong anti-slavery leadership in DuPage.

Blanchard also assumed the pastorate of the Wesleyan Methodist congregation. He combined it with local Congregationalists to form the First Church of Christ. Within seventy years that body divided three times. In 1862 the Wesleyans separated. In 1878 the First Church split into the First Congregational Church and the College Church of Christ over the issue of Freemasonry and secret societies. Because of its change in membership composition, the Congregational church became First Presbyterian Church in 1909. While College Church continues to the present, in 1929 a group from it formed the Wheaton College

*Sympathy for runaway slaves. Avis Blodgett was a DuPage settler whose Abolitionist convictions led her to assist those who were caught by a bounty hunter.*
*Art by Lester Schrader*
*Courtesy Naperville Heritage Society*

*Francis A. (Franz) Hoffman.*

Interdenominational church, the Wheaton Bible Church of today. Each of these then could trace its origin to that antebellum Wesleyan church.

The Germans who had come to this country to escape the limitation of freedom contributed much to Abolitionism. The Churchville congregation was pastored from 1842 to 1847 by Francis Arnold (Franz) Hoffmann who, by the time of the Civil War, had become an attorney, helped organize the Republican party, and begun service as lieutenant governor of Illinois.

The turning point in sentiment toward this support of liberation occurred in 1850 with the passage of the Fugitive Slave Act. This law stringently enforced penalties of $1,000 fines or six months in prison for harboring runaways. The legislation came as such a moral challenge to the people of DuPage that the means of hiding slaves became even more developed than before.

Most of the fugitives came into Illinois from Missouri and followed the rivers north. Along the West Branch of the DuPage River in the West Chicago area, a hideaway site was discovered in 1981 in the basement of what had been the John Fairbank's home. This discovery was confirmed by a group of researchers from Northern Illinois University. Farther north, the home of the Guilds in Wayne Center was a well-known place of concealment.

Overland routes from west to east included stops at the William Strong's, located on Aurora Road just east of Eola Road, at Blodgett's home and blacksmith shop in Downers Grove, and also at Pierce Downer's home just off today's Ogden Avenue. The Graue Mill, north of Ogden on York Road, contains an exhibit illustrating its participation in the fugitive operation. Along St. Charles Road Thomas Filer's home served as an ideal hiding place, as it lay adjacent to the East Branch of the DuPage River. A tunnel ran between the house and barn on this property, which was purchased in 1872 by Frederic Barnard. Farther east, where St. Charles crosses Grace Street, Sheldon Peck his as many as eleven runaways at a time in his home. His son Frank recalled conversations with the slaves from whom he learned a number of southern songs. This experience he reported to his daughter Alyce Mertz, who still lives at that location.

Glennette Turner, author of *The Underground Railroad in DuPage County, Illinois,* reports that once the slaves reached the Tremont Hotel in Chicago, the black barbers acted as conductors on the last leg of the trip to Detroit. After crossing into Canada at Windsor, they found certain areas provided for the establishment of black households.

An additional manifestation of fermenting sentiment was the establishment of the Plow Boys in Downers Grove. Prior to the election of Abraham Lincoln in 1860, this group of forty-five young men, riding on a massive wagon to neighboring towns with a great flag flying from a forty-foot pole, organized support for the new Republican party. They were to offer themselves as early recruits in the Civil War, once it began.

## ANSWERING THE BUGLE

There were forty regiments served by men from DuPage, and $180,000 in bounties was raised. Four companies from the county, along with six from DeKalb, made up the 105th Infantry Regiment of Illinois Volunteers. The S. F. Daniel Company of Volunteers, the so-called Bryan's Blues, had been funded largely by Thomas B. Bryan of Chicago and Elmhurst. He was also active in the war effort as the builder of Bryan Hall in Chicago, where mass meetings would be held.

Also directly involved in the conflict were

*The Sheldon Peck Home.*
*Courtesy Lombard Historical Society*

those serving in the 7th Illinois Infantry, including Alan Bates of Wayne, a casualty at Shiloh, who had bought his own guns for $50 on a $13-a-month pay. Captain Walter Blanchard of Downers Grove served in Company K, 13th Illinois Volunteer Infantry, having left his position as a probate judge. He was killed in action at Chattanooga, Tennessee. Marcellus Jones, a resident first of Danby (Glen Ellyn) and later of Wheaton, was purportedly the first to fire at Gettysburg.

An offspring of one of the original German settlers in Addison Township, Frederick Fischer, enlisted as a nineteen-year-old in 1861 and participated in all the battles of Company B. 33rd Regiment, including the Seige of Vicksburg. His parents sent him a folding chair made by an Addison Township cabinetmaker; he carried it, strapped to his blanket roll wherever his company marched.

Describing the conditions and actions of these young men was Benjamin Franklin Taylor from DuPage County; he became an internationally known war correspondent. His stories were distributed to both national and overseas newspapers. He had taught briefly at

*Glenette Turner, authority on the Underground Railroad — at the Graue Mill.*

the Warrenville Academy prior to the Civil War; then he became a correspondent for the *Chicago Evening Journal*, writing letters from Union camps, including the names of the young men whom he had visited at their campfires. After the war he dedicated a book of his collected correspondence entitled *In Camp and Field* to his friend Thomas B. Bryan, with whom he commuted into the city on the Chicago & North Western Railroad. The *London Times* called Taylor "the Oliver Goldsmith of America." His house at 203 East Seminary in Wheaton is still referred to today as "Poet's Corner," a fitting tribute to this man whom latter-day commentators have referred to as "the Ernie Pyle of the Civil War."

Roselle Hough, a resident of Bloomingdale Township and a founder of Union Stock Yards in Chicago, also served in the Union army. When the body of the assassinated president was brought to Chicago, Hough served as grand marshal of the funeral parade.

Another to distinguish himself in the war was William Plum. Born in 1845 in Ohio, he excelled as a telegrapher and was one of only three to hold the secret cipher that coordinated the Union campaigns. Later, after finishing a law degree at Yale, he moved to Babcock's Grove (Lombard) in 1867, whence he commuted into his city office. He and his wife Helen traveled extensively; they brought to Lombard over 200 species of lilac bushes and thus began what is today Lilacia Park.

The final person to be noted in this sequence of Civil War participants was one whose life stretched across that era into the next, one who was prototypical of nineteenth-century forces. T. S. Rogers, the son of pioneer Joseph Ives Rogers, came as a teenager from St. Lawrence County, New York in 1844. At nineteen he was teaching school in present-day Glen Ellyn for $13 a month. In 1851 he began farming in Downers Grove and in 1856 became involved in Republican politics. He was captain of the Plow Boys and an original Lincoln supporter in 1860. He enlisted in Company B, 105th Illinois Volunteer Infantry in 1862, having organized the first company of one hundred men in DuPage for service in the war. Before it ended he had participated in Sherman's March to the Sea. Upon his return home, he served as the county sheriff until 1866, then as the president of the board of trustees of Downers Grove. That same year he went into the meat business in Chicago, subsequently suffering the loss of his property in the Great Fire. He quickly reestablished his enterprise and continued in it for another thirty-eight years. By 1890 he was involved in a lawsuit with E. H. Prince, the land developer of the century's last decade, which led to the condemnation of

*105th Illinois Volunteers on Lookout Mountain. DuPage soldiers include Willard Scott of Naperville, far left; Theodore S. Rogers of Downers Grove, far right.*

Roger's Downers Grove property in opening up Main Street north of the Burlington tracks. This railroad and land development were the harbingers of a new age, which had followed the signing of the Treaty at Appomattox.

## ALONG THE LINES

It is ironical that the first engine to bring trains into DuPage was called The Pioneer. For this newest product of mid-nineteenth century technology marked the end of the pioneer era.

The originally projected route had been from Elmhurst, where Gerry Bates had given the right-of-way adjacent to his store, continuing through Lombard, with plans calling for its following St. Charles Road. However, the Wheaton brothers entertained Galena & Chicago Union (G&CU) Railroad president William Ogden in Jesse's home in 1848 and promised the right-of-way land without cost, thus winning a more southerly route for the line. They were joined in their offer by Erastus Gary, who had moved to Wheaton in that same year.

Thus the development of what became Glen Ellyn, Wheaton, Winfield, and West Chicago was assured. As the G & CU track was laid through today's Winfield in 1849, John Hedges built the first depot and post office. In 1854 the railroad built a station, briefly called Warren, showing the influence of Julius Warren in the Winfield area. The Besch family owned Hedges' home from 1897–1977; then it was moved to its current location on north Winfield Road.

In West Chicago John B. Turner, president of the G & CU, platted the twenty-two acres, the first in the community he called Junction, because the Burlington and the St. Charles Branch line joined the G&CU at this loca-

*William Robbins.*
*Courtesy of Hinsdale Historical Society*

tion. The town was later called Turner, after him. In 1857 William Currier (related to the Currier and Ives lithographers) built the *Gone With the Wind*–style house, subsequently occupied by Congressman Chauncey Reed. Comparable economic activity was also evident in Babcock's Grove, newly organized and named Lombard in 1868 after developer Josiah Lombard, who had bought the property of Reuben Mink.

By 1864, because of cooperation between communities in the southern part of the country, the Burlington track was laid from Aurora through Naperville, Lisle, Downers Grove, and Hinsdale. The families from Fullersburg had hoped to have the line extend through that community, but the grade to the east was an insurmountable forty feet; therefore the roadbed followed the valley between hills to the south, through what is now the center of Hinsdale.

The man to anticipate that direction was William Robbins of Chicago, who had previously gone to California during the Gold Rush. Upon his return he purchased 800 acres from Alfred Walker, including the right-of-way for the incoming Burlington. The platting of land was opposed by area farmers who saw it as a threat to their established pattern; but eventually they accepted the iron horse as inevitable.

To the east of DuPage the problem of laying the railroad bed was complicated by what were called "The Flats." The ground between Hinsdale and today's Western Springs was so marshy that the first train sank eleven feet into the bog. Engines had to be brought in from both sides to lift it, so that the roadbed could be filled.

Other aspects of economic growth besides the railroad included the A. S. Jones Plow Company and Stenger Brewery in Naperville. There were also the enterprises of Ernst Von Oven, who had immigrated in 1852 after his two sisters had married the Hammerschmidt brothers, Adolph and Herman. Following the Civil War, Von Oven purchased the Martin and King Tile and Brick Works, which soon expanded rapidly because of the new use of field tile to drain wetlands in the Midwest. Within fifteen years one million tiles were being produced annually. Ernst's real love, however, was the Naperville Nurseries, established in 1866 and operated until 1918. He brought this interest from his native West-

*Pioneer at Cottage Hill Station.*
*Courtesy Elmhurst Historical Society*

phalia where trees and shrubs ornament both elegant and modest homes.

Adolph Hammerschmidt began in this same period to purchase quarry sites in Lombard and in Elmhurst, while having his son William develop the tile and brick business in Lombard as well. The Elmhurst site became the Elmhurst and Chicago Stone Company. In the twentieth century these holdings have expanded to locations in Greene Valley and Warrenville. This family's enterprise indicates how influential the German population had become during the Civil War era.

## THE GERMAN GROWTH

The 1850 census showed that out of a population of 9,290 there were 2,553 United States–born residents eighteen years or older in the county and 1,859 foreign-born. Of those from abroad the German population numbered 878, the largest single group, not including the 200 German-speaking persons from the Alsace-Lorraine region of France. Next in number were 354 from Ireland.

The 1860 figures show 4,672 foreign-born out of a total of 14,701, with 2,680 from Germany. That comparison indicates how the growth of German population accelerated during the period just prior to the Civil War.

Factors at work from earlier in the nineteenth century accounted for this dramatic immigration pattern. One was the economic disruption following the Battle of Waterloo in 1815. Promotional literature like Gottfried Ouden's travel narratives, painting a rosy picture of the Middle West, led John Glos, Jr., to bring his family from Bavaria to York Township. The liberalizing movement in Germany had been thwarted in 1830 and again in 1848. After the latter aborted uprising, the Hammerschmidt brothers left. The potato famine in Ireland also had its counterpart on the continent. Conscription of young German men into the military for long terms of service

*Fischer Mill.*

provided still another impetus for emigration, as was the case with Franz Hoffmann. As a result DuPage had a variety of German groups arriving.

The northeastern corner of the county was settled primarily by those from Protestant northern Germany; those from Prussia were mostly of the Reformed faith while those from Hannover were Lutheran. In 1838 the German United Reformed Lutheran Church was formed in the Churchville area of today's Bensenville. The name was later changed to Zion. The Reformed group established its own Emmanuel Church in the same vicinity in 1859. Zion served as the founding church for Lutheran congregations within a ten-mile radius. St. Paul's in Addison, St. Luke's in Itasca, Trinity Church in York Center, Immanual in Elmhurst, and Calvary in Wood Dale were among the offshoots.

Immigrants from southern Germany and Alsace-Lorraine settled in Lisle and Naperville townships. SS. Peter and Paul Church, as previously noted, was composed primarily of immigrant families from Alsace-Lorraine, although its first pastor was Italian (Father Raphael Rainaldi), its first wedding French (Beaubien), and its first baptism Irish (Wheeler). The second Catholic church was to start in the southern part of Bloomingdale and the northern part of Milton townships. St. Stephen's began in 1852 in the pioneer community of Gretna, at the end of Main Street and St. Charles Road, in today's Carol Stream. It continued as a mission church until its closing in 1911. A church that has continued, however, is St. John the Baptist in Winfield, organized in 1867, with its first pastor, Father John Wiederhold, serving from 1869 to 1921. It is significant that there was no Catholic church in Addison until 1913, a sign of how the patterns of settlement persisted until a relatively late date.

One family who typified these waves of settlers was the Dieters. The first of the group to come from Kleinhausen in Hess Dormstadt was Valentine Dieter Sr., who arrived in 1846, just in time to become a charter member of the

*Martin and Von Oven Brick & Tile Works.*
*Art by Lester Schrader*
*Courtesy Naperville Heritage Society*

Naperville parish. He farmed near Belmont and Hobson Road. His grandson Valentine Dieter Jr. became Naperville's mayor at the turn of the century. Meanwhile, the Nicholas Dieters arrived in 1854, and by 1867 had mortgaged their farm at the Bloomingdale-Winfield township line to help start the St. John parish.

While the Catholic German settlers tended toward farming, their Protestant counterparts were engaged in more commercial ventures. Among these were the four "Dutch Windmills" that once graced the DuPage landscape. These grinders of flour/feed and sharpeners of tools included the Fischer Mill, previously mentioned and the only one left standing in DuPage County. It was constructed by Dutch workmen at Grand Avenue and County Line Road. The Old Holland Mill in York Center was completed by Louis Backhaus in 1851, purchased by Colonel Fabyan in 1918, and moved to his Fox River estate, now part of a Kane County forest preserve. The Holstein Mill in Bloomingdale, south of Schick Road, was destroyed by a tornado in 1899. The largest, Heidemann Mill in Addison, had a wing span of ninety feet; fire destroyed it in 1958.

It was also from Holland that the Germans borrowed the Christmas custom of St. Nicholas gift giving and combined it with their own Tannenbaum festivities. In marked contrast, those of Puritan background held to the strictures against Yuletide celebrating; Wheaton College President Jonathan Blanchard required class attendance on Christmas Day. This practice, however, did not long endure.

## RAID AND GRADES

What has continued, however, is the New England pattern of townships. The year 1850 marked the transition from pioneer governmental structures as the nine townships were established in DuPage. This development was the result of former Connecticut Yankee Warren Wheaton's efforts when he was a state legislator from 1848–1850.

The other major change of this period was

*Nocturnal seizure. Wheatonites confiscate county records from court house in Naperville in 1868.*
*Art by Lester Schrader*
*Courtesy Naperville Heritage Society*

moving the county seat from Naperville to Wheaton. An initial attempt in 1857 to relocate to Wheaton's more central and rail-serviced location was defeated. A second effort in 1867 succeeded, with the referendum carrying 1,686 to 1,635.

Naperville, however, refused to turn over the records. The transfer, therefore, necessitated a midnight raid in which a contingent of Civil War veterans from Wheaton seized the records from the old court house. When the men were making their escape, the alarm was sounded. A few books were dropped. These were taken into Chicago for safekeeping, but were consumed in the Great Fire.

The governmental move to Wheaton also caused Naperville's plank road to lose out to the railroad. By the time the planks had warped and had been discarded, the mainstream of public life had already shifted to the towns along the G & CU. The mail, for instance, had to be brought to Naperville by way of the train station at Winfield; at this point it was transferred to stagecoach and taken down Winfield Road through Warrenville. The mail route in Downers Grove depended upon a comparable service from Lombard, until the Burlington line was finally completed in 1864.

A final aspect of the governmental evolution was establishment, in 1856, of the state requirement for public education. Previously, schools had operated on a subscription basis. Typical of these was the Churchville School across from the Zion Lutheran Church. It was built in 1850 for eight grades and one teacher on land donated by August Fischer. After its conversion to a public school, it continued in use until 1931. The Naperville Academy, built in 1851, became a public school in 1860; the building stood until 1928. Gleaner's Hall (now the Pleasant Hill School) was erected in 1852, just to the west of the cemetery on Geneva Road, where Revolutionary War veteran Gideon Warner had been buried nine years earlier.

In the mid-nineteenth century the school

*Churchville School.*
*Art by H. Gilbert Foote*

year lasted six months; during the other half children could work on farms. Teachers were paid at the rate of $20 to $40 a month. Young men often found teaching a stepping stone to other vocations. For example, Myron Dudley taught in Addison in 1853 and later became a judge.

It is also significant that the 1850 census shows only three teachers in the county. This low number resulted from women's vocations not being counted in the census, a practice corrected in the 1860s.

The 1850 census did, however, show Clarissa Hobson to be the wealthiest individual in DuPage with $18,000 in property value. Her husband, Bailey, had died that year. His demise was yet another sign of transition from the pioneer era. In contrast, the wealthiest person in the 1860 census was Thomas B. Bryan of Elmhurst; his real estate was valued at $300,000 and his personal property at $25,000. He represented the gathering forces of modernity in post–Civil War DuPage.

York Road in 1900 Elmhurst.

# CHAPTER 4 The Tap Root

## INTO THE MODERN ERA: 1870–1920

The period from 1870 to 1920 functioned as the tap root for the modern world. In that period the inventions which were to give shape to modernity came into play. While it is often said that necessity is the mother of invention, it can also be said that invention is the mother of necessity, since modern people have become dependent upon technology to sustain new lifestyles. This broad historical force was clearly manifested in DuPage.

Infatuation with innovation is portrayed in *The Cottage on Maple Avenue,* a film produced by the Lombard Historical Society dramatizing a typical day at 23 West Maple Street in 1876. Newell and Flora Matson are shown entertaining William and Helen Plum by demonstrating the newest devices they had brought back from the Philadelphia Centennial World's Fair.

But it was the Chicago World's Fair which triggered the next chain reaction of life-style change. Not only did the Columbian Exposition of 1893 demonstrate how Chicago had emerged as the fastest growing of all cities (from 100,000 in 1860 to one million in 1890, despite the Great Fire of 1871), but it also revealed the wonders of new technology, especially electricity. Electrical demonstrations led quickly to the installation of public utilities in suburbs to the west.

The same impetus carried over into the first two decades of the twentieth century as the automobile replaced the horse and buggy, although they could still be seen side by side at the turn of the century. The 800 cars in the nation in 1900 became 8 million by the end of World War I. By 1920 motion pictures had become prevalent enough that a version of the

_ _ _ _ _ *CHICAGO & NORTH WESTERN,* 1849 (FORMERLY GALENA & CHICAGO UNION)

——..·—— *BURLINGTON NORTHERN,* 1864 (FORMERLY CHICAGO, BURLINGTON, & QUINCY)

- - - - - - - - *MILWAUKEE ROAD,* 1873 (FORMERLY CHICAGO, MILWAUKEE, ST PAUL, & PACIFIC ALSO CHICAGO & PACIFIC)

——— ——— *ELGIN, JOLIET, & EASTERN,* 1888

———————— *CHICAGO GREAT WESTERN,* 1888 (FORMERLY CHICAGO, ST. PAUL, & KANAS CITY)

——— ——— *ILLINOIS CENTRAL GULF,* 1891

—— —— —— *C.A.&E.- CHICAGO, AURORA, & ELGIN,* 1902 (TODAY THE ILLINOIS PRARIE PATH)

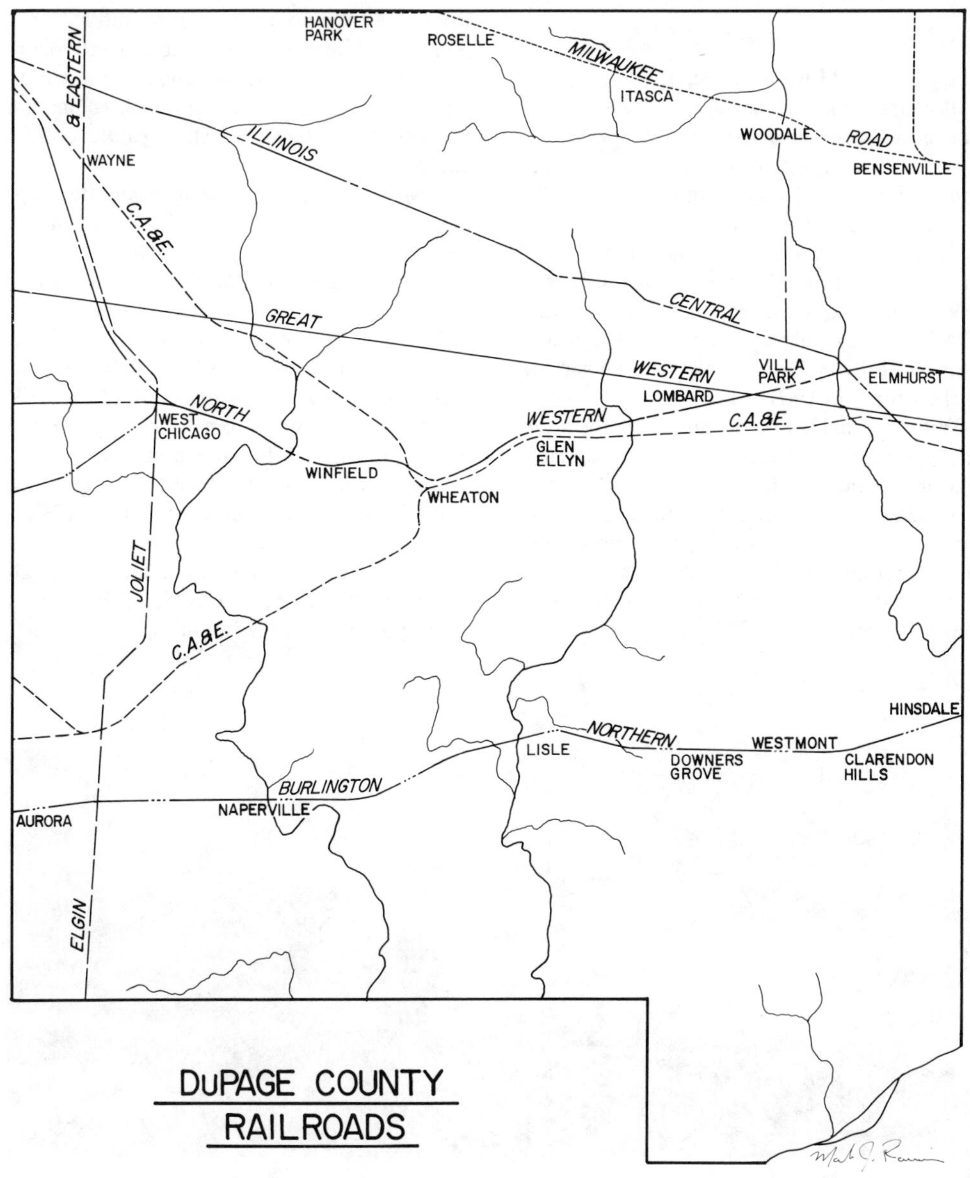


*Art by Mark Ravanesi*

Black Hawk War was produced on the edge of Lake Ellyn, with Indians giving chase to frontiersmen up Honeysuckle Hill.

The mechanical inventions of this half century found their counterpart in the realm of ideas, such as those pertaining to the women's movement and to the growth of colleges and schools. Both the offspring of original settlers and those from outside DuPage secured a significant place for the county in society's intellectual, social, and economic soil.

## RAILS, PAILS, AND SALES

The Chicago, Milwaukee, St. Paul & Pacific Railroad, later known as the Milwaukee Road, was established in 1873; it cut across the northeast corner of DuPage. The Elgin, Joliet and Eastern (EJ&E) was established in 1888, the same year in which the Chicago Great Western was laid across the county. The Illinois Central completed its line in DuPage in 1891, and the Chicago, Aurora & Elgin (CA&E), first called the Aurora, Elgin and Chicago Railway, brought electric rail service to the county in 1901.

With the final laying of rails came the great increase in dairy production and in commercial, industrial, and land sales. The railroads were both cause and effect of DuPage's transformation from a crop to a dairy producing area. After the Civil War, as wheat production moved to the western states, corn reemerged as the main staple crop. Milk and cheese production, however, became the predominant element in the economy until the 1920s. The growing population of Chicago during this half century accounted for the large-scale shipment of dairy products from neighboring DuPage.

Along the Milwaukee Road, Bensenville, Lester's Station, Itasca, and Roselle were pickup points for milk pails. Bensenville had been a quiet German farming community prior to the coming of the railroad in 1873. Following the establishment of the Milwaukee Road, 400,000 pounds of cheese and 150,000 pounds of butter were shipped annually from that town. By 1910 the roundhouse and switching yards had also been constructed in that community, further diversifying its economy and population.

Residential and other commercial developments followed quickly. Dr. Elijah Smith's 1874 platting of Itasca anticipated the imminent new home construction. Roselle Hough had 300 acres surveyed for the "Roselle Addition," in addition to his flax factory for linen and rope production. It was Hough who also was responsible for the directing of the Milwaukee tracks away from Bloomingdale and northward through his own property.

Ontarioville, too, benefited from this rail route. This southern part of modern-day Hanover Park had been called Ontarioville from as early as the 1840s, for it lay on an Indian trail connecting Lake Ontario to Green Bay. With its original post office in DuPage and its first

*CB&Q Lisle Milk Stop.*
*Courtesy of Holleye Riedy Purcell*

*Ontarioville Historical Museum — in Hanover Park.*

school in Cook, it served farmers in both counties. The Wanzer and Wieland dairy companies originated in this area. Other small butter and cheese factories arose before the advent of refrigerated railroad cars moved production farther north. Evidence of the prosperity was John Henry Harmening's construction of an Italinate-style home on today's Route 20 in 1871.

The Illinois Central and Great Western offered both passenger and freight service, while the EJ&E functioned strictly as a "belt line," connecting industrial sites on the perimeter of the metropolitan area from Dyer, Indiana to Waukegan. The Illinois Central (IC) made its 10:00 A.M. milk stop at Cloverdale at Gary and Army Trail roads, where Tedrahn's Grocery began its ninety-five year history in 1888. A hundred people lived on the surrounding dairy farms.

By 1894 at the eastern end of the county an equal number of people would be riding just one of the three commuter lines serving the

*John C. Neltnor House.*
*from* 1874 Atlas & History of DuPage County, Illinois

*Elbert Gary and John Gates. The prominent industrialists' portraits are featured in the DuPage Heritage Gallery.*

1,500 residents of Elmhurst. The Great Western was among these. This line was intersected at the turn of the century by the CA&E. Thus the rural community of Prince Crossing was formed. The Country Home for Convalescent Crippled Children, later owned by the University of Chicago Clinic, was established nearby in 1911. This institution shipped its extensive dairy produce from this rail junction.

The EJ&E brought hope of rapid industrial development to Turner's Junction—not that the community had lacked enterprising individuals during its earlier years. J. C. Neltnor, whose parents had come to Bloomingdale Township in 1847, moved to Turner's Junction at the beginning of the Civil War. By 1874 he owned a nursery in partnership with C. W. Richmond, then county superintendent of schools and also author of the first history of DuPage County. In 1872 Neltnor started *The Fruit and Flower Grower,* a horticultural magazine. Active in national Democratic politics, he began publishing *The DuPage County Democrat* in the 1880s. This paper lasted until 1913. Neltnor himself lived until 1938, when he died at the age of ninety-six.

He was a contemporary of John "Bet-A-Million" Gates, who had grown up on the family farm outside Turner's Junction and who was nine years younger than neighbor Elbert Gary. In 1874 through family connections Gates was established in a hardware store, in which he fared poorly. After selling his interest, he became such a stunningly successful salesman for Joseph Glidden, the DeKalb inventor of barbed wire, that he began to buy steel companies.

This led, in turn, to his involving attorney Elbert Gary, by then the mayor of Wheaton and former county judge, in mergers which resulted in the formation of United States Steel Company. Although Gary became president, Gates was excluded by the conglomerate partners. He then turned his organizing abilities to the founding of the Texaco Company. All of this, however, occurred beyond the confines of DuPage.

Meanwhile, in Gates' hometown Civil War veteran and wealthy hide/tallow merchant C. E. Bolles built an 1894 "opera house," which featured plays and other entertainment. To further the prospect of a boom the name of the town was changed to West Chicago. It was not, however, until the mid-twentieth century that West Chicago fulfilled such promise.

The commercial development did, though,

materialize early along the Burlington line, particularly in Downers Grove. After the roundhouse for the Burlington was built in 1893, half of the suburban trains were serviced there and returned to Chicago; the other half were sent on to Aurora. This community had already undergone expansion, as another Civil War veteran and insurance magnet, A. C. Ducat, had come in 1885 to purchase 800 acres. He subdivided this land, south of 55th and west of Main, with the intention of making it a model community. A promotional booklet in that same year touted 50 foot by 200 foot lots ranging from $3 to $10 per frontage foot, "free from the odors of Bridgeport." He soon offered to install a water system in the mid-1880s if village trustees would have frontyard fences removed, an offer which they chose to refuse. He did eventually succeed in enticing his friend Marshall Field into buying the property, eighty acres of which became Maple Grove Forest Preserve.

The other major residential developer, E. H. Prince, also used the Burlington to bring excursion trains from Chicago to interest prospective buyers in the 250 acres he had subdivided north of the tracks. Prince Pond did, and still does, provide the focal point of that vicinity.

Just south of that neighborhood the first industry in Downers Grove, Dicke's Tool Company, which still makes equipment for electrical linemen, was established in 1889. Casper Dicke had won a prize for such innovations at the Paris World's Fair before coming to America from his native Cologne. Although Downers Grove residents at the time of Chicago's Columbian Exposition were still drawing water from wells and lighting by coal oil, they had made public improvements by the end

*Dicke's Tool Company.*

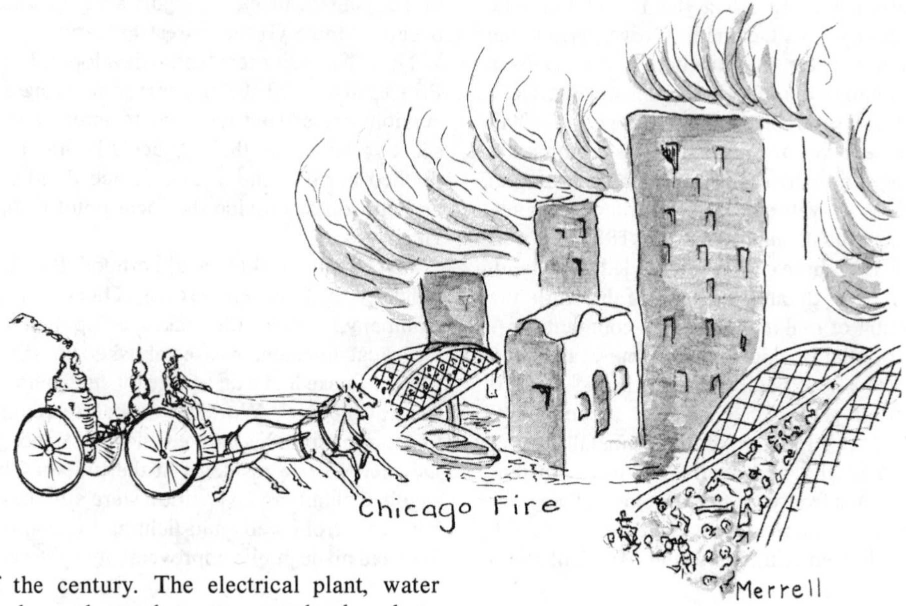


of the century. The electrical plant, water works, and paved streets were due largely to Dicke's leadership.

Other commercial developments of importance in that locality were the Austin Nurseries, the Washburn Greenhouse, and the Kidwell Greenhouse in Belmont, the largest in the county at the turn of the century.

Associated with this business expansion was the Polish settlement in East Grove, along Fairview Avenue. This area was also known as Gostyn, after the village in Poland, from which many of the 500 turn-of-the-century residents had come. St. Mary's Roman Catholic Church was founded in 1891 to serve these Eastern Europeans as well as the Irish residents. This was the only Catholic parish between LaGrange and Naperville, until St. Joseph's was built in downtown Downers Grove in 1906.

Altogether, this community's growth was among the most dramatic in DuPage. It grew from 586 persons in 1880, to 960 in 1890, to 2,103 at the beginning of the new century, making it among only four villages with populations of more than 2,000. The others in order of size were Naperville, Hinsdale, and Wheaton.

Naperville's development, to the west, featured the emergence of James Nichols, a leader not only of local significance, but also of worldwide importance. He had come as an immigrant from Germany in 1876, had graduated from North Central College, and had become the owner of a company that produced manuals for business. This made him the Dale Carnegie of his day. Nichols' self-help book, *The Business Guide*, sold four million copies; it was translated into German and Spanish. He was also instrumental in pioneering door-to-door salesmanship. One of the young men Nichols helped in particular was P. E. Kroehler, who took Fred Long's furniture shop and converted it into Kroehler Manufacturing Company. This was once among the world's largest furniture companies, although it is no longer in business in DuPage County.

In the same year that Nichols came to Naperville, the community purchased the Joe Naper Pumper, its first fire engine. This horse-drawn, hand-operated equipment was used until replaced by a motorized engine fifty years later. That single transition might be taken as the symbol of the whole economic transformation through which DuPage had passed.

At the same time the social scene assumed an elegance for a growing elite. Ironically, this development followed Chicago's greatest disaster until that time. Even citizens of Naperville could view the Great Chicago Fire thirty miles away from the widow's walk of Willard Scott's home, on the high land at Franklin and Washington streets.

*The Joe Naper Pumper. Present day students at the Naper Settlement learn first hand of early fire fighting effort, with the Paw Paw Post Office on the left, and the Martin-Mitchell Museum in the background.*

*Teamster George Stafford on his stake wagon, with the DuPage Courthouse in the background. The rig was used to move household furniture between Wheaton and Chicago in the 1885–1890 period, the round trip taking three days.*
*Courtesy Willis Stafford*

*William Greggs House.*

## FROM FIRE TO FAIR

The Great Chicago Fire had multiple effects on the county. After many had fled the flames, they began to make the area west of the city their home. Noted clothing merchant Henry W. King had purchased Hill Cottage in 1867, using the original tavern of Gerry Bates. It was to become Elmhurst's most famous residence. Not only had Thomas Bryan once owned it, but prominent portrait painter George Healy had also lived there. His "beardless" Lincoln is the only one of its kind of the president. King used it as a summer home until the 1871 fire. He describes the escape from his Lincoln Park home as follows: "As the dry leaves took fire beneath our feet, crossing a bridge on North Avenue and reaching the west side we found a conveyance at noon which brought us out to Elmhurst. We almost felt ashamed to be so comfortable." King subsequently established permanent residence in Elmhurst.

Thomas Bryan housed refugees from the fire on his estate, called "Byrd's Nest," named after his wife's family, the Byrds of Virginia. Elaborate balls and musicales would become common on such estates by the "Gay Nineties," although Elmhurst still remained a one-street hamlet, with prairie chickens so plentiful that they were called "food for newcomers."

Another area affected by the fire was Westmont, so called because of its location as a high point between Lake Michigan and the Mississippi River valley. The person to capitalize on this location was William Greggs, who established the Excelsior brick-making firm beside the clay pit there. The reconstruction of Chicago was facilitated by these building blocks from Gregg's Station, as Westmont was first called; they were placed on the Burlington cars and the gravity of the downhill slope drew the heavily laden train into the city.

Westmont's neighbor to the east, Hinsdale, also received its share of prominent fire refugees, such as H. L. Storey, founder of Storey and Clark Piano Company. As "Millionaires Row" was built in what some called the "Gold Coast of DuPage," the population rose from 500 in 1873 to 1,584 by 1890; thus it moved ahead of Turner as DuPage's third largest village. By 1900 it had replaced Wheaton as the second largest. It was the first community to establish water works, in 1890, and a power plant, in 1896, which it had purchased for $1.00 from J.C.F. Merrill, later president of the Chicago Board of Trade.

Hugh G. Dugan in his *Village on the County Line* describes this period of "crinoline and lace, broad acres and verandas, cupolas, sleighs, surreys, side-saddles, piano recitals, archery, costume balls, and calling cards." The bicycle craze was represented by races every Saturday afternoon in the summer. The Tennis Club was organized in 1893.

Also in this decade, Frank Osgood Butler

moved to Hinsdale. The Butlers of Oak Brook are descendants of those who came in the 1830s from Burlington, Vermont, and established the first paper mill west of the Alleghenies, in St. Charles. After purchasing a home in Hinsdale, Butler bought property in the Fullersburg area from George Robbins, son of Hinsdale's founder. The stands of oak trees along the Salt Creek suggested the Oak Brook name. The Natoma Dairy also became part of the Butler enterprise. Subsequently called Bowman Dairy, it was a pioneer in certified milk and thus anticipated Food and Drug Administration (FDA) regulations. By 1909 F. O. Butler's son Paul had organized the Chicago Polo Club.

The Butlers also had interests in what was first called West Hinsdale, but by 1873 was named Clarendon Hills, as suggested by Robert Harris. This president of the CB&Q Railroad sought with others to turn Clarendon Hills into another high-growth suburb. Oliver J. Stough had purchased Jarvis Fox's land south of the tracks in 1866. Henry C. Middaugh had purchased the 270 acres north of the railroad in 1869. In 1871 he drain-tiled the acreage and planted eleven miles of ash and elm. A designer laid out streets in the curvilinear fashion of Frederick Olmstead, the landscape architect famous for his Riverside Plan. One early commentary on this layout reads: "The peculiarity to this place is that no two streets are parallel and no two lots of the same shape or size. Only men of steady habits must settle in this place, for the serpentine appearance of the streets might prove too much for a head not evenly balanced."

Middaugh also built his own mansion at

*The Middaugh Mansion.*

*Chicago Golf Club Diamond Jubilee, 1892*

Norfolk and Chicago Avenue in 1892. But the anticipated boom did not materialize until after his day—in the 1920s. In the meantime the streets and parkways north of Chicago Avenue were formally vacated by ordinance in 1913, with the trees of today marking the original lines. What did survive the development lull was the Hinsdale Golf Club on Middaugh property, which the Butlers were later to purchase. Golfing represented still another component of the "Gay Nineties."

On New Year's Day in 1906, Marshall Field played at the Chicago Golf Club in Wheaton with Robert Todd Lincoln. According to Wayne Andrews' *Battle for Chicago,* he was back on the same links again a week later on one of the bitterest days of the year. By mid-month Field was dead from an illness contracted from the cold. The incident is illus-

*Burlington Park.*
*Courtesy of Mary Wehrli*

strative of DuPage at the turn of the century, not only in terms of the golf craze, but in what it represented in the pattern of wealth and class.

The World Columbian Exposition of 1893 precipitated the spread of the sport, with Charles Blair Macdonald laying out the first nine-hole course west of the Appalachians on a stock farm off Belmont Road in Downers Grove. Within a year the Chicago Golf Club, later to play host to Walker Cup and other major championship competitions, was founded on the 200-acre Patrick farm in Wheaton. This was the first eighteen-hole course in the U.S.

By 1900 twenty-six clubs were operating in the Chicago area, including those of Hinsdale and Elmhurst, the latter in old Duncklee's Grove along Salt Creek. To the west the Medinah Country Club would be established in Meacham's Grove.

Parallel to this development was the continued growth in estates. Again, Field was a case in point, having purchased the large acreage in Downers Grove in the mid-1880s. By 1920 Marshall Field II had sold the virgin maple stand to the DuPage County Forest Preserve and the balance to developers.

It was indeed the spread of disposable income to greater numbers that led to the opening of Burlington Park in Naperville, an early version of today's amusement parks. On a weekend as many as 10,000 people would ride out from the city on the train for recreation. A counterpart was the Roselle Park Club, established in 1898. Both parks provided for new-found leisure time.

Such modern trends could be related to that life-style-defining event, the Columbian Exposition. Thomas Bryan, who had given Cottage Hill its new name of Elmhurst after the row of elm trees he had planted there, had served as vice president of the World's Fair. His neighbor, banker Henry Glos, had visited the fair so often that one of the rooms in his 1893 Romanesque mansion was decorated with souvenirs from the exposition. A year earlier John Quincy Adams had built the Wheaton library in the same Romanesque style; today it is the DuPage County Historical Museum.

The fair's impact extended even to the westernmost edge of the county. The Dunham farm in Wayne, developed largely by Mark, the son of early pioneer Solomon Dunham, was among the largest horse farms in the country. It specialized in Percheron horses from France, a Clydesdale type needed to break up prairie sod. After a return trip from France, Mark had built what has been called a castle on the northwest corner of Dunham Road and Army Trail Road.

In 1893 during the Columbian Exposition, the Chicago & Northwestern trains brought visitors to the Dunham or Oaklawn farm to view the latest in agricultural technology, as demonstrated by International Harvester.

*Oaklawn Farm.*

*CA&E Ardmore Excursion.*
*Courtesy Villa Park Historical Society*

During the early 1900s the line brought guests for the horse shows, which continued to be featured in that vicinity.

The electric railroad, in itself, had such diverse and far-reaching effects in DuPage as to warrant particular treatment.

## CENTURY'S DAWNING

The first two decades of the twentieth century opened as dramatically as the preceding decades had ended. The acceleration of change was quite visible in 1905 Bensenville where an eight-mile-per-hour speed limit for automobiles was posted. Not quite so obvious, but just as much a sign of modern times, was Philip Lambert's replacing his team of plow horses with his first tractor in 1918 on the site of today's College of DuPage.

Not until the "Roaring Twenties" would motorized vehicles came to dominate the scene. In the meantime, the Chicago, Aurora & Elgin would literally electrify much of the county. Not only did this company in 1901 bring the last of the rail lines through the middle of DuPage, where it branched at the Wheaton switching yards, but its power station, south of Batavia, also served to provide electricity to towns served by the trains.

Among the communities virtually created by the CA&E were the twin developments of Ardmore and Villa Park. Just as Louis Meyer had donated land for the right-of-way to the Chicago & Great Western in 1886, so he did again when the CA&E came across his property at the St. Charles and Ardmore roads intersection; and so did neighbor, Florence Canfield.

In 1908 Chicago-based realtors, Bullard and Pottinger, purchased a part of the Canfield property and subdivided it into 203 lots. The name of Villa Park may have originated with its wealthiest resident, Charles C. Heisen, who owned an estate in Florida with the same name. It was named after the fashionable Philadelphia suburb. Free excursion trains were run on Sunday afternoons for prospective buyers.

The two subdivisions, in order to obtain tax revenues for public improvements, united in 1914, taking Ardmore as the name. By 1917 with the population east of Summit being of greater number, the name was changed to Villa Park. It was also in that part of the community that in 1917 the Ovaltine plant became operational. This company's malt extract had been widely distributed to allied troops, including those in German prison camps, during World War I.

The CA&E also served as a further stimulus to established villages. Glen Ellyn had already undergone its first expansion before the turn of the century under the leadership of Thomas E. Hill. He was a former mayor of Aurora and author of *Hill's Manual of Social and Business Forms,* an etiquette guide, which made him the "Emily Post" of his day. With Seth Baker he had developed Lake Ellyn and the health spa hotel overlooking it. In promoting his "Wildairs" subdivision south of the tracks, he would meet prospective buyers at the train with elaborate horse and carriage. Englishman John Foster was, at the same time, erecting many of the brick buildings still standing downtown. The CA&E added to this momentum as the Glen Oak Country Club was included as a stop.

*Glen Ellyn Hotel.*
*Courtesy of Glen Ellyn Historical Society*

Likewise, the Chicago Golf Club, in south Wheaton, was a favorite stop of the city's elite who came to stay in summer homes as well as to play on the course. The architect for many of these was Jarvis Hunt. His own home featured a parquet floor, the tiles of which were brought from the Chicago World's Fair.

Farther west, the pioneer homestead of Jude Gary lay on the CA&E route. Before his death in 1881, complete with a thirty-carriage funeral procession from the Warrenville Methodist Church, Jude had married a second time. It was this wife who provided a 100-foot-wide strip in exchange for the location of the Montview stop on the farm.

The Warrenville depot, built by William Rockwell, became the center of the settlement that arose north of the original section of town. Rockwell's family had come as tenant farmers to the area in 1853. By the 1900s he had become the largest property owner in the community, succeeding Julius Warren in this regard.

*Brilliant, the Percheron stallion.*
*from a drawing by Rosa Bonheur*

*Loie Fuller.
Courtesy Hinsdale
Historical Society*

These examples of the CA&E's impact along its southwest branch had their counterpart along the northeast fork. A hotel and inn were built for visitors who would come from the train stop to the horse shows and expositions at Oaklawn Farm. Mark Dunham's horse "Brilliant" was painted by Rosa Bonheur as a way of publicizing the 2,000-acre facility.

Such a spread was indeed part of the estate pattern that continued to characterize DuPage even after the World War I era. In 1912 commodities trader Arthur Cutten hired architect Norman Bridges, who had been affiliated with Frank Lloyd Wright, to build the mansion on his 525-acre estate. It was located just north of Joy Morton's Lisle Farms. To the east of them fuel oil and coal magnet J. Berrymans in 1910 built a three-story home, coach house, and 65-foot water tower at the southwest corner of today's Highland Avenue and East-West Tollway. Hand grenade manufacturer Frank Curran bought this complex and surrounding one hundred acres. His family continued to own it until 1979. It is currently being developed as condominiums by Sherman and Gwen Baarstad.

Betwixt and between these clusters of large land holdings, an increasing diversity of population groups were anticipating the proliferation of varying life-styles later in the century. Prior to World War I, the CA&E brought Cad Lewis Sublett, the first of a group of blacks who would build on the eastern edge of Wheaton. Called "The Hill," this area was the one place where blacks could buy without harrassment. Peter Hoy, a Danish immigrant who settled in Lombard, took in "knights of the road," hoboes from the railroad, whom he quartered in his Flowerfield barn.

But of all those from DuPage who represent

its penetration of the modern world, Loie Fuller may best exemplify it. Her mid-winter birth in Castle Inn, which had the only iron stove in the Fullersburg area in the 1860s, caused her to say later that she came into the world "with a cold she never got rid of." In contrast to those limited circumstances of her origin, she gained world-wide fame for her innovative, modern dance. After making her start on the Chicago stage, she won greatest admiration in Europe for her combining diaphanous apparel with electric lights. Her Serpentine Dance led Toulouse Lautrec to paint her whirling in "a mist of irridescent color," and Anatole France to extol her in the introduction to her autobiography, *Fifteen Years of a Dancer's Life.* That acclaim was evidence of the cultural and social growth that was evolving before and into the new century.

## MATTER OF MIND

The tap root of modern times had its intellectual and social fibres intertwined with the profound material change previously noted. Its institutional expression could be identified in the number of schools and colleges which suddenly appeared on the scene. In 1870 North Western College, originally Plainfield College and subsequently named North Central College, moved to Naperville, with Old Main built on an eight-acre site by Morris Sleight. By 1880 James L. Nichols was chairing its innovative Department of Commerce.

In 1873 Elmhurst College marked its beginning when the German Evangelical Synod accepted the thirty acres along prospect Avenue, made available through the generosity of Thomas B. Bryan. The first building, Kranz Hall, built in 1873, was named for the school's first president, Carl F. Kranz. As a proseminary, its main purpose was to prepare students for theological training and to train teachers for the schools of the founding denomination. Bryan's admiration for German culture and learning was also evidenced as he sent his sons to the second floor of the public school where

*St. Procopius College.*
*Courtesy Lisle Heritage Society*

*James Henry Breasted.*
*Courtesy Downers Grove Historical Society*

Herr Lussenhof taught in his native language, rather than to the English-speaking classrooms on the first floor.

Wheaton's first graded school, Longfellow, still standing at the Union and Seminary streets intersection, included high school classes. During the last quarter of the nineteenth century there were only four graded schools classified as high schools, the others being Naperville, West Chicago, and Hinsdale.

The next institution of higher education, St. Procopious in Lisle, did not come to DuPage until after the turn of the century, in 1910. It was founded in 1890 in Chicago by the Bohemian Fathers of the Order of St. Benedict. Their abbey followed in 1914, two years after the Sacred Heart Convent and Academy was built. Specialties in the Czech and Slovak languages and literature are still included in the curriculum of Illinois Benedictine College, as it is now called.

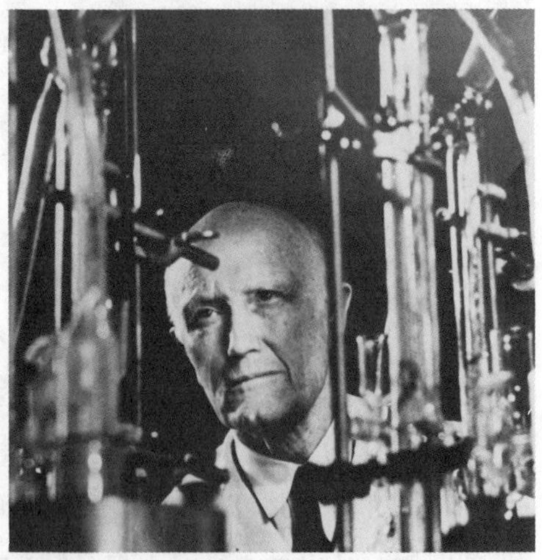

*Friederich Conrad Koch.*
*Courtesy Elmhurst Historical Society*

In this same pre-World War I period Avery Coonley School began its move from Riverside to the west end of Downers Grove. From 1912 to 1929 this country day school established a program and facility for preschoolers through eighth grade. From 1906 Mrs. Coonley and her colleague Lucia Burton Morse had applied the progressive principles of John Dewey in the Cottage School as it was called initially. Dewey, in turn, would describe this educational experiment in his *Schools of Tomorrow*.

Individuals from DuPage whose accomplishments bespeak an in-depth education include Herman A. Fischer, Sr., and Jr. The father's father, Conrad, was among the first settlers in Churchville and was the brother of Dr. Frederick Fischer, whose career has been previously noted. Herman A. Fischer, Sr., distinguished himself as professor of mathematics and philosophy at Wheaton College for forty-three years; Fischer Hall was named for him. His son, Herman A. Fischer, Jr., was one of five children to graduate from Harvard Law School.

Moving to Downers Grove at the age of eight in 1873, James Henry Breasted became famous as an archaeologist in the twentieth century. He first attended school at the two-story schoolhouse on the present site of Lincoln Center. After graduating from North Central College, Breasted seemed set on becoming a pharmacist. But his early participation in the Congregational church led him eventually to enroll in the Chicago Theological Seminary. There he immersed himself in antiquities. By 1919 he had founded the Oriental Institute at the University of Chicago, and in 1922 he was present at the opening of King Tutankhamen's tomb in Egypt.

Pursuing another field of scientific endeavor at the same time was Dr. Friedrich Conrad Koch. Also related to the Fischer family on his mother's side, Fred was born in 1876 in Elmhurst after his parents had fled the Chicago fire and built a home in the newly established Emerson Subdivision. After attending the German Lutheran School, he graduated from Oak Park High School because Elmhurst's high school was not yet accredited. Following his graduation from the University of Illinois in 1899, he became a noted research chemist for Armour Company and a distinguished professor of biochemistry at the University of Chicago. Before his death in 1948, he had become internationally recognized for his studies of enzymes and hormones, and was the first to show that ultraviolet light converted cholesterol into vitamin D.

Applying such new discoveries were persons in health services. Medical practice at the turn of the century was in pronounced contrast to what it had been when doctors first came to DuPage, usually following the railroads. A number of these first physicians were trained in homeopathy. Offices were in the doctors' own homes, and practice was often taken into patients' homes, with tonsils removed and legs amputated on kitchen tables. Embalming was also done in homes until the 1920s.

*Downers Grove Water Tower.*
*Courtesy Downers Grove Historical Society*

*Wood Dale Road, 1916.*

According to Dr. Raymond A. Dieter, whose *History of Medicine in DuPage County* is currently in preparation, the turning point for health care came at the turn of the century, when public utilities were installed. A high proportion of nineteenth-century illness was water-related. Once a clean water supply and sanitary sewers were installed, the fatalities from such diseases as cholera declined dramatically.

Following a system of "rational therapeutics," Henry Lindlahr purchased the Lathrop home at St. Charles Road and Prospect Street in Elmhurst in 1914 as a health resort. Among the notables who came for the nondrug treatment were novelist Sinclair Lewis and Socialist leader Eugene V. Debs.

The first hospital in DuPage was the Hinsdale Sanitarium, founded in 1905. Previously, in 1899, Drs. David and Mary Paulson had come from the Battle Creek Sanitarium in Michigan to establish a Seventh-Day Adventist mission and medical center in Chicago. After receiving care at that facility, Charles B. Kimball, manager of the Beckwith Estate, arranged for the transfer of that center to the Hinsdale property. The dedicatory address was delivered by J. H. Kellogg of Battle Creek.

Edwards Sanitarium in Naperville opened its doors in 1907 as "the torchbearer of just and efficient treatment of the consumptive." The words were those of Theodore Sachs, who had inspired Eudora Hull (Gaylord) Spalding to found the institution in memory of her first husband, Edward Gaylord. In 1909 the Jewish Charities of Chicago opened a tuberculosis sanitarium in Winfield, which eventually evolved into Central DuPage Hospital.

Parallel to the rising concern in the health field was that of child welfare. The first evidence of this was the orphanage established adjacent to the Evangelical Lutheran Seminary in Addison, in 1873. The preceding year, during the silver jubilee of the Missouri Synod Lutheran Church, eight congregations had joined together to build a facility accommodating a hundred youths.

In 1888 the county board of supervisors purchased 176 acres for the DuPage County Home and Farm, now the County Convalescent Center. In 1895 the Evangelical Home for Children and the Aged began in Bensenville. It still is in operation on York Road.

Business-inspired rest and recreation facilities for women employees came after 1913. In that year the Chicago Telephone Company purchased a forty-two acre wooded site in Warrenville for its "Hello Girls," who were suffering job-related stress. This program continued until 1939, when Our Lady of the Cenacle obtained the land. Nearby, the old Warren Mansion served as a summer camp for Montgomery Ward female employees between 1918 to 1925. Likewise, the Katherine Legge Memoral in Hinsdale was made available to the women workers of International Harvester.

As these accommodations were being provided, the feminist movement was realizing a significant breakthrough; for it was also in 1913 that women were allowed to vote in all elections in Illinois. Much credit for that development may be ascribed to Ellen Martin of Lombard. A native of New York state, she became the first woman law student in Chautaugua County, and began practicing in Chicago in 1876; however, she was not recognized officially as an attorney, because she was not an elector, a status not then granted to women.

On April 6, 1891, she and fourteen prominent women residents of Lombard marched into polling places and demanded ballots. The village charter did not explicitly use the word "male" in defining electors. It referred only to "citizens." The women's claim was then contested before county judge George W. Brown. Later that year women were allowed to vote in

*Evangelical Lutheran Orphan Home.*
*Courtesy Historical Museum of Addison*

*DuPage County Welcome Home for returning World War I veterans. 25,000 lined the streets in Wheaton on September 6, 1919.*

school elections. Ellen Martin died four years before the Nineteenth Amendment was passed in 1920, granting nationwide suffrage to women.

At the time of her death, the struggle with other sterotypes continued. Those of German descent were having to register in SS. Peter and Paul Roman Catholic Church and in other ways prove their patriotism during World War I, although sixty-one of the parishioners were serving in the armed forces. Yet even those parochialisms would soon be giving away to the broader view that came with the unprecedented influx of newcomers in the following decades.

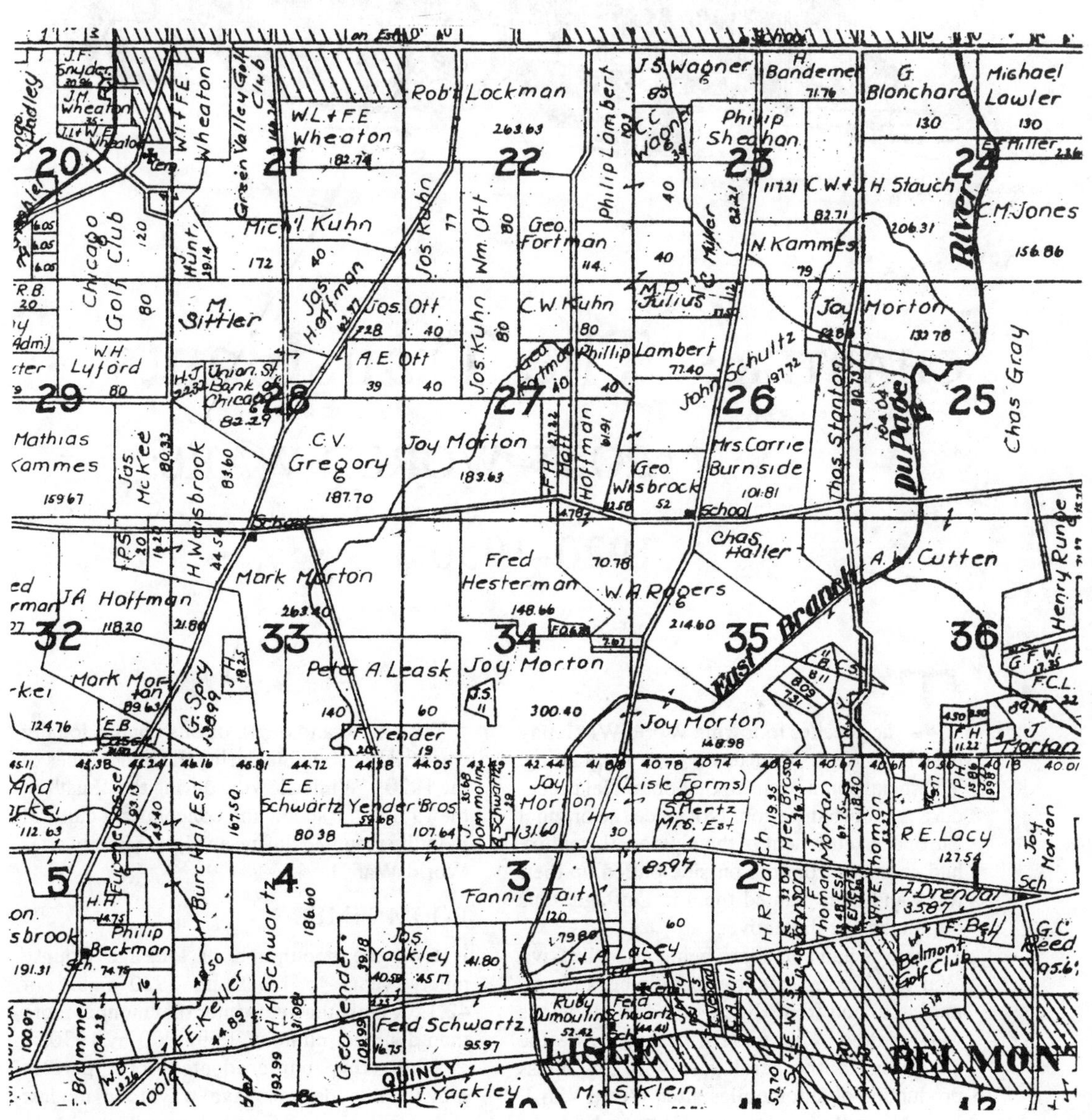


World War I era map.

*Louis Place.*

# CHAPTER 5 The Transplants

## POST–WORLD WARS: 1920–1950

The decades following World War I may best be thought of in terms of transplanting. The social counterpart to that botanical procedure is suburbanization. Not since the original European settlement of the nineteenth century had so many from the outside pulled up their roots and then planted them in DuPage, thus outnumbering the natives.

Suburbs had come into being after the Civil War to a limited extent as people began commuting to and from Chicago and subdivisions were platted. This pattern ceased to be the exception to the rural rule with the mass production of automobiles after World War I. In 1900 automobiles were counted in the hundreds. By 1920 they were numbered in the millions. That kind of geometric progression made the automobile the predominant invention of the era, thus creating the moving-van phenomenon.

The extent and depth of this change locally was strikingly visible during the boom times of the 1920s. While slowing during the "bust" of the 1930s, the social and concomitant cultural mobility resumed during and immediately after World War II.

### BOOM TIMES

It took the population of DuPage County ninety years to reach its 1920 figure of 42,120. Only ten years later that number more than doubled, climbing to 92,000 by 1930.

While this unprecedented 118 percent growth in a decade gave way to a modest increase during the Great Depression, with the county attaining only a 103,000 level by 1940, a 40 percent spurt followed in the 1940s. The next chapter will recount the resumption of a doubling growth rate in a decade after the 1950 record of 154,000 people.

*Bloomingdale Garage, 1915.*

The areas that were most heavily affected by the larger numbers in the 1920s were the townships of, in order of size, York, Downers Grove, and Milton. By 1930 Downers Grove Township had taken second place to York Township. The population of Downers Grove Township grew 250 percent from 1920 to 1930, from 7,925 to 25,396. During this decade Elmhurst leapfrogged into first place as the largest community in the county, increasing from 4,594 inhabitants to 14,055. Another sign of the land development bonanza was the increase in real estate agencies in Glen Ellyn, from three in 1920 to twenty in 1928.

Arthur T. McIntosh was the individual who most typified this period's "land-office" business. He was the largest real estate developer in DuPage after World War I and into the post–World War II era. Originally from Iowa, he founded his Chicago land development company in 1907. He also was involved in major developments in Cook, Lake, and Will counties, as well as in Florida and Iowa. In 1920 he bought property in Westmont, laying out streets and sidewalks and selling land for as little as $5 an acre. Within four years, he had 1,800 buyers, and Westmost experienced its initial surge of growth.

Among these purchasers were persons of various ethnic backgrounds who had first settled in Chicago and were working for such companies as International Harvester and Western Electric. They were looking for places on the outskirts of the city. These "transplants" from abroad continued to have a feeling for the soil and so sought room for gardens. They would often drive to the suburb after working hours or over the weekend to build their own homes, aided by the headlights of their cars. That practice indicates how the automobile was becoming the dominant means of transportation and how inseparable it was from the building boom.

In 1922 McIntosh bought the property of

Henry Middaugh in Clarendon Hills. He converted it into the McIntosh Golf Addition, because of its proximity to the Hinsdale Golf Club. When laying the streets, he named three of them after himself—Arthur, Tuttle, and McIntosh. In the unincorporated community of Belmont, he bought property that included today's Downers Grove Golf Club, the area around Puffer School on Belmont Road. Altogether McIntosh had submitted twenty-five plats in Downers Grove Township by 1935, twenty-four such housing sites in Lisle Township, and an equal number in Milton. To promote the McIntosh Lisle Farms south of the Morton Arboretum, trainloads of people were brought on excursions. North of the arboretum Walter A. Rogers, a founder of the Bates-Rogers Construction Company, established the estate of Warwood. Upon his death in 1955, the McIntosh Company purchased that land.

Parallel to expanded home ownership was growth of horticulture, long a strong element in the DuPage economy, which took on fresh impetus during these postwar decades. George Ball, a Spanish-American War veteran, began the Ball Nurseries in Glen Ellyn in 1905. By 1928 he owned seven greenhouses in that community and had also started seven others in West Chicago. He then concentrated his holdings in the latter community, eventually selling only on a wholesale basis and becoming best known for hybrids and seeds. The George Ball calendulas won a far-reaching reputation. In 1938 he was elected president of the Society of American Florists. At its height, George J. Ball, Inc., operated seventeen companies, including six overseas.

By 1939 Ball had diversified his interests, purchasing the North Avenue Airport and developing it into the largest airfield between Chicago and the Mississippi River. During World War II it was called the Air Activities Airport. It later became the DuPage County Airport, and it now operates as the Fox Valley Air Authority.

Others were also interested in the new field of aviation, including Emile and Herbert Miller. Theirs was the American Eagle Airport, west of Finley Road and south of Roosevelt, on the site of today's International Village. These brothers had come to DuPage in 1913 from Berwyn with their cabinet-maker father. He subsequently helped establish them in Willie Knight's Auto Repair. In 1921 Emile, at nineteen, took spare parts from automobiles and used them to build an airplane. At seventy-nine he still could strip down a plane and reassemble it. The airfield lasted from 1929 to 1964. Another airport, Mitchell Field in Addison, also lasted until the 1960s. A hardware warehouse is now located on that site.

*Arthur T. McIntosh. Courtesy of Northwestern University Archives*

The busiest of all the nation's airports was to have its beginning in this same period. Extending into Bensenville, Douglas Field, previously called Orchard Park (still evident in the ORD on baggage tags), was begun in 1942 with the aircraft plant delivering 655 large cargo planes to the armed forces by October, 1945. At the war's end, Chicago purchased the field in 1946, along with an additional 6,300 acres of neighboring farmland, and O'Hare International Airport, named after a World War II flying ace, came into being. During this decade

*The Ball Nurseries in the mid-1950s (from left) George K. Ball, G. Carl Ball, G. Victor Ball.*
*Courtesy of George G. Ball Inc.*

*First Air Mail from Westmont, 1938.*
*Courtesy of Westmont Historical Society*

*Dan and Ada Rice — with Liberace and Don Ameche.*
*Courtesy Forest Preserve District of DuPage County*

Bensenville doubled its 1940 population of 1,875.

Despite this swift development in the northeastern corner of the county, neighboring Wood Dale remained rural; electricity had not been brought into that area until 1923 and phone service not until 1927. Until 1948 Police Chief Adolph Soska was having his wife take calls at their home. There are now nineteen on the staff of that department.

Just to the south of Wood Dale, however, a foretaste of things to come was visible as early as 1918. It was then, on the east end of Addison at Lake and Villa roads, that Hungarian immigrants Louis and Mary Bosworth started their own restaurant. Louis' Place remains the oldest continuing restaurant in DuPage. Such as establishment testified to the growing use of the automobile, because customers would drive out from the city.

During Prohibition eating places on the edge of the metropolis also served as "roadhouses." In Winfield Township "Whiskey Creek" was associated with more than one "still." Another was located on Lambert Road, north of today's College of DuPage and across from Berger's fox farm.

Among the most notorious bootleggers was Roger Touhy, whose widower, policeman father, and eight children had moved to Downers Grove from Chicago in 1908. After graduating from St. Joseph's parochial school in 1911, he served in the military and taught code to naval officers at Harvard. After returning to Chicago, he established a trucking company which lent trucks for transporting "moonshine." Touhy subsequently engaged in a protracted feud with Al Capone.

The automobile accounted for still another kind of service in the county—the first ice cream drive-in. This innovation was the result of collaboration between two Downers Grove boyhood chums, Walter Fredenhagen and Earl Prince. In 1928 the latter opened up the initial Prince Castle in DeKalb. Meanwhile, Walter, whose family business dated to the nineteenth-century Fredenhagen grist mill in Warrenville, bought a wholesale ice cream company in Naperville. In 1931, during the Depression, he opened four ice cream drive-in stores in DuPage and called the chain Prince Castle. These friends also knew paper-cup salesman Ray Kroc, who later founded McDonald's. Because the cooperation between the two DuPage county men did not result in a merger, Fredenhagen renamed his operation Cock Robin in the 1950s.

## STILL ESTATES

There were still estates in the midst of this land and commercial development, representing the continuation of a "country gentleman" life-style. Previous mention has been made of Robert McCormick's assuming ownership of his grandfather Medill's Red Oak Farm, changing the name to Cantigny because of his participation in that World War I battle. His cousin, Chauncy McCormick, in the 1920s purchased the land just to the south, calling it St. James Farm, now owned and operated by his son, Brooks McCormick. They cooperated with owners of neighboring estates to begin the DuPage Hunt, which lasted into the 1950s. The fox chase began at Cantigny with Colonel McCormick serving as master of the hounds. The Wayne Hunt was launched in 1935 by Joy Morton II, whose father, Mark, owned property in Wayne Township. A subsequent merger resulted in the Wayne-DuPage Hunt.

There were others aspiring to such equestrian activity. In 1919 Francis Stuyvesant Peabody, of the Chicago-based Peabody Coal Company, bought property in the Fullersburg area for a country home. Over three years he built a Tudor mansion on the 848 acres. On Sunday morning, August 17, 1922, a fox hunt had been arranged by his son, Jack. When the chase ended on the south end of the estate on Ogden Avenue, someone noticed that Mr. Peabody was missing. He was found lying on a grassy knoll, dead of a heart attack at the age of sixty-three. In 1924 Mrs. Peabody sold the property to the Franciscan Fathers, who have since used a portion of it for the Mayslake Retreat Center. Senior citizen housing is now located on another part of the site.

Another example of persisting elegance was that of Danada Farms, named for its owners Dan and Ada Rice. He had been born in 1897 in Chicago, later rising in the commodity business to become one of its most successful dealers. The Daniel F. Rice Company flourished for thirty years, from the 1930s to the 1960s, surviving the Depression and World War II and merging with the Haydyn-Stone Corporation in 1960.

His fellow trader, Arthur Cutten, persuaded Rice to buy Mark Morton's nearby holdings in 1929. Danada eventually grew to encompass 1,300 acres. He planted no fewer than 5,000 trees in his apple orchard.

The Rices' real claim to fame was their twenty-five-horse stable and racetrack, where their Kentucky-born horses were trained. One of these, Ada's Lucky Debonair, won the 1965 Kentucky Derby. Among the horse enthusiasts entertained in their 1939 home were Don Ameche, Jimmy Durante, and Liberace.

Joy Morton, on his adjacent Lisle Farms, had more than commercial interest in his land. After making the initial purchase of farmers' wood lots in 1909 and building his "Thorn-

*Brooks McCormick — by cross country jump at St. James Farm.*

hill" home in 1911, he turned increasing attention to his estate, leaving the day-to-day operation of the Morton Salt Company to his son Sterling, nephew Carl, and treasurer, Daniel Peterkin. With his father, J. Sterling Morton, having founded Arbor Day, Joy had a long-standing interest in establishing "an outdoor museum of woody plants." Judge Win Knoch, in an interview just before his death in 1983, reported that Joy Morton asked his advice prior to starting the arboretum. Wanting the public to enjoy the acreage, he was considering donating it to the forest preserve. Knoch advised him to set up a foundation instead, to avoid the possibility of future political vagaries. The Morton Arboretum was established as a privately controlled trust in 1922.

## OLD AND NEW DEALS

Knoch also provides the connecting link to the governmental developments which transpired during this thirty-year period. While the New Deal had considerable impact on the local scene, the Republican dominance continued as it had since the Civil War, except for renegade Republicans who had won as "Bullmoosers" during the Theodore Roosevelt years.

Knoch's grandparents on both sides had immigrated from Germany. His father, William, a cigar manufacturer in Naperville, had served on the county board and was one-time mayor of Naperville. Knoch came from a politically active family.

After graduating from SS. Peter and Paul parochial school and Naperville High School, Knoch earned his law degree from DePaul. He then served with the infantry in World War I.

Upon his return, he entered law practice with Chauncey Reed and Russell Keeney. Reed soon became state's attorney with Knoch's organizational support. Between 1934 and 1956 Reed served as United States congressman from DuPage, followed in this office by Keeney. These victories were due in large measure to Knoch's helping consolidate

*Win Knoch greets Ohio Senator Robert Taft.*
*Courtesy Doris Knoch Wood*

*Joy Morton. After commuting from Chicago, the founder of the Morton Arboretum walks the Joy Path.*
*Courtesy Morton Arboretum*

the power of the Republican party locally, although he never sought the chairman's role.

Knoch himself ran for the office of county judge in 1930. He won, in part, because of the post-World War I support of the American Legion, which in addition to being a veterans' organization also functioned as a community voting bloc. Knoch would frequently campaign with veteran Clarence V. "Pegleg Pete" Wagemann, who was also the county clerk.

Knoch went on to distinguish himself in the judiciary. In 1958, upon the nomination of his friend Senator Everett Dirksen, President Dwight Eisenhower named Knoch to the United States Appeals Court, covering Illinois, Indiana, and Wisconsin.

In Naperville, there were four accomplishments for which Knoch wished to be remembered. The first was the organizing of the Naperville National Bank in 1934, in the midst of the Depression, thereby helping local citizens maintain solvency. Secondly, he served as general chairman of the Naperville Centennial Committee, which led to the purchase and development of Centennial Beach. By 1938 he had also become the chairman of DuPage's Centennial. A third contribution was persuading Caroline Martin Mitchell, descendant of

*Lottie Holman O'Neil.*

George Martin, to bequeath the twenty acres of homestead as a perpetual museum, the Martin-Mitchell Museum, and site for Naperville Central High School. Finally, in 1955, after the invention of antibiotics ended the need for Edwards Sanitarium as a tuberculosis treatment center, Knoch led in its conversion to a general hospital. Another law partner, Melvin J. Abrahamson, oversaw its formation as the only tax-supported hospital in the county.

At the same time that Knoch was beginning his career, another of considerable importance was being launched in Downers Grove. There Lottie Holman O'Neil was becoming the first woman ever to be elected to the state legislature in Illinois. This was a result of the Nineteenth Amendment to the Constitution, which granted the franchise to women. A resulting development, the formation of the League of Women Voters, helped to create the support needed to assure her election in 1922. She served consecutive terms until 1963, except for two years when she made an unsuccessful bid for the United States congressional seat. Also of significance is that the minutes of the DuPage League of Women Voters, in February 1929, reported a distribution of leaflets titled "Shall Women Serve on Juries in Illinois?" Two years later, November 28, 1931, women were allowed by law to serve on juries, and the county jury list for the first time had women's names on it.

In the 1930s the New Deal of Franklin D. Roosevelt was defining new political realities throughout the land. Although the devastation experienced elsewhere in the country was not so severe locally, suffering was felt nevertheless. In May 1933, $10,911 in public aid was distributed to the unemployed. Downers Grove received the largest share, $3,159. Wayne received the least, $174. The township of Lisle had 223 families receiving

*Remnant of Camp McDowell. Courtesy Forest Preserve District of DuPage County*

public assistance and a soup kitchen operating at the Morton Arboretum.

By 1936, when the national unemployment rate rose to 16.9 percent, it was only 4.7 percent in DuPage County. Yet all but one of the New Deal programs were represented. Graue Mill was a case in point. It had operated as a mill until 1929. The Butler family owned it at that time, then sold it to the forest preserve district. Through a combination of Works Progress Administration (WPA) and Civilian Conservation Corps (CCC) efforts, the dam and millrace were reconstructed and the building restored. Reforestation and erosion prevention were undertaken on this forest preserve property.

Along North Avenue, at the Salt Creek, a CCC camp was established. This program, administered by the United States Army, with the help of Army Reserve officers, resulted in the paving of North Avenue in 1933, with trees planted beside the roadway.

Another location where the effects of the New Deal were particularly evident was McDowell Grove, the forest preserve between Naperville and Warrenville. The CCC came to McDowell in the 1930s, shortly after the preserve had been purchased by the district. There were as many as 300 men working at that camp, a site for construction of bridges and dams as well as for state and county flood control projects. In April 1938 a group of older workers, veterans of World War I, were brought in from the Fullersburg Preserve where they had been stationed previously.

After the bombing of Pearl Harbor in 1941,

*Westmont Railroad Station, W.P.A. Project.*
*Courtesy of Westmont Historical Society*

McDowell Grove became the site of a secret installation for radar equipment, the second largest such collection in the world during World War II. The army built Camp McDowell in twenty-eight days, taking the old CCC barracks, adding to it guard houses and a radar school building. The person in charge of the camp was a priest, Father Claridge. As many as 400 men trained at this camp during the course of the war. The security was tight; even refuse collection followed a special format. Because the camp had no food disposal, a local resident was recruited to remove and elminate the refuse without leaving any clues of the camp's existence.

At war's end the district bought the remaining government land at McDowell Grove, in 1946. Today the only evidence of this operation is an H-shaped concrete slab. At one time the school structure was twenty-eight feet high, with a false roof which concealed radar dishes and screens from view during the day. At night trainees folded away this facade to expose the equipment for use. Only shortly before the war Wheaton College student Grote Reber had invented a dish-shaped device to eliminate excessive static on his ham radio band. From this invention came the first radio telescope.

One person whose life accents the New Deal period was Seymour "Bud" Waterfall. Next to Argonne National Laboratory is Waterfall Glen Forest Preserve, named after him. He came to DuPage in 1928, at the age of ten. Before his life's end, he had become chairman of the county board and president of the forest preserve district. His place in county govern-

*1936 County Board (from left, bottom row) Charles L. Gary, Jonas R. Foster, Nick W. Lies, Theodore F. Hammerschmidt, Adam W. Kohley, Frank J. Bogan, Anton Dudek. (Middle row) William Senf, Seymour Waterfall, Jr., Donald R. Murray, Harold P. Dunton, Joseph F. Yackley, Lewis F. Mechan, John J. Kelly. (Top row) Henry H. Zainginger, A. H. Beckman, Frank W. McCabe, Walter R. Youngberg, Clarence V. Wagemann (Clerk), Charles C. Kautz, John H. Horstman.*

ment as a "Johnny-come-lately" to the community was in contrast to others on the board, who came from nineteenth-century families. Nicholas Lies, for example, was from a Prussian family who had settled in Bloomingdale Township in 1853. Adam W. Kohley lived on the same property at Route 53 and 83rd Street that his grandfather farmed in 1847.

Certainly Waterfall's arrival did not presage such political involvement. He lived in Westmont, having been trained as a civil engineer, and worked for the street and sewer department of that village. When the Depression hit, he was soon out of a job. Then he obtained the position of administrator of relief funds for the New Deal programs. He also became more actively involved in politics after the Depression. Again, the political success he enjoyed was related to his connections with the American Legion, which supported him. He was never defeated in candidacy for office between the 1930s and the 1960s.

*An Adam Emory Albright Painting, Photo by Barbara Natzke Courtesy Warrenville Public Library District*

## FLOWERING ARTS

Likewise, it was the New Deal that contributed to the career of Ivan Albright, who represented the artistic flowering in the decades between the World Wars. But it is first necessary to review the way he was transplanted to DuPage.

He was the son of Adam Emory Albright, a Wisconsin native, who had studied at the Chicago Fine Arts Institute, with Thomas Eakins at the Fine Arts Academy in Philadelphia, and in Europe where he was influenced by Impressionism. He then moved to the Chicago area, and eventually to a picturesque location along the West Branch of the DuPage River in Warrenville. In 1924 he purchased what had been the Methodist church in Warrenville as a studio and a nearby home on Aurora Avenue. His twin sons, Ivan and Malvin, moved to Warrenville in 1927, having first tried their hand at other fields, but ultimately following in their father's artistic footsteps. Yet they choose a decidedly different style from that of Adam Emory, whose idyllic childhood scenes, including those of the twins as boys, made him the precursor of Norman Rockwell. In contrast, Ivan and Malvin, the former in particular, portrayed the decay of life and flesh. The two would later turn their father's pictures toward the wall of the studio when visitors came.

During the Depression, Ivan was involved briefly in the Public Works Art Project (PWAP). For it he painted the pictures of his neighbor across the street, Mrs. George Stafford (1933–1934), called "The Farmer's Kitchen." The series is close to the Regionalist theme of such other artists as Thomas Hart Benton, but it is unique in its detail and complexity of patterns. This painting now hangs in the Smithsonian. In 1943 Ivan was asked to paint the portrait of Dorian Gray for the movie of that name. He journeyed to Hollywood, and brother Malvin painted the younger versions of that Oscar Wilde character.

Although the brothers left DuPage County after gaining fame, their father continued as a resident until his death in 1957, at age ninety-five. Both brothers died in 1983, Malvin in September and Ivan in November. Most of Ivan's paintings on exhibit at the Chicago Art Institute are of DuPage County subjects. In

*The Albright Studio. Originally the Warrenville Methodist Church, the 1858 building is used today as the Warrenville Historical Museum and cable television facility.*

*Carl Sandburg — at the rededication of the Junior High School named after him, with Elmhurst historian Helmut Berens.*
*Courtesy Elmhurst Historical Society*

contrast to his often morbid subjects, he was a cheerful, fast-talking man who sometimes joked about his art. He once answered a reporter who asked him to explain his art, "Explain it? It's hard enough to paint it!"

Another artist of note, the originator of "Little Orphan Annie," was Harold Gray who lived in Lombard in the 1920s at the time he devised the cartoon. He subsequently bought the expansive Victorian home on North Main, built by Dr. William LeRoy, for his parents, with whom he lived for a while. In 1929 he married Winifred Frost, who had worked in the ticket office of the local movie house. They moved to Connecticut soon after.

Growing up in Elmhurst during the same period was Margaret Chant, who was also to marry a person of prominence. In 1948 in a Minneapolis dentist's waiting room, she met George Papandreou. She subsequently married this economics professor, who has become Greece's prime minister.

One of the best-known literary figures of the time, Carl Sandburg, lived on York Avenue in Elmhurst during the decade of the 1920s. After commuting home from the city, where he was a columnist for the *Chicago Daily News,* he would continue writing in his "Happiness House" residence. At night neighbors would hear him on the typewriter, not knowing until later that the effort resulted in *Rootabaga Stories* for children; *The American Songbag* in 1927; and *Good Morning, America,* a 1928 book of poems, as well as *The Prairie Years,* the first part of his Lincoln trilogy. By the end of the decade, traffic had increased so much on York Avenue that he thought it too congested and moved to Harbert, Michigan.

While Sandburg changed his residence to Michigan, two other writers of prominence continued working in Downers Grove. One was Sterling North, who wrote the novel *Rascal* in 1934. Alice Tisdale Hobard wrote *Oil for the Lamps of China,* which was made

*World War II ship named for the county.*

into a movie. Another author in Elmhurst, Rosamund DuJardin, was concurrently writing short stories and children's works of note.

Living in the area for a short time was Katherine Dunham, identified as the Mother of Black Dance. Following her birth in 1914 in Chicago to a French-Canadian Indian mother and a black father, she moved with them to a subdivision in Glen Ellyn. There Katherine attended an elementary school. During that period homemade bombs were thrown at their windows, but the family persisted.

A later move to Joliet was followed by her receiving two degrees in anthropology from the University of Chicago, starring in Ruth Page's 1933 Martinique ballet, choreographing and dancing in the 1940 stage and film production of "Cabin in the Sky." The 1943 production of "Stormy Weather" ensued. Before her death in 1983, she had established a Performing Arts Training Center in East St. Louis for ghetto youths.

Another event which highlighted the racial issue occurred in York Center. After the outbreak of World War II and the imposition of gas rationing, Louis Shirky, a ten-year resident of that community, found it impossible to drive into Chicago to attend the First Church of the Brethren. He then took a first step in establishing that denomination locally and also in purchasing the Goltermann farm for a housing cooperative. When blacks were allowed to buy into the co-op and two families did in 1948, a hundred neighboring citizens gathered to protest in the District 49 school. By March 1950, however, spokesman Jesse Ziegler could write ". . . there is new friendliness and quite likely a more general support for the right of the Co-op to carry on its own business according to its principles." By 1957 Bethany Theological Seminary, the divinity school for the Brethren, was located at Meyers and Butterfield roads.

The cultural flowering in the county was in large measure a result of the cross-fertilization which characterized this era of social transplants. It is fitting, then, to conclude the description of this period with the lyrics of "Judge" Frank Earl Herrick, who has been called the "Poet Laureate of DuPage County." From a family whose Warrenville roots dated to the 1830s, this justice-of-the-peace was in the 1930s catching the sense of excitement of a county becoming more aware of its own uniqueness, blending old and new, commerce and estates, art and politics. Calling DuPage "A star upon the breast of great Chicagoland, a jewel in the crest of Illinois the grand . . . ," he wrote in "The Song of DuPage County":

There's a Spirit fine and gentle
Who goes with me night and morning . . .
And he tells me all the stories
All the lore and all the legends
of DuPage and its good people . . .
Clear from Signal Hill to Bartlett
From Lake Street to Copenhagen
From the Airport down to Downers
From Army trail to Ogden.
And he knows all of its cities
All its villages and hamlets,
Knows Roselle, Nick Lies Kingdom,
And he knows all West Chicago
(little replica of Dublin)
With its railroads and its freight yards;
Knows great Elmhurst and its lordly
Avenues of shade and beauty,
The Goliath of the county.
And he knows Lombard, the splendid,
Lombard and its lovely lilacs . . .
Knows Hinsdale, of kingly glory,
Great estates and trees and landscapes . . .
Rocky Glen and leafy Wood Dale
Herrick Lake and the Bird Refuge
And Glen Ellyn's crystal mirror . . .
And great Morton Arboretum
A crown jewel of the Nation . . .
Westmont, wide awake and coming,
Winfield, in its Sleepy Hollow,
Wayne, a wild rose on the prairie . . .
Knows Lisle township's rural beauty,
Adam Kohley's lovely country;
Warrenville, the grand old rustic . . .
Naperville, renowned in legends . . .
Warrenhurst and Swift and Belmont,
Bensenville and small Eola,
Frontenac and Lace and Granger,
Cloverdale and Lisle and Ardmore,
Addison and fair Itasca
And young Villa Park, the giant.

For a thousand years hence forward
May this DuPage County Spirit
Watch and keep our noble homestead . . .

Fermilab.

# CHAPTER 6 Succession Community

## SINCE 1950

"Succession" is the description of the way plant communities evolve both in number and diversity. This ecological process, first formulated by Henry C. Cowles of the University of Chicago in 1899, was popularized by May Theilgaard Watts of the Morton Arboretum in her book *Reading the Landscape of America*.

This evolutionary model of simpler life forms giving way to the more complex also provides an interpretative framework for post-1950 DuPage. A comparable transformation in the county's population, economic, political, and cultural composition occurred in the wake of World War II.

### POPULATION EXPLOSION

The 1980 census put this transformation in dramatic perspective. Of DuPage's 658,858 people, 75 percent had been gained in the preceeding thirty years. The increase of 171,000 from 1970 represented the largest absolute growth of population in any county outside the Sunbelt. DuPage is currently the sixteenth fastest growing county, the others being located south of the Mason-Dixon line. It has become larger than the cities of Boston, Cleveland, New Orleans; it has a population greater than five states. For most of the history of the six-county Chicago area, DuPage was least in population. It is now second largest in the state.

Even since the turn of the decade, there have been marked developments. This has been particularly evident in Naperville which, according to a special count in 1983, has become the most populous community in DuPage with a total of 49,196 people. That increase of 6,600 persons amounts to a 15.5 percent growth in three years. Elmhurst, which had

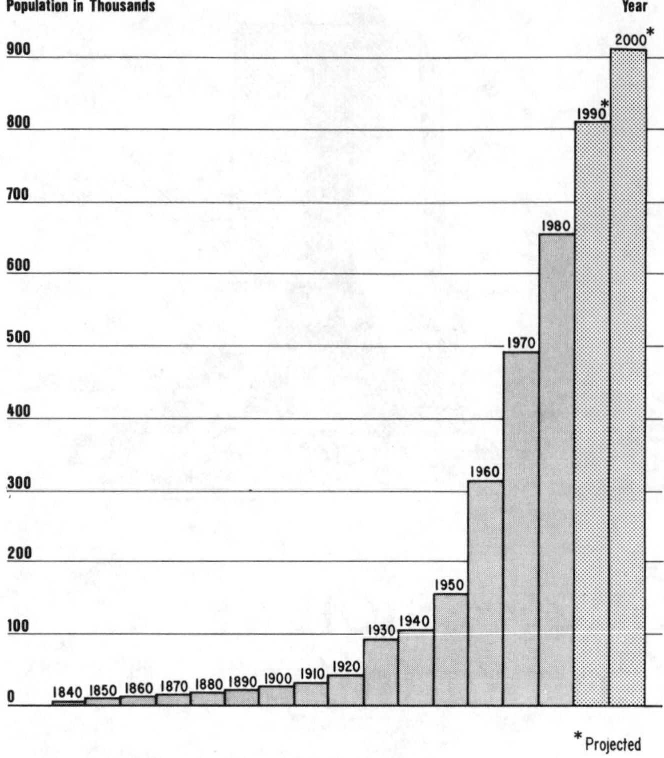


**Du Page County Population Growth, 1840 - 2000**

*Courtesy DuPage County Development Department*

held the lead as the largest city in the county for most of the century, is now well behind in second place. In relative terms, the village of Bloomingdale showed the biggest gain between 1970 and 1980, from 2,974 to 12,659, a fourfold increase.

This numerical expansion found its counterpart in spatial annexation. Naperville doubled in size virtually overnight in 1960, while William Zaininger was mayor, in the largest single annexation in DuPage history. This action followed the state legislature's adoption of the one-and-a-half-mile jurisdictional review rights for the purpose of preventing separate incorporation by adjacent subdivisions. Builders would often seek incorporation with a minimum of residents to escape the requirements of the county's or city's building code. In the 1970s the incorporated city again expanded from twelve to twenty-two square miles. In DuPage as a whole, unincorporated areas decreased correspondingly from encompassing 23 percent of the population in 1970 to 18 percent in 1980.

Three other characteristics of the changing demographic scene must be noted, each a sign of the times in society at large. The increased percentage in nonwhite residents presents itself first. The overall pattern was from less than 1 percent of the population in 1970 to more than 5.2 percent ten years later. Hispanics represent 2.6 percent of the total, Asian-Americans 1.4 percent, and blacks 1.2 percent. Among communities with higher-than-average nonwhite groups are West Chicago and Bensenville with Hispanics comprising 16.7 percent and 8.4 percent of these communities respectively. Glendale Heights is 12 percent nonwhite with 7.8 percent of these being Asian. Carol Stream's population is 4 percent black.

A survey of 800 Hispanic families in nine

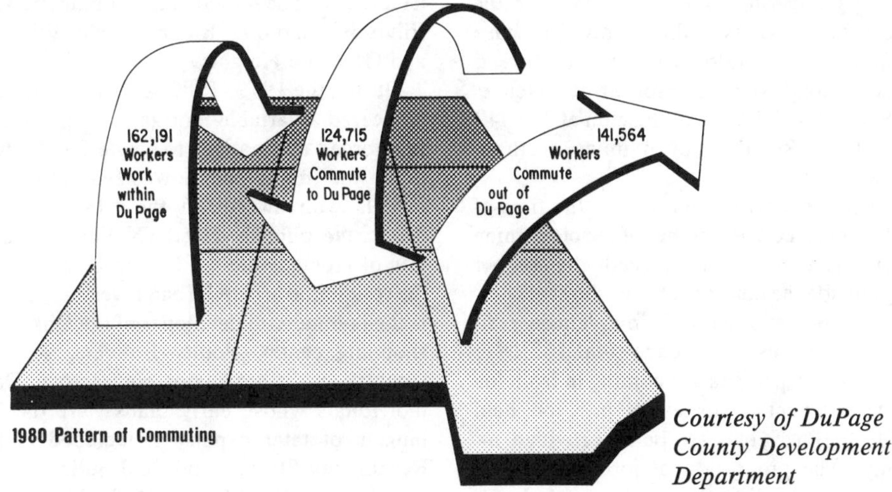


*Courtesy of DuPage County Development Department*

Addison Township Catholic parishes showed that most had come from four states of Mexico, although Puerto Ricans, Cubans, and Guatemalans were also represented. Most have been in this country less than ten years. There is a generation of older Hispanics who came to work on the railroads in the 1920s and 1930s and whose children are actively involved in all aspects of community life.

A large number of Asian-Americans live in the southeast corner of the country, including the villages of Burr Ridge, Hinsdale, Oak Brook, Willowbrook, Darien, Clarendon Hills, Westmont, Downers Grove, Woodridge, and Lisle. People of Asiatic descent in that area include Chinese, Japanese, Korean, Filipino, Vietnamese, and Asian Indians. Because many of them have specialized in engineering and scientific fields, they have found employment in Argonne National Laboratory. Westmost resident Tirupataiah Tella is president of the Federation of India Association, which oversees fifty groups serving approximately 50,000 Asian Indians in the Chicago area. She estimates that 90 percent of this population has migrated within the last ten to fifteen years.

Two other characteristics of the changing population pattern pertain to the composition of households. The increase of single-parent homes from 6.8 percent to 10.8 percent during the 1970s bespeaks the effects of an increase in the society's divorce rate. The aging of the general population in DuPage is seen in the median age rising from 26.1 years in 1970 to 29.4 years in 1980. While the "Graying of America" is not happening as rapidly locally as elsewhere in the nation, it has already meant the closing of a number of schools.

The implication of these shifts in demographic features will be noted now in other aspects of the contemporary social landscape. The foremost factor to be considered is economic, serving as both cause and effect of population increase.

## ON THE MOVE

Long identified as a "commuter's paradise," DuPage has now become increasingly the place of employment. An early turning point in this direction was construction of the Eisenhower (Congress) Expressway in 1956. The concomitant closing of the CA&E railroad symbolized the end of the preceding era. Previously the settlement pattern was villages growing up around the railroad stations. The new pattern became a proliferation of housing subdivisions beyond village centers, reachable only by automobile. The vast conversion of farms into "dormitory" tract developments continued without letup from the mid-1950s until the late 1970s, with residents commuting elsewhere in the metropolitan area for employment.

As a result of such growth, Harold Dunton, assistant Milton Township supervisor, devised a house numbering system in 1953 for the unincorporated areas of the county. The base line for east-west addresses was State Street, and north-south was Madison Street. Hence, the Wood Dale Historical Museum at 7 N 040 Wood Dale Road is seven miles north of Madison.

A further mutation occurred by the time of the 1980 census. The number of people coming to work inside the county exceeds the number going outside the county. Those who still commute to work number 141,564. Those residents working inside DuPage total 162,191, while 124,715 persons are coming in from the outside. Currently, for every one job held outside DuPage, two are being provided internally. The proportion of jobs in the six-county metropolitan area generated by DuPage doubled, from 4.4 percent in 1970 to 8.5 percent in 1980. Median family income rose to $30,431—the highest in the state and the twelfth highest nationally.

Housing continues to be the focal point of the area's economic development, although it no longer enjoys the near monopoly of capital spending it held through the 1950s.

Two-thirds of the county's 211,710 acres are currently developed with residential use constituting 36.8 percent of the acreage developed between 1970 and 1980. During that same period 13 percent of the land was devoted to commercial, industrial, and ORD (office, research, and development).

Among the earliest of the developers was Harold Moser, who came to Naperville in 1917 at the age of two when his osteopath father moved to that community. By the mid-1930s, young Moser had started the *Naperville Sun*, which he soon sold. He subsequently purchased the Kluckhom Coal Company and later converted it into a lumber yard, leading Moser directly into construction. He began his housing development in 1951 with Moser Highlands. This was followed by Naperville Plaza, Cress Creek, West Moser Highlands, representing a total of 9,000 power connections.

Coming from outside the DuPage area, the first of the large tract builders was the Hoffman Group, originally called Hoffman-Rosner. The company came to Chicago from Arizona in 1955 and started with the construction of Hoffman Estates. It then moved into DuPage County, with developments in Lombard, Glen Ellyn, Bolingbrook, Bloomingdale, Wheaton, and Glendale Heights.

During the 1979–1982 recession, Hoffman pioneered a variable mortgage plan. As inflation forced alternatives to single-family dwellings and made for downsized homes, its models won awards in the 1982 *Builder's Magazine*, published by the National Association of Home Building. United Development, the residential arm of Urban Investment, which is the commercial developer of the Oak Brook shopping center, Poulty Builders, Town & Country are other major contractors. Other individuals whose early plans were the harbingers of later expansion included Harold Reskin, Jay Stream, and Paul Butler.

Following World War II Reskin and his father, Charles, after completing projects in North Lake and Villa Park, looked farther west along North Avenue and identified the area to be incorporated in 1959 as Glendale Heights. It was so named because of its location between Glen Ellyn and Bloomingdale.

In that same year, Carol Stream was incorporated and named after the daughter of developer Jay Stream. Like Glendale Heights, it included an increasing number of multifamily units. For DuPage as a whole, 69,502 units are in multiples, housing 30 percent of the population, compared to 18 percent in 1970.

Jay Stream also planned varied land use, as did Paul Butler for the village of Oakbrook. In Carol Stream provision was made for industrial development to keep homeowners' property taxes low. Container Corporation of America, Crown Zellerbach, and Fiat-Allis were among the companies to locate in that community. Jay Stream left in the early 1960s to become business manager for entertainer Wayne Newton, with whom he shared an interest in Arabian horses.

Oakbrook celebrated its twenty-fifth anniversary in 1983, after its transformation from a 7,000-acre rural area, owned by Paul Butler, to the commercial, if not geographical, center of the county. A quarter of the Fortune 500 companies maintain offices in the community, including the headquarters of fifteen major companies, such as McDonald's and Chicago Bridge & Iron.

Among the other communities celebrating their silver anniversary recently were Oakbrook Terrace, Willowbrook, and Woodridge. In 1958 the city of Utopia was incorporated, thus continuing the name that had been associated with the area around Butterfield and Summit roads since 1881. In that year Elmhurst postmaster Dr. Frederich Bates gave it that name after receiving complaints from around Albert Knapp's creamery/cheese factory that residents were not receiving their mail. That missing correspondence included bills, which made "Utopia" seem an appropriate name. In 1959, however, by referendum vote (101 yes, 84 no) the name was changed to Oakbrook Terrace, thus indicating its proximity to the new shopping center.

The name for Willowbrook came about in a different manner. According to the county's *Reference and Yearbook*,

> In 1959 a homeowners' group decided to incorporate as a village. Changes in the law scheduled to become effective January 1, 1960 which would require a population of 400 for incorporation, caused this group of 167 people to expedite its request. In fact, while the case was before court, the attorney called the association's president, Anton Borse, frantically asking a name for the new village. Borse looked out of his window at the willow trees along the edge of a creek on his property and promptly gave the village its name. Willowbrook became one of the state's smallest villages on January 16, 1960.

*Argonne experiment. Biologist Patricia Irving demonstrates the acid rain simulation to members of the Forest Foundation of DuPage County.*
*Courtesy Argonne National Laboratories*

*Director, Leon Lederman (Rear) and high energy physicist John Yoh are pictured in one of the laboratories at Fermilab.*
*Courtesy Fermi National Accelerator Laboratories*

This community also contains one of several pet cemeteries in DuPage County. In Willowbrook the grave sites are at 64th and Bentley roads. Another, the Illinois Pet Cemetery, founded in 1926, is on Jefferson Road, south of Hanover Park.

Neighboring Burr Ridge took its name from the Burr Ridge Estates, as it joined Woodview Estates, the village of Harvester, and the International Harvester Center in 1961. This combination of subdivisions and Harvester facilities is located in both Cook and DuPage counties.

The most recent community to be incorporated was Darien in 1969. Its name was taken from Darien, Connecticut.

There are unincorporated areas which continue to resist annexation. Keeneyville residents, near Hanover Park, still maintain horses on their property, a practice prohibited in municipalities. The only civic institution in Eola, adjacent to Aurora at the Kane County line, is the post office. Each of its households depends upon its own well water and septic field.

The macroeconomic picture of the county would not be complete without surveying the variety of other commercial and industrial growth, particularly in the last fifteen years.

The first research institution in the county was Argonne National Laboratories. It opened in 1947 as the peaceful spinoff from the original atomic fission experiment under Stagg Field at the University of Chicago (the military counterpart is in White Sands, New Mexico). It has since expanded its research to cover a broad range of projects, such as the effects of acid rain and, until 1981 federal cutbacks, of toxic metals in the Great Lakes.

The 6,800-acre Fermilab, opening in 1973, houses the largest high-energy particle accelerator in the world. Subatomic particles are orbited at the rate of 50,000 times a second in a ring four miles in circumference. When these smash against the target area, the basic structure of matter is explored, yielding results in such fields as cyrogenics and super-conductivity. Five hundred scientists from the United States and abroad conduct their experiments at any given time on this site of the short-lived post–World War II village of Weston.

Commercial research and development is represented by the "High Tech Corridor" along the East-West Tollway. Largest of these "R & D" facilities is AT&T Laboratories with 6,146 employees. This number does not include the 2,000 persons working in its adjacent software center, AT&T Technologies (formerly Western Electric Company).

There are thirty-eight industrial parks in DuPage, the largest being the 1,500-acre Santa Fe Argonne Park with 600 acres developed. Second in land acreage but first in development is the Carol Stream Industrial Properties, with 980 of its 1,100 acres developed. The cluster of industrial parks in Addison contains United Parcel Service's (UPS) largest sorting facility; this hub handles 1 million UPS packages a day.

There are a total of 222 companies in DuPage with at least 150 employees. Retail sales in DuPage rose from 8 percent of the total in the six-county metropolitan area in 1970 to 12 percent in 1980 and are estimated to reach 17 percent in 1990. The fourth regional shopping center, Stratford Square, was completed in 1981 on 873 acres. Oakbrook opened first in 1962, followed by Yorktown in 1968 and Fox Valley in 1975.

## ENVIRONMENTAL IMPACT

Whenever officials speak at public forums, the most frequently mentioned issue is water. This topic signifies that the most obvious effect of post–World War II change has been environmental.

The water issue is succinctly summarized by the fact that the two-thirds of a million residents, along with institutional users, consume 80 million gallons of groundwater per day, compared to 50 million that can be extracted without depleting the water supply. The esti-

*Flooding at Route 83, south of St. Charles Road.*

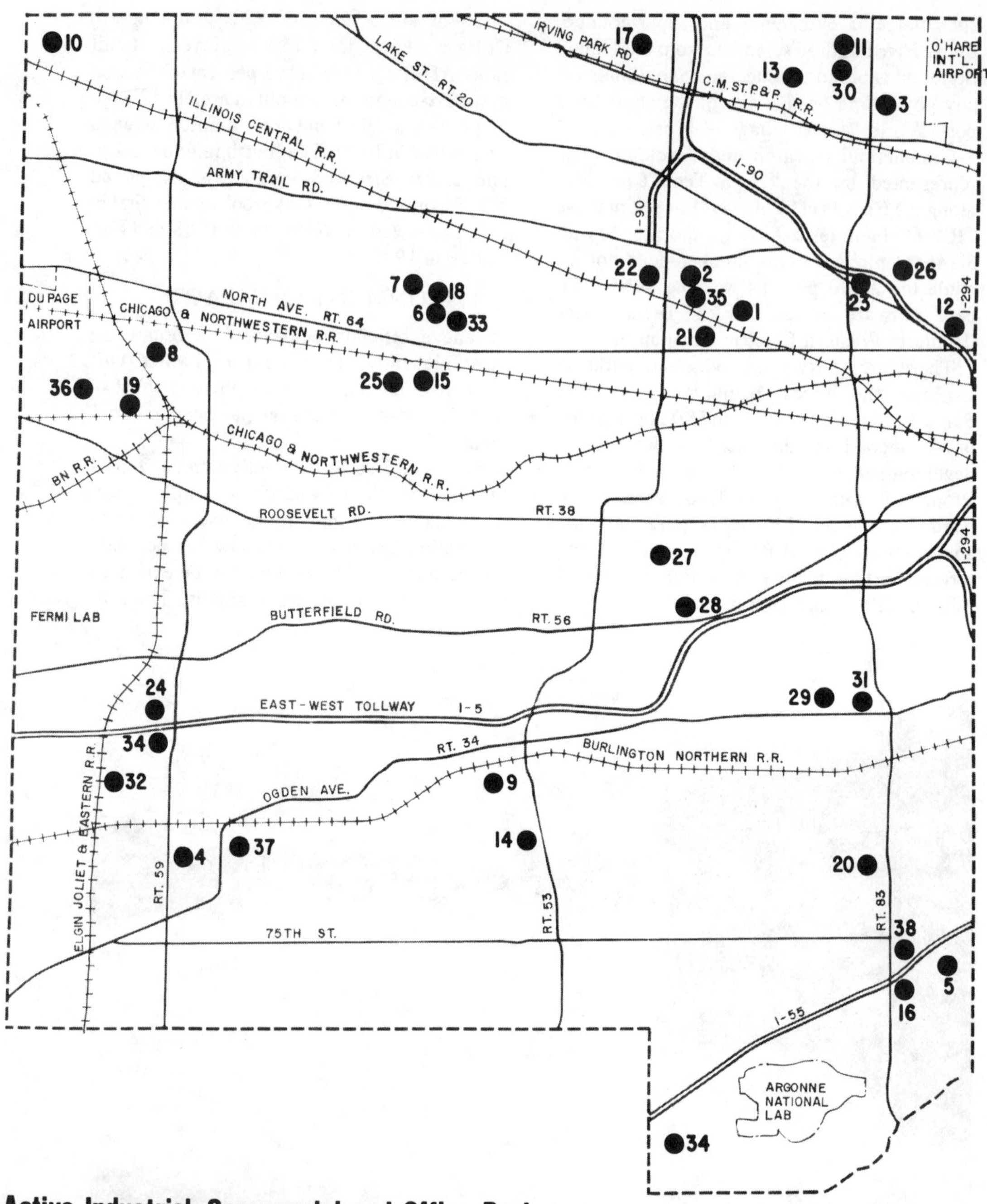


**Active Industrial, Commercial and Office Parks Locations in DuPage County**

**Source: Chicago Association of Commerce and Industry.**

DuPage County Regional Planning Commission

*Courtesy of DuPage County Development Department*

# DuPage County Active Industrial Parks - Total Acres, Acres Available and Agency Handling the Property 6/1982

| Map Location* | Industrial Areas | Location | Total Acres | Acres Available |
|---|---|---|---|---|
| 1. | Addison-Grace Industrial Park<br>Bennett & Kahnweiler, Assoc.<br>(671-7911) | Addison | 43 | 30 |
| 2. | Army Trail Industrial Center<br>Kenroy, Inc. (583-0900) | Addison | 64 | 54 |
| 3. | Bensenville Industrial Park<br>Trammell Crow (773-4100) | Bensenville | 150 | 106 |
| 4. | Burlington Northern/Naperville Industrial Park<br>Burlington Northern, Inc. (435-4346) | Naperville | 594 | 402 |
| 5. | Burr Ridge Industrial Common<br>Pain/Wetzel (559-0600) | Burr Ridge | 45 | 18 |
| 6. | Carol Stream Industrial Park<br>Nardi & Company (544-9010) | Carol Stream | 1,100 | 120 |
| 7. | Carol Stream Industrial Properties<br>Bennett & Kahnweiler Assoc.<br>(671-7911) | Carol Stream | 85 | 60 |
| 8. | Carolina Acres<br>Bennett & Kahnweiler Assoc.<br>(671-7911) | West Chicago | 110 | 80 |
| 9. | College West Industrial Park<br>Calmark Realty (963-9000) | Lisle | 58 | 20 |
| 10. | EJ&E Properties<br>Elgin, Joliet & Eastern Railway<br>(815/740-6641) | Multiple Location | 780 | 780 |
| 11. | Elk Grove Industrial Park<br>Trammell Crow Co. (773-4100) | Elk Grove Village | 250 | 25 |
| 12. | Elmhurst Tri-State Industrial Park<br>Bennett & Kahnweiler Assoc.<br>(671-7911) | Elmhurst | 41 | 6 |
| 13. | Forest Creek<br>Bennett & Kahnweiler Assoc.<br>(671-7911) | Wood Dale | 273 | 264 |
| 14. | Four Lakes Research Park<br>Nicolson, Porter & List, Inc.<br>(299-9400) | Lisle | 43 | 43 |
| 15. | Gary St. Charles Business Park<br>Coldwell Banker (655-7374) | Carol Stream | 40 | 21 |
| 16. | Hinsdale Industrial Park<br>Berggren Realty Corp. (887-9600) | Hinsdale | 110 | 5 |
| 17. | Itasca I-90 Center for Industry<br>Harrington, Bateman, O'Leary & Co.<br>(346-1322) | Itasca | 75 | 27 |
| 18. | Kimberly North Industrial Park<br>Coldwell Banker (861-7812) | Carol Stream | 66 | 55 |
| 19. | Kress Road Properties<br>Terrance O'Brien Co. (729-1310) | West Chicago | 360 | 150 |
| 20. | Lake Hinsdale Business Center<br>Nardi & Co. (544-9010) | Willowbrook | 23 | 23 |
| 21. | Lombard Industrial Park<br>Bennett & Kahnweiler Assoc.<br>(671-7911) | Lombard | 184 | 84 |
| 22. | Mitchell Field Industrial Park<br>Pain/Wetzel Assoc. (559-0600) | Addison | 74 | 20 |
| 23. | Mourekson Industrial Center<br>A. Mourek & Son (279-3770) | Elmhurst | 115 | 8 |
| 24. | Naperville Business Park<br>Western Investments (325-9000) | Naperville | 522 | 342 |
| 25. | Narco-Carol Stream Center<br>Nardi & Company (544-9010) | Carol Stream | 80 | 6 |
| 26. | Narco-Elmhurst Industrial Sites<br>Nardi & Company (544-9010) | Elmhurst | 37 | 24 |
| 27. | Oak Creek Industrial Park<br>Simborg Industrial Real Estate<br>(371-2150) | Lombard | 90 | 15 |
| 28. | Oak Grove Center of Commerce<br>Berggren Realty Corp. (887-9600) | Downers Grove | 130 | 11 |
| 29. | Oakwood Industrial Plaza<br>Podolsky & Assoc. (671-7600) | Westmont | 170 | 40 |
| 30. | O'Hare Thorndale Industrial Park<br>Blanco Construction Co. (595-8300) | Wood Dale | 30 | 30 |
| 31. | Pasquinelli Properties<br>LaSalle Partners (782-5800) | Westmont | 20 | 9 |
| 32. | Prudential Industrial Park<br>Nicolson, Porter & List<br>(299-9400) | Naperville | 200 | 140 |
| 33. | St. Paul Center for Commerce<br>Coldwell Banker (861-7812) | Carol Stream | 77 | 60 |
| 34. | Santa Fe Argonne Industrial District<br>Atchison, Topeka & Santa Fe R.R.<br>(427-4900) | Lemont | 1,500 | 950 |
| 35. | VanDer Molen Industrial District<br>Coldwell Banker (861-7812) | Addison | 36 | 26 |
| 36. | Western Industrial Park<br>Coldwell Banker (861 -7812) | West Chicago | 130 | 70 |
| 37. | Willoway Industrial Park<br>Arthur Rubloff & Co. (399-7070) | Naperville | 22 | 12 |
| 38. | Willowbrook Executive Plaza<br>Gottlieb Properties (782-6735) | Willowbrook | 100 | 25 |
| | DU PAGE COUNTY TOTAL | | 7,827 | 4,161 |

SOURCE: Chicago Association of Commerce and Industry, Commerce, July, 1982.

*Hamilton Lakes — The Stouffer Hotel (left), and office building in Itasca.*

mate is that water usage will increase 60 percent, to 130 million gallons per day, within forty years. The water table is already dropping as much as ten feet per year in parts of the county.

Because of the growing shortage, the Tree Towns Water Commission was founded in the 1950s. Its successor, the DuPage Water Commission, was composed of representatives from 22 municipalities. This in turn, was superceded by a body composed of 11 members, five named by the municipalities, and six by the county board. A proposal has been formulated to bring water from Lake Michigan in a seven-foot diameter pipe to a point just south of Elmhurst. Thence it would be distributed throughout the county at a total cost of $350 million.

If water shortage is one pressing problem, another is water surplus— when it comes to flooding. Following the devastating innundation of 1972, a floodplain ordinance was enacted by the county within a year. A subsequent program of water retention has been undertaken; one example is the 870-acre reservoir near Spring Brook Creek north of Bloomingdale. This, in turn, feeds into Salt Creek, which is part of the Des Plaines River watershed.

A third water-related issue deals with recycling. Environmental engineer John R. Sheaffer, a Wheaton resident and co-author with Leonard A. Stevens of *Future Water,* contends that the need to recycle water is urgent. An example of such conservation is found at Hamilton Lakes, a new hotel and office complex in Itasca. The 274-acre project is hydrologically self-sufficient as well water, pumped from a shallow aquifer and once used, is then piped to two lagoons where bacteria and micro-organisms begin disposing of the waste. The water is then used to irrigate the landscape through an underground sprinkler system. The nutrients from the treated waste water provide $13,000 worth of free fertilizer annually as the water filters through the soil. By the time it reaches the aquifer again, it is clean enough to be used for drinking.

The problem of waste disposal is, of course, broader than water management. In DuPage, as elsewhere, there is the challenge of running "out of out" in a throwaway society. Two landfills, Mallard Lake in Hanover Park and Greene Valley in Woodridge, following the pattern of "Mt. Trashmore" in Blackwell Preserve, have capacities to receive enough waste to continue in operation until after the turn of the century. However, there are twenty-five municipalities outside of DuPage, mostly from Cook County, that use these facilities. Cook County is slated to close some of its own sites in the meantime. Moreover, the disposal of toxic wastes has been a continuing source of contention. An Oak Brook–based waste management company received national publicity in 1983, the year of the "Sewergate" controversy. The presence of thorium contamination in Kress Creek, produced by owners of a plant in West Chicago from 1931 to 1973, resulted in a 1984 cleanup order from the Nuclear Regulatory Commission.

The public response to the ecological threat

of rapid population growth often has been made through the Forest Preserve District of DuPage County. Its land acquisition program has resulted in an increased amount of land in the public domain from its first purchase of sixty-one acres in 1917, two years after the State of Illinois passed the enabling statutes to allow the formation of forest preserve districts, to 17,500 acres at present. DuPage was the second county in the state and the fifth in

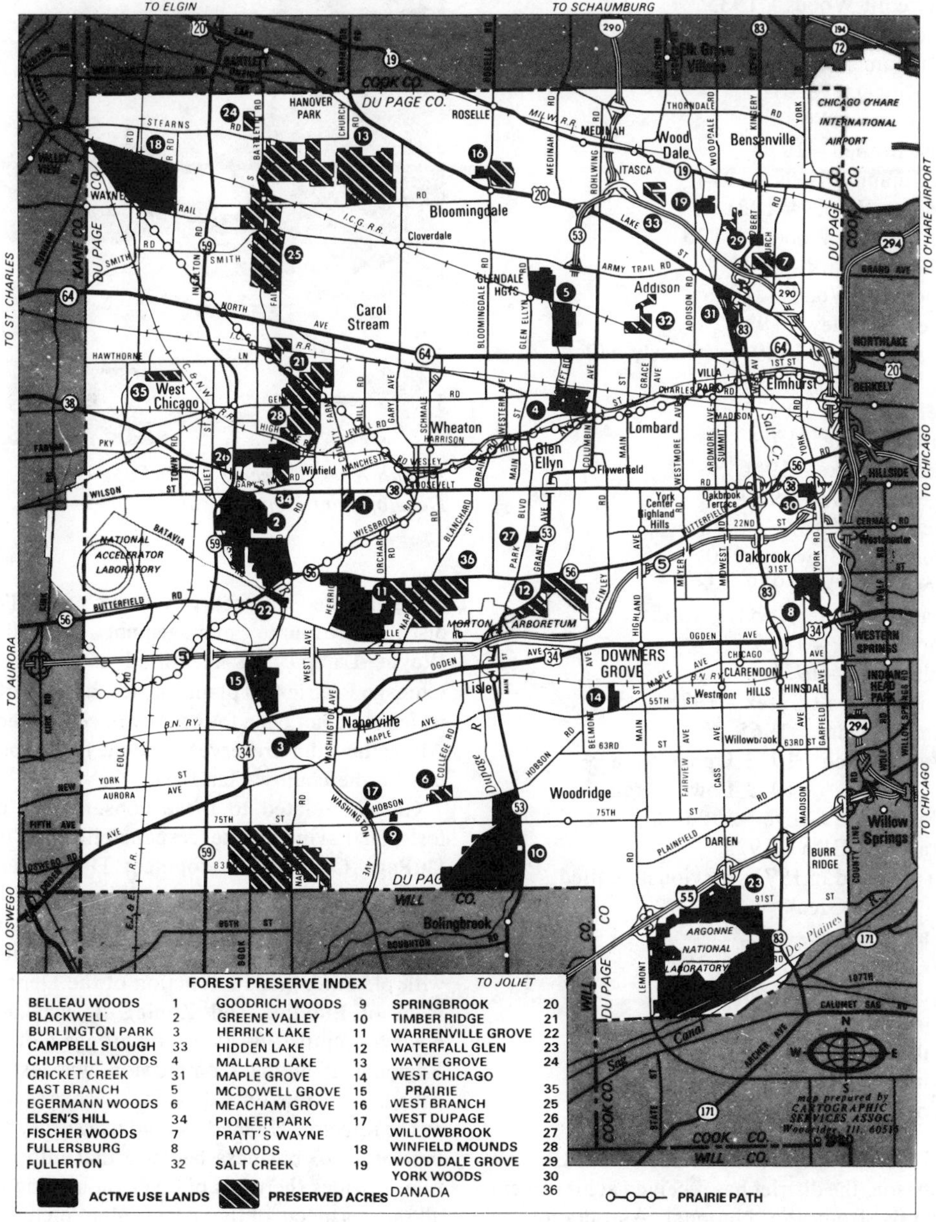


*Courtesy of Forest Preserve District of DuPage County*

the country to establish a district. Commissioner Roy C. Blackwell offered particularly strong leadership in promoting the cause of conservation. The date of acquisition of each of the preserves is as follows:

Belleau Woods – 1965
Roy C. Blackwell – 1961
Burlington Park – 1922
Campbell Slough – 1977
Churchill Woods – 1935
Cricket Creek – 1974
(renamed 1978; previously called Kingery West)
Danada – 1980
East Branch – 1970
Egermann Woods – 1974
Fischer Woods – 1921
Fullersburg Woods – 1920
Fullerton Park – 1974
Goodrich Woods – 1926
Greene Valley – 1926
(renamed in 1969; previously called Hinterlong)
Herrick Lake – 1925
Hidden Lake – 1976
Mallard Lake – 1956
Maple Grove – 1920
McDowell Grove – 1930
Meacham Grove – 1920
Pioneer Park – 1929
Pratt's Wayne Woods – 1965
Springbrook – 1975
Salt Creek – 1931
Elmhurst/Salt Creek – 1978
Timber Ridge – 1965
West Branch – 1973 Upper Area
1979 Lower Area
Warrenville Grove – 1923
Waterfall Glen – 1925
(renamed in 1973; previously called Rocky Glen)
Wayne Grove – 1923
West Chicago Prairie – 1979
West DuPage Woods – 1919
York Woods – 1917
Willowbrook – 1956
Winfield Mounds – 1976
Wood Dale Grove – 1929

Under the administration of H. C. "Chuck" Johnson, the district has received achievement awards from the National Association of Counties for the Blackwell Recreational Preserve and the Fullersburg Nature Center. The districts resource management specialist, Wayne Lampa, has identified in the West Chicago Prairie 450 plant species, a number of which have not been found growing elsewhere. Altogether, the preserves account for 20 percent of the county's land use.

*Joseph Abel, Director of DuPage County Development Department.*

Closely related to these conservation efforts, but having broader responsibilities, is the DuPage County Development Department. DuPage was the first county in Illinois to adopt a zoning ordinance in 1933. A comprehensive rezoning of the county occurred in the 1950s, with planning made a function of the Department of Building and Zoning. It was not, however, until 1969 that the DuPage County Regional Planning Commission was established. Since that time, Joseph Abel has served as the director. He made a land use survey the first order of business because that information provides the basis of decision making for all other aspects of the master plan, including its housing and transportation components.

These, in turn, have generated considerable debate.

## CONTROVERSY

In 1971 HOPE, Inc. (Homes of Private Enterprise), an advocacy group formed in 1968 to provide increased housing opportunities for lower-income and minority persons, filed suit against the DuPage County Board on the grounds of exclusionary zoning practices. Headed by former Catholic priest, Bernard Kleina, the group was represented by attorney R. Dickey Hamilton, son of former Wheaton mayor, Margaret Hamilton.

Ten years after the initial complaint, Federal District Judge Herbert L. Will ruled in favor

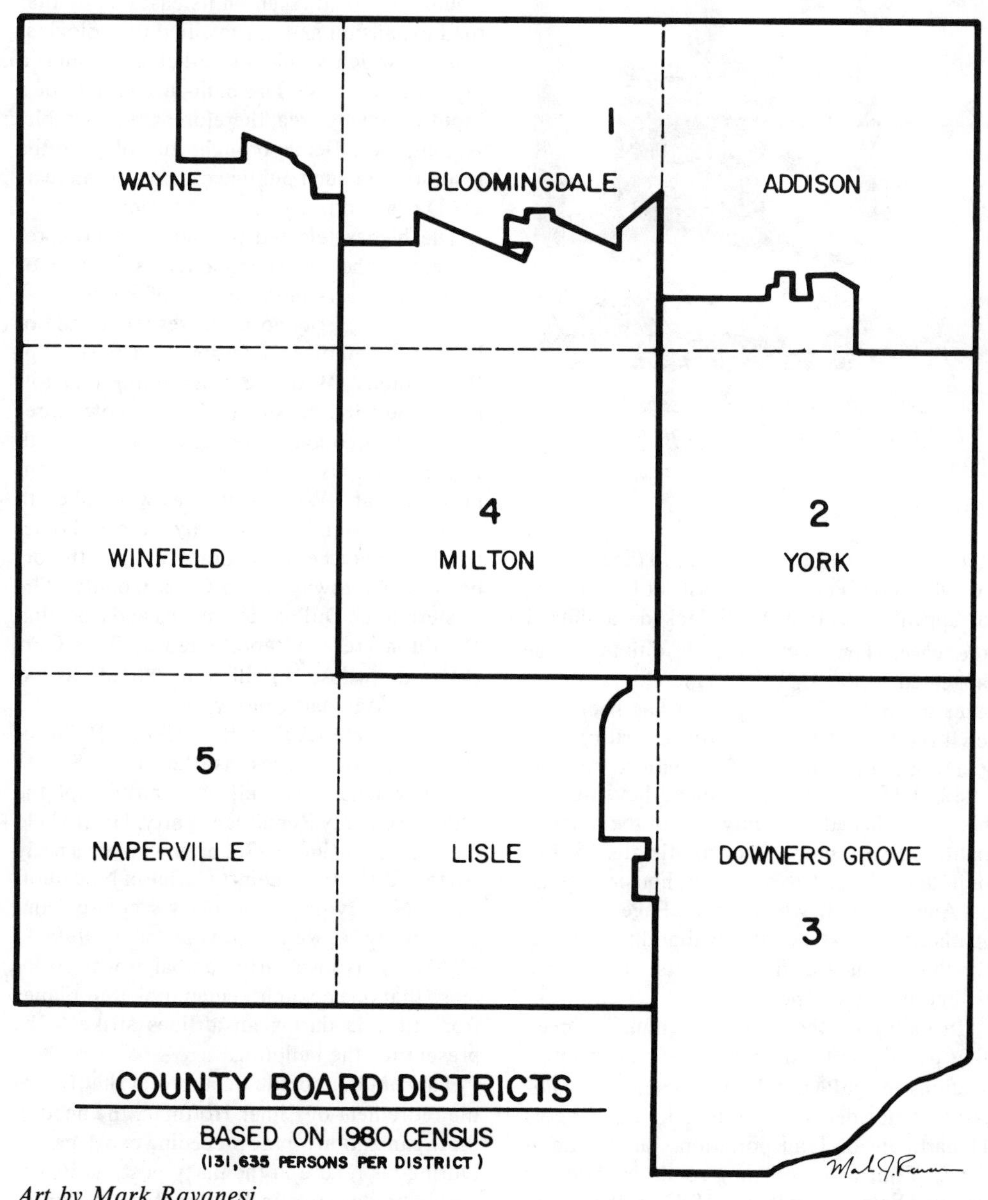


*Art by Mark Ravanesi*

*John Erlenborn with his successor to the 13th Congressional district seat, Harris Fawell*

of the fair housing organization. In the summer of 1984, however, the 7th District U.S. Court of Appeals ruled that HOPE lacked standing in the case. The decision may ultimately be appealed to the U.S. Supreme Court. Whatever the outcome, the dispute has become a civil rights landmark in DuPage history.

During the period of litigation, through 1982, 4,154 units of subsidized housing had been established in twenty-five of the municipalities. By the county's own estimate, 15,000 units are still needed to meet the housing needs. In August 1983, when the DuPage Housing Authority announced the availability of funds for thirty rent subsidy payments, 700 people waited in line to apply.

In addition to the housing dilemma has been that pertaining to highways. Seventeen intersections in DuPage fall into the highest category of accidents, according to the Illinois Department of Transportation. The traffic at Army Trail and Rohlwing roads in Addison doubled between 1978 and 1983, with 61,000 vehicles entering and exiting at the nearby Interstate Route 90 terminus each day.

Relieving that congestion would be the proposed North-South Tollway which would make connection between Army Trail Road and I-55. With the Northeast Illinois Planning Commission projecting 20 percent of the region's population to be living in that corridor by the year 2000, the need for FAP 431, as the projected expressway has been called, is apparent. The Morton Arboretum, however, would have land taken on its east end by that road expansion and has testified to ecological damage which would be inflicted by such a high-speed artery. The built-in conflicts of a rapidly growing area, therefore, are inevitable. Among the officials brought into play on the resolution of such public collision of interests are DuPage office holders at various levels.

The highest elected officials are those representing the county in Congress. For six of his twenty years in the House of Representatives, John Erlenborn represented all of DuPage County, in addition to a portion of Will County, With the redistricting that followed the 1980 census, DuPage is now represented by three congressmen. Erlenborn's 13th District extends across its southeast quadrant into Cook and Will counties as well. The 6th District, currently served by Henry Hyde, covers the northeast quadrant along with portions of five townships in Cook County. The western three DuPage townships and a portion of Milton are now represented by Tom Corcorcoran, whose jurisdiction extends as far south as Marshall County.

At the state level, James "Pate" Philip of Elmhurst now serves as the State Senate minority leader as well as chairman of the DuPage County Republican party. He has held the latter post since 1970, after winning a hotly contested election against Carleton Nadelhoffer of Naperville at the party's county convention by a weighted vote of 31,990 to 31,552. This intraparty campaign was so intense that one committeeman took four planes from Florida during an airlines strike to be present for the balloting.

This political battle occurred at the time of the retirement of Elmer Hoffman, the head of the organization for the preceding two decades. During his tenure in the party post, as Erlenborn's predecessor in Washington, as Illinois state treasurer, and officeholder in a variety of other positions, Hoffman had been the dominant political figure since World War II. During the Richard J. Daley era, Hoffman claimed that the Chicago mayor was the best campaigner the DuPage Republicans ever had because the opposition to the Chicago "machine" was a common denominator among suburbanites.

The state's attorney's office has been the springboard for a number of the recent generation of leaders. Under William Guild's administration in the late 1950s, these attorneys first served and later held the following positions: William Bauer, federal judge; John Erlenborn, congressman; Harris Fawell, state senator and congressional nominee. Helen Kinney, the first woman to serve as circuit court judge, likewise, had worked in that office. In 1960 Phoebe Dutcher was the first woman ever elected to county-wide office.

A three-part series in the *Suburban Tribune* from October 22–24, 1980, delineated the three networks which sustain the near monopoly that the Republican party enjoys in DuPage: the business-political axis, the precinct committeeman system, and loyalists who hold county jobs. Illustrating these interconnections, the series notes that fifty-six corporate contributors to the party received seventy-three county contracts. There are 112 elected state, county, and township officials in DuPage. At that time sixty-nine of them, or members of their immediate families, served as committeemen.

The dominance of the GOP is also to be accounted for by its three-to-one voter registration advantage over Democrats, although 55 percent of the county's electorate are undeclared independents. A record four Democrats served on the twenty-five-member county board in the wake of the Watergate scandal; however, Jane Spirgel of Elmhurst is the only one to survive elections subsequent to 1976. Democrat William Redmond of Bensenville served as speaker of the Illinois House of Representatives before his 1982 retirement.

Jack Knuepfer also served at the state level of government before his successful race for county board chairman in 1976. In that capacity, he leads in overseeing its tax-supported human services.

## CARE AND CULTURE

Both publicly and privately supported services provide the collective response to the human impact of post–World War II social change in DuPage.

The county's Mental Health Department has grown to the point of offering satellite

*1982–1983 DuPage County Board (Seated, from left) Jay C. Bennett, County Clerk, Jack T. Knuepfer, Chairman of the County Board, R. Lloyd Renfro. (Standing, from left) Norbert R. Fencl, Frank C. Urban, Lenore Davenport, Richard A. Carlson, Charles G. Kaelin, Paul W. Weber, Mary B. Price, William R. Bates, Barbara Broderick, J. Russell Swanson, Julius T. Hankinson, Jane Spirgel, Don G. Prindle, Charles Vaughn, Pat Trowbridge, Harold J. Bollweg, Ange B. Mahnke, Frank H. Bellinger, Barbara R. Purcell, Herbert C. "Bud" Kirchhoff, Ruth Kretchmer, Robert J. Raymond, Ray R. Soden.*

*President Reagan visits DuPage College in 1984.*

counseling services in Addison, Lombard, Westmont, and Wheaton in response to 400 calls a month. DUI Program (Driving Under the Influence) is treating those referred by the courts. It services 3,000 cases instead of the originally estimated 1,000 cases, according to Gary Noll, director.

Mobility, in itself, generates the need for varied services. Within the schools, for example, with the high degree of turnover in the county's population, the 275 counselors, social workers, and psychologists find continuity of service difficult to provide to 112,000 students. Only 18.8 percent of those living in Carol Stream in 1980 had resided in that community five years before. The figure was 24.7 percent for Lisle and 28.20 percent for Naperville. While length of residence was up to 62.47 percent in Elmhurst and 71.06 percent in Wayne, the average stay in one place in the county as a whole was less than 50 percent over the preceding five years.

The increasing mixture of national origins is reflected at the College of DuPage. This two-year community college, which has grown to 28,000 students since its 1967 opening, provides English as a second language to students from thirty-nine countries. Thirteen of the county's forty-five school districts offer bilingual education.

The DuPage Library System serves twenty-eight schools, seventeen public, sixteen special, and eight academic libraries in the county. Established in 1966, this is one of eighteen cooperative systems in Illinois. It makes possible the interlibrary loan program, computer searching, and a variety of other services.

In the private sector, two of the social agencies date from the nineteenth century. The **Lutherbrook Children's Center, now part of the statewide Lutheran Child & Family Services**, dates back to the Addison orphanage. The eighty-eight-year-old Bensenville Home Society now offers retirement as well as adoption, foster care, and counseling services.

The Family Service Association, begun during the Depression years, devotes half of its resources to divorce problems as the rate of marital dissolutions nears the 50 percent mark. Drug-related and financial counseling have assumed a larger portion of staff time in recent years.

A service for the mentally handicapped came to an abandoned 1916 school building at the corner of Park and Butterfield roads, south of Glen Ellyn, in 1952, after having made an initial start that same year in LaGrange. Taking the name Bonaparte from above the door, it moved to Lincoln School in Bensenville in 1956 and merged with the Ray Graham Rehabilitation Center in 1972. Today, with seventeen sites in DuPage and a $6 million budget, the Ray Graham Association for the Handicapped is the largest agency of its kind in the country. It was named after the founder of such rehabilitation services for the State of Illinois.

Begun in 1965, Little Friends, Inc., of Naperville also serves the disabled and handicapped and occupies the former Kroehler mansion. The Attention Group (TAG), an emergency shelter for teens in Naperville and Downers Grove, and the Family Shelter in Glen Ellyn for battered women and their children reflect a grass-roots response to problems about which society is becoming increasingly aware.

Compassionate Friends, headquartered in Oakbrook, is an international organization with 350 chapters around the world providing support to grieving parents. The local expression of a national movement is Hospice Volunteers of DuPage, a support service for the terminally ill and their families. It cooperates with the county's seven hospitals, three of which have been established since 1950—Glendale Heights Community, Good Samaritan in Downers Grove, and Marianjoy Rehabilitation in Wheaton. Each of these has had particular impetus from the religious community.

Mixed with its social service involvements, DuPage religion has been characterized by three recent developments. The first is the marked increase in the number of Catholics, now constituting the largest religious body with 255,000 adherents out of the 675,000 population. (The Missouri Synod Lutherans with 26,374 are next in size.) This is up from 30,000 adherents when the Joliet Diocese split off from the Chicago Archdiocese in 1949. The number stood at 180,370 in 1971. There are forty parishes and thirty-one elementary and five secondary schools. This growth is due in large measure to the influx of people from the predominately Catholic western suburbs of Cook County, as distinct from the earlier pattern of transferees from across the nation. The largest parish is still SS. Peter and Paul in Naperville, with 3,700 families. There are 3,500 families in Glendale Heights' St. Matthew's Church, including a sizable number of Vietnamese, with a Mass in that language.

Cloverdale's Parish of St. Isidore changed little after its founding in 1920 until the 1950s. By 1978 it had 450 families registered. Within two years that number almost quadrupled. The Rev. Stanley Orlikiewicz is the dean of priests in DuPage. He has served three different parishes and is currently at the 3,000-family church in Roselle, a church which had doubled in size over the last decade.

Also of note is the work of Father Thomas Peyton, a Maryknoll priest, who in 1967 organized a Roman Catholic group called REC (Religious Education Community), patterned along Vatican II guidelines. Drawn from different parishes, the group was instrumental in the establishment of the Peace and Justice Center in Wheaton, which provided draft

*Father Stanley Orlikiewicz.*

*Billy Graham, with Wheaton College officials — at the dedication of the Billy Graham Center.*

counseling during the Vietnam War. This agency is now called People's Resource Center. Director Dorothy McIntyre reports that it is now one of twenty-eight pantries in DuPage, double the number from the preceding years. It serves 5,000 persons annually.

As these numbers have grown, Sister Rosemary Burrin has established Bethlehem Center, a food depository serving pantries in DuPage and neighboring counties. It makes available government surplus food as well as Second Harvest donations from large food companies. It is supported by the DuPage County Building Trades Council composed of twenty-eight construction trade locals, such as Sheet and Metal Workers Local 265 of Carol Stream. These efforts recognize that there are currently 5,900 county residents over the age of sixty who live below the poverty level. Altogether 20,000 persons, or 3.5 percent of the population, lives below that $4,300 annual income figure.

The second characteristic of religious life has been evangelical expansion. The opening of the Billy Graham Center in 1980, across from Wheaton College's Blanchard Hall, represents that movement. This $13.5 million structure contains the evangelist's memorabilia and papers and serves as a museum, a conference center, and quarters for the Wheaton Graduate School of Religion. It is near neighboring Carol Stream which provides headquarters for such groups as MAP (Medical Assistance Program), Tyndale House (publishers of *The Living Bible),* Youth for Christ, and the National Evangelical Association, publishers of *Christianity Today,* which has the largest circulation of all Protestant journals. In 1967 Calvary Temple began in Naperville as the work of the Assemblies of God denomination and has grown to 2,000 members. Christ Church in Oakbrook has become a 3,000-member nondenominational congregation.

Finally, the increased religious diversity of the most recent decades must be considered. There are two Jewish congregations—Beth Shalom in Naperville and Etz Chaim, an older congregation of 220 families in Lombard. The Zorastrian Center, at 8615 Meadowbrook Drive in Hinsdale, is the first such temple built in North America and serves 300 adherents in the Chicago area. In 1983, at the Odeum Stadium in Villa Park, there was a celebration of the Moslem holiday of Ramadan with 6,000 people attending in the sports facility that accommodates only 4,000. The traffic was backed up for a considerable distance on neighboring Route 83. The Hindu community has purchased the American Legion hall in

Glen Ellyn. A Nachiren Shoshu (Buddhist) temple has been built at the intersection of Joliet Road and Route 59, across from the original site of Gary's Mill.

The cultural aspect of DuPage since World War II likewise features a diversity, variety, and complexity unknown in previous decades. In 1979 the College of DuPage sponsored a community project called Century III, which compiled a list of art-related activities in the county. The resulting booklet, "The Arts in DuPage," showed that there were, at the time, nineteen groups in the field of graphic arts. The DuPage Art League was the first to have a gallery and a school. It met originally in the Albright building in Warrenville in 1957 and subsequently opened a gallery on Front Street in Wheaton.

Also listed are three dance groups, fourteen drama groups, sixteen music clubs, twenty-seven musical performance groups, including four orchestras. The most recently formed of these in the New Philharmonic at the College of DuPage. Perhaps the best-known vocal group is the Glen Ellyn Children's Chorus, which has sung with the Chicago Symphony and has appeared elsewhere in this country and abroad.

The DuPage County Historical Museum was established in 1967 through the 1965 purchase of the old Wheaton Library building by philanthropist Edwin Deicke. Margaret Dunton served as first director, the position now held by Patricia Wallace. There are now twenty-six historical societies, the most extensive of program and facilities having been developed by the Naperville Heritage Society. In cooperation with that community's park district, an eleven-and-a-half-acre site has been made available as a historic pioneer village with fourteen authentically restored buildings representing DuPage life in the 1831 to 1865 period. This volunteer group has 700 members and operates on an annual $50,000 budget.

Among the unique cultural institutions is the Lizzadro Museum of Lapidary Art. Its collection of precious stones and rocks was acquired over a forty-year period by Joseph L. Lizzadro of Elmhurst, owner of Chicago's Meade Electric Company. The museum, established in 1962, includes such items as a green jade pagoda fashioned in eighteenth-century China.

*Sherill Milnes.*

Perhaps the best-known performing artist to come from DuPage since World War II is Sherrill Milnes of Downers Grove. His father, James, came to Downers Grove in 1940 with his wife, Thelma, whose father, Charles K. Roe, had left her a 250-acre dairy farm. Sherrill was five years old when they arrived. In 1945 his mother became the director of the choir of the Congregational church, and it was through her that he gained his initial training and continuing inspiration. As he later recalled, "I heard all the 'big dads' sing on the Metropolitan Opera broadcasts. . . . But it never occurred to me that one day I would be singing with them."

After graduating from Downers Grove High School in 1952, he attended North Central for a year, before transferring to Drake University. He did graduate study at Northwestern, doing commercials from 1958 to the early 1960s. His was the big baritone voice singing, "When you're out of Schlitz, you're out of beer." By 1965 he had made his Metropolitan debut with his performance of Valentin in

Gounod's "Faust." He has taken his place in the succession of great lead baritones including Lawrence Tibbett, John Charles Thomas, and Robert Merrill. He continued to return to Downers Grove for years for Christmas oratorios at the Downers Grove Congregational Church, conducting the "Elijah" in 1969 in memory of his mother, who had died that December.

Other notables from the county in the post–World War II era include two who graduated from Wheaton Central in the 1960s. Both won fame in the mass media. John Belushi became a popular television and movie actor, while Bob Woodward followed a journalistic career on *The Washington Post,* where he was one of the two reporters to crack the Watergate conspiracy,

The DuPage Heritage Gallery, with its exhibits at the DuPage Center and with its oral history library and series of biographies, publicizes the lives of outstanding personalities from the locality. With the rate of change continuing unabated, there has been no climax to the area's development. The need to chronicle the deepening, broadening, and ever more varied DuPage roots continues.

## CLIMAX

While no historical counterpart to the climax forest yet has occurred in the county, still the human parallels to the latter stages of plant succession are clear.

New life forms appear quickly once a former stage is superceded. Hardwoods moved into prairie cleared of grass so swiftly that pioneers could not let time lapse unduly before planting their crops.

In comparable fashion, as the auto age superceded former means of transportation, new communities appeared in rapid succession. To be sure, efforts continued to retain small town atmosphere in the midst of suburban sprawl. One Wayne resident stated, "We're two miles west of Illinois 59 and two hundred years behind the rest of the world."

Oakbrook Terrace retained its previous name, Utopia, for only a year. It became an

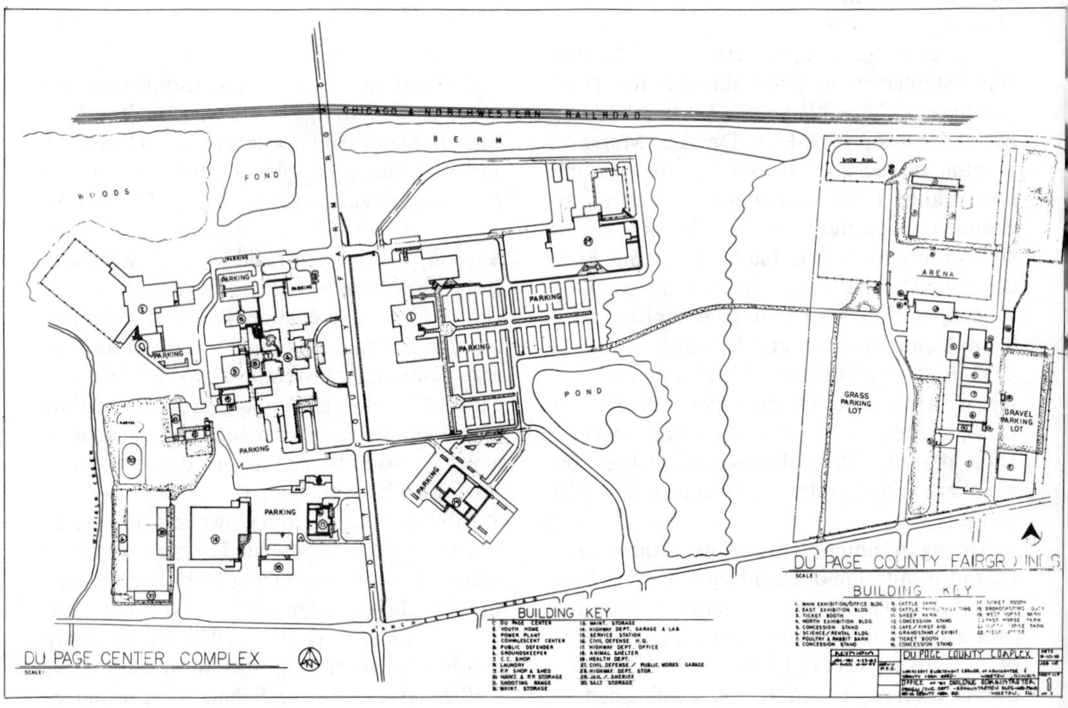


*DuPage Center Map.*
*Courtesy DuPage County Central Services*

*Author John R. Sheaffer autographing copy of* Future Water *for Sierra Club member Margaret Simpson.*

"instant community." Still, "Utopia" describes the economic and social aspirations of the multitude of new residents. Refugee Resource Networks of Wheaton has assisted the relocation in DuPage of 3,000 refugees from Afghanistan, Cambodia, Ethopia, Laos, Poland, and Vietnam. The *Daily Journal,* in its annual Business and Industry edition under Alyce Bartlett's editorship, details the broadening economic base which makes absorption of such newcomers possible.

Even with the full potential of the county yet to be realized, DuPage is inevitably caught up in all the major issues confronting society. Although twenty-eight of its municipalities now have black residents, the increase of that part of the population from 1,652 to 7,809 during the 1970s was not in proportion to the total population growth, an irony in the county which was at the forefront of pre-Civil War Abolitionism.

Yet evidence abounds that preservation efforts are not simply for the sake of indulging in nostalgia. Alex Haley's *Roots* was a recent bestseller because of growing appreciation that the sense of past gives perspective and hope for the future. *DuPage Roots* has been written with that conviction.

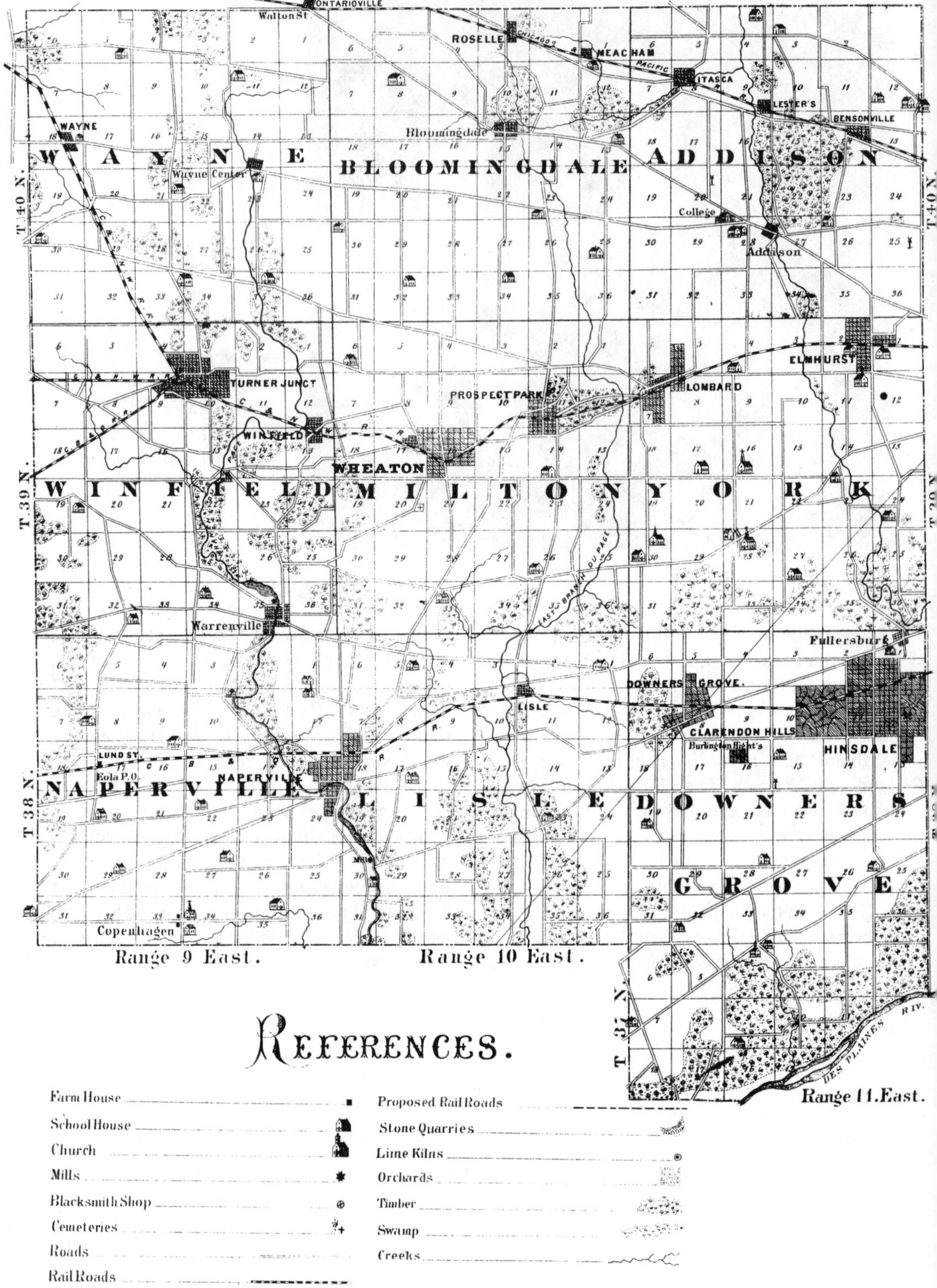


# REFERENCES.

| | |
|---|---|
| Farm House | Proposed Rail Roads |
| School House | Stone Quarries |
| Church | Lime Kilns |
| Mills | Orchards |
| Blacksmith Shop | Timber |
| Cemeteries | Swamp |
| Roads | Creeks |
| Rail Roads | |

# Part II

# Local Highlights

EDITED BY RICHARD A. THOMPSON

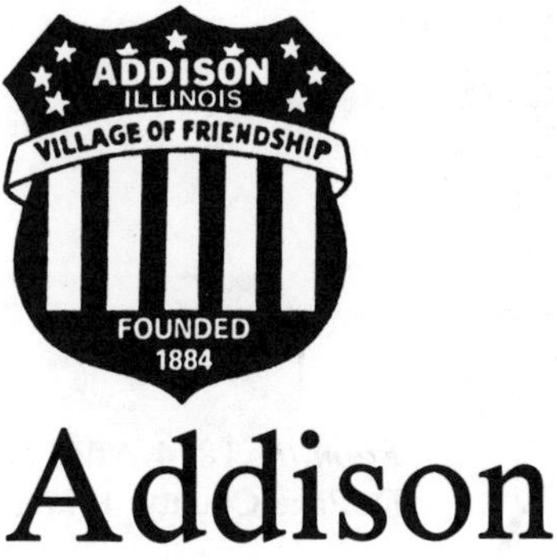


# Addison

*Pearl Morris*
*Vivian Krentz*

Like the Indians before them, the first white settlers made their homes near rivers and groves of native timber that gave them the fuel and water needed for survival. The first pioneers in what is now Addison Township were Hezekiah Dunklee (also spelled Duncklee) from Hillsborough, New Hampshire, and Mason Smith from Potsdam, New York. They arrived in Chicago September 3, 1833, having travelled by land from Detroit. They left Chicago five days later, and following a northwest trail made the year before by General Winfield Scott's army through twenty miles of flat, grassy marshland and prairie, they came to a large grove of trees located on the eastern bank of a river, which later became known as Salt Creek. After surveying the land to the west of the river, they returned to the north end of the grove.

On May 25, 1834, Bernhard Joachim Koehler and his family settled east of Dunklee's Grove on the present site of the River Forest Country Club. On that same day the Friedrich Graues settled south of the grove. These two families were the first of a large German influx during the next few years. Others to follow were the Stuenkels, the Krages, the Rotermunds, the Kruses, the Fienes, and the Buchholzes.

Most of the necessities of life were produced on the farms, but often the pioneers had to travel to Chicago to buy other provisions. With no roads through the prairie, travel was difficult. Many walked the eighteen miles to Chicago. The Des Plaines River flooded after heavy rains, and at those times such travel was impossible. Wells were dug by hand, often to a depth of thirty or forty feet, and a windmill was built to pump the water. If there was not enough wind, pumping was done by hand.

In 1839 Dunklee's Grove became part of Washington Precinct. When township organization was adopted in 1849, Washington Precinct became known as Addison Township.

*From the* 1874 Atlas & History of DuPage County, Illinois

After the first pioneers settled, other friends and relatives came to claim lands. In 1837 there were thirty families living in the Dunklee's Grove area. By 1844 there were 200 people living in the vicinity. Gradually businesses were established, such as a steam grist mill, a general store, a cobbler's shop and a blacksmith shop. In 1867 the Heidemann Mill was constructed in Addison to serve the residents who had been taking their grain to surrounding communities to be ground.

By 1853 state laws enabled school districts to be formed, and District 4 came into being with the building of its first public school in 1858. Peter Nikel was the teacher. The building was located on the southwest corner of Addison and Army Trail roads. Today it is part of the Edward Green home. The German population of Addison township formed a church in 1838 which was called the German United Reformed Lutheran Congregation of Dunklee's Grove. In 1849 the first church school building was erected in Addison, near the corner of Army Trail Road and May Street.

In 1864 the Evangelical Lutheran Teachers' Seminary was built in Addison to train teachers for the Lutheran school system. Their lecture hall, which opened in 1885, included a chapel, and it was here that the residents of Addison worshipped from 1893–1906. In 1906 the Lutheran congregation built the St. Paul Church along Army Trail Road near Lake Street.

In 1874 the Evangelical Lutheran Orphan Home was built to "raise, train, and educate orphans, half orphans and other children entrusted to its care." All children from the Orphan Home who were of school age went to St. Paul's Christian Day School. After graduation from the eighth grade, the girls would remain in the Home for work and future training. The boys were placed on farms, truck farms or in greenhouses to work.

In 1884 the village of Addison became incorporated. The population at the time was 400. The first president was Henry Buchholz, who served in that position from 1884 to 1891. In 1890 five Addison men formed the Addison Railroad Company, Inc. These were William Leeseberg, Louis Stuenkel, Edward Rotermund, Professor Johann Backhaus, and H. Z. Zuttermeister. Stock capital amounted to $5,000. A charter was issued on July 16, 1890, for the right to a stretch of land from today's North Avenue into Addison to build a railroad track. An agreement was made with the Illinois Central Railroad officials to provide the railroad bed and equipment and to maintain and operate the railroad for fifty years from that date. The cost of the whole right-of-way was

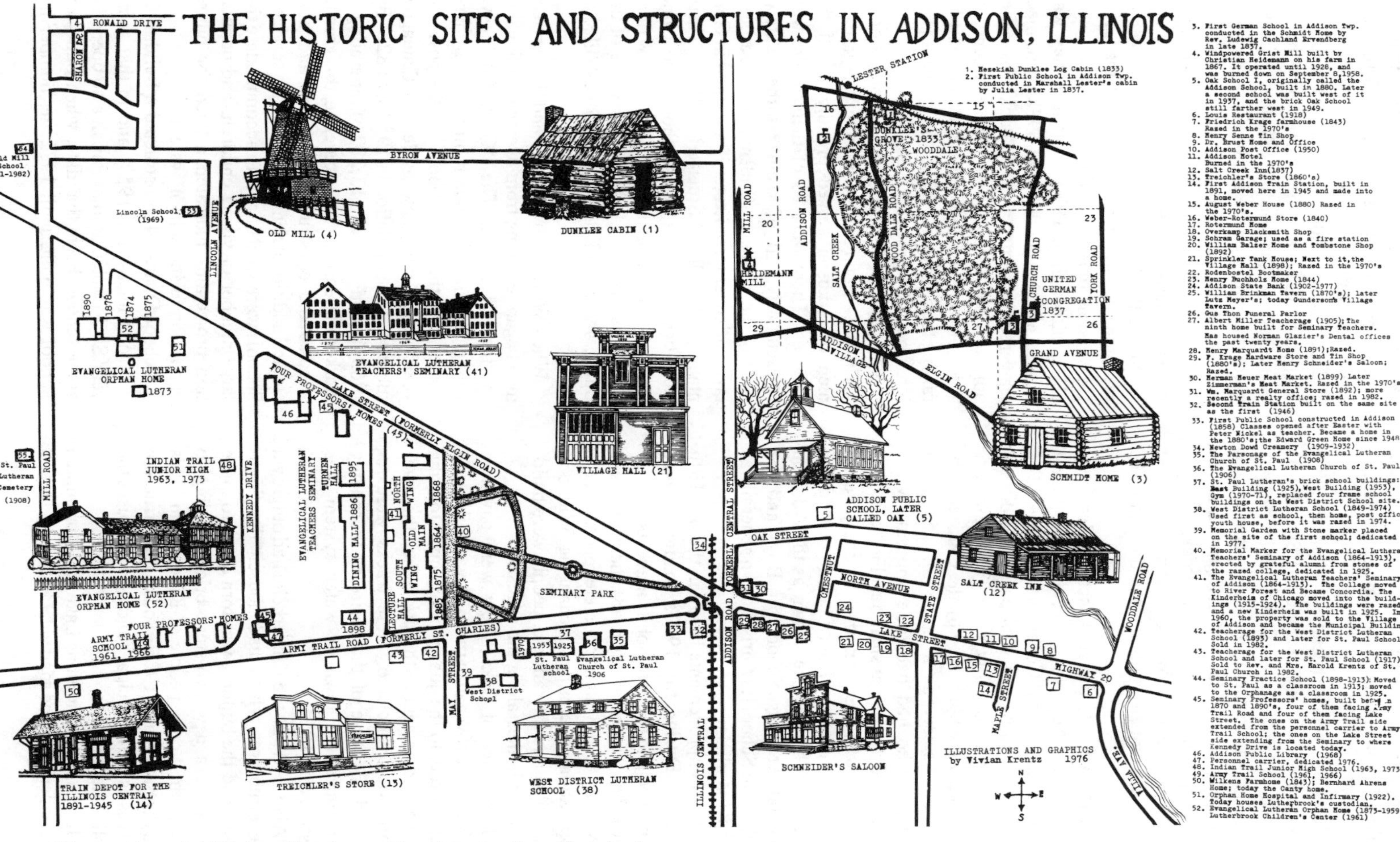


3. First German School in Addison Twp. conducted in the Schmidt Home by Rev. Ludewig Cachland Ervendberg in late 1837.
4. Windpowered Grist Mill built by Christian Heidemann on his farm in 1867. It operated until 1928, and was burned down on September 8,1958.
5. Oak School I, originally called the Addison School, built in 1880. Later a second school was built west of it in 1937, and the brick Oak School still farther west in 1949.
6. Louis Restaurant (1918)
7. Friedrich Krage farmhouse (1843) Razed in the 1970's
8. Henry Senne Tin Shop
9. Dr. Brust Home and Office
10. Addison Post Office (1950)
11. Addison Hotel Burned in the 1970's
12. Salt Creek Inn(1837)
13. Treichler's Store (1860's)
14. First Addison Train Station, built in 1891, moved here in 1945 and made into a home.
15. August Weber House (1880) Razed in the 1970's.
16. Weber-Rotermund Store (1840)
17. Rotermund Home
18. Overkamp Blacksmith Shop
19. Schram Garage; used as a fire station
20. William Balzer Home and Tombstone Shop (1892)
21. Sprinkler Tank House; Next to it,the Village Hall (1898); Razed in the 1970's
22. Rodenbostel Bootmaker
23. Henry Buchholz Home (1844)
24. Addison State Bank (1902-1977)
25. William Brinkman Tavern (1870's); later Lutz Meyer's; today Gunderson's Village Tavern.
26. Gus Thon Funeral Parlor
27. Albert Miller Teacherage (1905); The ninth home built for Seminary Teachers. Has housed Norman Glazier's Dental offices the past twenty years.
28. Henry Marquardt Home (1891);Razed.
29. F. Krage Hardware Store and Tin Shop (1880's); Later Henry Schneider's Saloon; Razed.
30. Herman Heuer Meat Market (1899) Later Zimmerman's Meat Market. Razed in the 1970's.
31. Wm. Marquardt General Store (1892); more recently a realty office; razed in 1982.
32. Second Train Station built on the same site as the first (1946)
33. First Public School constructed in Addison (1858) Classes opened after Easter with Peter Nickel as teacher. Became a home in the 1880's;the Edward Green Home since 1948.
34. Newton Dowd Creamery (1909-1932)
35. The Parsonage of the Evangelical Lutheran Church of St. Paul (1908)
36. The Evangelical Lutheran Church of St. Paul, (1906)
37. St. Paul Lutheran's brick school buildings: East Building (1925), West Building (1953), Gym (1970-71), replaced four frame school buildings on the West District School site.
38. West District Lutheran School (1849-1974) Used first as school, then home, post office youth house, before it was razed in 1974.
39. Memorial Garden with Stone marker placed on the site of the first school; dedicated in 1977.
40. Memorial Marker for the Evangelical Lutheran Teachers' Seminary of Addison (1864-1913), erected by grateful alumni from stones of the razed college, dedicated in 1925.
41. The Evangelical Lutheran Teachers' Seminary of Addison (1864-1913). The College moved to River Forest and Became Concordia. The Kinderheim of Chicago moved into the buildings (1915-1924). The buildings were razed and a new Kinderheim was built in 1925. In 1960, the property was sold to the Village of Addison and became the Municipal Building.
42. Teacherage for the West District Lutheran School (1893) and later for St. Paul School. Sold in 1982.
43. Teacherage for the West District Lutheran School and later for St. Paul School (1917); Sold to Rev. and Mrs. Harold Krentz of St. Paul Church in 1982.
44. Seminary Practice School (1898-1913): Moved to St. Paul as a classroom in 1913; moved to the Orphanage as a classroom in 1925.
45. Seminary Professors' homes, built between 1870 and 1890's, four of them facing Army Trail Road and four of them facing Lake Street. The ones on the Army Trail side extended from the personnel carrier to Army Trail School; the ones on the Lake Street side extending from the Seminary to where Kennedy Drive is located today.
46. Addison Public Library (1968)
47. Personnel carrier, dedicated 1976.
48. Indian Trail Junior High School (1963, 1973)
49. Army Trail School (1961, 1966)
50. Wilkens Farmhome (1843); Bernhard Ahrens Home; today the Canty home.
51. Orphan Home Hospital and Infirmary (1922). Today houses Lutherbrook's custodian.
52. Evangelical Lutheran Orphan Home (1873-1959); Lutherbrook Children's Center (1961)

*Illustrations by Vivian Krentz* *Graphics by Ron Carringi*

$16,488.90. The first train came to Addison for the Orphan Home Picnic on September 12, 1890.

Telephone service became available in 1895. Addison's first bank, the Addison State Bank, opened in 1902. In 1912 the Public Service Company of Northern Illinois brought in light and power lines. Electric street lights burned in Addison for the first time on February 1, 1913. That same year the Western United Gas and Electric Company brought gas lines into the area.

In 1913 the Lutheran Teachers' Seminary moved out of Addison to River Forest, where it is now known as Concordia College. The Seminary had been a vital part of Addison's history for almost fifty years. The Seminary buildings were purchased by the Chicago City Mission Society as a home for dependent children who had had little opportunity for moral, mental or physical development. The children, who were referred by the juvenile courts, were moved from Chicago to Addison in 1916. This became known as the Addison Manual Training School for Boys and the Industrial School for Girls, known generally as the Kinderheim.

Street improvements began in the late 19th century. During the 1920s roadways were improved and the automobile made its appearance. The former muddy roads and dusty trails gave way to gravel and concrete roads, and the population patterns began changing. With better routes and the railroad, people were building their homes along the roads.

Two lanes of Lake Street were paved in 1922. A narrow gauge railroad was built along Lake Street to the quarry in Elmhurst to bring gravel and cement to the site. When the roadwork was completed, these tracks were removed. Because of the desire to thoroughly modernize the town, a water system was installed in 1924.

Also, by 1924 the Kinderheim had outgrown the structures which had housed the Seminary, and the building was torn down to make room for a new two-story brick building to house the young people of Kinderheim. This was completed in 1925. Today that structure serves as the municipal building and houses the police department.

Increased traffic along Lake Street prompted the widening of the road in 1930 to forty feet all the way from Cook County line to Ontarioville, a distance of 12½ miles, and the constructing of a three-span bridge over Salt Creek at Lake Street. Addison was served by the Marigold Bus Line, which came from Chicago every hour on the hour. It followed the same route that had been used in 1837 by the Frink and Walker Line on its way toward Galena, these stage coaches having stopped for a change of horses in Addison.

During the 1930s Addison, as well as the rest of the country, was plunged into the Great Depression. In Addison the bank was forced to close, although in 1933 enough money was raised (between $8,000 and $9,000) to meet legal requirements, and the bank was again able to open for business. The residents of Addison were able to weather the lean years by raising food for their tables, and by taking any job, no matter how small the pay.

The years of World War II brought prosperity once again to the community. Again the men of Addison served proudly in all the services. There were 86 of them in the war. Miraculously, all of them returned safely. Among the Addison residents who had been taken prisoner were Lester Rotermund in Germany, and William Stuenkel in Italy. There were two casualties among those who came from the area outside of Addison: Wilbur Backhaus, who was killed in the Battle of the Bulge; and Ernst Ellerbruch who was killed in Sicily.

When World War II ended and the servicemen began returning from overseas, a housing shortage developed. The "G. I. Bill" gave young families the opportunity to purchase homes, and the "baby boom" of the post-war years brought many new residents to Chicago's suburbs. The population in 1950 was 823. By 1963 it had reached 13,272. Generating a marked increase in village revenue, this growth affected the construction industry and also created additional demands for village services. Schools were soon unable to accommodate the large number of young children, and population projections indicated a need for future expansion of the school system.

School District 4 constructed a building in a second location in 1957, and in that same year St. Joseph Catholic Parish also opened a grade school. From that date, when Fullerton School was built, until 1972 the number in-

*Illinois Central Train in Addison on "Orphan Home Festival Day."*
*Courtesy Historical Museum of Addison*

*Plass Garage. Arthur Krage, George Rathje, George Plass, Warren Web stand before the Ford Agency in 1925.*
*Courtesy Historical Museum of Addison*

creased to nine public grade schools and one junior high school.

In 1965 a second Catholic grade school, St. Philip the Apostle, was built. In 1966 there were two secondary schools built, Addison Trail High School and Driscoll Catholic High School.

Additional religious facilities were added to serve the increased population. Originally most of the residents had been German Lutherans, and the few Catholic families attended church in Elmhurst. As the number of families increased, so did the diversity of faiths. Between 1954 and 1965 there were seven churches of different denominations built.

The "G. I. Bill" was also used by many of the returning servicemen after World War II. Addison established an industrial park with a railroad line that ran into the area. Highways were being improved , and the short distance from O'Hare Airport was an attraction to many manufacturers who built in the park. These additional plants, in turn, brought more people to Addison to live. Many of the farmers surrounding Addison began to sell their farms as property values rose and their taxes increased accordingly.

Prior to 1950 there were few parks and playgrounds in Addison; however, as developers subdivided the land, they were encouraged by village officials to set aside areas in each subdivision to be used as parks. In 1958 the Central Park Committee was formed. This was a volunteer group of homeowners who helped establish and maintain parks. The Addison Recreation Club, another volunteer group, began working with Addison's youth in the early 1950s. In 1965 Addison voters approved a referendum to establish a park district, which now owns over 200 acres of land at eighteen sites and offers activities for residents of all ages, from tots to senior citizens.

In 1962 a public library was established in the municipal building. In 1968 a new building was constructed along Lake Street at Kennedy Drive to house the Addison Public Library.

The banking industry also grew along with the population. Before 1950 the Addison State Bank was the only bank in Addison. As population and businesses increased, the need for additional financial services brought the opening of six other banks or saving and loan associations to the village.

The building industry that began flourishing after World War II concentrated on single-family homes in Addison. More recently developers have obtained permits to build multiple family homes, apartments, townhouses and condominiums. Decreasing availability of land and rising construction costs have contributed to this trend. Today shopping centers have replaced the earlier "general stores." Shops and restaurants have opened specializing in ethnic goods for an increasingly diverse population.

Also, the schools, with an increased enrollment of children from families new to this country, have had to include bilingual courses in their curriculum. High technology advances have caused many services and business establishments to turn to computers and new training programs for their personnel. Addison's special education organization, the Ray Graham Association, its Lutherbrook (successor to the Evangelical Lutheran Orphan Home), its assistance programs through the Community Switchboard, its support for cultural growth through the arts programs are all a part of Addison's response to varying needs.

To summarize, during the past 150 years Addison has grown from a few hardy settlers planting their crops to a town of 30,000 citizens engaged in a multitude of occupations. The quiet hamlet where everyone knew everyone else has given place to a suburb bustling with activity. Today, as it has been throughout its history, Addison is a caring community.

**The Authors**

Pearl Morris and Vivian Krentz are co-authors of *Addison— Village of Friendship,* the community's centennial book.

# Bensenville

*Kenneth Ritzert*

Bensenville is located in the extreme northeast corner of DuPage County in Addison Township. The village is seventeen miles from downtown Chicago. It is touched by O'Hare Airport, is flanked by major expressways and is on the Milwaukee Railroad.

Bensenville's story can be divided chronologically into five periods: the Indian period, from the earliest times to 1833; the early settler period, to 1873; the railroad village, to 1916; the transition, to 1945; and the O'Hare challenge, to the present.

Bensenville, located on the low-level watershed divide, between Salt Creek and the Des Plaines River, was the hunting and trapping preserve for Indian settlements located along both rivers. In the early 1800s Chief Black Partridge of the Potawatomis moved close to the trading post of John Kinzie and to Fort Dearborn at Chicago. The chief's village on the Des Plaines River was a short distance from his hunting preserve in the Bensenville region. This was the legendary Tioga, a word reported to mean "The Gate." Perhaps this hunting ground was a gateway to enjoyment for the Indian hunter.

The first assault against Fort Dearborn in 1812 came from Winnebago Indians from the upper Rock River, who stopped to camp along Salt Creek at the present site of the Elmhurst Country Club. Here they had a ritual meal and put on their warpaint. Then the eleven braves followed an animal trail, today called Grand Avenue, to Chicago, and massacred the Lee family in their home on the Chicago River.

Later in 1812 Black Partridge attempted without success to restrain the bloodshed in the Fort Dearborn Massacre. He was only successful in protecting the family of his friend, John Kinzie. As the War of 1812 ended, most Indians in the region realized they would now have to relate to the United States rather than to the agents of Great Britain.

During the Black Hawk War more Indians than ever flocked to camps in the Des Plaines Valley, anxious to disassociate themselves

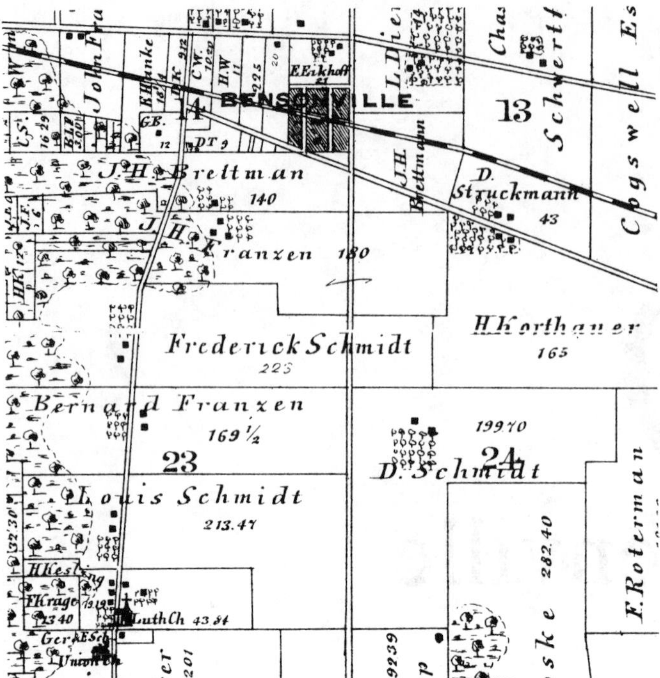


*From the* 1874 Atlas & History of DuPage County, Illinois

from the violence of Black Hawk. After Black Hawk was defeated at the Battle of Bad Axe and Illinois was finally secure against Indian attack, the loyalty and help of the Potawatomi to the white settler was forgotten. White resentment against Black Hawk was transferred to all Indians. They would pay for the actions of Black Hawk by being forcibly removed from Illinois.

A few Indians remained behind for a while. They befriended the early settlers in the Bensenville area, teaching them how to stalk game, fish through the ice, and grow crops. Their instructions in wilderness life included the process of "jerking" meat. In jerking, deer meat was cut into thin strips and stretched over a scaffold. A small fire burned beneath, slowly smoking and drying the meat.

By 1836 all Indians had vanished from the area. Bensenville's Indian legacy survives today in the names of its schools called Tioga, Mohawk, Blackhawk, and Chippewa, and in a number of its present roads and streets which were once Indian trails.

The first permanent white settlers in the Bensenville area came in 1833 from New England. Hezekiah Dunklee and Mason Smith decided to build their log cabin homestead on the east side of Salt Creek at the edge of a wooded area they named Dunklee's Grove. This forest was bordered by what is today Church Road on the east, Third Avenue on the south, Wood Dale Avenue on the west and Lawrence Avenue on the north.

By 1834 Hezekiah Dunklee was joined by the rest of his family. His brother Ebenezer, noticing the lack of fresh fruit in Dunklee's Grove, brought in three barrels of apples and planted them in 1836.

The Yankees from New England were followed by German settlers. By 1835 numbers of Hanoverians, Prussians and Pomeranians began arriving. Conrad Fischer was one of the earliest German settlers near Dunklee's Grove. Mr. Fischer had been a saddle maker in Napoleon's army in the 1812 invasion of Russia. With the help of his sons Augustus, Frederick, and Henry, he built a cabin where West Avenue runs north of Grand.

A feeling of cohesion existed among the families, forming a solid basis for community life. They spoke "Plattdeutsch," or low German; and later they erected the Plattdeutsch Guild Hall in Bensenville. These early Ger-

*Franzen Linseed Mill grinding stones.*

man families intermarried, so that everyone eventually seemed to be a relative of everyone else.

Church meetings were first held in settlers' homes. In 1847 Rev. E. A. Brauer was called as pastor of the German United Reformed Lutheran Church. The group included Lutherans from Hanover and Reformed members from Prussia. Forty-eight acres were purchased from Louis Schmidt on Church Road on a plot, which came to be known as Churchville. By 1848 the group split, with Reformed members leaving to begin St. John's Church, on a site north of Irving Park Road. In 1858 another split occurred, when the Franzen family built Immanuel Church across the street from Zion.

The Chicago and Galena Stage Line selected Grand Avenue, once called Whiskey Road, as the best route to Chicago since that old Indian path was the highest and dryest trail at all times of the year. Lead from mines in Galena was hauled along this road. The stage line had stopping points every ten miles.

One of these was the Buckhorn Tavern, built by Charles Holt and located at the corner of York and Grand. The tavern provided food and lodging for drivers and passengers, feed and water for the horses. Here the stagecoach would sometimes change teams.

Travelers on early roads sank their wheels in bottomless mud. Following the lead of Russia and Canada, private interests west of Chicago began constructing plank roads in the 1840s. Irving Park Road was once known as Plank Road. These private thoroughfares filled a transportation need until maintenance problems and the coming of the railroad bankrupted the companies.

Saw mills in the area soon made frame housing possible. All foundations were made of fieldstone. The Schmidt house on Church Road was built in 1854 from stone hauled by oxen from Aurora. In 1862 the present landmark Zion Church was built with brick, but most dwellings were constructed with framing lumber. The Churchville frame schoolhouse was built between 1843 and 1849.

In 1847 John H. Franzen constructed his flax mill and brick factory at the present location of St. Alexis Church on Wood Street. The two millstones, currently displayed in front of the Bensenville Library, were used to grind flaxseed to produce linseed oil. Flax became an important cash crop for farmers in this area. These farmers often came from a long distance to grind their flaxseed, and were welcomed to stay overnight at the Franzen farm. Women used the flax fiber to make linen cloth. The Franzens continued to make flax tow after they had shut down their mill. Their mill is said to be the first of its kind in Illinois.

The Fischer windmill on Grand Avenue was also begun in 1847. This landmark is located in front of Mount Emblem Cemetery. Henry Korthauer, a cabinet maker and builder of spinning wheels, helped construct the mechanism. Men from Holland also aided in the three-year construction. The family of Edward Ehlers lived in the mill, which was in operation for seventy years.

A steam engine powered the grist mill of Frederick Wolkenhauer on Center Street. This mill was in continued operation until 1922.

The Civil War tended to stimulate grain production in the area. Some settlers joined the army, fought and died on Civil War battlefields. Louis Schmidt held a reunion for fellow Civil War veterans after the war. People felt strongly about the Union cause. A mob of angry farmers came to Zion Church with pitchforks and a rope after Pastor Franke had said that President Lincoln deserved to be shot because he was attending the theatre on Good

*Auguste Asche's Cheese Factory — about 1900.*
*Courtesy Bensenville Historical Society*

Friday at the time of his assassination, when he should have been in church.

Between 1860 and 1880 agriculture in the Bensenville area was changing from diversified subsistence farming to specialized cash crops, then to commercial dairy farming. Settlement patterns were also changing from dispersed to clustered dwellings near railroad lines, which had come to the area by 1873.

By 1874 the Chicago and Pacific, later the Chicago, Milwaukee and St. Paul Railway Company, was already hauling 300,000 gallons of milk a year from Bensenville to Chicago. Over three times that volume was kept in the vicinity with much of that milk being made into cheese.

The coming of the railroad brought about a need for a nodal center to serve as a shipping point and to provide services for the agricultural hinterland. In 1872 a group, including Dedrich Struckmann, Henry Korthauer, and Frederick Heuer, purchased the present site of Bensenville. The plat was recorded and subdivided into lots in 1873. The name "Tioga" appeared on some old maps, but the name "Bensenville" was selected after Henry Schuette said the small community was similar to his former home in Bensen, Germany.

On April 5, 1884 a public meeting was called at the Korthauer Hardware Store where a committee was appointed to investigate the advantages of incorporation. A petition was sent to Judge Elbert Gary in Wheaton, the county seat of DuPage. On May 10, 1884, the proposal for incorporation carried by a vote of 42 for and 7 against.

The turn of the century found new developments in the village. The bank of the Franzen Brothers, later called the First State Bank of Bensenville, was started in 1911. A telephone switchboard was installed in Korthauer's hardware store in 1902. In 1903 concrete walks were built to replace the town's wooden sidewalks. By 1910 electricity came to Bensenville. Gustave Gutsche, the village shoemaker, no longer had to be hired as lamplighter of the kerosene lamps on the town streets.

Changes were taking place in the Bensenville school system. Science replaced German in the school curriculum in 1906. Those who still wished to study German could do so in summer school. The new brick Green Street

School was completed in 1916. On the second floor of this landmark structure, the first Bensenville High School was started in 1916.

The Milwaukee Railroad expanded its facilities in the early 1900s. In 1912 a huge water tank was erected. The roundhouse at the Milwaukee yards was built in 1916. This became the railroad's main shop. The roundhouse employed three hundred people. This brought a new population to town, and the German monopoly in Bensenville was broken. There was resentment against the newcomers, and social tension felt. By 1919 Mexican railroad workers were living in six boxcars on railroad property. Mexican culture would become an important part of Bensenville's history.

By World War I the community's culture was strongly German. Bensenville's young men, however, demonstrated their American patriotism by willingly going to war to defeat Germany and Kaiser Wilhelm.

Following the war, Prohibition became an issue. Prior to the passage of the 18th Amendment, there had been five saloons in Bensenville, including one run by Max Fensky, who also dished up the biggest ice cream cone in town. During the bootleg era, the town was in the national news with reports that two men from Minnesota were being held for ransom by the Ma Barker gang. Dances at Shane's ballroom on Higgins Road sometimes resulted in fisticuffs.

During the early 1920s, Fred C. Fenton became school superintendent, while continuing to teach high school classes at Green Street School. Community High School District 100 was established by the Illinois Supreme Court, after its boundaries had been contested by some residents. A referendum for a new high school was successfully passed, and in 1927 grades seven through twelve moved into the new Community High School at York and Memorial. The orphans from The Bensenville Home, across the street, by state law now had to attend public school. Mr Fenton was superintendent of District 2 and 100 until his death in 1943. At that time Wesley A. Johnson assumed the position.

The Depression years made their impact on Bensenville. Large dairies in Chicago making pasturized milk displaced the independent dairy farms around Bensenville. Grist mills closed down. "Drag days," with a shorter work week, were designed to keep men employed on the railroad. Still there were layoffs. Families lost homes, and children went to school without anything to eat. In 1931 there were no funds for teachers' salaries, so payments were delayed.

Residents would often pick flowers and berries in the dense woods east of Route 83. This became part of the Grove Farm, which in turn became known as Plentywood Farm. In 1932 the Plentywood Farm restaurant opened in log buildings constructed from trees cut on the property. Later, part of the property of the Grove Farm was purchased by Fenton High School by right of eminent domain.

Two unincorporated residential communities were eventually annexed to Bensenville. One was Georgetown, which included property north of Irving Park Road and east of York Road. St. John's Church, which served the spiritual needs of farmers north of Bensenville, was the main landmark of Georgetown. The other area was Edgewood, located south of First Avenue and west of York Road.

Stresen-Reuter brought industry to Bensenville in 1937, manufacturing paint, varnishes, and chemical sand. It also engendered controversy over the issue of air pollution. The Campbell Soup Company contracted with farmers living north of Irving Park Road to raise tomatoes, which were harvested by Mexican-American migrant labor and hauled to Chicago. Potatoes became another large cash crop. Farmers from a wide geographic area, including those living on Washington Island, Wisconsin, shipped their potatoes to Edward J. Anderson's Potato Factory, located at Green Street and County Line Road.

1940 Bensenville had a population of 1,200 people. German was still spoken in the butcher shops. Changes would soon come to the community, however, because of World War II. The U. S. Government was looking for a site to build Douglas C-54 *Skymaster* cargo planes. An interior location was needed since the West Coast was considered vulnerable to Japanese attack. The two-million-square-foot building constructed nearby for this manufacture was the largest all-timber plant in the world, until fire gutted it on July 18, 1944.

The VFW became one of the most active organizations in town. It was here that ethnic

*The Milwaukee Road Yards — looking toward Chicago Skyline. Courtesy Bensenville Historical Society*

barriers between people of the community were broken down. Later Ray Soden, one of its leading members, was elected national commander of the VFW.

Beginning in 1946, the Douglas-Old Orchard location was converted into an airport, soon to be called O'Hare Field. The Village of Bensenville petitioned that Chicago, located in Cook County, had no right to acquire property in DuPage County, where Bensenville was located. This effort came to naught. The jet age continued to have an increased impact on Bensenville. Due to new flight patterns and a third landing system, the level of noise from O'Hare continued to increase. In the spring of 1969 Bensenville, with sixteen other suburbs, formed the O'Hare Area Noise Abatement Council. This group called for more industrial and less residential areas in the path of flights, and demanded that planes eliminate "fanning out" on takeoffs. Bensenville Village President John Varble became the leader of N. O. I. S. E. This organization lobbied at all levels of government for laws on air and noise pollution. The group was successful in having high density rule restrictions imposed to limit the number of evening flights at O'Hare.

The population of Bensenville doubled betwe 1940 and 1950. Between 1950 and 1960 it nearly tripled. An industrial district began to develop as a buffer between O'Hare Airport and the village's residential area. Industrial development also took place on east Green Street. In 1959 the Mohawk Country Club became a part of a 700-acre industrial park purchased by the Chicago, Milwaukee and Pacific Railroad. By 1981 land zoned for industrial use occupied 25% of the developed area of the village.

The Illinois Manufacturers Directory lists more than 230 manufacturing plants in Bensenville. As of 1981 the largest employer was the Bally Electronic Pinball Division, maker of pinball and video games. Jovan, Inc. produces perfumes, soaps and cosmetics. Griffin Wheel makes railroad wheels. Precision Extrusions converts aluminum extrusions into fabricated and finished parts. Bee Line Fashions deals in direct clothing sales and has its national center at its Bensenville location. Bensenville is also the national headquarters of the Flick-Reedy Corporation. The Miller Fluid Power Corporation, a division of Flick-Reedy, is the nation's leading manufacturer of hydraulic and pneumatic components. Warehousing is a major growth industry of the industrial district.

Bensenville has had direct contact with individuals prominently involved in politics. John Kennedy's campaign stop in the village in 1960 was a memorable occurrence. Representative William Redmond of Bensenville became Speaker of the Illinois House of Representatives in 1975, serving until his retirement in 1982. Gene Hoffman, Chairman of the Social Studies Department at Fenton High School, was elected to the Illinois General Assembly in 1968 and continues to serve in the Illinois House. Congressman Henry Hyde, U.S. Representative from the 6th District, has made Bensenville his home.

From Indian hunting grounds to pioneer farm settlement, from railroad village to a residential/industrial component of the Chicago metropolitan area, Bensenville's history has been rich and varied.

The Author
Kenneth Ritzert is chairman of the Social Studies Department at Blackhawk Junior High School in Bensenville. He is recipient of the Valley Forge Teacher's Medal and the Freedom Foundation Award. He has also written the play, *Bensenville Story*.

# Bloomingdale

*Thomas J. Perkins, Jr.*
*Patti Lee Perkins*

When the last glacier began its retreat from the area we now call Bloomingdale, it left behind ridges of material which it had pushed all the way from Canada. Along Schick Road runs the terminal moraine left behind as the glacier melted. In among the rock and debris were the materials needed by early settlers to produce fine stone tools: flint, sandstone and granite.

Unearthed artifacts show that early settlers lived in the Bloomingdale area for about five thousand years before white explorers arrived. The major settlement was west of Bloomingdale Road and south of Schick Road. Here a natural spring broke from the ground, and the land provided a good view of the surrounding territory, mostly prairie and marsh, with a huge grove extending to the south side of present-day Lake Street.

The first white settlers, coming from Vermont and upstate New York, had forced the Indians out of their lands. Originally from Rutland County, Vermont, the Meacham family left in the mid-1820s to live in western New York. In 1830 the Meachams were living in Richland, Sandy Creek Township, Oswego County, New York. Lyman Meacham left that area and came to Illinois ahead of the family to scout the Chicago area for good land to settle. On March 11, 1833, the Meacham family arrived in what would become Bloomingdale Township. Lyman was soon followed by his brothers: Harvey, Daniel and Dr. Silas Meacham. They pitched their tents near the grove that was soon to bear their name.

The Meachams lived among the Indians for their first year in the area, and found them to be quite trustworthy. Harvey Meacham loaned a valuable rifle to one of the Indians for several days, on the promise he would return it on a certain day. The Indian did.

The Meacham family claimed an area of about 1,200 acres. Two men with four horses could till one hundred acres, while three men

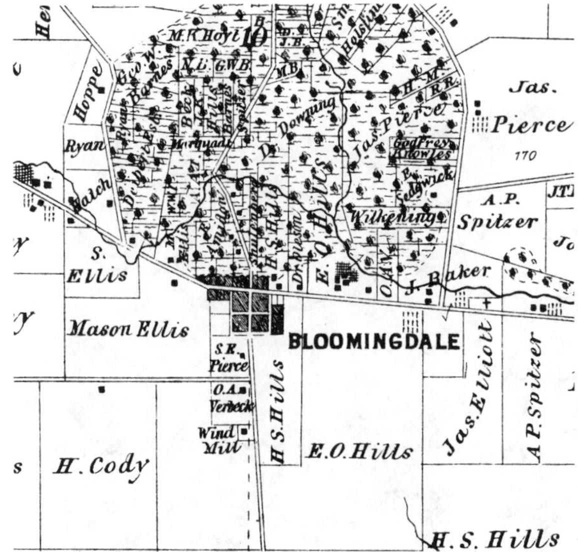


*From the* 1874 Atlas & History of DuPage County, Illinois

with five horses could do 160 acres, or a quarter section. A good day's work for a man with a single team of horses was two acres of ploughing. Much of the Meacham claim was woodland, which provided posts for fencing in their claims and farms, as well as lumber for housebuilding.

Lyman Meacham's wife died in the fall of 1833 and was buried in the grove. However, in 1834 the population of the area increased with the arrival of more families. Woodworth, Stevens, Bangs, Maynard and a Major Skinner were among those listed in the party. By the end of the year the settlement had increased to twelve or fifteen families. From the time of its settlement in 1833 until early in 1839, Bloomingdale was located in Washington Precinct of Cook County. Elections were held in Elk Grove, eight miles northeast of Meacham's Grove.

The legislature in January of 1836 authorized the laying out of a State road from Meacham's Grove to Galena. There was already an established road from the Grove to Chicago. By 1837 two daily stages ran through Bloomingdale to Elgin. On July 20, 1837 the post office at Bloomingdale was established. Frink and Walker's Stage Line ran through town, with travel from Chicago to Rockford taking twenty-four hours. The stage left Chicago at two o'clock in the morning and by daybreak had reached the Bloomingdale area. By the end of the 1830s, several hundred wagons and travelers came through Bloomingdale each day. According to the rates established by Cook County officials, breakfast or supper could be obtained for 25¢, dinner for 37½¢ and a night's lodging for 12½¢.

By 1839 Bloomingdale was an established village. The origin of the name of the township and village remains obscure. It was not named for the Meacham's hometown in Vermont because there has never been a town by that name in Vermont. The only existing clue may be the 1840 notes and map made by the man responsible for the survey of this township. This surveyor, L. D. Ewing, had been Governor of Illinois in 1824. On his map and in his notes Ewing mentions another grove on the Bloomingdale-Addison Township line. The grove, to the east of Meacham's grove, is called Bloomingdale's Grove! No other record of the name has yet turned up in the 1830 or 1840 Census. Perhaps the Meachams were not the first settlers, but rather the first permanent settlers in the area.

The year 1840 was most important to the settlers of the entire region. By original intent, this area was not to be settled until the Federal government had surveyed the land into thirty-six one-mile squares called "sections." However, "squatters" had settled this area prior to

*Original Baptist Church Building, currently Bloomingdale Park District Museum.*

the survey of these lands. These "pioneers" had no claim legally to the lands and many claim disputes developed, such as the "Kent Tragedy" of 1840.

Milton Kent had leased land from Dr. Silas Meacham about 1836 and had built a tavern on the north side of Lake Street, near the Fairfield Way intersection. Dr. Meacham then moved to the Des Plaines area, selling his claim to Ebenezer Peck. Ebenezer Peck, in turn, sold the claim to George W. Green of Chicago. Kent was then told to move out of the tavern by the new landowner, Green. Angry, Kent and his son made a midnight raid against Green, who now had moved into the vacated tavern. In the ensuing scuffle Milton Kent was mortally wounded by Green, and Lorenzo Kent, the son, was also badly wounded. Lorenzo and some of his friends subdued Green and forced him to sign a quit-claim to the property and retitle it to Kent. The Kents then ran him off the property.

The sheriff was summoned and soon arrested Lorenzo and his friends. While awaiting trial, they escaped and fled the state. Mr. Green, found "not guilty" in Milton Kent's death, kept the property for another four years, and after selling it, moved back to the city of Chicago.

Lyman and Harvey Meacham had also purchased most of Section 15, where "Old Town" is located today. On March 10, 1843, almost ten years to the day of their arrival, they sold the northeast quarter of Section 15 to Erasmus O. Hills, a founder of the Village of Bloomingdale. Lyman moved to DuPage Township in Will County.

Other early settlers purchasing lands in the early 1840s included these: Lloyd Sterns, Captain E. Kinne, Harry Woodworth, Moses Elliot, James Barnes, Asa W. Clark, Richard K. Swift, Moses Hoit, Huit B. Hills, Elijah Hough, Waters Northrup, Noah Stevens, Hilamon S. Hills, Parker Sedgwick, Hiram B. Patrick, William F. Bloom, Milo F. Meacham, Cyrus H. Meacham, Rowland Rathbun and Moses Stacey. All 640 acres of Section 36 was purchased by Marcellus Farmer. When she purchased her land in November of 1844, development in the area had pushed the price from $1.25 to $3.00 per acre.

The Village of Bloomingdale grew throughout the 1840s. In August of 1840 the Congregational Church was organized by Deacons Elijah Hough, Allan Hills, C. H. Meacham, and others. Construction of their church began in 1851, and the first service was held on June

13, 1852. The congregation sold the building to the St. Paul's German Church in July of 1878 for $850. No known records of this Congregational Church exist.

On March 24, 1841, at the home of Noah Stevens, the First Baptist Church at Bloomingdale was organized. Seventy members were soon signed up, with A. W. Bulton and Joel Wheeler officiating. After meeting in different homes, they decided to build a meeting house. A lot at Franklin and Bloomingdale was deemed a suitable spot, and on January 25, 1848, Hiram Goodwin gave the property to the Baptist Society. Hiram had purchased the land from Dr. Silas Meacham and his wife Rebecca for $1,100 on May 20, 1844. The building was completed early in 1849. The growing congregation built still again in 1855 on Lake Street, where local lore has it that Abraham Lincoln spoke in his 1858 senatorial race against Stephen Douglas.

Erasmus O. Hills, Hilamon S. Hills and Hiram Goodwin platted the Village of Bloomingdale on January 11, 1845. It was the first village to be platted in the northern part of DuPage County. On November 6, 1849, Bloomingdale Township of DuPage County was organized. The major occupation in the Bloomingdale area in the 1850s was agriculture. The only industry in the township worth more than $500 was that of shoemaker Hiram Cody, age 52. He employed three people and paid wages of $88 per month for their labor.

These residents of northern DuPage County were served by the stage coach which left Chicago for Elgin at 9:00 a.m. each Wednesday. The first stop in the township was Kinne Post Office, a now unknown location. The postmaster at Kinne was Waters Northrup, the former postmaster at Bloomingdale. The Village of Bloomingdale's postmaster in 1850, Sherman P. Sedgwick, operated the post office out of his drug store at the northeast corner of Bloomingdale Road and Lake Street. The route ended at Elgin, thirty-two miles from its start. The mail began its return to Chicago at 6:00 a.m., arriving at 4:00 p.m. on Thursday.

Colonel Benjamin Franklin Meacham came in 1855 to join his uncle, Harvey Meacham, in Meacham's Grove. With him came his wife Rebecca, 18-year-old son George William and 12-year-old daughter Elizabeth (Lizzie).

In 1860 the Bloomingdale Academy opened. It was probably some form of high school, but the records are unclear. The two teachers taught seventy-five students. On April 22, 1861, the First Baptist Church sold its old building at Franklin and Bloomingdale to the Bloomingdale Academy trustees. But fifteen days earlier an event had taken place at Charleston, South Carolina, that would affect the people of Bloomingdale and limit the life of the Academy. The War Between the States had begun!

In September of 1861 many men from the village and surrounding area enlisted in the Eighth Illinois Volunteer Cavalry. Some, like Robert Wales Gates, served throughout the war and came home to make many contributions to their community. Others, like 25-year-old William B. Pierce, were not as lucky. Pierce was one of two DuPage County soldiers to die at Andersonville Prison in Georgia.

The people who stayed behind were not idle. On September 1, 1861, a meeting was held at the Academy building in Bloomingdale, "for the purpose of rendering assistance to the sick and wounded soldiers of the Army of the United States." School teachers were requested to take up collections in the schools. One of those on the committee, Elizabeth Meacham, was the daughter of Colonel B.F. Meacham. A student at Wheaton College at the time, she would eventually marry veteran Frank Woodworth in 1873. The war probably drained the Academy of students, for on October 1, 1861, the school trustees sold the building to the trustees of Bloomingdale School District 7, 13 today.

As the Civil War dragged on, there were not enough volunteers to keep the ranks of the Union Army filled. To meet this need for manpower, the first military draft was instituted in July 1863. Men between the ages of 18 and 45 were required to register for the draft. By June 27, 1863, there were 157 men in Bloomingdale Township so registered.

The fall of 1864 brought the reelection bid of President Lincoln. At the home of Henry Moore, on November 8, the men of the township cast 218 votes. Of these, Peace Democrat George McClellan received 79 votes, while Abraham Lincoln received 139. Sherman P. Sedgwick of Bloomingdale was elected Representative in the Illinois State Legislature.

The war ended in April of 1865. On the 15th

news came of the murder of President Lincoln. On the 19th memorial services were held at the Lake Street cemetery for the "martyr to slavery."

Major changes took place in the area to affect the village in the 1870s. The Chicago, Milwaukee and St. Paul Railroad came through the northern part of the Township in 1873. B. F. Meacham and Roselle M. Hough both donated large tracts of land for the railroad construction. Colonel Hough was the largest landowner in the area, with 1,122 acres. In 1875 Bernard Beck platted the Village of Roselle along the railroad right-of-way.

Industry increased in the Village of Bloomingdale during the 70s. Hiram Cody was still making boots and shoes, 250 pairs a year of the former and 150 pairs of the latter, but he now had competition in the person of John Roehler, producer of 250 pairs of boots and 800 pairs of shoes. Robert Wales Gates was the wagonmaker/blacksmith for the village. During the year he produced twenty-six wagons and nine buggies. The well-dressed townsman might visit merchant and tailor Francis X. Neltnor, whose shop still stands at the northeast corner of Lake Street and Bloomingdale Road. For house building, cabinet making or general carpentry, one could employ John Dumper or Oscar Verbeck at a cost of $1.50 for a ten-hour working day. The farmers could sell their milk, 120,000 pounds of it produced annually, to Oscar C. Woodworth, who operated his cheese factory only six months per year.

B. F. Meacham died in 1879. His son, George William, sold the family lands early in 1880 and moved to Chicago. In 1885 the family moved to Green Lake, Wisconsin. They returned to Illinois in 1896, finally settling in Glen Ellyn. Rebecca, the Colonel's widow, remained with her son-in-law and daughter, Frank and Lizzie Woodworth, until her death in 1891.

By the 1880s few of the early settlers were alive or in the area. Asa Clark, 85 and disabled, lived with his son Seth. Anthony Kinney, 69, was the bed spring manufacturer in the village. At 82 Hirman Cody was still making shoes. The early pioneers had done quite well. The farms of Waters Northrup and Moses Hoyt alone produced 42,000 gallons of milk per year.

The late 1870s and early 1880s marked the westward migration. The Congregational Church building was sold to the Germans in the area and renamed the German United Evan-

*Looking West on Lake Street. Second Baptist Church building was built in 1855. Courtesy Mr. & Mrs. Thomas J. Perkins Jr.*

gelical Lutheran St. Paul Church of Bloomingdale in 1878. The membership of the Baptist Church declined from 300 in the early 1860s to 73 in July of 1880. On its 1882–83 roll many names are followed by notations, "Went to Iowa," "Went to Kansas," and "Went to Nebraska."

A petition was sent to County Judge Elbert H. Gary on January 30, 1889, to allow an election for purpose of officially incorporating a Village to be called Bloomingdale. On March 5, 1889, in the tailor shop of the late Francis X. Neltnor, the people of the area voted 47 to 12 in favor of the proposition. The first trustees elected to the village board were Frank Holstein, Dr. Henry Vanderhoof, John Bagge, William Wangelien, Joseph Fiedler and William Rathje. Dr. Vanderhoof was chosen as the first president and John H. Rohler as village clerk. The first village included the North Section (Roselle), and the South Section (Bloomingdale). Total expenses for 1889 were $1,080.56.

The new schoolhouse at Lake and Third Street was constructed in 1890, the first building to be built as a school. On May 7, 1892, the township board met at the old Baptist church and school at Franklin and Bloomingdale to purchase it at a public auction. In 1895 the village passed an ordinance granting the Chicago Telephone Company the right to place poles and wires along the Chicago and Elgin Road (Lake Street). The first cement sidewalks were placed in the village on Charles Hollenbach's lot in 1899.

The arrival of the 20th Century brought more changes to the village. Automobiles were common enough for the village to pass a 1904 ordinance establishing speed limits of 8 mph on streets (4 mph in alleys). Drivers were required

*Randecker Hardware — 1910*
*Courtesy Mr. & Mrs. Thomas J. Perkins Jr.*

to sound a bell or gong at every street crossing. Gas street lamps were purchased for both parts of the village. From 1903 to 1905 the village board met at Hollenbach's bowling alley.

A proposal was made in June of 1904 that the village set aside $200 to establish a library. According to the proposal, half of the books would be kept in Bloomingdale and half in Roselle. One third on the first purchase would be printed in German. The village purchased its first fire engine on August 18th for $350. The committee agreed that the engine would be located for six months in Roselle and six months in Bloomingdale.

In 1910 the township purchased a portable steel jail cell for installation in the township hall. Around this same time William Randecker left the house-painting business to his partner, Fred Hillman, and built a hardware store at the southwest corner of Franklin and Bloomingdale, which is today known as Old Town Hardware.

The Western United Gas and Electric Company began to lay its gas lines in the village in 1916. In 1917 the village began purchasing street oil to keep down the dust on the gravel roads in the area. With the passage of the 19th Amendment, Bloomingdale women were allowed to vote in the 1920 election. Prohibition was ushered in by the 18th Amendment, and at least one "speak-easy" was located in the village, on Lake Street east of First Street.

Operating two villages as one caused friction. Accordingly, on May 22, 1922, a majority of the voters agreed that "the Village Organization of Bloomingdale Shall be Dissolved." Property was divided between the two parts, and the last meeting of the "old village of Blomingdale including Roselle" was held on August 19, 1922. By a vote of 81 to 15, the people in the south part of the old village established a new village of Bloomingdale on June 16, 1923.

Electricity came to the village in 1924; however, many would not enjoy this convenience or that of the telephone for years. Fifteen electric street lights were installed on a trial basis in 1934 as replacements for the gas lights. Construction on Central School was completed in 1937. The old school was rented to the village, and the first meeting of the village board was held there in August 1938. The building was purchased a decade later.

After the United States was thrust into World War II, the Civilian Defense and Air Raid Black-Out Ordinances were passed early in 1942. The War Ration Board operated out of the township hall. In 1944 tin can collections were set up for the war effort. Bloomingdale men served in the armed forces. Alvin Koehn and Roy Fuller were among casualties.

The 1950s were years of growth. The village purchased its first marked police car. Prior to this time the village marshall drove his own car while he was on duty. The Bloomingdale Fire Protection District 1 was formed in 1954. The same year indoor plumbing was added to the village hall. The Indian Lakes and Suncrest subdivisions were built in that decade, as the population tripled from 338 in 1950 to 1,262 in 1960.

The larger population in the 1960s led to the creation of a full-time police department. The new post office was completed in 1962, but patrons continued to pick up their mail. Because a second school was necessary, DuJardin School was built in 1964. Bloomingdale Township offices were moved to new quarters in 1965; and on June 14 the old Baptist Church was again sold, this time to the Bloomingdale Park District, for one dollar. The Illinois Sesquicentennial in 1968 saw the building and grounds dedicated as "Pioneer Park Hall."

A time both of growth and destruction occurred during the 1970s. Tree lined Bloomingdale Road was deemed too narrow for the growing community. Despite much protest from concerned citizens, the trees that had stood for hundreds of years were axed in 1974.

The first class graduated from the new Westfield School in 1975. The first library opened at Fairfield and Bloomingdale roads in that same year.

The year of the bicentennial brought more changes. The death of George Bender on February 8 ended the family ownership of the village's oldest hardware store. "Bloomingdale Grove" was renamed "Meacham's Grove." A special census that year showed that the village had a population of 9,934. Its new village hall opened on Valentine's Day, 1977. Three shopping centers were under construction or in the final stages of approval: Old Town Square (on top of the Indian Village), Springbrook, and Stratford Square.

The sesquicentennial of the Meacham's

arrival in the Township in 1983 brought a focus upon the history of the area. Old and new residents participated in the 150th Anniversary. Through tours, student government day, and a presentation of crafts called "The Way We Were" students learned about the village's past. Old Town was revitalized through the renovation of historic buildings and construction of new replicas. It was a time to remember the past and look toward the future.

**The Authors**

Thomas J. and Patti Lee Beckermann Perkins have lived in the Bloomingdale area since 1972; he has taught in that community's Junior High during that time, she has been self-employed.

# Carol Stream

*Jean Moore*

Like the surrounding land in the county, Carol Stream was once inhabited by Indians. The farmland which lies between Shawnee Drive and North Avenue was one of several Indian camp sites in central DuPage County. St Charles Road was little more than a footpath for the Indians.

The early settlers in the north Milton, south Bloomingdale and east Wayne townships were residents from New England and New York state. Most of them had traveled along the Erie Canal via the Great Lakes to Chicago, while others had taken the overland route through Ohio and Indiana.

Among these pioneer families of the early 1830s was that of Anning S. Ransom, a veteran of the War of 1812 and a New York resident. He brought with him his bride, Melissa Bingham Ransom, an Ohio resident. They traveled by wagon with an ox team, often used to pull wagons at that time because oxen were less expensive than horses. Entitled to a tract of land in the newly acquired Indian territory due to his military service, Ransom selected a slight knoll in north Milton Township along St. Charles Road as the site for his first home, a log cabin. Like many families, the Ransoms lived in their wagon until the cabin was completed. Later, he built a larger home on the north side of St. Charles Road near Pleasant Hill Road.

The Ransoms made an annual marketing expedition to Chicago to trade their produce and grain for the staples needed to operate a home on the northern Illinois prairie. The trip to the city on the lake was made over St. Charles Road, improved to a wagon road in 1836. In order to cross the Des Plaines River west of Chicago, the Ransoms would unload the bags of grain and carry them across the river on their backs to keep them from getting wet. After leading the cow and wagon across

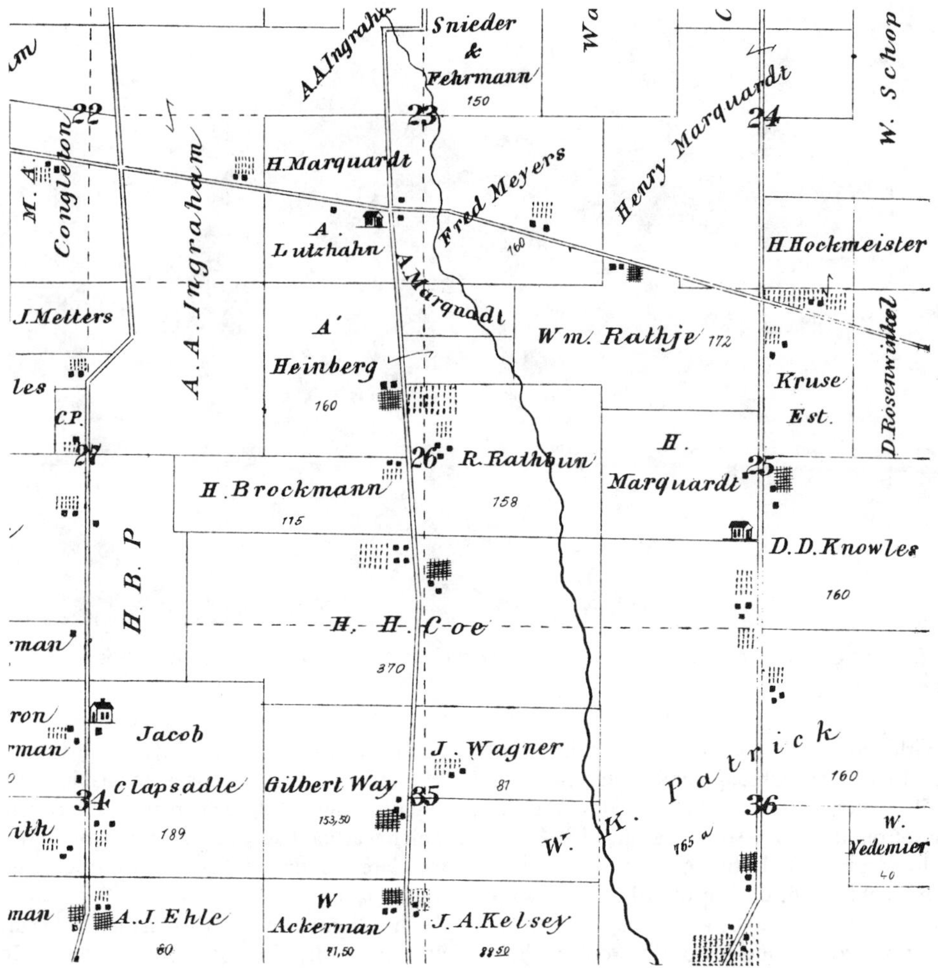


*From the* 1874 Atlas & History of DuPage County, Illinois

the river, they would reload the wagon and continue the journey into Chicago. The return trip would be made in much the same fashion.

In 1842 Daniel Kelley came west on a land purchase trip. Returning to his home in Danby, Vermont, he obtained enough funds to return the next year and acquire 1,400 acres of land in north Milton and Bloomingdale townships. He began construction of a home for himself and his bride-to-be, Mary Elizabeth Huls of St. Charles, a former Vermont neighbor. Today the home, known as Tall Trees, still stands on the north side of St. Charles Road at Main Place.

Kelley and several of his brothers and sisters moved to this area. A brother, David, was stationmaster and postmaster for the Village of Danby (now Glen Ellyn) in 1849. Daniel brought Merino sheep from his father's herd in Vermont to his home in the community of Gretna. The Merino sheep, originally imported from Spain, were noted for their fine wool and for their hardiness in warding off attacks by wolves which still roamed the area in the 1850s. Kelley founded the Illinois Wool Growers Association.

Kelley was an active member of the Wheaton Community. He donated land for the original First Baptist Church of Wheaton, now the Geneva Road Baptist Church, at the northeast corner of Seminary Avenue and Main Street. His wife and daughter lived in the small house which later became the church parsonage. He also donated a new right-of-way for St.

*Visitors at Gretna Cemetery. Container Corporation is located to the north of this pioneer site.*

Charles Road when the original roadbed was acquired by the Chicago and Great Western Railway for its tracks. Moving slowly eastward from the Minnesota area since 1854, the railroad came to Gretna in 1885.

By that time the destiny of Milton Township had been determined by a generous land donation from Warren and Jesse Wheaton and their brother-in-law, Erastus Gary; they had offered land to the officials of the Galena and Chicago Union Railway in 1849 if the railroad would be platted through their adjoining farmlands near Roosevelt Road rather than following a course which at the time would have taken it through Gretna.

Despite the loss of the railroad line in 1849, the community in north Milton continued as a small service area serving the farmers of the area who continued to use St. Charles Road.

The Daniel and Mary Kelley family had eight sons and three daughters, all of whom played a major role in the political and business development of the Wheaton area in the latter quarter of the 19th century and early part of the 20th century.

Another change came to the Gretna area in the late 1840s when a number of German farm families, fleeing the political oppression and famine in their homelands, arrived in north Milton and Bloomingdale townships. Frequently they took ownership of farmlands which earlier had been acquired by settlers who later continued their westward search for open space.

The Germans who settled in the Gretna area were primarily Catholics from southern Germany. At the time, there was no Catholic church in the county other than Sts. Peter and Paul in Naperville. Once a month one of the priests from the church would gather his religious articles for the journey across the prairies to Gretna. By 1852 the bishop of Chicago had authorized construction of a wooden Catholic church and school with a churchyard cemetery. St. Stephen's Catholic Church was dedicated the same year by Bishop James Oliver VandeVelde.

It continued to serve the vast German Catholic parish of central DuPage County from Roosevelt Road north to the county line near Schaumburg. In 1867 St. John the Baptist Catholic Church was opened in Winfield to serve that growing area. The bishop ordered St. Stephen's closed, except for special services, with families transferred to St. John's for worship. When St. Michael's Catholic Church

*Joseph Kuhn threshing grain — about 1932.*

and School opened in Wheaton in 1872, the parishioners from St. Stephen's were transferred to that church, along with their records. The cemetery at St. Stephen's continued to be used until 1911. Today, only the old cemetery remains as a reminder that once a major Catholic church was located at Gretna. Six area churches all trace their roots to the original St. Stephen's Mission Church at Gretna.

The vast farming area around Gretna and in Bloomingdale and Wayne townships continued in use as rich agricultural land in the county until after World War II. The family names remained the same, it was merely the generations that changed. Included among these area farmers were the Kramers, Kuhns, Dieters, Nagels, Hahns, Klocks, Paulings, Starks, Neddermeyers, Barnes, Lies and Kammes. Very few of the young men were called upon to serve in military service since they were already involved in a vital wartime industry — that of providing food for the armed forces abroad and for the people on the home front.

Following World War II, a few changes were made as the older farmers retired in order to give their offspring a chance at a place to live and work. The slow but steady migration of city dwellers into the suburban countryside was underway. However, for central DuPage County it would be another few years before the cornfields would come alive with new homes almost overnight. It was in this same period that another miracle of communication found a spot in the rich farmlands of DuPage County.

In the spring of 1953, the Illinois Department of Agriculture began a search for a farm and a farm family who would become the stars of a new television show on the National Broadcasting Company. One of the thirty-five farms on the itinerary was the Harbecke Farm on Gary Avenue, rural Cloverdale in Bloomingdale Township, operated by Harbecke's daughter and son-in-law, Bertha and Wilbert Landmeier. Tracing their roots to pioneer German farm families, the young couple had moved to the Harbecke Farm to operate a dairy farm. They had recently installed dairy equipment which carried the milk in refrigerated tubes from the milking machine to cooling tanks on the milk truck, which transported the commodity to an Addison dairy. The farm also had a hay drier which was another piece of modern machinery not found on every farm in

1953. These advantages, plus the fact that the location was considered one of the best between Chicago and the Fox River for beaming the television waves, made the selection of the Harbecke-Landmeier Farm ideal for the show. Thus, "Out on the Farm" began the first of a two-year run from the Harbecke-Landmeier Farm in the summer of 1953.

During the second season the first outdoor network colorcast originating from Chicago was the pickup from the Landmeier Farm. At the end of the 1954 season, the show was over, as Cloverdale and all of DuPage County were due for rapid change. The emphasis would shift within another year from the fine agricultural county of the past 124 years to a prestigious area of new homes for veterans of both World War II and the Korean War.

It was about this time that Jay Stream of Durable Construction Company, and a long-time Wheaton resident and businessman, began looking for a place to create his own town, one in which industry and residence could exist side by side. Returning to his home town after service in the armed forces during World War II, he turned to the home construction business. One of his business partners was Gordon Oury, whose family had an interest in the Imperial Service Company of Melrose Park. They began their new home venture by constructing three homes along Geneva Road.

Durable continued its construction of new homes on scattered sites in Wheaton during the first years of its organization. Then Stream acquired two major tracts for conversion to new homes. These included the old Greene Valley Golf Course, south of Roosevelt Road between Main Street and Naperville Road, and the Hawthorne area, which lies east of Main Street and north of Hawthorne Avenue.

But there was one continuing problem for the families to whom Stream sold homes — high taxes. Many of the homeowners sought advice from the developer. The only answer Stream could offer was that the community had to obtain a broader base for the collection of real estate taxes, which escalated as the need for public services increased. He felt the simplest way to help defray the cost of public services in the City of Wheaton would be to have business or industry help share the tax burden. However, city officials did not want to rezone for light industry.

Thus, by the summer of 1956 Stream and his staff were looking in the Wheaton vicinity for land which could be used to develop a new community, one in which industry would be a built-in part. One of his requirements was that there should be sufficient land for his planned community to expand in years to come. After a number of air flights over the central DuPage area, Durable officials felt they had located the ideal spot for their future town. The land lay generally to the northwest of Geneva Road and Main Street in Wheaton. There was plenty of it, and the views from the air indicated that the sites were adequately drained.

In the summer of 1957, Stream and his crews were completing work on the Hawthorne Shopping Center on North Main Street. This would be a service center for his new community in its early years because it was less than two and a half miles away. Land acquisition began with three farms belonging to the Nagel and Mittmann families as well as the Giesers. This was raw land which had to be cleared, graded, and sectioned off into units. New streets were cut through and sewer and water lines installed. Then a developer could begin to lay foundations for the new homes. Stream reasoned that the homes had to come first since industry would not be attracted to an area which did not offer a work force.

While the basic engineering and work were under way in the new community, a personal tragedy struck the Stream family. Daughter Carol, age fourteen, was visiting at the family summer home in southern Wisconsin when she and her friends were involved in an automobile accident. One person was killed, the others had lesser injuries, but Carol was critically injured and lay in a coma for days.

Meanwhile work on the new village continued. When time came to file plats of subdivision with the county, the engineer asked Stream what name should be given to the small stream which ran through the southern section of the original units. He mumbled the name "Carol" and thus the name was pencilled on the plat. However, when it was filed at the county offices, the name "Carol Stream" was applied not only to the small stream but to the entire new subdivision.

In his next visit with his young daughter who was still in a coma, Stream told her the new town had been named for her. As he recalled

*Carol Stream Historical Museum — formerly the Gretna Station.*

later, the motionless youngster opened her eyes for the first time since the accident months before. Her rehabilitation continues to this day.

By November 1, 1958, Roy and Jeanne Blum, with their infant son, Roy Jr., had moved into the first home to be occupied in the village. Within weeks there were more than 100 inhabitants residing in the new community. Under state law at the time, this was a sufficient number of residents to hold a referendum to incorporate the community as a village. Stream felt this was the only way to make certain that he would be able to carry out his dreams for a well-planned community. Six trustees, a village president and village clerk were elected in a special election held January 31, 1959.

The village was the ninth in the State of Illinois to pass a 5% utility tax during the first months of incorporation. The tax continues in effect today with no village property taxes levied, except for library purposes, sewer and water bond issues.

By 1960 Durable had provided the community with a private swimming pool club. When the company fell victim to the financial recession of 1962, the private swim club was operated by a small group of interested individuals. By 1964 a drowning of an eighth grader, and the problems inherent in maintenance of such a facility led to formation of the Carol Stream Park District.

Today the park district oversees more than 150 acres of parklands, a community center, a museum, and enclosed year-round swimming pool, and a system of waterways for the village.

In 1961 and 1962, the office and industrial parks began to develop in Carol Stream. Today sixteen religious businesses call Carol Stream home as do more than 140 industries, ranging from the large Container Corporation complex to smaller industries which may employ as few as six or eight individuals. The dream of the developer that business and industry could live side by side with good homes, sharing the costs of a well-planned community has come true.

As the community has grown to the southeast and northwest, it has found itself involved with school districts other than the original one in the village. Students in the southern sector of the village attend schools in the Wheaton-

Warrenville Unit District 200. Students in the southwestern sector attend schools in Carol Stream and West Chicago High School districts, while those in the northwestern sector of the village find themselves attending classes in the Elgin-U-46 schools of Kane County. Glenbard North High School, which opened in 1968, is located in Carol Stream. The elementary district has grown from one school in 1958 to four elementary schools and a junior high school.

The village is served by a network of major highways, most of them four lanes wide. In addition, the industrial park is served by two railroads, the Illinois Central-Gulf on the north side of North Avenue, the Chicago and North Western Railway on the south side, successor to the Chicago and Great Western Railway. The village is located eight miles from the DuPage Airport.

While it is a community with only a quarter century of life, its roots go deep into the early history of DuPage County; thus it had a stability which lends itself to future growth patterns for the Village of Carol Stream.

**The Author**

Jean Moore is president of Carol Stream Historical Society, and was chairman of the village's bicentennial commission. She also serves on the board of governors of the DuPage Heritage Gallery, and was president of the DuPage County Press Association.

# Clarendon Hills

*Celia Perry Shockey*

It was in the 1830s that a speculator and early settler, John J. Monell, purchased 320 acres that is today Clarendon Hills. Then in 1839 he was issued a patent to 640 acres. He sold one-third of this to Alfred Belknap, and later a portion to Myron P. Bush and George Howard.

This land was subject to the rights and privileges of the Chicago, Burlington and Quincy Railroad. In 1863 the building of the railroad began. It was completed in 1864, bisecting the area which became Clarendon Hills. In 1867 Bush and Howard conveyed 370 acres, which were south of the tracks, to attorney and president of the CB&Q, James M. Walker. Henry C. Middaugh took charge of the 270 acres north of the tracks in 1870. He farmed this land for many years.

This vicinity, 18.3 miles west of Chicago, was platted in 1873. The name of Clarendon Hills was suggested by Robert Harris, a former president of the CB&O Railroad, after a Boston suburb.

In the early days trains stopped mostly for milk, hay and wheat. Through the years the CB&O developed a commuter service. By the seventies the Burlington changed its engines from woodburning to coal, and eventually from steam to diesel.

The men who platted Clarendon Hills were interested in developing the area as a real estate venture. Frederick Law Olmsted, the prominent landscape architect, laid out the village, according to an early president of Clarendon Hills, Paul Rickert, who kept a detailed scrapbook of village history. A more recent hypothesis is that the community was laid out according to Olmsted principles. The village does have two trademarks of Olmsted's work: winding streets fitting the contours of the land, and individual lots of different shapes and sizes.

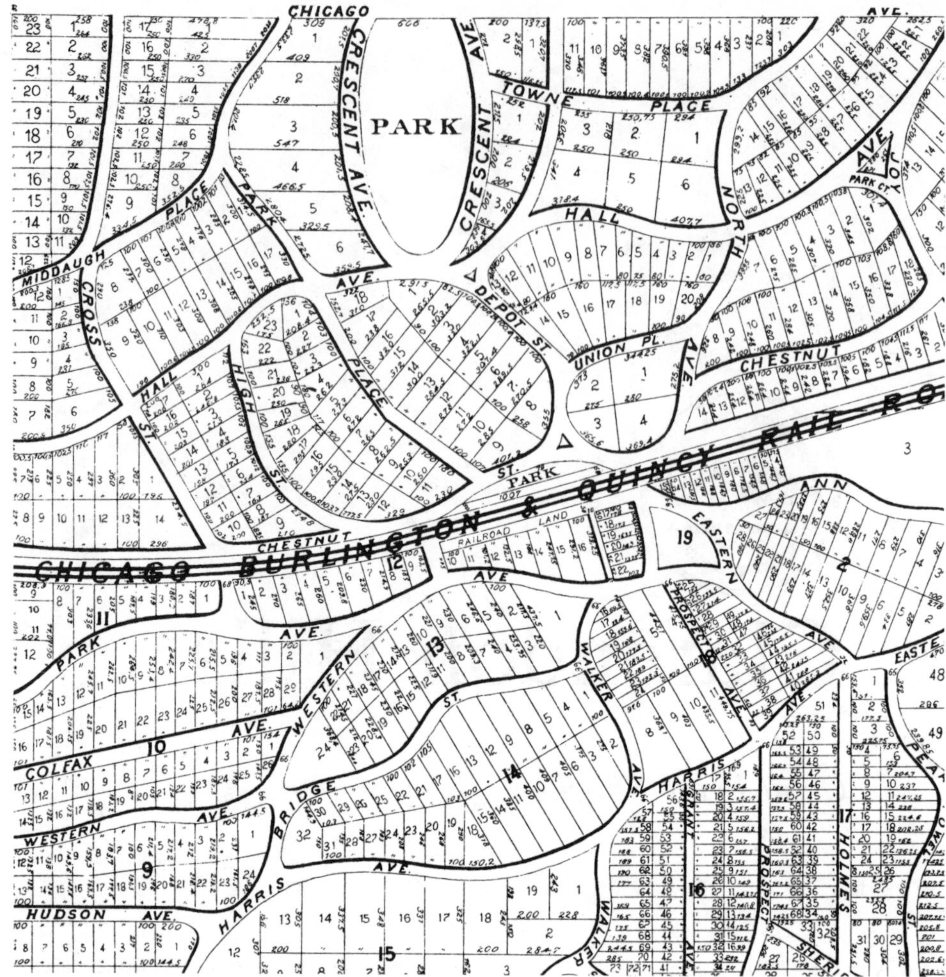


*From the* 1874 Atlas & History of DuPage County, Illinois

Speculators kept investing in land, but little happened. Middaugh tile-drained his land and planted eleven miles of trees along proposed streets which follow the contours of the land.

In 1893 he built a stately mansion as his home. He expected others to follow, but such development did not happen in his lifetime. The village lay dormant until the 1920s.

Among homes over 100 years old are two structures built in 1870 — the Middaugh foreman's home at 148 Norfolk Avenue, and sheepherder's cottage at 58 Chestnut Street. Middaugh acquired an additional 80 acres, kept several hundred horses, a large herd of cattle and sheep for which he built an imposing group of barns. He served as a DuPage school director. The 1913 history of DuPage County records that he served eight years as a member of the DuPage County Board of Supervisors, the last four of which as chairman.

Clarendon Hills became noted in those years for its daisy fields. People from Chicago and many other places came to see and pick the daisies in bloom. Daisy seeds had mistakenly been supplied to Middaugh in his seed order.

Henry Middaugh was instrumental in persuading the Hinsdale Golf Club to establish its course on 133 acres within the village limits of Clarendon Hills. It is one of the early golf courses in the great metropolitan area, with water hazards and sand traps formed like the characters appearing in the cartoons of the *Chicago Tribune.*

The residence and farm of Mr. Middaugh was occupied later by Albert E. Cook. After the Middaugh home was vacated by Cook, it

*Henry C. Middaugh*

*Windmill — west of Prospect Avenue. This supplied water for the Middaugh herds.*

was taken over by the Sisters of Christian Charity of the Convent of Maria Immaculata. It was used as a retreat for those of the Roman Catholic faith until 1954. At that time the newly formed Notre Dame parish took possession. Middaugh House, owned by the Catholic Church, is now listed in the National Register of Historic Places.

Many of Clarendon Hills streets bear the names of early landowners. Other street names cross over from Hinsdale. Ogden Avenue was originally a well-traveled Indian path. Through the years residents have found many arrowheads and spearheads on their properties, evidence of early Indian habitation and travel.

In 1922 the plat of the A. T. McIntosh & Co. Clarendon Hills subdivision was recorded. In 1923 the McIntosh Golf Club Addition was recorded. When McIntosh took over the north end of town, he was not aware of the Olmsted plan. Therefore he proceeded to straighten out all streets. McIntosh soon learned that some of his residential lots were peat bogs, and he had to buy back the land. Fire broke out frequently in the bogs and, in some cases, lasted for two years. Today the bogs have been made into park areas.

At the turn of the century, Mr. Robert Hamill bought forty acres in the village and moved his family to one of three houses on the property. Part of the property was later used by the Lion's Club for a park and swimming pool. A small residential area became known as Hamill Lane.

Recently the Clarendon Hills Village Board has annexed parcels of developed lands south of 55th Street. Few open areas remain, and Clarendon Hills has become a contained village.

In 1923 there was great need to establish a public agency overseeing the welfare of Clarendon Hills citizens. There was much discussion among the natives, whether to annex to Hinsdale, or to remain a separate entity by incorporating. A vote for self-government carried, 81 to 57. The first election was held and Mr. Orrin Goode became the first president. The village was incorporated early in 1924. The board appointed A. G. Hines as treasurer, who served in that capacity until his death.

It was in 1944 that the village adopted the caucus system for naming candidates for election to village offices. The party system of the previous twenty years had become a divisive one that had caused much bitterness among

*First store and Post Office — 1916.*

people. There is representation on the caucus from every organization in the village and from nine neighborhood sections. The candidates nominated are to fill vacancies on the village, park and library boards, and the office of village clerk. These nominations are submitted for approval at the annual meeting and voted upon at the next election.

This village has long been known as "the volunteer community." Volunteers have created and maintained the parks. The fire department continues to be a volunteer undertaking. The public library began and has remained a volunteer operation for twenty years, now using the talents of sixty or more dedicated individuals. It now has one paid librarian and one part-time assistant librarian. In 1981 the library statistics for the state of Illinois showed that the Clarendon Hills Public Library was at the top in its category, with circulation 50% higher than most libraries in villages of this size.

Lloyd Church was appointed village superintendent in 1952, and in 1959 was named village manager. He served the village until his retirement in 1973. In 1978 the new village hall building was dedicated to him.

Ed Mochel was appointed the first police officer. From a one-man department, begun in 1924, it has grown to a fully-paid force of twelve today.

There are approximately fifty acres devoted to parks located in four sites. In 1946 an election was held to form the Clarendon Hills Park District. In 1957 a referendum gave the district authority to issue bonds for park planning.

In 1956 the businessmen and women of the village formed a Chamber of Commerce for the advancement of business interests, to promote home trade and to enforce higher business standards. It spearheaded a 40th anniversary celebration in 1964. Each year it promotes a spring festival and periodically publishes a booklet about the village. At Christmastime it sponsors a Christmas Walk. It has urged architectural uniformity in the business district, better lighting and improved landscaping. The village has only a few small manufacturing activities.

In 1870 a one-room church/schoolhouse was built in Clarendon Hills. It accommodated one teacher and about twenty pupils during the week. On Sunday it provided a place for twenty-five Methodists to have religious services. In 1887 this building was destroyed by fire and a new one-room schoolhouse was built. In 1927 this schoolhouse was replaced by a two-room brick building to accommodate ninety pupils and two teachers, with an addition made in 1930.

When Clarendon Hills was experiencing a boom in 1947, the school was seriously overcrowded and some pupils had to commute temporarily to Hinsdale. It was at this time that the two school districts were combined. Now Clarendon Hills and Hinsdale are in the same district.

The first church to be organized became Community Presbyterian, meeting in homes and the Walker School. In 1929 the group had grown to thirty-four persons, affiliating with the Presbytery of Chicago. The Reverend Robert Bell served as the organizing pastor.

For eighteen years the Roman Catholics in the village met in a rented store front. A mission church, it was served by clergy from the St. Isaac Jogues Roman Catholic Church of Hinsdale. In 1954 Bishop Martin McNamara of the Joliet diocese established the Notre Dame Parish, after purchasing the Middaugh property.

In 1954 an Episcopal church, the Church of the Holy Nativity, was founded. It was a mission church of the diocese of Chicago. Parishioneers worshipped in a rented store until 1958, when a new building was completed. Episcopal churchwomen operate a business for the benefit of the church and its missions, the "Tween the Towers Shop."

In 1951 a Lutheran congregation also began in Walker School. By 1955 a new building was completed, Christ Lutheran Church of Clarendon Hills.

In the early life of the village people formed various clubs. In 1927 there was a civic club established. In 1940 a popular garden club sponsored an annual flower and garden show each fall, continuing through the 1950s. Also in that decade two women's clubs were formed, one meeting in the evening and the other in the afternoon. The evening club gave money for an ambulance. The afternoon club helped start the village library. The Infant Welfare Society sponsors the sale of luminarias for the Christmas Eve decoration of village streets. Originating as an old Mexican custom, the luminaria have made Clarendon Hills a showplace on Christmas Eve, attracting many visitors and celebrants.

The Lions Club was formed in 1950. The Lions chose as their major project a swimming pool for the village, buying land and doing most of the work themselves. The pool was dedicated in 1953, and the organization continues to maintain it. Since the loss of so many American elm trees to the Dutch Elm disease, the Lions also set up a program for replacing trees on the village streets.

There were 132 residents in 1920, and 934 in 1930. By 1960 the community had grown to 5,885 inhabitants, to 7,300 in 1970. In 1974, after the addition of the Blackhawk Heights subdivision, the total was about 8,000 persons. The 1980 census figures, however, showed a population decrease to 6,709 persons, as the children of families remaining in the village matured and moved elsewhere.

Clarendon Hills continues to be a village in which residents take pride and enjoy one another as neighbors.

**The Author**

Celia Perry Shockey is a thirty-year resident of Clarendon Hills, who was Administrator of the Clarendon Hills Library from its opening in 1963 to 1971, and currently maintains its historical files.

# Darien

*Anita Elbe*
and
*Eisenhower Junior High*
*Social Studies Department*

The first group to settle in the Darien vicinity traveled from the New England states by water, using the Erie Canal and the Great Lakes. They settled along an old stage coach route which is now roughly I–55. Among the first to arrive was Thomas Andrus. Andrus was born in Vermont in 1801, and first came to Chicago in 1833. He worked, driving oxen teams and helping on construction jobs. He went back to Vermont and returned to Illinois in 1835 with his second wife Melissa and three children from his first marriage.

Andrus decided that it would be a good idea to build an inn for travelers on the Ottawa stage coach line. Each day fifteen coaches traveled the line. The spot he chose for his inn was at the entrance to today's Carriage Way subdivision, on the North Frontage Road near the intersection of Cass Avenue and I–55. He planted a tree next to his inn, which included a tavern and a post office, and named the area Cass. The tree he planted was felled to build the stone entrance to Carriage Way.

Andrus' inn was a busy place. He even held dances in his dining room. Andrus was elected to several government positions, including that of justice of the peace. However, Melissa did not like the fact that people attending court sessions would spit tobacco juice on her living room carpet; so Andrus did not seek reelection as justice of the peace. He also served as the town clerk, as assessor and as a county commissioner. Andrus' son, Edgar, born in 1835, is believed to be the first child born in this area. The boy rode his horse each day to the Illinois and Michigan Canal and swam across it to get the mail for his father.

One of the early needs of a pioneer community was for a church. With Thomas Andrus' help The Rev. Stephen Beggs established the Cass Methodist Episcopal Church on the North Frontage Road east of the Andrus

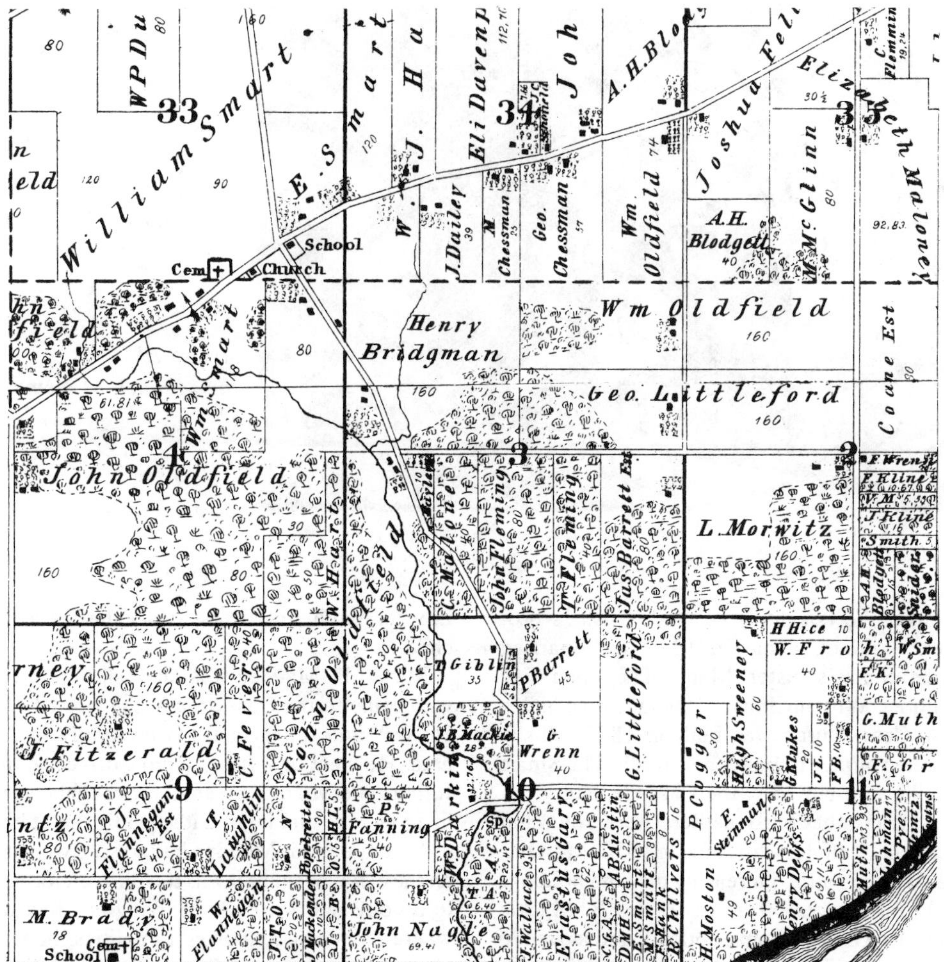


*From the* 1874 Atlas & History of DuPage County, Illinois

property. Beggs traveled back and forth from Plainfield to Chicago. He was a circuit riding minister, serving more than one church. He wanted the Cass church built because he felt the ride between Plainfield and Chicago was too great a distance to cover in one day. The Cass Methodist Episcopal Church was a log cabin. Its cemetery, located west of the church, can still be seen today.

Beggs was a very colorful person. He wrote a book titled *Pages from the Early History of the West and Northwest.* He was six feet tall and weighed over two hundred pounds. He had a reputation for being the strongest man in the entire county. According to one account, he preached so loud that he could be heard from a distance of three blocks. The church was also used by the community as a schoolhouse, the first school in Cass.

Elisha Smart and his wife Eliza arrived in 1838. Elisha had come to America from England in 1825. The Smarts settled on a farm located between the Cass church and Andrus' inn. They had ten children, eight of whom lived. In 1853 after gold had been discovered in California, Elisha got "gold fever' and left for California to strike it rich. He left Eliza and their children to take care of the farm. At the time he left, their oldest daughter was fourteen, their oldest son was eleven, and their youngest child, Josephine, only a year old.

Elisha did strike it rich in the California gold fields and returned to the Cass community seven years later a very wealthy man. When he

*Aylesford, the Madden Mansion.*

returned he bought more land. Elisha's brother, William, came in 1839 and married Eliza Smart's sister Mary. They had five children. William donated the land on which a new Cass church was built in 1870. Elisha donated money to build the church. The Smart families are buried in the Cass Cemetery.

Among other early settlers were John and Hannah Oldfield, who came in 1850. Mr. Oldfield raised cattle, increasing his land holdings from forty to 2,000 acres. James B. Mackie came to America from Scotland, and moved to Cass in 1857. He lived with his uncle John Mackie. James married Elizabeth Dunn of Cass in 1864. Charles and Catherine Austin came to Cass in 1848, becoming farmers and operating a nursery and orchard. During the Civil War Charles served in the Illinois Volunteer Infantry.

Franklin Blanchard was one of Cass' few businessmen. He operated a cheese factory or creamery, which was located on Plainfield Road. Franklin was born in Cass in 1838, two years after his family had arrived. He opened the cheese factory in 1881. Both Franklin and his father served in the Illinois Volunteer Infantry in the Civil War.

Abram Wells was a Cass farmer who also served in the Civil War. His wife Abigail had ten children from her first marriage, only one of whom, John Pitcher, lived beyond childhood. Pioneer families often had to face the death of a child.

Martin B. Madden was an Irish immigrant who came to the Cass area in the late 1800s. He was an orphan and had no family in the area. He went to work as a mule driver on the Illinois and Michigan Canal. He caught his leg in a tow rope and injured it so badly that it had to be amputated. Madden had to stop working on the canal because it was too difficult for him to do physical work. After living in Chicago, where he became involved in politics, he was elected to the House of Representatives. When he married Josephine Smart, her family gave the couple property on which to build a home. Congressman Madden liked to do things in a grand way; so he built his home in 1903 to look like the White House in Washington, D.C. He called it Castle Eden.

After Madden's death in 1913, the mansion served as a restaurant for a while. Following a period of vacancy, the Carmelite Order of the Roman Catholic Church purchased it and forty acres around it in 1959. Today Castle Eden is part of the Aylesford Retreat Center of the Carmelite Fathers. Many of the original Smart family farm buildings still remain on the property, including the original farm house, built in 1838.

Parallel to the growth of Cass was that of the Lace community to the north. A group of

*Lace School.*

German Lutherans came to this area in the 1840s. In 1859 they purchased three acres of land at 67th and Clarendon Hills Road for $30.00. During that summer they built the first St. John's Lutheran Church on this property and laid out the cemetery behind the church. In 1899 a new church was built on the northeast corner of 75th Street and Cass Avenue. In 1969 the second church was torn down and the present St. John's Church was built on the west side of Cass Avenue north of 75th Street.

By the 1860s the Lace community had also established a school of the northwest corner of the intersection of Cass Avenue and 75th Street. This school was the first Lace School.

The people in the Lace community did well, and by the 1890s the village of Lace was established. The most important location for the Lace community was the triangle of land bordered by Cass Avenue, Plainfield Road and 75th Street. This location was called "The Point." The town hall, which was called Lace Hall, was located here. There was also by 1884, a general store, a blacksmith shop and a postoffice.

There are two versions of how the Lace community got its name. One is that 1880s storeowner John Keig named the postal station for his grandmother, Mrs. Tom Lace. The other version is that Gainsburg, the next owner, was asked to come up with a four letter name to identify the area for mail delivery. He looked up in his store and saw a bolt of lace on a shelf and named the community Lace.

Among Darien's oldest residents is Malinda Anderman Wehrmeister. Her grandparents, Fred and Sophia Anderman, came from Hanover, Germany, in the 1850s. Her parents owned farm property in Lace. In fact, Eisener Junior High School is built on land once owned by the Andermans.

For a long time the Cass and Lace communities had little contact with each other. they were divided by different backgrounds, languages and religions. The people of Cass were closer to the people of Lemont. Slowly the name Cass began to fade and the name Lace became better known. Eventually, the Cass mailing address disappeared and Lace began appearing on local maps.

In the 1860s the Burlington Northern Railroad laid its tracks north of Lace. This slowed the growth of the community. Several Irish Catholic families, however, left Ireland and settled south of Lace near what is today Argonne National Laboratory. When the Illinois and Michigan Canal stopped carrying trade, most of the Lace residents became farmers.

The area remained a quiet farm community until the period following World War II. Then people who were living in Chicago were able to

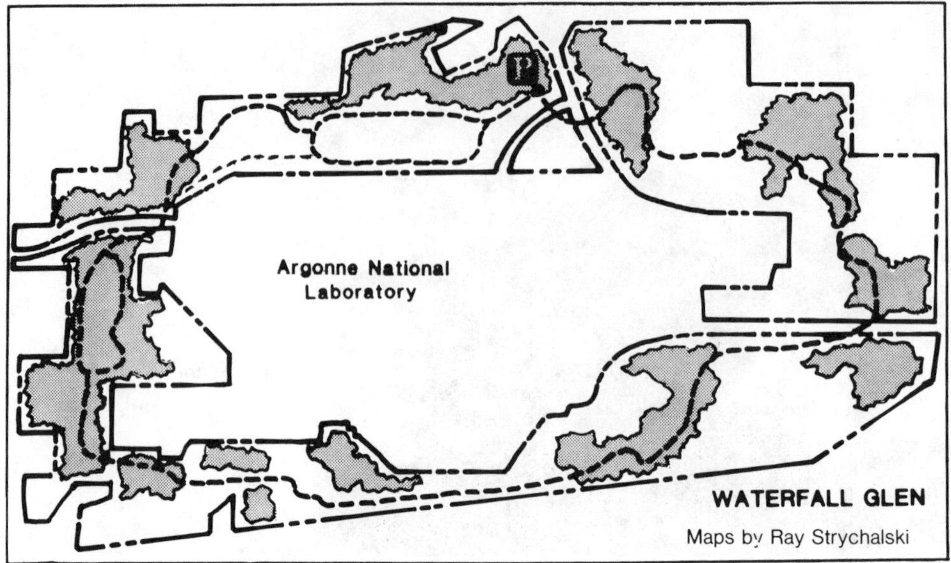


*Courtesy Forest Preserve District of DuPage County*

move to the suburbs because of the availability of automobiles and improved roads. Many of the Lace farmers had been struggling to keep their farms profitable. Instead of continuing that struggle, many of them decided to sell their land to developers to be divided into homesites. The first two subdivisions built were Marion Hills and Brookhaven, followed by Clairfield and Hinsbrook. As more people moved into the area, businesses were established to meet the needs of a growing population. Many farmers were sad to see fields of wild asparagus paved over, or fruit trees ripped out to make way for the new construction.

For a while the remaining farmers and the newcomers did not get along; nor did the four subdivisions. Finally, in the 1960s the four subdivisions decided to merge, lest each subdivision become a part of a surrounding town. Also, many tired of depending on the county for police protection and road maintenance. In December 1969, the city of Darien was incorporated.

The name Darien was chosen after Major Sam Kelly had returned from a visit to Darien, Connecticut. Because he thought it a pleasant town, he suggested naming the new community after it. His idea was accepted. The flag for Darien, Illinois, is blue and white, with four stars representing the four subdivisions that united to form it.

The Darien Historical Society was formed in 1976 to preserve the local history. Shortly after it was founded, the society acquired the use of Old Lace School as its museum. The first Lace School burned down in 1924; the present building is the second one. It was the only school in the area until Marion Hills School was built in 1951. As District 61 grew, a new Lace School was built in 1957, next to the old one. The school district still used the old building, however. It continued as a bandroom until 1968. In 1969, when Darien became a city, Old Lace School became the first City Hall. It served for municipal functions until 1970, after which it was the police station until 1972. During that time the girls' washroom became a jail to hold troublemakers until the deputies of the DuPage County Sheriff could arrive.

In the 1930s Erwin Freund, a wealthy Chicago industrialist, and his wife Rosalyn bought 200 acres of land in the southeastern part of DuPage County to build a summer home. He was the first person to own a patent on casing for sausage. Mr Freund also loved the story of *Alice in Wonderland* by Lewis Carroll. He named his estate Tulgey Woods after the woods in that story. Three miles of bark trails wandered through the estate. Carved wooden figures of *Alice in Wonderland* characters were placed along these. In 1941 the Freunds arranged to have seven white deer brought to the estate. Over 300 descendants of these deer still remain here.

In 1946 the United States government began acquiring over 1,000 acres of land, including the Freund property, to build Argonne National Laboratory, a nuclear research laboratory. In 1973 most of the Argonne property was transferred to the DuPage County Forest Preserve for public parks and recreation purposes. Today it is the Waterfall Glen Forest Preserve.

Argonne, Lace and Cass together define the Darien vicinity, with its history of interest both to present and future generations.

**The Author**

Anita Elbe was a member of the Darien Bicentennial Commission, has prepared a history of the local school district, and has developed a slide presentation for use in the community.

# Downers Grove

*Virginia A. Stehney*

The first settler in Downers Grove was Pierce Downer, who arrived in 1832. This Vermont native, but long-time New York resident, camped alone in a grove of oak trees at the fork of two ancient Indian trails. He staked his claim to the surrounding 160 acres of prairie and timberland, for which he paid $1.25 an acre. Enroute, Downer had visited his son Stephen, who was a mason helping to build Chicago's first lighthouse. He had written his father about the rich land to the west of Chicago.

In that same year the Black Hawk War ended and more settlers came. Three years later Israel Blodgett left a homestead near Naperville to establish a farm and blacksmith shop south of what was to become Maple Avenue. Some of his earliest customers were Indians who brought firearms to be repaired. Then Samuel Curtiss laid claim to land just north of the Blodgett homestead, which is now in the center of the village's business district.

In order to facilitate travel into that area, Blodgett and Curtiss hitched six yoke of oxen to a heavy log to level and widen a trail between their land which intercepted the trail from Chicago to the Naper Settlement. They planted sugar maples along this road, some of which still stand.

By the early 1840s two blacksmith shops were operating. Henry Carpenter had opened the first store and post office in 1842. Carpenter also subdivided his land, resulting in growth of the village near his store on Maple Avenue just west of the future Main Street.

By 1850 Europeans from England, Ireland, Germany and Alsace-Lorraine were arriving the area. Some worked on the Illinois-Michigan Canal, construction of which began in 1836.

Downers Grove was represented on the Brush Hill committee which petitioned the Chicago, Burlington, and Quincy Railroad to build a line from Aurora to Chicago. It was

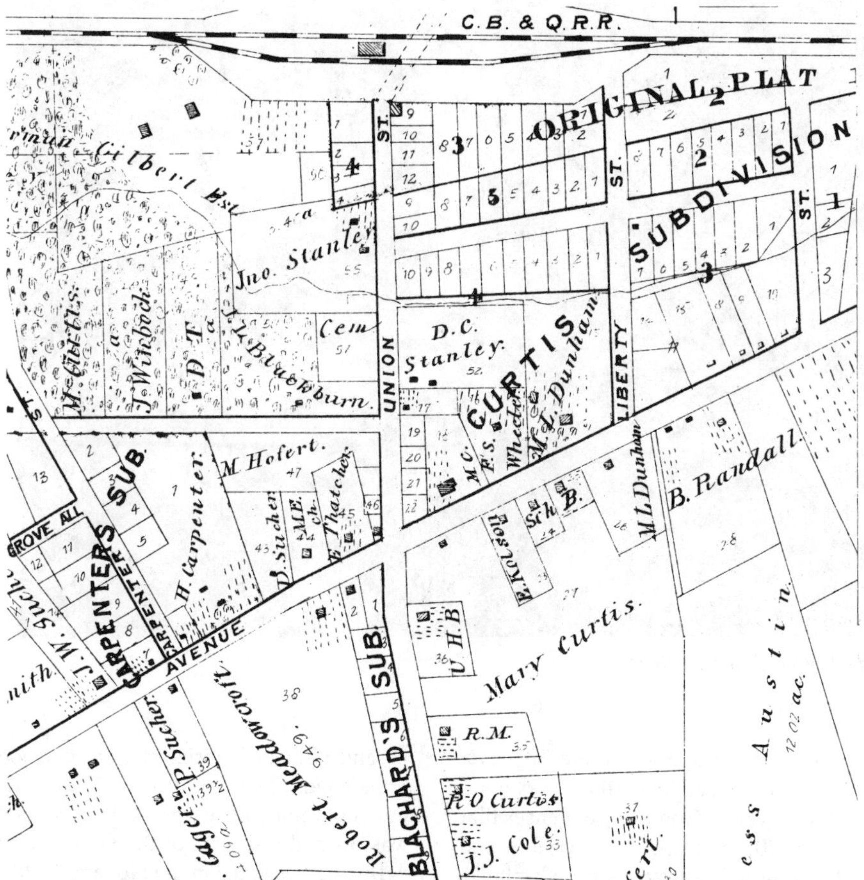


*From the* 1874 Atlas & History of DuPage County, Illinois

emphasized that Downers Grove was a well-established farming center with produce to send to Chicago. The first train arrived in 1864. For a number of years one train a day traveled in each direction, with passengers often having to ride in freight cars. With the coming of the railroad the first plat of the village was made, and Main Street, then called Union Street, was opened north of the railroad.

In 1860 a political group called the "Plow Boys" campaigned for Abraham Lincoln. Led by DuPage County Sheriff Theodore S. Rogers of Downers Grove, they were spectacular in their red and white uniforms, as they rode on a wagon drawn by eight black horses. From the wagon's tall flagpole was suspended a large American flag. They took part in rallies in neighboring communities. A blue silk banner presented to them by the village ladies now hangs in the American Room of the Smithsonian Institution.

A few years later Rogers was commissioned a captain to organize the first company in the county for service in the Civil War. Nearly 140 men enlisted. Captain Walter Blanchard, 54 years old, commanded another company of Illinois men. Blanchard was killed in the war. His grave as well as a number of others of local Union dead, may be found in the Main Street Cemetery, in the center of the village.

The remains of the founder, Pierce Downer, and his wife Lucy, who died within a day of each other in 1863, are on Linscott Avenue. They had to be buried on their farm because spring rains had caused St. Joseph Creek to flood, making the downtown inaccessible from the north.

In 1873 approval was given for village in-

*The Pierce Downer Home.*

corporation, with 49 aye votes and 38 nays. T. S. Rogers was chosen first village president, serving sixteen years. Operating expenses that year were $600, half spent for streets and alleys. The first sidewalk of two inch planks was built along Maple Avenue.

Village population had grown to 500 by 1885. A promotional piece on the village by the CB&Q gave information about real estate and the numerous daily trains. The first sewers were built by village ordinance in 1888.

The *Downers Grove Reporter* celebrated its 100th anniversary in 1983. It is the oldest paper continuously published in DuPage County, and the oldest business in Downers Grove.

German-born Casper Dicke started the village's first industry. He manufactured fine quality tools for electrical linemen and received a grand prize for his products in the 1889 Paris World's Fair. The company, owned by one of Dicke's grandsons, still manufactures special equipment for the telephone company.

In the 1890s E. H. Prince subdivided land in the northwest section of the village, improving a pond there and adding small parks. The World Columbian Exposition opened in Chicago and villagers' horizons were considerably broadened. The Belmont Golf Course, the first nine-hole golf course west of the Appalachians, was opened just west of the village in 1893.

Businesses listed in the November 28, 1895 *Reporter* included a piano factory, ice/coal/wood business, blacksmith/livery/wagonmaker, lumber company, general stores, drug store, laundry agency, bank, hotel, hardware store, tailor shop, and a furniture store.

A volunteer fire department was organized in 1898. A fire destroyed Dicke Tool buildings in 1906. The factory was rebuilt, and Casper Dicke's seven sons became active in the department. One of these, Grant, served as Chief for thirty-seven years.

Toward the end of the century, the immigrants to the area reflected the ethnic change as more East Europeans came. An annual directory of 1899 listed 575 names in Gostyn or East Grove. This predominantly Polish settlement was located between Downers Grove and Westmont along Fairview Avenue.

During the World War I era, the life of the village was centered on the war effort with Red Cross work, vegetable gardens and Liberty Loan bonds. The village now had three hotels, two banks, and four major industries: the Dicke

Tool Company, the Kelmscott Press, the Illinois Heater Company and the Austin Nurseries. The village adopted the commission form of government in 1917.

Downers Grove resident Lottie Homan O'Neill was in 1922 the first woman elected to the Illinois legislature. She served in the House and Senate until 1963, except for two years.

On Christmas Day, 1928, the Tivoli Theater opened. Four thousand people waited in line! It was the second theater in the U.S. designed and built for talking pictures. It still is in operation.

The village celebrated its centennial on July 4, 1932, with a parade and pageant helping to raise spirits a little during the Depression. Federal civil works projects for the schools, village, sanitary district, as well as for county forest preserves, gave employment to local people.

Again, there was an all-out civilian effort during World War II, with residents engaged in Civilian Defense, victory gardens, scrap drives, and Red Cross work. Downers Grove honored its servicemen by posting their names on a billboard at the railroad station downtown.

When World War II ended, Downers Grove was bordered on the southeast, south and west by productive farms. Its population numbered 11,300. Today the village is a sprawling municipality of over 42,500 people, spread over thirteen square miles.

What has caused this growth? Over the last three decades several factors stand out: the Burlington-Northern Railroad, expressways/toll roads, and Argonne National Laboratory.

From the time the Chicago, Burlington & Quincy Railroad was built through the village in 1864, it has been important. At first grain and other produce were the important commodities it carried to Chicago, but by 1869 the first commuter trains were operating; and by 1895 twenty-five trains ran daily between Chicago and Downers Grove. Until 1952, Downers Grove was the end-of-the-line for half of the commuter trains, served by a turntable, switching yards, water tower and coal yards.

In the 1980s the railroad, now called the Burlington-Northern as a result of a 1970 merger, is as important to the community as ever. Main Street station was the line's most heavily-used commuter stop until recently, when Naperville moved into the lead. However, the three Downers Grove stations together provide more commuters than any other suburb.

*St. Mary's of Gostyn.*

Expressways and tollways have been a strong force for change, providing good vehicular access, and helping attract new residents as well as industry to the area.

By the mid-60s Ellsworth Industrial Park was being developed at the western edge of the village. Then through the seventies shopping centers appeared, and businesses along Ogden Avenue and eventually along Butterfield Road greatly increased. In recent decades an increasing number of apartments, condominiums, and senior citizen housing units have been built.

Recently, changes in the ethnic background of newcomers have resulted in greater community diversity. East Indians, Southeast Asians, Filipinos and Blacks are among the groups represented.

Growth of the village was also affected by the Argonne National Laboratory on marginal farmland in the southern edge of the county. Established in 1947, Argonne attracted employees with high-level technical and scientific skill who were very supportive of good schools, the arts, youth activities, and many community groups. Today Downers Grove has the largest concentration of Argonne employees, with Joliet second and Naperville third.

As the village changed, so did the government. The largely volunteer mayor-commission form continued until 1962. By that time the population had reached 22,000. Residents then voted in the council-manager form of government, with a mayor and four council members overseeing the administration of professional staff.

The village has been innovative in dealing with problems of growth. Downers Grove was the first community in northeastern Illinois to initiate a self-supporting commuter shuttle bus service. Downers Grove was the first community in the area to employ a specialist for Cable TV programming and for training community residents to do programming for their organizations. In addition, the village elected its first woman mayor, Betty Cheever, in April, 1983.

*Mayor Betty Cheever.*

School developments also reflect the recent change. The local elementary district consisted of four crowded elementary schools in 1950. In that year the most inclusive referendum in the village history was held. The ballot included no less than forty-three propositions, covering eight school building sites, three new elementary school buildings, one new junior high school, additions to four existing elementary schools, and improvements to the sites! All of these propositions won by a three to one vote.

The peak enrollment was reached in the elementary district in 1971–72, with 6,267 students, thirteen elementary schools, and two junior high schools. After the second high school was built in 1964, high school enrollment reached its high point of 6,064 students in 1974–75. By the late seventies the downward student population trend had resulted in the closing of three elementary schools.

Among the particular institutions responding to new needs was the Downers Grove Public Library. The standard two-story Carnegie Library, opened in 1915 at the corner of Forest and Curtiss, was enlarged in 1956 by a wrap-a-round addition designed by local resident George Steckmesser, a student of Frank Lloyd Wright. Eventually, a referendum was passed for a new, larger two-story building which was opened on the corner site in 1977.

Downers Grove became a college town in 1966 when George Williams College moved from the Hyde Park section of Chicago to its location on 31st Street. The college's new campus was built on 200 acres which had been previously annexed to the village. The Downers Grove Committee for International Students at the college was organized to meet the special needs of the foreign students and offer them opportunities to get acquainted with American families.

Established in September 1959, the newly-formed Downers Grove Area YMCA began to offer activities for adults and children in schools and parks. Indian Boundary YMCA moved into a new building in 1969.

The community gained a hospital in 1976 when Good Samaritan Hospital opened on

Highland Avenue. This 287-bed facility, owned and operated by the Evangelical Hospital Association, brought a wholistic approach to medical care to the surrounding area.

Not surprisingly, considerable change has occurred in the local park district since it was formed in the early fifties. In the early eighties the district's holdings include 350 acres in twenty-five sites, and its services include a year-round recreational program for people of all ages and interests. The ten-acre Belmont Prairie has been preserved largely through the efforts of Margot and Alfred Dupree and The Nature Conservatory/Illinois Chapter. The historic Lincoln Center houses an active senior citizens program. In 1983 the district won the national Gold Medal Award given by the National Recreation and Parks Association for excellence in its services.

A number of cultural organizations were formed over the years: Downers Grove Artists Guild in 1941, Grove Players in 1946, Downers Grove Concert Association in 1946, Village Forum in 1948, and Oratorio Society in 1958.

Most of the churches were still located near the center of town in the 1950s. The following decade, with their congregations increasing in size, some churches moved to outlying areas to have more land. New congregations were also organized. By 1983 there were thirty one houses of worship. These served as social as well as religious centers. Many churches offered programs for children and youth. These services included nursery schools and day-care centers as more mothers entered the labor market.

In 1947 the village enjoyed its first Fall Festival, organized by the newly-formed Kiwanis Club and held at the high school, to benefit the youth of the community and feature their talent. Often celebrities, such as Mahalia Jackson and Harry Belafonte, appeared on the program. Some informal activities have proved particularly enduring. Rose Guthrie, a long-time resident of the village, reported that "Our neighborhood is very friendly, really like a small town. We have had block picnics for over thirty-five years!"

Special to the village is a beautiful bicentennial quilt depicting local history, made by local women, now hanging in the historical museum. "An Evening with Mr. Lincoln" slide presentation by local resident Thomas Dyba shows Dyba's historically perfect replica of Lincoln's Springfield Home. This replica has been on display at the National Park Service's Visitors Center for Lincoln's home since 1977. It is viewed annually by a half million visitors.

One of the best attended local events ever held was the Downers Grove 150th birthday celebration in 1982, called Heritage Fest. The village council presented plaques containing pieces of the Old Plank Road, uncovered in 1981 during reconstruction of Ogden Avenue. Participating in the Fest were members of the Downers Grove Historical Society. Begun in 1966, the society grew so much that its museum moved into the historic Blodgett home at 831 Maple Avenue a decade later.

A concluding note comes from the special edition of the *Suburban Life Graphic* saluting the village's 150 years of progress. "The celebration has been planned to involve as many participants as possible, continuing the tradition of citizen involvement that has made Downers Grove one of the most livable of communities in America."

**The Author**

Virginia A. Stehney is historian of the Downers Grove Historical Society, and served as chairman of the Downers Grove Bicentennial Commission.

# Elmhurst

*Margaret Franson Pruter*

In the early 19th century, prior to white settlement, the region that includes today's Elmhurst was inhabited by the Potawatomi Indians. Although there is no archaeological evidence to indicate there was ever a permanent Indian settlement in Elmhurst proper, a Potawatomi village was located on Salt Creek between Elmhurst and Hinsdale. White migration to the region began in the 1830s following the end of the Black Hawk War.

Settlers came from the East, mainly from the state of New York, and from abroad, and were predominantly of English and German extraction. Two diverse cultures planted roots, giving Elmhurst a dual character. For decades it would be a bilingual village, with both English and German being spoken, written, and taught.

The first settlements were made along Salt Creek in what became York and Addison townships. The Germans settled mainly in the north, the settlers of English ancestry in the south. Elisha Fish was the first known settler in York Township, building a cabin along the west bank of Salt Creek near Butterfield Road in 1834. Frederick Graue settled along the Creek near the present Elmhurst-Addison boundary, also in 1834. They would be joined during the remainder of the decade by many others who would play important roles in the development of the community. Among those pioneers were Jesse Atwater (1834), Nicholas Torode (1835), Edward Eldridge (1835), David and John Talmadge (1836), and Conrad Fischer (1836). In 1837 John Glos, Sr. came with his family to settle on land acquired earlier for him by his son John Glos, Jr., in what is now Crescent Park, south of St. Charles Road. His descendants became influential in the economic, social, and political life of the community during much of its history.

In 1842 Gerry Bates arrived from Ohio and staked claim to a treeless tract of land in what was to become the center of Elmhurst, the land along Salt Creek already having been occu-

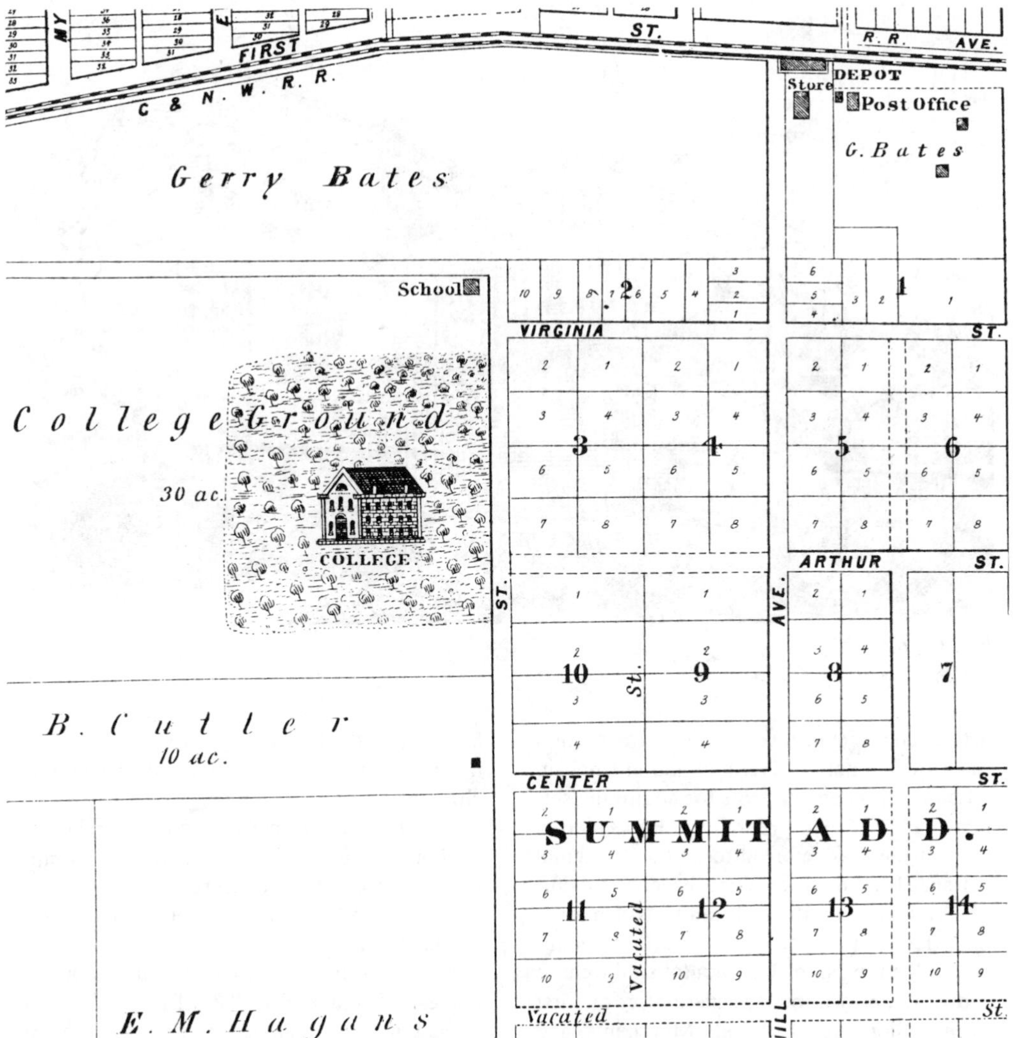


*From the* 1874 Atlas & History of DuPage County, Illinois

pied. Bates is often referred to as Elmhurst's founder because it was he who gave the settlement its first sense of community consciousness. Although Bates soon returned to Ohio to dispose of his interests there, he engaged his brother-in-law, John L. Hovey, to construct a building for him at the present intersection of St. Charles Road and Cottage Hill Avenue. Hill Cottage Tavern, as Bates named his structure, opened in 1843 and served as a stage stop, an inn for travelers, and a gathering place for local residents. In 1845 the community was officially named Cottage Hill, after the tavern.

In 1845, when the Galena and Chicago Union Railroad (today's Chicago and Northwestern), established a station in Cottage Hill, on land given by Gerry Bates just west of York Street and along Park Avenue, growth of the fledgling settlement was spurred. The Cottage Hill station gradually became the most important stop along the route, providing easy access to and from Chicago for farmers, their produce, commuters, and new residents.

In 1850 York Township was created, so named because of the large number of settlers in the area originally from New York. Also that year, School District 1 was formed, and a small, one-room schoolhouse was opened on St. Charles Road west of Cottage Hill. In 1857 a new school, a two-story structure, was built

*Hill Cottage*
*Art by H. Gilbert Foote*

on Church Street just west of York. Instruction was provided both in German and in English.

Land was made available for additional settlement in 1854. That year Gerry Bates platted lots in what was referred to as the "Original Cottage Hill," between York Street and Addison Avenue, from the railroad to North Avenue, which at the time was the northern boundary of the township. The first lot sold went to Ludwig Graue, who built a general store on First Avenue along the railroad. Merchants and tradesmen purchased lots near the railroad and York Street for commercial purposes, with York Street eventually becoming the village's main thoroughfare.

Bates later subdivided the southeastern section of his land. It was sold in large tracts and became the site of several imposing estates, built mainly by wealthy and socially prominent businessmen from Chicago. The village attracted such settlement because of its proximity to Chicago; as DuPage County's easternmost community, it was only sixteen miles west of the city. It also was easily accessible by train and other transportation routes — St. Charles Road, North Avenue, and Lake Street. Another factor was its favorable topography being located on a ridge seventy feet higher than the Des Plaines River. This elevation allowed for better drainage and a healthier climate.

The first to purchase land was Thomas Barbour Bryan, a Virginia-born lawyer and entrepreneur, who is often referred to as "The Father of Elmhurst" because of the pivotal role he played in its formative years. Bryan bought 1,000 acres from Bates and built a country home in Cottage Hill. "Byrd's Nest," as he named it, was located at what is now the southwest corner of St. Charles Road and York Street. He then induced some of his wealthy friends to move to the village, which can date its suburban beginnings to this time. In 1857 Bryan sold land to Elisha Hagans, a real estate developer, who moved into a home on the southwest corner of York and Arthur. Also that year, Bryan's friend, artist G. P. A. Healy, called "The Painter of the Presidents," occupied the original "Hill Cottage," renaming it "Clover Lawn." At the end of the 1850s the community numbered about 200 people, out of a total of about 1,500 in York Township.

During the next decade, other estates were established. In 1860 John R. Case, Sr., who in 1851 had bought the west half of a 160-acre plot of land south of St. Charles along York, moved to Cottage Hill. He founded "Cherry Farm," so named because of his planting of some 1,000 cherry trees on the property. Jedediah H. Lathrop, Bryan's brother-in-law, built "Huntington" on the south side of St. Charles west of Cottage Hill in 1864. In 1867 Henry W. King, a clothing manufacturer, moved into "Clover Lawn." The following year Seth Wadhams, an ice manufacturer, came to Cottage Hill and built "White Birch" on land that is now Wilder Park. In 1868 Lathrop, with the aid of Wadhams and others, had a large number of elms planted along Cottage Hill. It was from these plantings that Elmhurst took its present name, at Bryan's suggestion in 1869.

Meanwhile, development of the community as a whole was slow. At the outbreak of the Civil War, Cottage Hill was a "one-street" country village, with the railroad running down the center, east to west. The "one street" was York Street. The war, with its general depletion of economic and human resources, further retarded growth.

Nonetheless, several events occurred in the 1860s that had significance for the community. Mammoth Spring, which was to supply Elmhurst with water for decades, erupted on the Talmadge farm in 1861. In 1862 the first Protestant congregation was formed by Thomas Bryan, who was an Episcopalian lay reader. Also that year, St. Mary's Catholic Church (later Immaculate Conception Church) was built. In 1864 the first brick building, the second Graue store, was constructed. After the Civil War, Dr. George F. Heidemann, a surgeon, settled in the community, becoming its first physician. Population totaled 329 in 1870, an increase of about 100 persons during the preceding decade.

After the Great Chicago Fire of 1871, Elmhurst became a permanent refuge for a number of Chicago families. Some new homes were built in the northwest section, on a tract of land called the Emerson subdivision. In 1871 the German Evangelical Synod of the Northwest bought land from Thomas Bryan and established the Proseminary that later became Elmhurst College. Several new businesses opened along York Street, including Louis Balgemann's blacksmith shop (1870), the hardware store of Adam S. Glos (1872), and Henry L. Glos' general store (1874). In 1876

*Thomas Bryan.*
*Courtesy Elmhurst Historical Society*

St. Peter's Evangelical and Reformed Church was built. Immanuel Lutheran School, Elmhurst's first parochial school, was constructed in 1879, at Larch and Third streets. The first Roman Catholic school, Immaculate Conception , was opened in 1899.

The 1870s also saw the beginning of what has been called Elmhurst's Gilded Age, an era of elegant socializing by the owners of the great estates that lasted into the 20th century. Prominent Elmhurst and Chicago families were entertained at garden parties, musicales, amateur dramatic productions, and elaborate balls. Among the estates of the period, in addition to those previously named, were Lucian Hagans' "Hawthorne," Fred Rockwood's "Hollywood," George Runsey's "Sweet Briar" (later owned by Frank Sturges), Lee Sturges' "Shadeland," and John R. Case, Jr.'s "Orchard House."

Until the early 1880s, Elmhurst was governed only by county and township. In 1882, at the urging of Henry L. Glos, an election was held to vote on incorporation of the village. Sixty votes were cast in favor; 28 in opposition. Elmhurst was incorporated, with its legal boundaries being St. Charles Road to North Avenue, and one-half mile west of York Street to one-quarter mile east of York.

At the time of incorporation Elmhurst was, ethnically, predominantly German and English; politically, overwhelmingly Republican; religiously, mainly Lutheran and Roman Catholic. There were about a dozen large estates, some forty businesses, and a number of farms. In 1883 a major industrial development was begun near the village's western limits by Adolph Hammerschmidt and Henry Assman, who founded the Elmhurst-Chicago Stone Company to quarry the dolemite limestone that underlay the region.

Soon after incorporation, Henry Glos was elected president of the village. He served for all but one term during the next twenty years. During this period numerous municipal improvements were made. Streets were named and platted. Plank sidewalks were laid on the principal streets. A police marshal was chosen, and a jail built in 1882. A village hall was constructed in 1884. The Cottage Hill School (later renamed Hawthorne School), a two-story brick structure located at Cottage Hill and Arthur, was completed in 1888, providing both elementary and secondary classes. In 1893 the first sewers were laid, and a volunteer fire department established. A health department was organized in 1896.

During the latter part of the 19th century, private companies brought a variety of services to the community. The Elmhurst Spring Water Company provided running water in 1889; the Elmhurst Electric Light Company furnished electric power in 1892; and the Chicago Telephone Company supplied telephone service in 1897. The coming of the Chicago Great Western Railroad in 1887 and the Illinois Central in 1888 stimulated commercial and residential development in south Elmhurst. In 1894 the *Elmhurst News,* the village's first weekly newspaper, started publication. On its front page, it proclaimed, "Elmhurst – A Village of Beautiful Homes and Progressive People."

Elmhurst's population had reached 1,050 in 1890. To aid expansion, additional land was annexed in 1892 — a parcel east of York between North Avenue and Lake Street and an area west of York between the Chicago and Northwestern tracks and St. Charles Road. The latter was the Elm Park subdivision developed by Wilbur Hagans, son of Lucian Hagans. Hagans had a large residence, called "Villa Virginia," built for himself (1886–90) at the corner of what is now Hagans Avenue and St. Charles Road. Hagans, an avid equestrian, also built a racetrack, which he named Hawthorne, southwest of his home on what is now the athletic field of York High School. (After it closed in 1896, two grooms took the name and the horses to Cicero, where today's track was established). Others with an interest in horses helped to organize the Elmhurst Saddle Club in 1890.

Around the turn of the century, there was more time for social activities in the community. Many Elmhurst residents enjoyed the annual Elmhurst picnic in Graue's Woods, dancing at Mahler Hall, church socials, presentations by amateur dramatic and choral groups, buggy and sleigh rides, and a variety of sports, including ice skating, croquet, golf, and baseball. The Elmhurst Golf Club, designed by local resident and internationally prominent architect Walter Burley Griffin, was built on the site of what is now York High School in 1900.

In Elmhurst's last decade as a village, a street numbering plan was adopted (1900), and several major streets were renamed. The Chicago, Aurora and Elgin Railroad, an interurban line, was routed through the village in 1902. In 1903 a gas franchise was granted to H. W. Darling. In 1907 the Cherry Farm subdivision, laid out by John R. Case, Jr., was opened south of St. Charles and east of York.

By 1910 the population had climbed to 2,360. Village government, with its reliance on voluntary services, was no longer adequate. Incorporation as a city was proposed. A special election was held (1909), and incorporation narrowly was approved. In 1910 a city-council form of government was adopted. Henry C. Schumacher was elected mayor, and other city officials were chosen. Elmhurst's boundaries in 1910 were North Avenue on the north, St. Charles Road to the south, Poplar and Avon on the east, and Myrtle and Villa to the west. The business district had continued to expand along York and adjacent streets. Busi-

*Stone Quarry, Elmhurst*
*Art by H. Gilbert Foote*

ness establishments included the Baethke General Store, Weber's Bakery, Heinemann's Butcher Shop, Poulos' Ice Cream Parlor, the Wilcox Drug Store, Frieda Mahler's Park Avenue Variety Store, Mrs. Blau's Candy Store, the "Dew Drop Inn," the Schwass Saloon, the Wendland and Keimel Greenhouses, the Robillard Funeral Home, and Wandschneider's Hotel Edelweiss.

In 1911 F. W. M. Hammerschmidt, co-owner of Hammerschmidt & Franzen's Grain, Fuel, Coal, Ice and Lumber Company, was elected mayor. He held office until 1919. Many changes occurred during this period. The school system was expanded, with the building of Field School in 1911 and Lincoln School in 1916, and the establishment of York Community High School in 1918, which opened in 1920. A municipal sewage plant was constructed at Rex and Crescent, and additional land parcels, including the East End and Oaklawn subdivisions, were annexed during 1911–15. Several social and service organizations were founded, among them the first woman's group, the Elmhurst Woman's Club (1913). Other organizations included the Boy Scouts (1914), the Camp Fire Girls (1917), the Elmhurst Booster's Club (1918), and the Girl Scouts (1919). In 1916 a public library opened in one room of the Glos Building (the present site of the Elmhurst National Bank), with a collection of some 800 volumes. A few years later, in 1922, the Wilder mansion became its permanent home.

World War I (1914–18) was a difficult time for Elmhurst, with its population largely German and English in ancestry. As in the rest of the nation, the conflict provoked anti-German sentiment, and misunderstanding lingered in the community at war's end. Nonetheless, after the United States entered the fighting, many young men from Elmhurst, including those of German-American descent, served their country in the armed forces. Following the war, American Legion T.H.B. Post 187 was chartered (1919) to serve as a fraternal organization for the returned servicemen.

The 1920s in Elmhurst, as elsewhere, were a boom period. It was the time when the city lost its rural character, when it ceased to be a farmer's shopping center, and became a suburban community. Between 1920 and 1930 population more than tripled, rising from 4,594 to 14,055. The city had become the county's largest during this decade. The driving force behind much of the development of this era was Elmhurst's third mayor, Otto Balgemann, who held office from 1919 to 1931. Balgemann, a real estate broker, was the candidate of the newly formed People's Party (1919) and campaigned on the slogan "Get Elmhurst out of the mud," the community having no paved streets at the time of the election. York Street became the first street to be paved, in 1921. Other civil improvements included establishment of the City Water Department, which eventually took over the privately owned water works. To oversee development, a zoning board was established in 1924, and a city planning commission in 1930. In 1925 a police department, consisting of a chief and a motorcycle officer, was organized. Elmhurst Community Hospital (later Elmhurst Memorial Hospital) opened in 1926 to serve the city and surrounding communities, its creation due largely to the efforts of Dr. E. W. Marquardt.

To provide recreational area for Elmhurst's growing population, the Elmhurst Park District was founded in 1920. It soon began to acquire land for parks and playgrounds. Its first acquisition was Wilder Park, secured in 1921. The city's boundaries were expanded during the 1920s with the annexation of the Pick Subdivision along St. Charles near Salt Creek, and the platting of Tuxedo Park in the southeast. Closely associated with the city's growth during this period was the Elmhurst Booster's Club, which became the Chamber of Commerce in 1926. It sought to make Elmhurst the business, social, and cultural center of the county. Perhaps the city's most famous resident at this time was author Carl Sandburg, who had moved to Elmhurst in 1919 to find a peaceful place to write. By 1930 the bustling community had grown so that York Street, where his home was located, became too noisy for his creative efforts.

The boom began to bust following the financial crash of 1929, and the Great Depression enveloped the nation. Housing construction in Elmhurst ceased. Vacant lots dotted the city. Unemployment was severe. However, most of Elmhurst's 200 businesses weathered the lean years, and the city continued as the county's leading retail shopping center. While bank closings were occurring throughout the area, no banks failed in Elmhurst. For the jobless and other citizens in need, the city and a variety of private groups provided assistance. The Elmhurst Community Chest, organized in 1930, coordinated private welfare efforts. To distribute aid to the needy, the Elmhurst Welfare Relief Committee was established by the city in 1932. The city, with tax revenues reduced, cut the municipal payroll. It also applied for federal funds for public works projects, such as sewer construction.

When Elmhurst celebrated its centennial in 1936, the worst of the Depression had passed. The mayor for much of this time was Claude L. Van Auken, a civil engineer, who served from 1933 through World War II. During the decade 1930 to 1940, population increased by only 1,403 and totaled 15,458. Growth was virtually at a standstill, but recovery gradually began in the late 1930s.

During World War II, Elmhurst's experience was similar to that of most communities. Hundreds of its young men went into the armed forces. On the home front, a civil defense system was organized; Victory Gardens were planted; and rationing of such staples as meat, canned goods, and gasoline was endured.

The decades immediately following the war were another period of significant growth and development for Elmhurst. Population increased from 21,273 in 1950 to 50,547 in 1970. To provide a long-range development plan for the city, the Elmhurst Plan Commission was created in 1946. The city-manager form of government was adopted in 1953. That year Robert Palmer was named the first city manager.

Demands for new housing led to the construction of the St. Charles West Apartments in 1947 and the development of the Emery Manor and Brynhaven subdivisions in the 1950s. In addition to housing, new schools were needed. During the 1950s and 1960s, several elementary schools were built, including Jackson, Jefferson, Emerson, Edison, Madison, and Eldridge public schools, Visitation and Mary Queen of Heaven parochial schools. Sandburg Junior High School (originally Elmhurst Junior High) and Bryan Junior High School were constructed in this period. During 1963–73 the Timothy Christian schools were moved from Cicero to Elmhurst. In 1974 all Elmhurst schools were consolidated into the newly created School District 205.

To provide organized recreational programs for the community, a YMCA was founded in 1953. In 1960 a large, million-dollar facility was constructed on First Street. A variety of cultural organizations and institutions were established, enriching community life. The Elmhurst Artists Guild was organized in 1946; the Elmhurst Children's Theater in 1947; and the Elmhurst Symphony Orchestra in 1961. Two museums were founded — the Elmhurst Historical Museum in 1957, and the Lizzadro Museum of Lapidary Art in 1961.

To attract industry to the city, the Elmhurst Industrial Park was created by the annexation of 600 acres stretching north to Grand Avenue in 1962. Within a few years some 120 companies had located in the area. The retail shopping areas of the city expanded, including the downtown district and the areas along Spring Road, South York and Butterfield, St. Charles and Route 83, Lake Street, North Avenue, North York and Grand. Much of the latter area became an "auto dealers' row."

For the nation's bicentennial celebration in 1976, the long-deserted Great Western passenger station in Wild Meadows Trace was restored. On nearby York Street the Bicentennial Fountain was dedicated. In 1977 the underpass under the tracks of the Chicago and Northwestern Railroad was opened. Greatly facilitating traffic flow in the center of the city, it proved to be a major municipal improvement.

The census of 1980 revealed that the population had dropped to 44,276, a decline of 12%. It was the first decrease in the city's history, but not an uncommon occurrence for the time among older communities. Several factors were responsible for the lack of growth in the 1970s, including a declining birthrate, high interest rates that effectively barred younger families from purchasing homes in Elmhurst, and a lack of additional land for development. As a result of the decrease in the number of school-age children, seven elementary schools were closed from 1977–83. A faltering economy nationwide led to several business closings in Elmhurst, including the failure of one of the city's largest retailers, Long Chevrolet.

In the 1980s, citizens and city officials alike strove to maintain and enhance the quality of life in Elmhurst, despite limited growth potential. That quality was exemplified by the selection of York High School in 1983 as one of two high schools in Illinois to receive an award from the U.S. Office of Education as "representative of excellence in education." In 1983 the city and business community, aided by the DuPage County Planning Department, initiated a revitalization study of the downtown area. A branch campus of MacCormac Junior College was opened on West Avenue, in the former Cornille Elementary School. By the mid-1980s, an improved national economy had significantly aided home purchases and retail sales in the city.

At mid-decade, nearly 150 years had passed since Elmhurst's founding. A few small homesteads and a handful of settlers had been replaced by a residential community of nearly 45,000 persons. The city's 9.8 square miles stretched from Roosevelt Road on the south to Grand Avenue on the north, and from County Line Road on the east to Villa Avenue on the west. Within its boundaries were nineteen elementary and secondary schools, serving some 9,500 children; two colleges, enrolling approximately 3,400 students; thirty churches, representing most major denominations; two libraries, one public and one academic (Buehler Library at Elmhurst College), with a combined total of about 300,000 volumes; two museums; a hospital, with a 455-bed capacity; some 1,900 commercial, professional, and industrial business concerns; and twenty park sites, covering 328 acres of recreational land and facilities. Upon the sturdy foundation laid by its early settlers, succeeding generations of Elmhurst residents had built well for themselves and for the future.

**The Author**

Margaret Franson Pruter is Senior Editor in the Social Science Department of *New Standard Encyclopedia* in Chicago and serves as a commissioner on the Elmhurst Historical Commission.

# Glen Ellyn

*Janice Perkins*

Descendants of the first settlers in Glen Ellyn remember stories told of Deacon and Mercy Churchill, who journeyed from New York State in 1834. Their wagons traveled slowly through the tall prairie grass, following tracks of the future St. Charles Road. They chose a homesite along the side of the East Branch of the DuPage River. Oak trees were felled to build a log cabin, and the large Churchill family settled down to the challenges of frontier life.

News from the east was eagerly awaited, and weeks-old copies of the *New York Tribune* were passed from hand to hand. New neighbors homesteaded around the crossing of Indian trails called "The Corners," and shared in the work of putting up community buildings, including a school and blacksmith shop. Until the church could be built, the smith swept out the ashes and welcomed everyone for Sunday Sabbath School.

The Churchills, Ackermans, and Christians were among those who gathered to dedicate the first church, a plain white building reminiscent of their New England heritage. When the weather permitted, Sunday worship was led by circuit rider preachers who traveled for hours to serve scattered congregations many miles apart. After two or three hours of sitting on hard pews, the people enjoyed relaxing in the grass beside the wagons, and digging into basket lunches of simmered prairie chicken, cucumber pickles and bread specialties.

Taking produce to the Chicago market was a trip of at least two days, and a much longer one for those who lived farther west. When Moses Stacy built his inn-farmhouse in 1846 at Stacy's Corners he served farmers from as far away as the Rock River. These were charged 50¢ for supper, lodging, breakfast, and hay for two horses. As the first stage coach service of the 1830s was succeeded by evermore brisk traf-

From the 1874 Atlas & History of DuPage County, Illinois

fic, weary, dusty travelers gratefully quenched their thirst and exchanged news of the road in the warm comfort of Stacy's Tavern. Ladies were segregated in their own private parlor and were given separate second floor bedrooms, while men and boys crowded together in a large area above the dining room.

The fate of an inn and a town sometimes rests upon short distances; the hubbub of Stacy's Corners diminished considerably with the building of the Galena and Chicago Union Railroad, now the Chicago and Northwestern, only a mile and a half to the south. The right-of-way, purchased for $111, ran through land owned by Dr. Lewey Q. Newton. He foresaw that with regular passenger service a town would follow and so put his own money into a station and water tank, piping water from a reservoir-swimming hole south of the tracks. Everyone who could get there was on hand October 24, 1849, applauding old Deacon Landy as he ran down the tracks ringing a welcoming cowbell. Dr. Newton waved the American flag, and an assortment of drummers and fifers escorted the first train into the station. Probably Miss Almeda J. Powers, who later married Judge Seymour Dodge, took her school pupils to see the awesome ten-ton locomotive as it slowly pulled coaches filled with waving passengers.

The name of Newton Station lasted only until the first station master arrived in 1851.

David Kelley declared, "Since there is already a Newton, Illinois, the name should be changed to Danby — after my hometown in Vermont." He, too, saw the local economic possibilities of the railroad and built the Mansion House Hotel on the northeast corner of Crescent and Main. The town pump was also situated on this corner; thus the rocking chair crowd on the veranda had front row seats for the daily village happenings.

During the Civil War years more homes were built in the new center of town, and businesses like Joseph R. McChesney's grocery store supplied their needs. Children attended the white frame school on Duane Street, and the small church from Stacy's Corners was moved to Main Street between Crescent and Pennsylvania. The wagon and team maneuver took three weeks to accomplish this feat, with the horses inching carefully down the hill, since it was much steeper then than it is today. A few judicious bets were placed on whether or not the church would slide off into the mud.

When the bloody Civil War battles finally ended in 1865, red, white and blue bunting was strung on front porches to greet the Men in Blue happily returning to a normal life. As W. H. Churchill reminisced, "The swords that we carried so honorably have been deftly manipulated into corkscrews." Everyday life brightened. Young and old enjoyed hotel dances and skating parties on the pond east of Taylor Avenue. The veterans organized a baseball team, although the sport was so new that few had ever attended a game. After enthusiastically clearing a field on ground east of town, they challenged the Chicago Excelsiors to a contest. The wildly lopsided score of 102–2 was disappointing to the Danby boys, but they had the distinction of having lost to the team which later became the Chicago Cubs.

Everyone was concerned about fires during the severe drought of the early 1870s and watched with horror as the eastern sky was lit up for several nights by the spectacular blaze of Chicago's burning. For years after, what-not shelves displayed treasured souvenirs of fused

*Deacon Churchill Log Cabin.*
*Art by Ada Douglas Harmon*
*Courtesy Glen Ellyn Historical Society*

*Stacy's Tavern.*
*Art by Gerald A. Perkins*
*Courtesy Glen Ellyn Historical Society*

china and embroidered napkins blackened with soot.

In 1874 the townspeople observed their first forty years by changing the name of Danby to Prospect Park. No one seems to remember the reason for the new name exactly, but it was generally believed that a few rowdy young men had given Danby a bad image. This may have been what led village fathers to decide that a name change would be in order.

One of the first groups formed in Prospect Park was the Oak Grove Cemetery Association, now called the Forest Hill Cemetery Association, with property at Riford and St. Charles Road. School teachers today sometimes impress pupils with their heritage by helping them to make rubbings on the pioneer headstones there.

In the 1880s Chicagoans were attracted to the lovely setting of Prospect Park, as all day excursion trains had become popular. Favorite amusements of local adults included buggy rides to neighboring towns and attending lectures on spiritualism or war recollections; young girls cried over *Little Women*, while their brothers thrilled to novels by Jules Verne.

A few public spirited citizens were interested in forming a lake in the swampy valley east of Park; so Thomas E. Hill and Seth Baker spearheaded a drive to collect funds. The lake was created by damming the brook which ran through town north of the tracks, and Mr. Hill suggested calling it Lake Glen Ellyn — "Glen" for the natural terrain, and "Ellyn," for the Welsh spelling of his wife's name, Ellen. The *Wheaton Illinoian* described the area as "one of the most picturesque and charming locations in the whole west." Lake Glen Ellyn became so popular that in 1891 residents petitioned to change the name of their town to Glen Ellyn.

The Five Springs, just to the east of the lake, were believed to be of therapeutic help to those suffering from rheumatism, gout, and other such ailments. This belief led to the building of a large resort hotel high on Honeysuckle Hill between Crescent Boulevard and Lake Ellyn. National advertising put Lake Ellyn Hotel on the map, as vacationeers "took the waters" and enjoyed leisurely carriage drives around the lake and springs. The St. Lukes Society enticed clients with the "miracle cure" available in the "medicated mud and springs for the healing of disorders dependent upon a vitiated condition of the blood."

The hotel helped local business and the sale

of real estate boomed. More churches were built, classroom sizes doubled, and a long legal battle was fought over whether or not the village needed to extend its boundaries. The pros won, and 1,000 acres were added over the protests of pioneer families who said it was plain silly to think that village homes would ever replace the good farmlands. This argument must have enlivened conversation at the birthday party for Luriana Church Ackerman and Christiana Church Christian in 1893. At the age of 91, they were the oldest living twins in the United States. Mrs. Christian proudly quoted the Bible verses to prove that her mind was still young.

After the turn of the century, a few horseless carriages coughed and snorted along the narrow roads, but commuters were given an alternate choice of transportation with the opening of yet another railroad, the Chicago, Aurora and Elgin electric line. Residents discussed the new village water system and expressed gratitude for the twenty-two men who had volunteered to serve in the first fire department. The amount of $315 was considered expensive to pay for a fire truck. Citizens, nevertheless, wished it had been available in time to fight the flames when Lake Ellyn Hotel was destroyed by fire after being hit by lightning in 1906. In contrast to the constant anxiety over fire, crime was not a big problem, and only two policemen were needed to keep the peace.

By 1911 traffic was heavy enough to be considered hazardous to horses and dogs drinking from the fountain in the intersection of Main and Crescent, thus it was moved to the side of the road. Across the street the DuPage County Bank opened. Two blocks away from that intersection, the red brick Carnegie Library was built at Crescent and Park. A special article in *The Glen Ellyan* featured news of Dr. Frank Johnson and his generous gift of saplings, which he planted in parkways throughout the town. There was much interest among the ladies when Mrs. Charles McChesney was seen driving an automobile, but their husbands were more interested in the marvel of concrete pavements on sections of Pennsylvania, Main, and Crescent.

Civil War veteran Philo Stacy, son of Moses the inn-keeper, died in 1917, one month before the United States entered World War I. Village families prayed for the 166 men who volunteered to be Doughboys. Citizens sold Liberty Bonds, worked for the Red Cross, collected tinfoil, and tried not to grumble over the need for Daylight Savings Time. On November 11, 1918, when news of peace rang out with the fire whistle blowing at 3:00 a.m., a joyous crowd gathered to laugh and sing around a bonfire at the railroad station.

During the postwar years, the numbering of houses aided the postman on his twice-daily rounds, the first auto licenses were issued, and the town rang with the sounds of new construction spreading out like fingers from the older business district. A village hall was built on Pennsylvania. Commercial buildings rose south of the tracks. Eleven acres of Lake Ellyn were filled in for a football field, and Glen Ellyn teenagers excitedly moved from classrooms above the DuPage Bank to the new Glenbard High School. The standard of excellence for this "Castle on the Hill" was initiated by Principal Fred L. Beister. People read all about it in the new *Glen Ellyn News,* with its editorial comments by Lillian Shattuc, whose red hat was said to look like a beacon in the print shop window.

Mortgage foreclosures were common during the Depression of the 1930s. Neighbors were kind to each other, and civic pride was high.

During this time bird watchers wandered through the Benjamin Gault Sanctuary north of Hawthorne between Forest and Main. The famous ornithologist had brought in over one hundred species of birds indigenous to this climate, and the wooded area became a symphony of sound and color.

Telephone lines hummed with plans for the 1934 Glen Ellyn Centennial. Miss Ada Harmon presented to the village her native wild flower paintings, later loaned to the Morton Arboretum. A bronze marker was placed near the site of the Churchill cabin as part of the week-long celebration which drew to a close with a Grand Parade.

Soon after young parade watchers grew up to carry guns in the Second World War. Windows of their homes displayed blue service stars; neighbors gathered sadly when gold stars mutely told of a good friend's death. The food shortage was eased with the planting of Victory

*Frank Johnson, Glen Ellyn's "Johnny Appleseed."*
*Courtesy Lee Hesterman*

Gardens, and with village officials' allowing backyard chicken coops. Leisurely Sunday afternoon drives were frowned upon as more and more fuel was needed for the war effort. On V–J Day Main Street once again exploded with shouts and tears. Fred Beister led an impromptu parade with Glenbard Band Director, Orth Baer, beating a brass drum while everyone held up both hands in the "V-for victory" sign.

The men who did not return home were honored by such groups as the Veterans of Foreign Wars and the American Legion. As the sad notes of Taps faded from mind, villagers turned to the needs of an increasing number of children, organizing Little League baseball teams, chaperoning camping weekends for scouts, and hosting skating meets at Lake Ellyn. Traffic seemed to double overnight as prewar cars were replaced; simple stops signs gave way to four-way traffic lights at Main and Roosevelt; and automatic gates were installed at railroad crossing. Old timers shook their heads over the newfangled parking meters and muttered dolefully about the so-called benefits of progress.

When Mrs. Florence Robey Kroeger retired as principal of Ben Franklin School, a large crowd gathered to show their appreciation of this favorite educator. Mrs. Kroeger's career spanned three generations of students, and her special skill had touched hundreds of young minds.

After many years of sitting at the curbside, the old cast iron horse trough once again was moved back to the middle of the intersection of Crescent and Main. Water was replaced with flowers and the ornamental landmark was much admired.

The village love affair with trees continued. In spite of the ravages of Dutch Elm disease, many other varieties were planted. Along Riford Road friends of Judge Sam Perry were amazed when workers, enlarging his small lake, discovered a 10,000 year old mastodon skeleton. Experts painstakingly relocated the near-perfect specimen to Wheaton College where it was mounted and displayed on a revolving platform.

The 1960s saw further transition from farmlands to suburbia. Sport enthusiasts applauded when village officials created the Village Links golf course and the recreation area. Glenbard South High School was built to meet the needs of this expanding area.

Partly because of its central geographic location in the county, open land between Park Boulevard and Lambert Road was recommended for the site of the College of DuPage. Built to serve 2,000 students, with a ten-year projection of 7,000, the use of the college surpassed all expectations. The 1983 fall enrollment exceeded 27,000 pupils.

At the nearby site on Park Boulevard and Butterfield Road, the Village Theater Guild contributed resources to lease the old Bonaparte School. Their first production, *The Haunting of Hill House,* was well received. Productions have continued over an eighteen-year period.

Children with singing interests were given a rare opportunity for exceptional training when the park board invited participation in the Glen Ellyn Children's Chorus. Under the direction of Doreen Rao, the chorus has grown to 125 west suburban girls and boys. In addition to local appearances, they have performed in Carnegie Hall and at the Annual International Music Festival in West Germany. Concerts with the Chicago Symphony Orchestra have become frequent, and the chorus shared with it the honor of receiving a Grammy Award for the best classical recording of 1983.

In 1968 the celebration of the Illinois Sesquicentennial underscored the need for preserving original architecture of the Midwest. The village board authorized purchase of Stacy's Tavern and appointed a historic sites commission to encourage protection of historically valuable buildings. Restoration of the inn was begun by members of the newly formed Glen Ellyn Historical Society, who sought to remain faithful to the architectural details and furnishings of the original structure. This workmanship resulted in Stacy's Tavern receiving status as an Illinois Historic Site and a place on the National Historical Register.

The south side business district was given a boost in 1970 when the village government and police department outgrew the old Village Hall on Pennsylvania and moved to new quarters in the former Duane Street Junior High School. The building became known as the Civic Center, after extensive remodeling provided meeting rooms for organizations and senior citizens' activities.

Local residents will long remember the Chicago & Northwestern freight train accident in the spring of 1976. It was particularly shocking to those living in the St. Moritz Apartments who suddenly awakened to see a locomotive in the middle of their front yard. Hundreds of people in the area were alerted by police and firemen moving through the streets broadcasting the need for home evacuation. Quick response prevented human injury from toxic ammonia spillage. Acid fumes, however, seeped through the storm sewer system and killed all the fish in Lake Ellyn.

As vandalism became a growing problem locally, village officials worked within the school system to exert peer pressure. Glen Ellyn's Van Guard program won the Illinois Home Town Award for having achieved a 40% decrease in vandalism. Also, nation-wide attention was given to the passage of a teenage drinking ordinance. However, as evidence of the community spirit among youths, in 1983 Glenbard West student organizations raised funds for a plaque listing the names of village men who had died in the Korean and Vietnam Wars.

Today 23,852 persons live in Glen Ellyn, which extends over 3,788 acres. The $350,000 price tag for a fire truck today would have been mindboggling to 19th century residents of the village. The community continues, however, to remember old traditions, while meeting new challenges.

As Glen Ellyn geared up for the 1984 Sesquicentennial Celebration, descendants of the first families joined with newer residents to plan a gala birthday party. Special memories were relived and conversations began with, 'Do you remember when . . . ?"

## The Author

Janice Keel Perkins has been a Glen Ellyn resident since 1951, and is a member of the Glen Ellyn Historical Society.

# Glendale Heights

*Amy E. Crisler*

"The pioneer looked toward the horizon and beheld a high, rolling treeless prairie. Here and there were traces of buffalo wallows and Indian camp fires . . . Nestled in the depressions were occasional ponds of clear water . . . Bright flowers mingled with the coarse grass, relieving the monotony with brilliant color . . . This was the land."

The pioneer was Hiram Blanchard Patrick. The words, which describe what was to become Glendale Heights, are those of his daughter, Ruth Patrick, written in *Story of a Pioneer Farm.*

Hiram Patrick came to DuPage County in 1843 from Courtland County, New York. In December 1845, he bought 760 acres of land from the government at $1.25 an acre. He eventually owned a thousand acres of land in the county, most of it in the Glendale Heights area. His land was on both sides of Bloomingdale Road, stretching north for a half mile from where Queen Bee School stands. The family home was on the west side of Bloomingdale Road at the north end of his land. He owned additional land on both sides of Schmale Road, about a mile north of North Avenue.

The family lived on the farm until 1873 when Hiram Patrick, with his wife and younger children, moved to Wheaton. One of his older sons continued to live in the house on Bloomingdale Road for many years. The *20th Century Atlas of DuPage County, Illinois* shows that the Patrick family still owned over 400 acres on both sides of Bloomingdale Road in 1904. Hiram died in 1906.

The Patrick house was built in 1860. It replaced an earlier two-story log house, and was a typical story-and-a-half Greek Revival frame house. The upright part was later moved to Glen Ellyn Road, and still stands on the west side of the street just south of Armitage Avenue.

Hiram's younger brother, William Kirk Patrick, came to DuPage County in 1850,

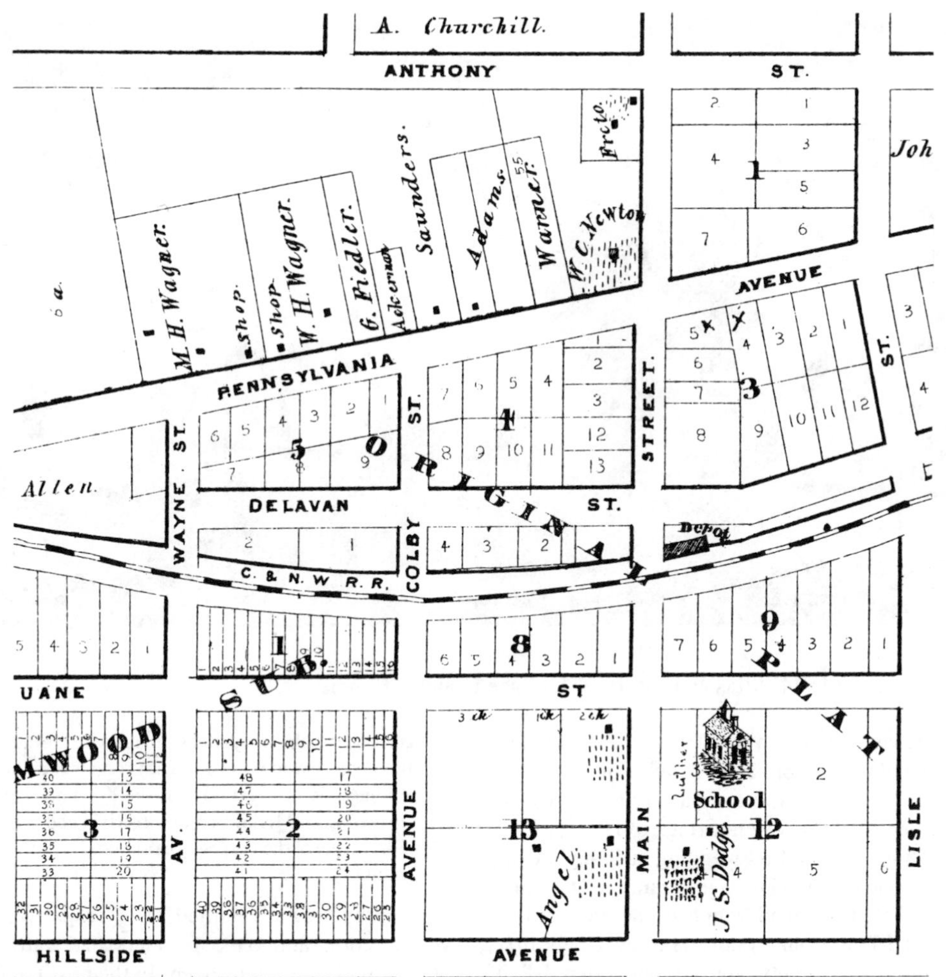


*From the* 1874 Atlas & History of DuPage County, Illinois

having previously bought 160 acres of land. He eventually owned all of Section 36 which is the square mile bounded on the south by North Avenue and on the east by Route 53. Most of this area is outside the village limits; but the *1874 Atlas and History of DuPage County, Illinois* shows that he owned property on the east side of Glen Ellyn Road between what is now Easy Street and Armitage. The home which he built still stands on the west side of Swift Road, just south of the Illinois Central tracks. Members of the family lived there until 1942.

Both Patricks were active in community affairs. W. K. was Bloomingdale Township supervisor from 1864 to 1873, and twice was president of the DuPage Agricultural and Mechanical Society. Hiram and two of his sons were also active in this organization, which operated the county fair from 1865 until 1900.

Another early settler was Rev. Milton Smith, whose land was on the west side of Bloomingdale Road and north of North Avenue. He came to DuPage County in 1835. He was one of the founders of the Wesleyan Methodist Church in Wheaton, and also one of their early pastors. The local historian, Rufus Blanchard, lists him as an active Abolitionist and says that he had a station of the underground railroad at his home in Bloomingdale Township, "... making great sacrifice of time and expense in conveying them (the slaves) stealthily in the night to Chicago to steamers that carried them to Canada."

*Coe Farm.*
*From the* 1874 Atlas & History of DuPage County, Illinois

Along Glen Ellyn Road three men who were original owners of land, or their families, continued to live in the area for many years. Gilbert Way, whose marriage to Harriet Fish in 1840 was the first wedding at Stacy's Corners, had come to DuPage County in 1837 and preempted the land which is the east end of Glen Ellyn Countryside. Harvey Coe's first holding was eighty acres along Glen Ellyn Road north from Winthrop Street; but he later owned the land on both sides of Glen Ellyn Road for one half mile, a total of 370 acres. His house still stands at 1688 Glen Ellyn Road. Farther north Rowland Rathbun bought the land which is now the East Branch Forest Preserve on the east side of Glen Ellyn Road. All three families continued in the area for many years. By 1904 the Coe farm had changed hands, but the other two families were still on the land.

After the first settlers had arrived, the area developed rapidly. Prosperous farms with large houses and big barns, orchards, and gardens dotted the landscape. In the *1874 Atlas and History of DuPage County* the Coe farm is thus described:

> The homestead place consists of three hundred and seventy acres, very handsomely situated, in fact one of the very finest places in northern Illinois. It is well improved with good fences and buildings. It lies just east of the dividing ridge between Lake Michigan and Fox River and in the midst of one of the best neighborhoods in DuPage County.

Farming was diversified. The crops were wheat, corn, and oats. Farmers had cattle, horses, pigs and often sheep. In the post-Civil War era milk was sold to the creameries and cheese factories, which sprang up in almost every town. Blanchard's 1882 history reports, "There is a cheese factory in the southeast part of the township which consumes 4,000 pounds of milk and makes 135 pounds of butter and 280 pounds of cheese daily. William Rathje and Fred Stuenkel, proprietors." The exact location of the factory is not known.

After the coming of the railroads, milk was shipped to Chicago, and the dairy industry flourished. The Illinois Central Gulf, put through in 1888, had milk stops at Cloverdale and on Swift Road. Farmers along Glen Ellyn and Bloomingdale roads shipped their milk on the Great Western, built in 1887. This line had a milk station at North Glen Ellyn, just west of Main Street on the south side of the tracks. Both lines ran milk trains which went into Chicago in the morning, carrying cans filled with milk, and returned in the afternoon with the "empties." The milk trains on both lines carried one passenger car. This was the only local passenger service on either railroad.

Early roads often followed paths which animals and the Indians had made. The only well-known road from pioneer days touching Glendale Heights is Army Trail Road.

When new routes were put through as the land was settled, the north and south roads did not follow section lines but ran approximately in the middle of the sections, probably because the land was settled before the survey was made. Glen Ellyn Road was opened up in 1840; and Bloomingdale, soon afterwards. The first roads, of graded dirt, were impassable in rainy weather. Later they were topped with gravel. Glen Ellyn Road was straightened, widened, and paved in 1936. The hill just north of North Avenue on Glen Ellyn Road was much steeper than it is today. It was cut down when the road was paved.

The Illinois Central Railroad's crossing on Glen Ellyn Road was a steep grade until 1938 when the underpass was put in. It was widened to four lanes in 1976. A new bridge over the railroad on Bloomingdale Road was built in 1968, and widened to four lanes in 1970.

North Avenue, a new road in the area, was put through in 1928, the first forty-foot highway through the county. During the 1930s the borders of the new highway were landscaped and planted with trees and shrubs through a Civilian Conservation Corps project. As the plantings grew they provided unusually attractive surroundings for the street.

Until 1958 the area which is now Glendale Heights was largely rural, with the exception of a small subdivision, Glen Ellyn Countryside, the east side of Bloomingdale Road north of North Avenue, which had been subdivided in 1951. During 1958 Midland Enterprises, operated by Charles and Harold Reskin, bought two farms on Glen Ellyn Road north of North Avenue. The first houses were built that year on Glen Ellyn Road and Larry Lane near Fullerton. The population stood at 104 on June 16, 1959, when a petition to incorporate was filed. On July 13 the court declared the village organized, and the first election was held on August 2. The first village board met on September 1, 1959, at the home of the newly elected village president, Anthony Larry. Though incorporated as Glendale, the name was changed to Glendale Heights in March 1960, because there was another Glendale, in southern Illinois.

Growth of the village was rather slow at first. The Federal census of 1960 recorded only 175 persons. However, by September 1962 the number had risen dramatically to 2,020. Ten years after incorporation the population stood at 11,000. The most recent count, taken in April 1981, totalled 23,163. The number of residences has grown from 170 houses in 1959 to the current 4,216 single family dwellings and 3,424 multi-family units. The first apartments were built at 1270 and 1284 Glen Ellyn Road in 1961, and the first apartment complex, Valleywood, was completed in 1969.

When the village was organized, there was no provision for industrial development. However, it soon became apparent that for tax purposes it was advantageous to zone areas for industry and encourage its growth. Two large plants have been built: Chicago Blower on Glen Ellyn Road in 1966, and Spraying Systems at the intersection of Schmale Road and North Avenue in 1970. In addition eight smaller factories are in operation. The Industrial Site Inventory issued by the village in 1982 shows 283 acres of land zoned for future light industry. Several of these sites are along the Illinois Central Gulf Railroad, off Glen Ellyn and Bloomingdale roads.

Commercial growth has accompanied the increase in population. Small convenience shopping areas have been built along Glen Ellyn Road and along Bloomingdale Road. The first large development was on North Avenue, just west of Glen Ellyn Road. As the village extended its boundaries to the north, large shopping areas were developed at the intersection of Bloomingdale Road and Army Trail Road, with stores, offices and restaurants on three of the four corners. Commercial development has extended both east and west on Army Trail Road.

Schools have often been hard pressed to provide and pay for rooms and teachers for the increased enrollment. There are two school districts within the village: Marquardt, District 15; and Queen Bee, District 16. The original white frame, one-room Marquardt School building stood at the corner of Glen Ellyn Road and Army Trail. This was replaced in 1937 by a structure that was added to in 1954 and 1959. The one-room Queen Bee school, believed to have been 100 years old, was demolished in 1962, after the first part of a new building had been constructed.

By 1983 there were eight public elementary schools, one junior high school and one middle school. St. Matthew's Catholic School is an eight-grade elementary school. Developers dedicate ten per cent of the land they are developing for schools and parks.

The area is part of the Glenbard district, and students from Glendale Heights attend Glenbard North in Carol Stream. DAVEA, (DuPage Area Vocational Educational Authority), on Swift Road in Addison, which is supported by several DuPage high school districts, including Glenbard, provides advanced occupational training for students. They attend the home school half day, and spend the other half at DAVEA.

Before 1959 no churches existed within the area now comprising Glendale Heights. St. Matthew's Catholic Church was built in 1962 on land donated by the Reskins. There are currently six Protestant churches serving the people of the village.

Health care services are available within the village, which has a number of small medical centers and dentists' offices. Glendale Heights Community Hospital, which opened in 1980, has 186 beds, modern equipment, and a staff of 170 physicians in all specialties. In November 1982 the hospital was purchased by Adventist Health System North, Inc., the parent company of Hinsdale Hospital.

The police department, located in the Civic Center, has a complement of thirty-six officers. The village lies in two fire protection districts. The area south of the Illinois Central Gulf Railroad is in the Glenside Fire District, which is north of the railroad in the Bloomingdale District.

Water for Glendale Heights comes from nine shallow wells located throughout the area. The village is also participating in the Lake Michigan Water Allocation System.

Glendale Heights now has approximately eighty acres of park land on fourteen different sites, most of it dedicated to the village by developers. In 1983 the village received a grant from the Federal Land and Water Commission Program toward acquisition of a fifteen-acre park site. This is part of a larger tract of land of sixty-five acres which will be utilized as a central community park.

The village sponsors an extensive recreation program for both adults and children. The Glendale Heights Sports Hub, adjacent to the Civic Center, has an Olympic size swimming pool, tennis courts, racquetball courts, saunas, whirlpools, and many other sports facilities.

The Glendale Heights Polo Club, owned by Harold Reskin, is located on Bloomingdale Road north of the Civic Center. Its games are open to the public. These are played three times a week in season.

After a long period of make-shift facilities

*Marquardt School First Grade — 1913.*

*Glenside Public Library.*

for a village hall, the Civic Center at Bloomingdale Road and Fullerton was completed in 1975, and all offices, with the exception of public works, are concentrated in one building.

The Glenside Public Library, which moved into a new $2,000,000 facility at 25 East Fullerton Avenue on July 10, 1982, began in 1967 as a volunteer effort in a house at 1631 Glen Ellyn Road, leased to the village by Harold Reskin for $1.00 a year. The Glenside Junior Women's Club provided money and volunteers, as did several other groups. the volunteers, as did several other groups. The Glendale Heights Public Library District was created in February, 1974. In 1978 Glen Ellyn Countryside was included in the district, and the name was changed to Glenside Public Library District. A $2.4 million referendum in 1980 provided the funds to purchase a three-acre site and to construct a facility. After fifteen years and three different temporary locations, the library finally had a permanent home!

Great changes have taken place since Glendale Heights became a village in 1959. Population has multiplied 200 times. The geographical area has increased sixfold. Prices of homes have changed from $14,000 in the beginning to a median value of $68,000, according to the 1980 Federal Census figures.

As was true throughout DuPage County, most of the early settlers were from New York State or New England. By the time the 1874 atlas was published, German names had replaced many of the English names. The majority of the inhabitants were farmers of German ancestry until post-World War II. The 1980 census figures reflect another change. Of the 23,183 population, there were 377 blacks, 2,040 classed as Asian or Pacific Islanders, and 850 of Hispanic origin.

Instead of wide open spaces dotted here and there with farm buildings, there are thousands of split level and ranches, single family dwellings, apartment buildings, shopping centers, used car lots, and fast food restaurants. It is wholly a village of its time with virtually no reminders of the past. Gone are the corn fields, the herds of cattle, the big barns and silos. With the exception of a few farm houses, nothing of what had been before remains.

In another way it is a village of the time. There is no Main Street, no central business area, no "down town." It is very much a village of the present and future. Its motto "Proud and Progressive," reflects this orientation.

**The Author**

Amy E. Crisler has lived in what is now Glendale Heights since her family moved there when she was four years old. Having retired from teaching in 1968, she works part time at the DuPage County Historical Museum.

# Hinsdale

*Shirley Stitt*

In 1833 when the Ottawa, Chippewa and Potawatomi Indians ceded the last Indian-held land in Illinois to the U.S., Orente Grant staked his claim about eighteen miles west of Chicago in an area called Brush Hill, along the Southwest Trail, now Ogden Avenue. Orente's father, brother, and other relatives soon joined him. In 1834 Orente and his brother constructed a tavern which they named Castle Inn. The new hotel was a stop on the stagecoach route to Ottawa, and was also used as the Brush Hill post office, with Grant as its first postmaster.

Benjamin Fuller of New York arrived in 1835. He brought his wife, parents, brothers and sisters. The large family was to become an important addition to the little community.

The continuous westward migration of new settlers led to the addition of another inn, the Grand Pacific Tavern. It opened to house overnight guests and newcomers to the area, who lodged there while building their homes. A corral was available for transient livestock. The fact that there were two taverns in such a small town is evidence of the density of the traffic that passed through.

In 1837 Nicholas Torode erected a sawmill on the Salt Creek. In 1839 lumber from this mill was used to build the first schoolhouse whose first teacher was Mary Fuller Van Velzer, a sister of Benjamin. She is said to have used two large dogs to protect her from wolves in walking to and from her classes. Her husband was Barto Van Velzer, the first keeper of the toll gate on the plank road.

As more people arrived, there were added a church, store, blacksmith, shoemaker, doctor and carpenter. A town was born. In 1851 Brush Hill was platted by Benjamin Fuller, who by then owned most of it, and the name was changed to Fullersburg.

When Torode's mill burned down, Frederick Graue built a water powered grist mill which was finished in 1852. Before the Civil War Graue let the mill be used as a hiding place for

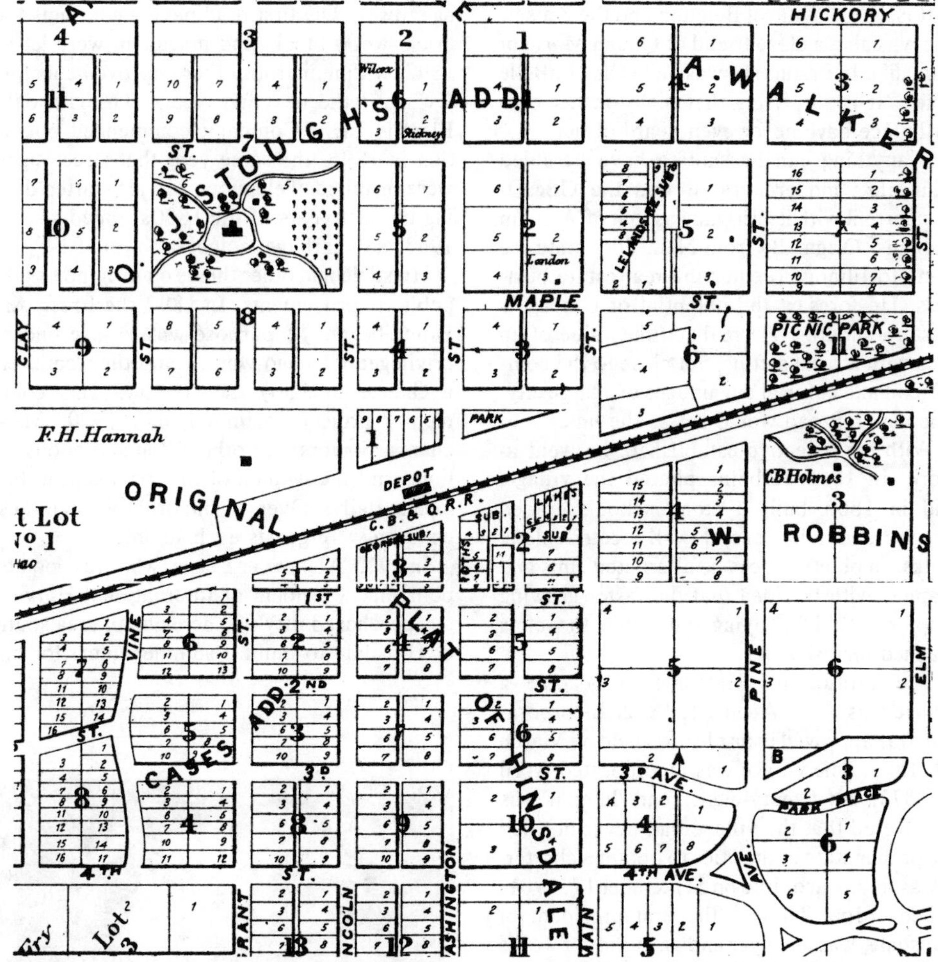


*From the* 1874 Atlas & History of DuPage County, Illinois

runaway slaves. When Fort Sumter was fired upon in 1861, Fullersburg set up a recruiting station in the school house and the fledgling community responded by sending ten men.

In 1854 Alfred L. Walker and his family arrived in Fullersburg from Vermont, and proceeded to buy from Benjamin Fuller 300 acres of land and the two taverns. A progressive farmer, Walker experimented with various farm produce, the preparation of meat, and the manufacture of cheese. His farm was considered a model farm by the Federal Government. It was also visited by Ineye Katsumasa, a Japanese student sent to learn American agriculture.

In 1858 civic leaders petitioned the Chicago, Burlington and Quincy Railroad to build a line into Chicago from Aurora, passing through their communities, including Fullersburg. Construction of the railroad began in October 1862, but it was hampered by the war, which caused a shortage of labor and scarcity of materials. Benjamin Fuller and Frederick Graue were among the petitioners for the new road. But the line was not run directly through their town because of engineering considerations. Thus the line was laid a mile to the south, through what was to become the village of Hinsdale.

In 1862 Loie Fuller was born in the stove-heated barroom of Castle Inn, where her family had gone to escape the bitter cold. A niece of Benjamin Fuller, she became an internationally famous dancer, appearing before the Czar of Russia, the King of Belgium and the Kaiser. She was also a close friend of Queen Marie of Rumania. In France she was hailed as "LaBelle Loie." It is surprising that many in her own birthplace have never even heard of her.

If anything can be said to have heralded Hinsdale's modern era, it was the CB&Q. Concurrent with its arrival was that of William Robbins. Originally from New York state, he came to Illinois to enter the real estate business. He foresaw the potential of Chicago's western suburbs. He realized the value of an area with a rural setting, yet close to the commercial and cultural advantages of a large city. The new railroad would act as the link.

With his objective established, he went to work. In 1865 Robbins platted the village, and in 1866 built a stone school, graded streets, and laid several well-located plank walks. In planting trees he alternated elms and maples, with the idea that the faster growing maples would be dying out when the elms reached maturity.

The petition for Hinsdale to become a village was dated August 1, 1872. Incorporation was approved in an election held on March 29, 1873. The village was incorporated April 3, 1873; but twenty-eight years later it was discovered that the village had never notified the proper state authorities to obtain a charter. It was finally acquired on September 17, 1901.

Judge Joel Tiffany, the first president of Hinsdale, was a lawyer and an author of works on law and religion. *Tiffany's Constitutional Law* was once used as a text book in many colleges. He was also an inventor, patenting the Tiffany railroad refrigerator car. The cost of operating the town in 1873 was $410.00, with total tax receipts of $600.00.

Until the 1890s water came from wells and cisterns; light, from coal oil lamps and candles; heat, from some early furnaces but mostly from barrel-shaped cast iron stoves, fireplaces, or kitchen ranges. Cows were kept in back yards, chickens were a familiar noise, and it was permissible to stable horses in the village. Hinsdale had no hard roads, sidewalks, electric lights, telephones, piped gas or public water systems until realizing that other towns were already enjoying some of these amenities.

In 1891 Hinsdale passed an ordinance providing for the issuance of bonds to cover a water pumping station, boiler house, and storage tower. The first road paving contracts for brick, wood block, and macadam were let in 1892, with numerous other improvements following in the next five years. The Hinsdale Electric Light Company commenced operation in 1896, the same year that street signs were installed. Telephone service started during the last years of the 1890s, piped gas, in 1903, and garbage incineration, in 1914.

Hinsdale had other things on its mind beside public improvements. In 1892 the Fresh Air Home began. Its purpose was to give underprivileged Chicago women and their children a chance to enjoy the country. This community project continued until 1920. Merchants, doctors and others donated goods or time, and the women of the town sent in hot meals daily. Over a hundred women and children were guests each summer.

In 1915 Alexander Legge, who was soon to be named President of International Harvester, purchased fifty two acres in an area south of Hinsdale to build a summer home for his

*Joel Tiffany.*
*Courtesy Hinsdale Historical Society*

*Hinsdale Sanitarium and Hospital.*

wife Katherine. Before this had happened, she died; and in her memory Legge built instead a Club House Lodge, turning it over to the female employees of Harvester to use as a vacation retreat. The KLM (Katherine Legge Memorial) Association used it until 1973, when Hinsdale fell heir to it as a gift. Today the Lodge is used for wedding receptions, benefits, and meetings. The grounds are used for jogging, cross-country skiing, seasonal festivals and art shows. Its most popular use is for the series of outdoor concerts held each summer.

The Hinsdale Sanitarium, which was founded early in the century, had its tenuous beginnings in Judge Beckwith's house, which was purchased by Dr. David Paulson in 1903. Now the Hinsdale Sanitarium and Hospital has 440 beds and a staff of 415 doctors.

The first issue of the *Hinsdale Doings* was published in October of 1895. It still serves as the town's weekly newspaper.

In 1899 the Hinsdale Club opened in the center of town; this was a turning point in the social life of the community. Meetings, dances, plays, lectures and bowling tournaments took place in the new facility. Old social clubs like the Cultivators, Baker's Dozen, the Cinch Club, and the Archers and Equestrians were giving way to the Women's Club, the new golf club and a tennis club. The churches had also become well established.

In 1923 the town celebrated its Golden Anniversary with a party in the high school gymnasium and a special edition of the *Hinsdale Doings.*

In that same year there was considerable discussion about a suitable war memorial; consequently, it was finally decided to erect a building to house village offices, the library and The American Legion. Efforts were organized to obtain land in the center of town. Philip R. Clarke undertook the task of raising funds. A total of $200,000 was collected in a community that had not previously exceeded $10,000 in any drive. The cornerstone was laid on Armistice Day 1927, and the dedication held on July 4, 1928. A statue by Oskar J. W. Hansen stands in the foyer.

In 1924 the Hinsdale Plan Commission was formed to create a master plan for the village and to suggest zoning ordinances. New housing areas were developed at this time. The remainder of Alfred Walker's farm became Radcliffe Park, and a new subdivision, The Wood-

*Hinsdale Historical Museum.*

lands, was laid out east of County Line Road. The village population had reached 7,500. In 1934 Hinsdale adopted the caucus system of selecting candidates for village offices.

The town survived the first year of the Great Depression fairly well; but after another eighteen months, unemployment rose. In December 1930 there were few Christmas decorations; Morris Flower Shop advertised a bouquet of one dozen roses for 50 cents, delivered. Jigsaw puzzles were for rent at the Parker Shop. Cattle rustlers were active in the county for the first time in sixty years.

During World War II the Hinsdale railway station was used as a depot for the collection and distribution of clothing and dressings. It served all DuPage County and part of Cook. The village also helped in keeping the Chicago Service Men's Centers supplied with food. Hinsdale's per capita representation in the services for both world wars was high by national standards.

Post World War II Hinsdale has seen a variety of changes. These are evident in the size of the police force. In 1945 there were eleven officers. Today there are twenty five. The appearance of the village has changed considerably. Ten thousands elms were lost in 1955, the year of the onset of Dutch Elm disease. Still, about 4,000 survived, plus five new disease-immune saplings.

In the 1950s a new community house was built, while old Castle Inn was torn down despite a last-ditch effort to save it.

In 1958, through the interest of Mr. and Mrs. Eugene Kettering, a health museum was established in Hinsdale. It represents an innovation in the field of health, family living and sex education. Having outgrown its facilities and with financial support from the Ketterings ending in 1970, a new era began for the museum. With contributions from many sources and a substantial gift from Mr. Henry Crown, in memory of his son Robert, the Robert Crown Center for Health Education was established. In 1974 the Center moved into a new building. It now serves 120,000 children annually from the Chicago metropolitan area and surrounding states. Programs on environmental quality and drug abuse prevention have been added. In 1973 the Wholistic Health Center came to Hinsdale.

In 1963 the Historical Committee of the Friends of the Library was organized. Because of its preservation of memorabilia, all was in readiness for the start of the Hinsdale Historical Society, created as a result of the 1973 Centennial and newly housed in an 1873 dwelling. Interest has spread to Oak Brook where old Fullersburg stood. An effort is underway to create an Historical Gateway linking the two towns, including Graue Mill, the Ben Fuller house and old St. John's Church. In 1979 the Ben Fuller Association was formed and is in the process of restoring the Fuller house, thought to be the oldest in the area.

After being abandoned for nearly forty

years, Graue Mill was restored in 1950. Here one can see displays of an old country store and barn, several furnished rooms of the period, and demonstrations of spinning and weaving. Corn is freshly ground and corn meal sold. It is the only operating waterwheel gristmill in the State of Illinois.

The village has doubled its population since World War II, with 16,700 counted in the last census. Revamping and remodeling of houses is continuous since Hinsdale can expand no farther; it is locked in by other communities on all four sides.

Hinsdale reflects the times. Mobility has increased. The population has grown so that residents no longer recognize most others seen in the village. Also many inhabitants are from the third world, with the grocery store often looking like the United Nations.

There are remnants, however. One is the Oak Street bridge, built as a foot bridge in 1875, and made large enough for cars in 1910. But the oldest remnant is perhaps the most unheralded. Wedged between Jackson Street and Route 83, withstanding the exhaust of thousands of autos a day, is a small, tough patch of original prairie, a treasured souvenir of long ago.

### The Author

Shirley Stitt has been a resident of Hinsdale since 1949, was active in forming the Historical Committee of the Friends of the Library, and currently serves as Chairman of Archives of the Hinsdale Historical Society.

# Itasca

*Joyce M. Usher*

The history of Itasca is inseparable from that of Elijah J. Smith. Its origin, therefore, must begin with his story.

Elijah J. Smith was born in Morristown, New Jersey, on May 8, 1815. Young Smith attended lectures at the College of Physicians and Surgeons in New York City and received a diploma on June 25, 1838. His health was not good. Friends in the profession advised him to leave his Boston medical practice and locate west, in a more agreeable climate. In May 1841 he set out to find a suitable site for doctoring, farming and raising a family.

Smith took a train to Detroit, then boat passage to the new city of Chicago, which was filled with land speculators and promoters. He bought a horse, saddle and saddlebags, and headed toward DuPage County, established two years earlier. Elijah selected an unclaimed eighty acres of high rolling prairie with a creek running through. His parchment government land title, dated March 10, 1843, was signed by John Tyler, President of the United States. The document gave Smith title to the land that is now bounded by railroad tracks on the south, Maple Street on the west, Cherry Street on the east and Division Street on the north.

The doctor returned to the East, settled his affairs, and brought his wife back to DuPage County, building a small house in 1843. In 1845 he bought his second parcel, 80 acres that increased his land holdings to a quarter section of land. The first parcel was $1.25 an acre. His second parcel was $5.00 an acre. The deed was dated October 9, 1845.

Smith's wife Jane died in May 1846. They had no children. In 1850 he married Mary Allen. He tore down the small house and built a ten-room home that provided not only living quarters but also a doctor's office and reception room. The couple had two sons and adopted one daughter.

In addition to a medical practice for the surrounding farm area, Smith started a dairy

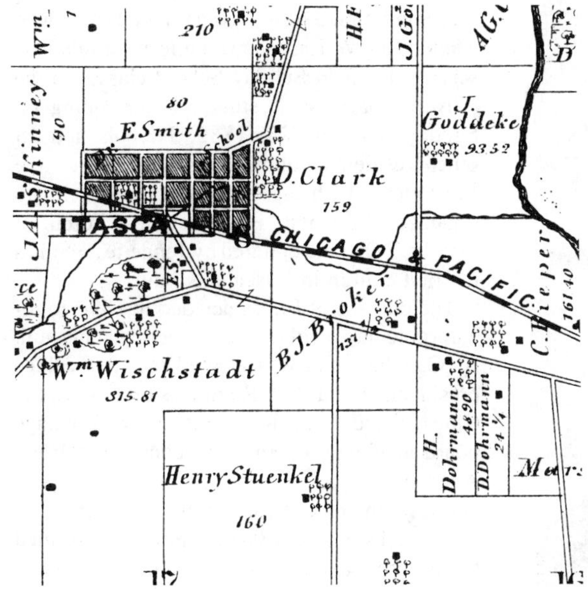


*From the* 1874 Atlas & History of DuPage County, Illinois

business and farmed. He had a large barn built from timbers cut and hauled from Elk Grove. They were hand hewn and fastened together with wooden pegs.

The post office that first served the area and the official map name that designated the cluster of farms surrounding the postal area was called Bremen. The post office was established in 1846 with Augustus Eddy as the first postmaster. In May 1850 the name was changed to Pierce in honor of Smith D. Pierce, who was postmaster from 1848 to 1864. Again the name changed, this time to Sagone, and the post office was in A. G. Chessman's home. In 1873 Chessman moved into Itasca, and the post office was temporarily located in the corner of his cheese box factory.

In that same year, the post office name was recorded as Ithica. Handwritten reports had probably caused the misspelling, because one month later, October 21, 1873, the post office and the community were recorded as Itasca. Early residents who knew the Smiths were interviewed for Itasca's first history, *This Is Itasca,* written in 1965. They substantiated the story that the name was selected after the doctor and his wife visited Lake Itasca in Minnesota. The Smiths so enjoyed both the trip and the name that they selected it for their settlement.

In the 1860s the first school was built. It was a small wooden structure with one room. The building was located on a site near the present First Presbyterian Church. In 1869 the Eddy family came from Limestone, New York. They settled on the farm that is now owned by the Mahler family on West Irving Park Road. Miss Carrie Eddy had taught in today's Roselle and Bloomingdale area before she and her family moved back to New York State. H. F. Lawrence was in charge of securing a teacher for the Itasca school. Discipline was lacking and Lawrence wanted to hire a teacher he felt capable of restoring order. He wrote to Carrie Eddy in 1876 and persuaded her to return and teach. Three years later Carrie became Mrs. H. F. Lawrence.

In 1873 Smith platted eighty acres of his land. The Chicago and Pacific Railroad was completed from Chicago to Elgin, with stations at Bensenville, Wooddale (called Lester) and Itasca. Smith gave the right-of-way to encourage location of the tracks through the settlement. He also donated $400 to help build a station.

In 1872 Ernst Schroeder moved to Itasca. The following year he set up a blacksmith shop. He invented the Schroeder plow, a potato planter, and a bobsled coupler. The Schroeder shop was located on the triangle of land now

*Elijah Smith.*
*Courtesy Itasca Historical Society*

bordered by East Irving Park Road and South Walnut Street. Schroeder's patent was sought by such farm manufacturers as the John Deere Company. The blacksmith preferred to make his equipment by hand, refused to consider dealing with the "giants" of the farm equipment industry, and thus his inventions went relatively unnoticed. Another blacksmith, Henry Droegemueller, located across from Schroeder on the east side of Elgin Road. Old timers tell that in clear weather the clanging of anvils could be heard for miles around. Droegemueller also built wagons and carriages.

Mary Allen Smith died in 1874. Some years prior to her death, her sister, Jennette, had become a widow. She moved from Texas to live at the Smith house. After Mary's death, Elijah married Jennette. They had no children. Elijah lived until December 7, 1888.

The Chicago and Pacific Railroad became "insolvent," as bankruptcy was then termed. In 1879 the road went into the hands of the Chicago, Milwaukee and St. Paul Railroad, a newly formed corporation combining several roads.

Edwin Nichols, the conductor of the Itasca Accommodation train, was a religious man who wanted to give Itascans some form of religious service. He held Sunday School classes in the railway coach as it stood on the siding on Sunday. On July 23, 1885, Nichols and 26 other residents submitted a petition to the Presbytery of Chicago requesting permission to organize the First Presbyterian Church of "Itaska." On land donated by Jennette A. Smith the first church in Itasca was built.

The citizens of Itasca decided in 1890 to incorporate into a village. At a meeting at his mill, A. G. Chessman was elected the first village president. Irving Park Road was first called the Chicago and Elgin Road. At an 1891 village board meeting the name was changed to Elgin Avenue.

Many unemployed began to follow the railroad tracks in the 1890s. They were termed tramps then, and the problem caused the village board to decide to build a "calaboose" or jail, and appropriate sums to provide daily food at a cost of 15¢ per inmate.

Dr. Smith had launched the community. Dr. A. R. Solenberger served on the first village board. Another doctor moved into Itasca in 1906 who would also contribute much to the village. He was G. F. Schroeder who, besides ministering to the physical needs of the community, served eight years as village trustee and twelve years as village president. He also found time to be president of the Lions Club.

The spire which is Itasca's most familiar landmark graces the top of what was formerly the Lutheran Church of St. Luke. This edifice was erected in 1907 by builder Fred Westendorf. Pastor Frederick Zersen served the congregation for thirty-eight years. Church services were in German. It was not until 1926 that English services were held twice a month. German was also taught in the church school.

By 1905 the dairy industry was flourishing in the county. Two milk shipments were made by train to Chicago each day. H. H. Geils bought a cheese and butter factory from Herman Wilk. The factory could process 2,000 pounds of milk daily. Geils also organized a corporation called "The Homer Squab Farm Co.," raising some 1,300 squabs each year for the Chicago markets.

Until 1916 there was no bank in Itasca, Herman H. Franzen took deposits for village residents to the Roselle Bank each morning, making the trip regularly on the 9:00 a.m. train. In 1916 two banks opened within weeks of each other. The Itasca State Bank had as its president H. F. Lawrence. The cashier was Elmer H. Franzen. The second bank was called the Dairyman's Bank of Northern Illinois, and was opened by F. N. Peck. Peck opened a total of four banks, but the Depression forced him to close them all. The Franzen banks in Itasca, Roselle, and Fox Lake were sound throughout the hard times of the 1920s, and emerged successfully from the Depression.

Telephone service had come to Itasca in 1899. Electricity was first installed in some homes in 1923. The bustling community soon gained another facility. The Itasca Country Club was opened in the spring of 1925.

A jovial, well-liked postmaster named George Pfaff gave pleasure to the youngsters when he dreamed up the idea of bicycle races. There was one difference between these races and conventional ones: in his, the youngsters rode as slowly as possible without losing their balance.

The rural village of the 1800s and early 1900s retained its atmosphere until the 1940s. A new word then began to enter the American vocabulary: suburb. The influence of the city increased as population increased. Commuting daily to the Loop became the routine for many of the village wage earners.

During the 1940s all village services were performed by two men. Frank Franzen was police chief; Carl A. Hanck was village clerk and policeman from 1945 to 1961. These men policed the village, read water meters, served as building inspectors, supervised the water system and pumping station, kept village records, maintained the sewage disposal plant and repaired the village streets. The population was 799 in 1950. There was little crime. The streets were waste oil over gravel.

By 1982 the population had grown to 7,129. Annexations had resulted in fifty miles of village

*Chicago-Elgin Road (Irving Park) — looking southwest, 1890.*
*Courtesy Itasca Historical Society*

*Itasca Historical Museum. Mayor Wesley Usher and Elbert Droegemueller inspect the original Milwaukee Road depot.*

streets, more parks, and two industrial areas to serve. Providing safety and service as population increased required the establishment of departments of public works, of sewer and water, of building and police. A park district, a library district, and a fire district were formed.

High school students from Itasca attended Bensenville's Fenton High School and Glenbard High School, a combined Glen Ellyn-Lombard school. A high school district, District 108, was organized in 1953. Lake Park High School, with students from Itasca, Roselle, Medinah, Keeneyville and Bloomingdale, opened in September, 1956.

Shopping centers were first introduced to the area with Bensenville's Green Meadow Shopping Center. Village residents with shopping needs that could not be met in Itasca or in Green Meadows traveled to the Loop, Elmhurst or Elgin. Shopping centers moved closer to the village from all directions during the 1950s and 1960s. A small cluster of stores was constructed at Irving Park Road and Route 53. Apartments were constructed. An industrial area was planned near the Route 53 and Irving Park Road intersection. The changing face of the community did not occur without protest. Loud disagreement from many residents followed the announcement of the plan to initiate each change. Apartments and industry were the most opposed features of change.

Modern industry was foreign to Itasca until 1961 when Central Manufacturing District (CMD) bought about 400 acres on the western edge of the village. An industrial park was established and such national companies as Continental Can and FMC soon moved in. Industry was limited to light manufacturing, distribution and warehouse facilities.

In 1970 the Itasca Industrial Park was established to the east of the village and attracted many more industries. These two industrial parks, in addition to providing a tax base for the community, also necessitated support services.

In 1973 the I-90 express highway to Chicago was now less than a mile away. During non-rush hours, it was possible to drive from Itasca to the Loop in twenty minutes, previously an hour's trip.

Anvan Corporation built a Holiday Inn on Irving Park east of Route 53. The building was of modular construction, the first such hotel in the nation to be built in this manner. Each room, stairway, corridor, and utility room was completed at an Elk Grove factory. Fully completed rooms, including carpeting, furniture, towels and pictures were sealed in plastic, delivered to the site, stacked and locked in place. The hotel opened in April 1972.

In 1969 Carson Pirie Scott purchased Nordic Hills Country Club. Two ten-story tower hotel buildings were constructed adjacent to the eighteen-hole golf course. In 1973 the Carson Inn/ Nordic Hills facility was annexed to the village.

In October 1979 Trammel Crow Company of Texas broke ground for Hamilton Lakes. A 420-room Stouffer Hotel and a ten-story office building, completed in 1981, constituted the first phase of the project situated on seventy-five acres on the northwest edge of Itasca. A sixteen-story office building was added to the complex in 1984.

In 1966 the village purchased sixty acres of land south of Irving Park Road. This established a green belt area to insure both open space and water retention. The area was the site of heavy flooding periodically from Spring Brook. In 1968 the Spring Brook Nature Center was formed. In 1980 a small barn on the property was expanded to become a museum, classroom, and living quarters for a naturalist. Nature trails were built and joint supervision of the Center was formulated by the village, the park and school districts. The three-fold purpose of the Center is recreation, education and flood control. In 1983 the State approved a $6.7 million grant for the development of a Spring Brook flood prevention reservoir.

Drinking water supplied by shallow wells is predicted to be in short supply. The long-range water supply by Lake Michigan water seemed a solution, but the high cost of participation for the small community caused the village board in 1982 to reject participation in the project until affordable funding could be found.

An inadequate sewage treatment system plagued the community development for most of the 1970s and into the 1980s. An upgraded sewage treatment plant, to handle the community's needs for twenty years of expansion, is scheduled for construction in 1985.

A Master Plan, adopted in 1965, continues to guide the community into its future. Itasca in 1984 also continues to control its development according to the individuality of its past.

**The Author**

Joyce Usher is the author of *This Is Itasca*, Managing Editor of F.E. Peacock Publishers, and former president of the Itasca Area Historical Society.

*"The Arboretum Village"*

# Lisle

*Marilyn W. Cawiezel*

In the fall of 1832, after the Black Hawk War had ended, the first two permanent settlers came to what is now the Village of Lisle. Luther Hatch (1804–1852), born in New Hampshire, lived on and farmed his claim south of Ogden Avenue. His brother, James C. Hatch (1806–1902), established a claim adjacent to Luther's and north of Ogden. Their parcels were bisected by what is now known as Main Street.

After improvising a shelter for the winter months, the Hatch brothers began farming preparations upon the raw prairie, using axes to chop grooves where they later planted corn. Plowing chores were eased somewhat by their using a team of oxen. Included in a letter Luther wrote to a brother in the fall of 1833 was this paragraph:

> We have built a small frame house, made our own shingles and did all of the carpentry and joining, dug a good cellar and a well, cut 18 tons of hay, put in our wheat (60 acres), cut up our corn (21 acres) and now are fencing our wheat, a rather tough job having to haul some of our rails nearly a mile.

Prior to 1842 Luther sold his claim and bought property on Warrenville Road, much of which is now Arbor Ridge subdivision. He farmed, had a saw mill, was director of the first school and was a township school trustee at the time of his death. His great granddaughter, June Frey, is a lifelong resident of Lisle.

James C. Hatch built a log house on his claim in 1833 and moved into a frame house in 1848. James kept a wagon and blacksmith shop on his farm, and built a creamery. One of the founders of the DuPage County Society for Mutual Protection, he also helped to organize the DuPage Agricultural and Mechanical Society in 1853, serving as its secretary. Luther too was active in the society. James was Lisle Township supervisor in 1855.

"Tomorrow I shall travel through the mud the distance of 23 miles to mail you this letter,"

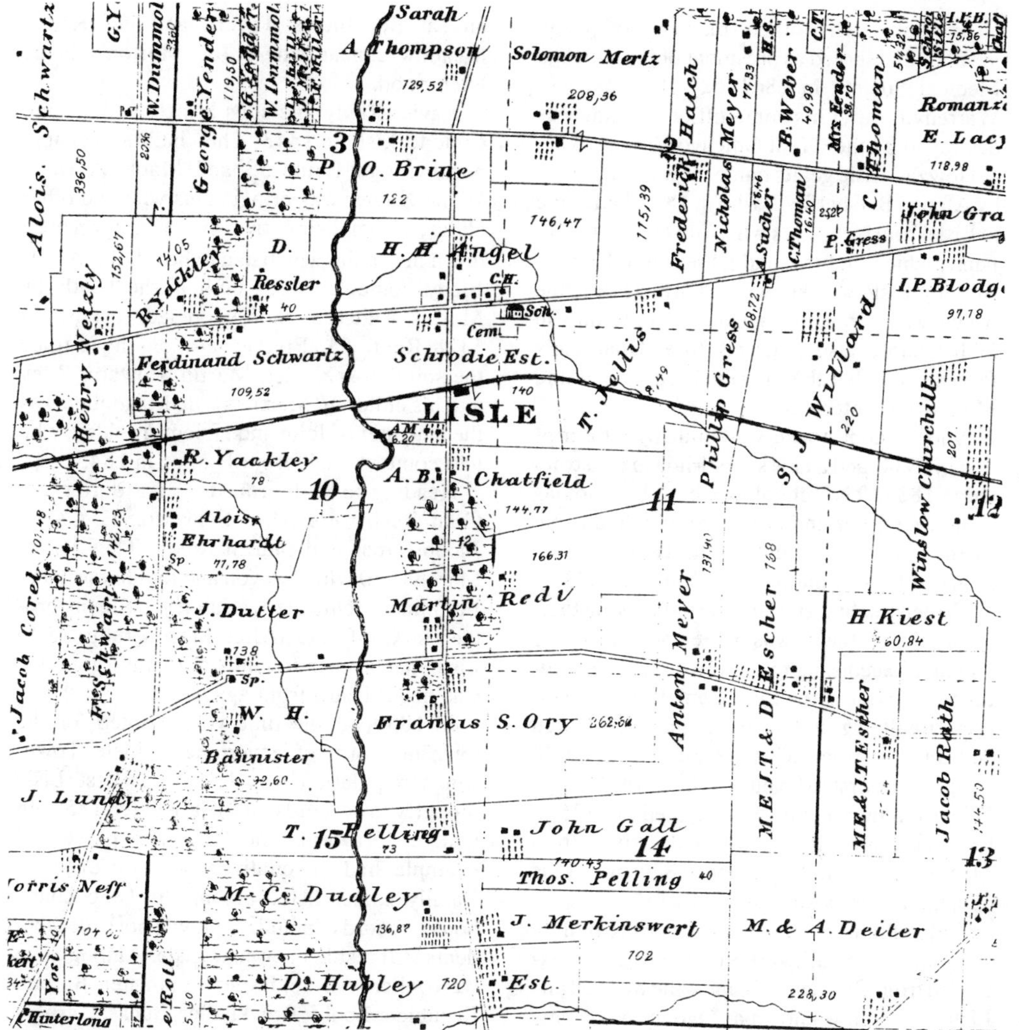


*From the* 1874 Atlas & History of DuPage County, Illinois

wrote Luther Hatch to his brother in 1833. He had to go to Chicago and later to Naperville to pick up or send mail. By 1834 John Thompson provided postal services in Lisle in his home, located on land now a part of the Morton Arboretum. He still was postal supervisor when Lisle Station was created in 1851.

Religion was important to the settlers. As early as 1833 members of the First Congregational Church of DuPage were worshipping in Lisle "on the first Sabbath of the month." In July 1982 members of Lisle's First Congregational-United Church of Christ observed the 140th anniversary of the formation of a congregation in the community.

In 1834 Jeduthan and Leonard K. Hatch joined their brothers in Lisle, taking claims to the north. Jeduthan was a representative to the Constitutional Convention in 1837, served as state legislator in 1842, was Lisle Township supervisor in 1851 and county judge in 1852. Leonard sold to John Thompson about 1835 and moved to Downers Grove. There he taught school and was the supervisor of that township by 1850. In 1855 he went into the grocery business with Henry Carpenter. Later he built a store in Lisle and purchased a farm east of the present Woodridge Golf Club. Some of the maple trees he planted along the road in that vicinity are still standing.

Another Hatch brother, Ira, went to Chicago in 1856, and served as president of the Chicago Medical Society in 1861–62. He moved to Warrenville after his home-office building was destroyed by the Great Chicago Fire in 1871.

How did Lisle get its name? It was suggested by Alonzo B. Chatfield, who in 1835 had come to Lisle from New York where an area bore that name, which, in turn, had its origin in France. Initially Lisle was known as DuPage, a name which was confusing because a township in Will County also had this title. Chatfield's farm surrounded the present Riedy Road and Main Street intersection.

A log school house was built by subscription in 1834, and a new school-house constructed in 1837. The school was built by Thomas Jellies, a farmer and carpenter who had come to the area from England in 1834. It was replaced by still another structure in 1873.

"When the first settlers started making their homes here, there was no cemetery in the vicinity," according to a foreword in the earliest record book of the Lisle Cemetery Association. Realizing the need, James C. Hatch dedicated a tract of his claim as a burial ground. The first to be buried there was George Willard, father of eleven, who died in 1835, a few weeks after the family had arrived from Massachusetts. In September 1836 two of his daughters were also interred there.

To facilitate travel plank roads were built in some places. Southwest Plank Road was extended from Chicago to Naperville by 1851; its Lisle path is now known as Ogden. A toll gate stood in front of Marc Beaubien's Tavern-Inn in western Lisle, a comfortable day's journey from Chicago. Marc had purchased the property in 1841 from Richard Sweet, and served as innkeeper in Lisle until 1865.

Jean Baptiste Beaubien, Marc's brother, was in command of twenty-five men who came from Ft. Dearborn to Naper Settlement during the Black Hawk War to fight Indians if it became necessary. In 1858 he retired to Beaubien Inn, died in 1863, and is among those buried in the small cemetery east of the building.

Patrick O'Brien, who came to Lisle in 1863, informed his granddaughter that an Indian burial ground was located on the Keller farm west of Beaubien's land. Joseph Yackley, in a 1916 interview, recalled seeing friendly Indians at Beaubien's Tavern and in "Round Meadow", near where Joy Morton's home later stood.

Xavier Riedy and sons Martin and Johann came to Lisle in 1843. They built a log cabin northwest of Route 53 and Maple Avenue. While Xavier was bringing his wife and other children from their native Alsace, a storm blew down his cabin, which had to be rebuilt. A new Riedy homeplace was built in the 1860s by Martin. Added to and remodeled, it stands at 5328 Route 53. Five generations have tilled the soil there: Xavier, Martin, Edward, Riley and his children. Martin's wife Magdaline was the daughter of John and Helena Yackley, who had come to Lisle from France in 1845.

Heading to California to mine during the Gold Rush were Alois Schwartz, E. Cable, Jacob Gross and Martin Riedy. They left in March 1850 with a wagon and four horse team. Ferdinand Schwartz left later, joining his brother in California. After Martin returned to Lisle, his brother Johann left to mine gold. He was never heard from again.

In 1850, at the time voters opted for the township form of government, Lisle Township's population was 1,137. Earliest Lisle property tax records on file are dated 1856. In that year Xavier Drendel's 24-acre parcel, for example, had an equalized valuation of $175. Family names listed among the 1856 courthouse records include many whose descendents still reside in or near Lisle. Among them were Allen, Alleso, Bailey, Bannister, Barber, Beaubien, Books, Bruckbeller, Bucks, Carpenter, Chatfield, Clancy, Drendel, Duck, Dumoulin, Dutter, Emory, Erhardt, Fender, Gall, Grafs, Griswald, Hatch, Heim, Helm, Horstman, Hunt, Jellies, Kaeffer, Kuenye, Lannis, Lehman, Lundy, Mertz, Meyer, Morse, Neff, Netzley, O'Brien, Ory, Parmer, Pelling, Potter, Reid, Rickert, Riedy, Schaerer, Schock, Schrodi, Schwartz, Sherwood, Sitter, Smith, Standish, Striker, Thoman, Thompson, Thorn, Weaver, Weber, Willard, and Yaeg. Other families who arrived through the 1860s were Corel, Haumesser, Hinterlong, Loring, Mueller, Rott, Schmitt, Tate, Yackley and Yender.

The first train came through Lisle on May 20, 1864 over tracks completed from Aurora to Chicago by the Chicago, Burlington & Quincy Railroad. After fire destroyed the depot built in 1863, a new one was constructed in 1874–75,

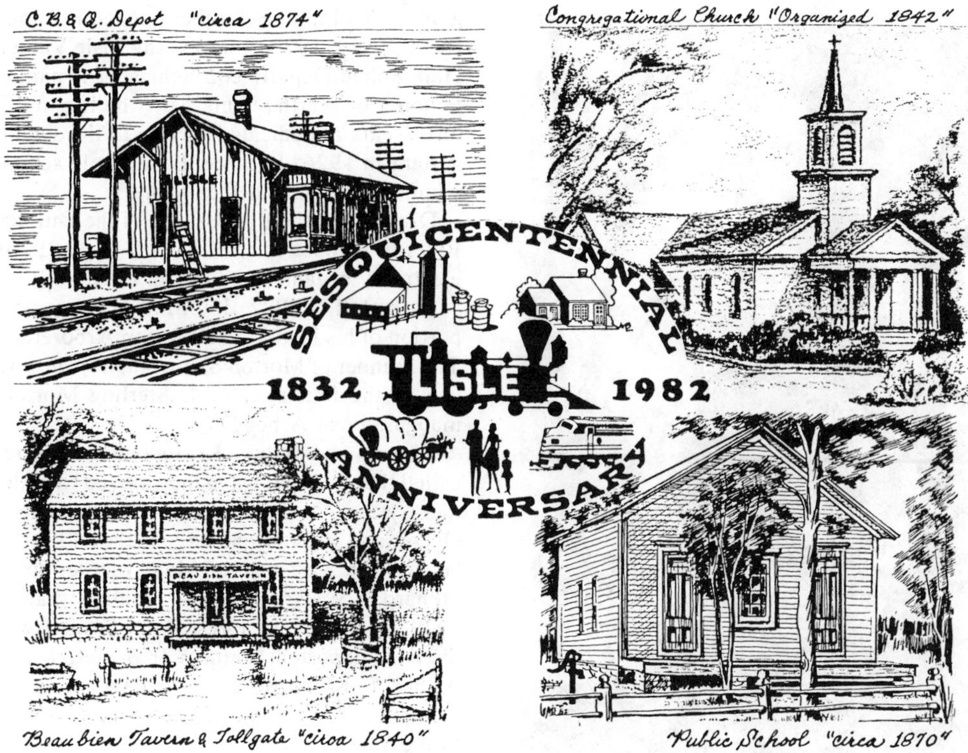


*Art by Marg Bryan*

according to documentation by Joseph Bennett. When Burlington Northern discontinued use of this historic structure in October 1978, it was donated for use as a museum. Moved about a quarter mile northeast and named the Doris M. Gurtler Museum in honor of a Lisle-promoting, long time *Sun* newspaper editor, the building is owned by the Lisle Park District, maintained by the Heritage Society and stands upon land leased from the Village of Lisle.

Riedy's Hardware, founded in 1889 and Lisle's oldest existing business, moved to a new building on Front Street in 1894, and then to a modern one on Main Street in 1968. The founder's grandson, Albert Cawiezel, is partner/manager. The Front Street structure has housed the Lisle post office, a Red Cross meeting room during the war years and, from 1968 to 1981, the Lisle Library. In 1981 it became headquarters for Multimedia Cablevision of Lisle.

In 1893 the first plat of Lisle was drawn up and recorded by members of the Lisle Improvement Company: Simon Engelschall, W. Spencer Green, H. H. Goodrich, W. F. Mitchell, Alfred and Lawrence Pelling, Albert Riedy and Joseph Yackley. Streets were graveled, trees planted and wooden sidewalks built in an area bounded by Front, Columbia, Division, and what became Route 53.

Before the turn of the century, a volunteer fire department was organized. In 1944 the Lisle Fire Protection District was formed; it took the name Lisle-Woodridge Fire Protection District in 1978.

Lisle Creamery was started in 1895. It later became the Union Dairy and then the Lisle Pure Milk Association. Lisle became the largest milk shipping center along the CB&Q between Aurora and Chicago.

St. Procopius College and Academy, founded in Chicago in 1887 by monks of the Order of St. Benedict, opened in Lisle in 1901. In 1967 the academy merged with Lisle's Sacred

*World War I Serviceman, Martin Reidy. Courtesy Albert Cawiezel*

Heart Academy, established by the Benedictine Sisters in Lisle in 1926. The school's name became Benet Academy. The college was renamed Illinois Benedictine on July 1, 1971.

In 1914 St. Procopius Abbey relocated in Lisle. In 1970 the monks moved into their new Abbey on College Road, a structure cited by the American Institute of Architects as one of the outstanding buildings in the United States for 1973. St. Procopius Seminary opened in 1916, but was closed in 1967.

After fire had destroyed the 1873 public school building on Halloween night 1909, a two-room brick building was constructed. Called Lisle Public School originally, and then Main Street School, it had three additions in forty years and served as Lisle's only public grade school until Schiesher opened in 1956. Renovated in 1979, it now is the Lisle Village Hall–Police Department. Schiesher is named in honor of Martha Schiesher, who began her forty years of dedicated service to the school system in 1926. She was Lisle's sole school administrator for nineteen years.

Dredging of the East Branch of the DuPage River took place in 1920. In the early 1920s electricity became available in Lisle.

In the fall of 1922, Joy Morton set aside a portion of his land for the Morton Arboretum. The founder of Morton Salt Company, he was one of the four sons of J. Sterling Morton, inaugurator of Arbor Day.

George and Sylvia Kostopoulos later recalled that in 1926, when they moved to Lisle, there were "no buildings on Main between Ogden and the railroad except the old farmhouse. The west side of Main was an apple orchard." Walker Gamble recalled that in 1929 Main had two stores. Dairy farming was the most important business. In the late 1920s Arthur T. McIntosh Co. was developing the Dumoulin farm south of Ogden and west of Route 53.

St. Joan of Arc Parish's first Masses were held in 1924 in the second floor meeting room of Riedy's Hardware-Lumber. Lisle Bible Church was founded in 1933. Faith United Methodist Church was organized in 1959. Lisle Trinity Lutheran Church's inaugural services took place in 1960.

In the 1930s the Lisle business district was augmented by buildings constructed on Main Street north of the tracks. A state highway plan called for closing the Main Street underpass when a Lisle link in Route 53 had been made and a new underpass built there. In 1938, however, merchants sponsored a street dance for the community to celebrate their successful campaign to keep Main Street open.

Volume 1 No. 1 of the Lisle *Advertiser* was published April 21, 1938. Charles and Marie Rice were editors. Volume 13, No. 15, appearing on October 6, 1950, was the first issue under the new and present owners, Harold and Eva White, owners and publishers of the *Naperville Sun.* Later the *Advertiser*'s name was changed to the *Lisle Township Sun.*

Improved telephone service came in 1946, when Lisle customers served by Naperville were able to signal the operator by lifting the

*May Thielgaard Watts — of the Morton Arboretum. Courtesy Morton Arboretum*

receiver instead of turning a crank. Dial service became available in 1956.

Lisle residents voted to incorporate in 1956. There were 606 ballots for and 287 against. In 1959 the appellation "Arboretum Village" was approved, reflecting Lisle's nearness to the world-famous Morton Arboretum.

Oakview subdivision, completed in 1956, was the first large post-World War II development. Others to follow included The Meadows in 1960, Four Lakes in 1964, Beau Bien in 1967, Shadowood (then Benedale Green) in 1973, and Green Trails in 1975.

The first financial institution in Lisle was Lisle Savings and Loan Association, which opened in 1959. The grand opening of the Bank of Lisle came in May, 1960.

Classes first convened at Tate Woods in January 1960. A new junior high was ready by December 1962. Lisle students who attended public high school enrolled either in Naperville or in Downers Grove except for several years in the 1930s when a two-year high school program was conducted in a portion of Main Street Grade School. Lisle Community High opened in September 1957 with 200 students. A new senior high was built, opening in September 1974. The first building became the junior high. The most recent grade school, Meadows, was started in January 1965. In 1972 voters approved combining the elementary and high school districts into Lisle Community Unit School District 202.

St. Joan of Arc school was open for classes in 1927. The parish junior high for grades six through eight opened in 1965. Both schools are conducted by Benedictine Sisters from Lisle's Sacred Heart Priory.

A referendum establishing a tax-supported Lisle Library District was approved in 1965. The Lisle Park District was approved by referendum in 1967.

Construction of the Western Electric plant in 1968 marked the beginning of a commercial, residential and research development which continues. Lockformer, Molex, Tellabs, Burroughs, Chicago Furnace, Victor Products and SWIB Industries are among Lisle's businesses. Corporate West office/research complex was approved by the village board in 1976. In that same year 2,400 commuters from Lisle boarded the Burlington Northern daily.

In 1981 the Hilton Inn in Lisle opened. Corporetum Office Campus, a sixty-acre office/research development planned for the strip of land east of Route 53 and south of the East-West Tollway, was approved in 1983. A few months later plans for a twenty-one million dollar Holiday Inn hotel-office complex were accepted by the village board.

Lisle has a wide complement of church, school, civic, service, sports and social organizations which reflect the many and varied interests of village residents. Participation in local government extends to service in the county. Julius Hankinson, president of Hankinson Lumber and Supply, has served on the county board for over twenty years.

Lisle's 1956 census reported 3,200 residents. There were 8,428 in 1975. The 1982 population totaled almost 14,000.

Lisle is still populated by pioneers of a contemporary sort, independent settlers who continue to improve and to add to the trails which had been skillfully blazed by those who preceded them.

**The Author**

Marilyn Cawiezel was an organizer of the Lisle Heritage Society, and wrote feature stories in Lisle newspapers from 1957–1979.

# Lombard

*Margot Fruehe*

The end of the Black Hawk War in 1832 signaled the beginning of the development of the area called Lombard. According to C. W. Richmond's 1876 *DuPage County History,* the earliest settler on the land of the town proper was Luther Morton, who built a cabin near the present rail depot, the heart of present day Lombard. But the town was originally named for brothers, Ralph and Morgan Babcock, who had settled farther west, near the DuPage River.

New Englanders were eager to take up the newly opened land sites, now that the threat of Indian attacks no longer existed. The year 1834 saw the arrival of the Deacon Winslow Churchill family. One son, Winslow Jr., settled on the east side of Babcock's Grove.

Another early settler, Sheldon Peck, a portrait painter whose primitive paintings still command high prices, established his farm on the eastern edge of Babcock's Grove, near the present Lombard Commons Park. His house, begun in 1837, remains standing, and is the oldest in the village. Alyce Mertz, the granddaughter of Sheldon Peck, occupies the house at this time. Her father, Frank Peck, reported in his journal that it took two years of dragging oak logs from a wood lot on the banks of the DuPage to complete the dwelling. It was here that the first school convened, and that runaway slaves were to find refuge during the Civil War.

Babcock's Grove developed along the trail from Chicago to St. Charles, Illinois. St. Charles Road today, old-timers in town remember, was once called Lake Street. Across the marshy prairie it followed the high ridges that the Indians favored; they, in turn, followed age-old buffalo trails. For eleven years the Frink and Walker Stage line used this trail from Chicago to St. Charles. But in time even this "comodious, efficient" method of transportation was to give way to something better.

The Galena and Chicago Union Railroad

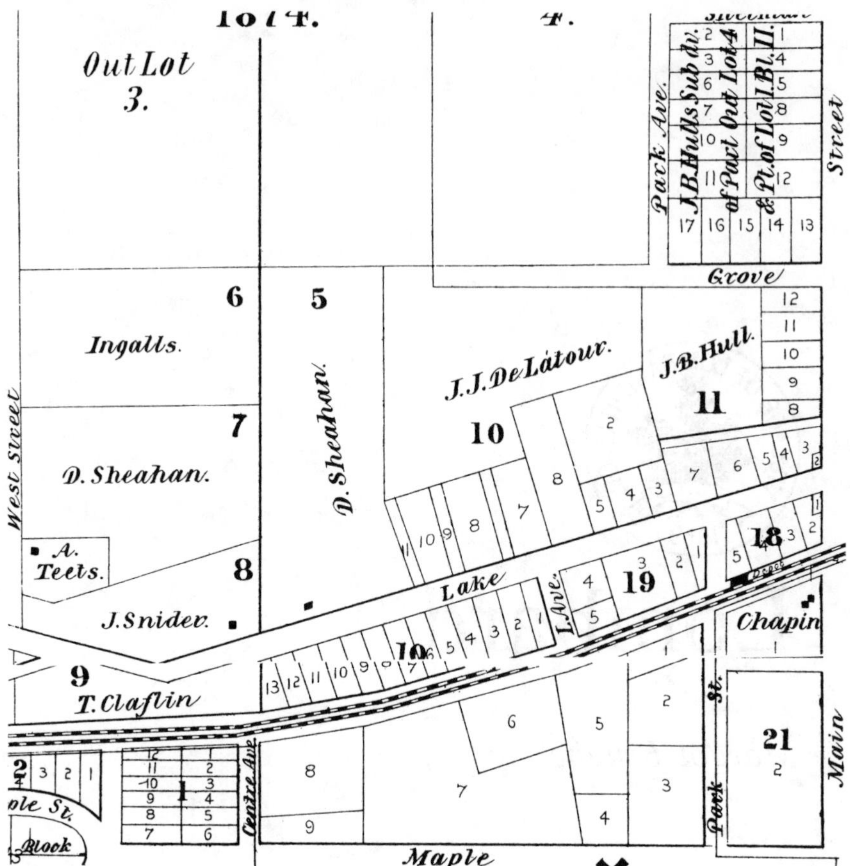


*From the* 1874 Atlas & History of DuPage County, Illinois

ran its first engine to Babcock's Grove in 1849, following the old stage line to St. Charles by slicing through the lands of Winslow Churchill Jr., Sheldon Peck, Hiram Whittemore, Reuben Mink and John Rumble. Farmers could see the advantages the railroad offered and eagerly accepted the $15 per acre for right-of-way. No more bogging down on muddy trails to the markets at Chicago! "The Pioneer," a second-hand steam engine now on display at the Chicago Historical Society, steamed westward at the admirable speed of 25mph. A temporary turntable was built west of town, and the train was hand-turned for its return run to Chicago. In time the line was extended to Newton's Station (Glen Ellyn), Wheaton, and beyond.

By 1851 the nucleus of a small community had begun to form around a makeshift depot and "railroad hotel." There were at least five frame houses and a store clustered around St. Charles Road and the future Park Avenue. Reuben Mink, a Pennsylvanian, purchased the Morton homestead and other land tracts. Either through luck or a sense of the future he found himself the possessor of much land in what was to become Lombard. But he was to give back to the town two pieces of property which were essential to its development. The first, located on Main Street at Washington Boulevard, was deeded to the small community for a burying ground. The earliest recorded burial was July 11, 1851. The second piece of property, located on St. Charles Road near Mr. Mink's home, was given for the first permanent schoolhouse, built about 1861. The schoolhouse, built in two sections, still survives in part. One portion, exhibiting Greek

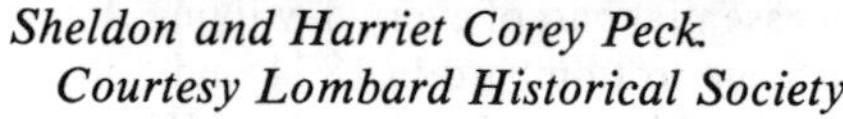

*Sheldon and Harriet Corey Peck.*
*Courtesy Lombard Historical Society*

Revival characteristics, is now a private home located at 210 South Lincoln, across the street from St. John's Lutheran School.

During the 1850s Babcock's Grove saw a period of development as a farming community. The earliest settlers in the area were from New York and New England states who had come west with the opening of the Erie Canal.

But soon names of other origin began to appear in the early land records. German immigrants, refugees from civil and religious strife in their native country, began to take up land. Soon York Township was dotted with farms owned by persons with names like Backhaus, Stueve, Meyer, Schoene, Klusmeyer and Heinberg. They would prove to be industrious and supportive of education. An early school was established by the German community on the Schoene farm, just east of Sheldon Peck's house, with Julius Schoene as teacher.

An influx of Irish settlers had its beginnings in this period as well. Although many came as laborers on the canals and railroads, others, with a typical love of the land and the money to purchase it, were able to pursue the occupation they knew best, farming. James Sheahan took up land on the western outskirts of Babcock's Grove. This farm, later purchased by Danish immigrant Peter Hoy, was to be one of the last operating farms in the area. Scheduled for development in the 1980s, the old Hoy barns, visible from Route 53 in Flowerfield are the last reminder of this period of agricultural growth. Of the early Irish settlers, only the names remain on the tombstones in little old St. Mary's Cemetery on Finley Road.

The 1850s saw other firsts. Dietrich Klusmeyer's three-story stone hotel, at the present intersection of St. Charles Road and Park Avenue was erected in 1858. It still stands today, housing a handful of commercial establishments. Its wide porches, bracketing and popular Dram Shop are gone; but the building has survived, a silent observer of years of Lombard's development.

Nearby, to the west, stands another survivor of those early days. J. B. Hull, the town's first postmaster, operated the first store, depot and post office in a small board and batten building next to the tracks.

Nationwide, the slavery issue had erupted into Civil War. The farmers of York Township joined the cause. While the women folk knitted and rolled bandages at home, a number of Babcock's Grove men marched off to war.

General Benjamin Sweet, a retired Civil War general, once charged with the direction of Fort Douglas in Chicago, where captured Southern soldiers were held, moved to a farm on the outskirts of Babcock's Grove. As pension agent in Chicago, he may have been acquainted with Josiah L. Lombard, a successful realtor who became interested in the yet untapped possibilities of the area. Joined by Captain Silas Janes of Danby, the three platted the town in 1868 and petitioned the state for a charter. The townspeople, impressed with Josiah L. Lombard's plans for the area, voted to name the town after him. The town of Lombard was organized in short order, after the granting of a charter in 1869. Isaac Claflin was named president and Colonel William Plum of Civil War fame, became clerk.

Josiah Torrey Reade followed Issac Claflin as president. He is remembered also for founding the first town library from his own personal collection of books. That first library had its beginning with a peach basket full of books carried by Reade between his home and the First Church, where a room behind the sanctuary was donated as a library.

That wooden Gothic chapel, a symbol of Lombard's beginning, still stands on the corner of Main and Maple Streets. When dedicated in 1870, it was the home of the First Congregational Church. Today it is known as the First Church of Lombard, United Church of Christ, a landmark which attracts photographers and artists alike with its board and batten exterior, lancet-shaped calico stained glass windows and classic lines. It is on the National Register of Historic Places.

By 1870 Lombard had become a "commuter" town, with many residents traveling by rail daily to Chicago. A small frame building on Park Avenue served as ticket depot, waiting room and freight office. Nearby was a small stockyard which held cattle being transported to the markets at Chicago.

Although the railroad offered a modern, up-to-date means of transportation between towns, the horse-drawn wagon and buggy were still an essential part of every day living. John Fisher came to Lombard in 1874 and built a carriage and blacksmith's shop at 19 West St. Charles Road.

Fisher served as the town's justice of the peace for twenty years, setting up a courtroom in the basement of his house. As there was no lock-up in Lombard, prisoners had to be taken

*Lombard Historical Museum and First Church of Lombard.*

to the jail in Wheaton. Fisher once averted what might have become the town's only lynching by spiriting his prisoner, a man named Bo Creek, who had killed his foreman in a dispute over wages at the stone quarry west of town, to the relative safety of the jail in Wheaton.

The temperance question continued to plague the townspeople. Dr. Richard Oleson, son of the town's first doctor, sums it up this way:

> The temperance-dram shop fights had been long and bitter. It always was an issue at election time. When the town was incorporated, the wets prevailed by one vote. The next year the opposition won by one vote. One year the town would have prohibition, the next year it wouldn't, until Rev. Caverno . . . got the boys together.

The Rev. Charles Caverno, pastor of First Church for many years after his 1870 arrival, pointed out to the New Englanders that the Germans who wanted their beer were honest, law-abiding citizens, and who were *they* to deny them. His argument prevailed. It was decided that dram shops might operate between the hours of 4:00 a.m. and 11:00 p.m. each day; the early opening accommodated farmers bringing their milk to town to meet the railroad "milk run."

In 1877 Dr. Charles Wilmot Oleson came to Lombard to serve for many years as the town's first doctor. Many people in later years remembered the compassion of this gentle man. He built a stylish Victorian home on North Main Street in a section of town which had come to be called "Quality Row." In later years Dr. Oleson suffered a stroke and was followed in his practice by his son, Dr. Richard Oleson.

Lombard continued to attract persons with leadership ability. In 1878 twenty-four year old William Hammerschmidt came from Naperville and bought land to develop a clay pit. He started manufacturing tiles and bricks. Many of Lombard's homes and commercial buildings were built of Hammerschmidt brick, which was sold widely throughout six midwest states.

In spite of the town's residential nature, a few small industries did operate in Lombard. There was a boot factory, with shoemaker Phil Carroll employing several men. Well drilling was an important business. Lightning rod salesmen did a brisk door-to-door business. Butter and cheese were made in the home until another early Lombard businessman arrived in 1879 and built a cheese factory on the south side of Lake Street, at the western edge of town. William Stuenkel's name appeared frequently in the town board minutes during the five years he operated his cheese factory. He had often to be advised to control the "offensive odors" coming from his establishment. But keeping 300 lbs. of cheese a day from smelling was an insoluble problem. The cheese factory continued after Stuenkel's tenure under the directorship of a corporation of local businessmen, including Frederick Marquardt. The name was changed to Lombard Butter and Cheese Company, and moved by Frederick Marquardt to the north side of Lake Street.

In 1880 Frederick Deicke operated a creamery near his home, adding to it a small general store. He married a local girl, Regina Goltermann, and took a special interest in the establishment of Trinity Lutheran Church at York Center, where he lived. His son, Edwin, has been instrumental in the development of many educational and cultural efforts throughout DuPage County.

Mention should be made at this point of those local craftsmen like William Zabel, Karl Mech, the Assmans, and others who used their hands and their talents to erect many of the homes and business establishments of Lombard. In many cases their names have been forgotten while Historical Society plaques commemorate the buildings which they embellished.

Telephone service in Lombard began in 1882. The town was fortunate in being situated on the Chicago-Geneva toll line, the Chicago Telephone Company's first experimental line.

Also in 1882 Colonel William R. Plum's *The History of the Military Telegraph Corps During the Civil War* was published. Copies were placed in the Federal Archives, and Lombard had its first published author!

In 1886 the town "saw the light" in the form of gas street lamps. The residents celebrated by hiring a band and holding a street dance. A tightwire was stretched from roof to roof of Gray's Hardware and Marquardt's Grocery, across the street, and a tightrope walker pranced across it.

The tracks were laid in 1886 for a second rail

line, the Chicago and Great Western Railroad. The first train arrived August 1, 1887.

Peter Hoy, a native of Denmark, came to America in 1880. By 1890 he had saved enough to buy the old John Sheahan farm southwest of town where he operated a dairy farm, bottling and selling the milk in Lombard and surrounding towns. He often invited the children of the Lombard School to his property to observe first hand the operations of a real dairy farm. At Christmas he would take Lombard schoolchildren for horse-drawn sleigh rides. His barn was often used to shelter vagrants, who had no other place to sleep. Jobless men often followed the rail tracks through Lombard, looking for work. Today Peter Hoy School commemorates this hard-working, gentle man.

Lombard enjoys the distinction of being one of the first towns in the nation where women voted before the passage of the 19th Amendment. However, this distinction lasted only for 1891. In that year, Ellen A. Martin, a woman attorney residing in the community, marched into the polling place and demanded to be allowed to vote, basing her claim on the fact that the town charter enfranchised *all* citizens, with no mention of sex. She and fourteen wives and daughters of prominent Lombard residents voted that day. But the men of Lombard won out by "reorganizing" the town charter in line with the state charter. The ladies did not vote the following year in the town election. As a result of ensuing litigation, women were allowed to vote in school elections. Unfortunately, Ellen Martin did not live to see the passage of the 19th amendment, since she died in 1916, having returned to her native New York State.

By 1893, after many long battles, Lombard finally reached an agreement with the Chicago and Northwestern Railroad, and a viaduct was constructed at Main Street under the tracks. Lombard was one of the earliest towns to deal with the problem of traffic flow in this manner.

In 1899 the Aurora, Elgin and Chicago Railway was authorized to build a railway through the south end of town. Begun in 1902, the railway, variously known as the Chicago Aurora and Elgin, the "Roarin' Elgin," or "the Third Rail," sped past the back yards of the town's residents at a decent clip, lights flashing and bells ringing warning stragglers to clear the track.

On October 19, 1903, Lombard was reincorporated, now as a village. Instead of a town council a board of trustees served the village.

At the turn of the century several churches were well established in Lombard. Diagonally from First Congregational Church, a Methodist Church organized in 1909, and a building subsequently erected. Several blocks west stood St. John's Lutheran Church with its two tall steeples and classic design; it has served the area's Lutherans since 1893. In fact, when the Roman Catholics erected their combination church-school on Maple Street at Elizabeth Street in 1912, Maple Street's name could as well have been changed to Church Street!

In 1959 Sacred Heart parish welcomed the grandson of Martin Hogan to the dedication of the new Sacred Heart Church, located on his grandfather's farm. The grandson, Rev. Martin D. McNamara, had grown up to become the first bishop of the newly-created Joliet Diocese.

Although a few automobiles were beginning to be seen regularly in town, throughout the early 1920s horses were still the common mode of transportation. When in 1914 the Methodists requested permission to set hitching-posts in front of their church, the request seemed reasonable.

But Lombard did have an up-to-date silent movie theater in a building on Parkside between Main Street and Park Avenue. And in 1928 the Parkside Theater, as it was called, was replaced by a new movie house on Main Street. The DuPage Theater, had gilded pillars, and a starlit sky, complete with drifting clouds. Outside, the "waterfall" marquee has been restored, recreating this Lombard landmark as it was in the thirties.

The end of World War I brought a return to simpler pleasures. One source of hometown pride was the comic strip "Little Orphan Annie," created by Harold Gray in 1924. The comic strip, which became a part of American life by way of the *Chicago Tribune,* was created by Mr. Gray when he lived in Lombard on South Stewart Street. He was later to purchase a spectacular Victorian home at 119 North Main Street for his parents, with whom he lived for several years between marriages.

*Courtesy Lombard Historical Society*

The house, which has retained nearly all of its original gingerbread trim and bracketing, was built by William LeRoy, one of the original town board members, and had formerly been known as "Chateau LeRoy."

With the return of soldiers from the war, a building boom was in the making. Townspeople began lobbying for a park and general beautification. On April 28, 1927, during lilac time, Colonel William R. Plum died, leaving his house and grounds to the village with the provision that they be used for a library and public park. Josiah Reade's small library, which had outgrown its quarters at the First Church, finally had a permanent home. Mr. Reade lived to see his collection of 3,000 books moved to the Helen M. Plum Memorial Library across the street.

Jens Jensen, a prominent landscape architect, having a special interest in Lombard and Lilacia, agreed to design the park for the modest sum of $600. His crowning touch was the limestone waterfall and pool designed especially for the new park.

In November 1929 plans were laid for holding the first annual Lilac Pageant. The highlight of the pageant was the choosing of the first Lilac Queen, Adeline Fleege.

In 1931, when the Depression was in full swing, both Lombard banks were forced to close, and several emergency measures were necessary to sustain the town. A canning project, set up by Father Jones of the newly organized Epiphany Mission, provided food for the needy, as well as assisting the townspeople. In a cooperative venture the churches lent pots and kettles, while the village supplied the gas. Canning equipment was procured, and farmers donated their surpluses. All who could pay were charged 3¢ per can, and every 20th can went on the shelf for the destitute. Government agencies like the WPA and the CCC stepped in to provide jobs for local men grading streets, removing and planting trees, and repairing village property.

Building in Lombard almost came to a standstill during the Depression, and many houses ended up on the market, or were repossessed when their owners were unable to meet monthly payments. Some residents argued for local beautification as a means of raising town morale. Shrubs and trees, dug from the Churchill farm west of town, were planted on the fringes of the village hall grounds, along streets, and around the sewage disposal plant by unemployed men. Seventy trees, purchased by individuals at $3.75 per tree, were planted along North Main Street between North Avenue and Pleasant Lane. Each tree was a memorial, and "Memory Lane" was the result.

In time the economy began to recover, and newcomers discovered the town, moving into the long-empty houses. The State Bank reopened in 1945. A Village Hostess program was initiated, with Estelle K. Wasz as the first hostess, greeting newcomers and answering their questions.

World War II brought the need for a Municipal Defense Council to Lombard. The East St. Charles Road pumping station was protected against sabotage by being fenced and lighted. Air Raid Wardens were appointed, and first-aid kits distributed. The townspeople were asked to salvage rubber, metals, waste paper and rags to aid the war effort. Even the cannon on the village hall grounds, a memorial to the veterans of the Spanish American War, was turned in for scrap. Ration coupons were carefully counted out on Lombard dinner tables, and even the smallest child in the family could aid the war effort by flattening tin cans.

As World War II ended and the veterans returned, there was a need for new housing. Shell houses with unfinished second stories, pre-fabricated housing, tri-levels and ranch houses were soon being built throughout the area. Lustron enamelled steel houses, introduced early in Lombard, became very popular. Public buildings, as well, were being erected or added to. Green Valley School, closed during the Depression because of declining enrollment, was re-opened in 1947.

The building boom continued into the fifties. The small shopping center on South Main Street was enlarged. Begun in the late twenties, it developed on both sides of the Chicago, Aurora and Elgin Railroad crossing at Main Street.

As the population grew, the school system began to feel the pinch. There was now a definite need for additional schools, and a number of present day Lombard schools had their beginning during this period.

In 1954 Mildred Robinson Dunning decided to record the history of her home town, as told to her by native-born and long-time residents of Lombard. Her effort, *The Story of Lombard, 1833–1955,* was a simple recounting of the highlights of the town's history. Others had thought the events of the town's growth of sufficient interest to preserve them for future generations. Frank Peck kept a journal for many years. Amy Collings wrote a series of newspaper columns in the 1940s for the local paper, *The Lombard Spectator.* Hubert Mogle chronicled the growth of American Legion Post 391.

Katherine Reynolds, editor of the *Lombard Breeze* and author of several novels, used thinly disguised local residents for some of her characters, much to the enjoyment of the townspeople. Her best-known work was entitled *Green Valley,* with the subdivision and school named for this work. Lillian Budd, also an established author and former Lombard resident, was approached in 1973 by the Lombard Historical Society to do an updated version of the town's history as a bicentennial project. The result of her labors was entitled *Footsteps On The Tall Grass Prairie.*

Lombard adopted the city manager plan in the spring of 1955. Lombard's first city manager, Hugh T. Henry, took office the following fall. A special census that year showed the village to have a population of 16,284. In 1962 the village received the highest rating in Illinois municipal waterworks operation from the American Waterworks Association. A design for a new village flag was selected, the result of a contest that year, with Susan Mills, a Willowbrook student, submitting the winning design.

In 1968 Yorktown Shopping Center was completed. It took four years of construction. Yorktown, encompassing 100 stores, covers 130 acres.

On the 100th anniversary of the founding of the town, the Centennial Lilac Parade depicted events and personalities reminiscent of the town's history. As the 1969 celebration drew to a close, Lombard Centennial, Inc. donated its assets to the establishment of a Lombard Historical Society. Today, the Lombard Historical Society maintains its museum in an 1870s style frame cottage at 23 West Maple.

Other recent changes include the closing of Lincoln School, built in 1916 near the site of the old brick Lombard School, and the still older frame school house. The village hall was also closed; it has been replaced by the Lombard Civic Center, a complex of modern buildings of pre-cast white quartz, located at 255 East Wilson.

Morris the Cat, star of Nine-Lives Cat Food commercials, has passed on to his reward from his home in Lombard. Morris' replacement also lives in Lombard.

Today Lombard is a village with a population of 38,500. It covers 10.5 square miles, on which 8,950 single family homes and 3,650 multiple family units have been built. Almost forgotten are the log cabins of the Mortons, the Babcocks and the Churchills. Faded into the past are the small clapboard cottages along the St. Charles Trail. Yet, in 1976, in celebration of the nation's bicentennial, a local group erected a permanent symbol of Lombard's past, a log cabin which is used today by all the groups in town. Thus the community has come full circle, from the little log cabin of the 1830s on the banks of the DuPage River to its sentimental recreation in a Lombard Park.

**The Author**

Margot Fruehe is Director of the Midwest College of Engineering Library in Lombard. She is a member of the Lombard Historical Society and DuPage County Genealogical Society.

# Naperville

*Helen Fraser*

Once a rich prairie teeming with wildlife, Naperville has become one of the fastest growing cities in the nation. Its growth began with the migration of settlers from the East. As timber was used up and farmland claimed, landless sons and daughters of earlier pioneers, as well as immigrants, came into the heart of the Illinois prairie to seek a better life.

Naperville is the oldest town in the county, founded by Captain Joseph Naper in 1831. Although Captain Naper was the founder of the village, then known as Naper Settlement, he was not the first settler in the area.

Stephen J. Scott and his son Willard, while on a hunting trip in 1830, discovered the DuPage River south of present-day Naperville and built a cabin at the fork of the east and west branches of the river in Will County. Other families soon settled in the vicinity, living peacefully with the Indians.

The first white settler on county soil was Bailey Hobson, who established a permanent home along the DuPage River near today's Pioneer Park. He came from Indiana with his wife, Clarissa, and five children. Within a few years he built a grist mill and a home, which served as an inn for many of the farmers who came great distances to grind their grain and often had to stay overnight while waiting for their turn. Legend says that farmers who came to the mill took delight in seeing the many peacocks who would feed upon the spilled grain around the mill. The Hobson home still stands on Hobson Road, east of Washington.

Captain Joseph Naper of Ashtabula County, Ohio, arrived in Chicago via the vessel *Telegraph* along with his brother, John, their families, and those of John Murray, Lyman Butterfield, Harry Wilson, and Ira Carpenter—about fifty people in all. After delivery of the ship to its new owner, they proceeded west to their new land. Captain Naper had met Stephen Scott on his first trip to the region a few months earlier and engaged him to break

*From the* 1874 Atlas & History of DuPage County, Illinois

ten acres of prairie land in the spring. Owing to the lateness of the season, however, the Napers could only plant buckwheat and rutabagas, while other provisions had to be purchased from established farms along the Wabash.

The winter was unusually severe. Despite this, after building a log cabin for his family, Captain Naper and brother John, also erected a sawmill during the first year. They used iron work which they had brought from Ohio. Christopher Paine, whom they employed, built a dam laying logs and stones across the river and then building up tne dam with mud and buckwheat straw. By the spring of 1832, the mill was in running order for sawing boards to build some of the first frame homes in the county. The mill stood at the foot of what is now Mill Street.

Upon completion of the sawmill, a crude grist mill was built. Christopher Paine had made the grinding stones from boulders, and each settler ground his own grain using his team of oxen for "horsepower." In the first year of settlement the Napers also established a trading post where they carried on a trade with both settlers and the friendly Potawatomi Indians.

Despite the hardships of daily life in the fledgling community, the settlers did not lose sight of the need for education. Along with several other families in and around Naper Settlement, the members of the community drew up a contract on September 14, 1831, establishing a school. Twenty-two scholars attended school in this first school house, which was a fourteen-foot square log cabin erected at the present intersection of Jefferson Avenue and Ewing Street. Lester Peet was hired as the teacher; he was paid $12 per month.

In the spring of 1832, the prospering community was threatened by the Black Hawk War. Half Day, a friendly chief of the Potawatomi, sent a messenger to Bailey Hobson advising the settlers to go to Fort Dearborn as rapidly as possible. He said that people were being massacred south of the settlement. Filled with fear and excitement, families quickly located one another in the vast prairie and packed their clothing and provisions for the journey to Fort Dearborn in Chicago. Crossing the prairie was slow and escape difficult. Roads were no more than muddy ruts. Wheels became embedded in marshy soil and fresh water was not readily available. The Hobson family's reminiscences speak of traveling thirty-six hours without food. Mrs. Hobson is said to have frequently used her shoe to dip water from the pools by the roadside in order to get a drink.

Joseph Naper was chosen as the captain of the first military organization in DuPage County to serve in defense against Black Hawk in northern Illinois. About the middle of June, General Atkinson detailed Captain Morgan L. Paine of Joliet and fifty volunteers from Danville to build a fort in Naperville. Fort Payne was a stockade about 100 feet square, surrounded by pickets set in the ground on two diagonal corners, which were blockhouses pierced with openings for a view of the prairies from all directions. While the fort was being built, there was one casualty — a soldier, William Brown, who was ambushed and killed while gathering wood for the fort in Sweet's Grove (near Odgen Avenue). No battles took place in the fort, for General

*James Nichols.*
*Courtesy* Naperville Sun

Winfield Scott made a treaty with the Sauks at Rock Island, thereby ending the Black Hawk War. The settlers once more resumed the task of subduing the wilderness.

Friendly Indians remained in the area for many years after the war. In subsequent years some of the much-used Indian trails formed the first roads used by the white man. In Naperville, Chicago Avenue was the Buffalo Trail and Ogden Avenue, the Ottawa Trail.

Fort Payne deteriorated after several years, but today a smaller reconstruction of the fort can be seen at Naper Settlement, Naperville's museum complex. The fort's original location was on North Central College's Fort Hill Campus, at Chicago Avenue and Ellsworth Street.

As Naper Settlement developed, it became a stagecoach stop for two important highways that formed a junction here. One ran south through Oswego, Yorkville, and Newark to Ottawa. The other was the southern stage route from Chicago to Galena laid out by Captain Joseph Naper. To accommodate the travelers, the Pre-Emption House was built. It was known far and wide for its hospitality. George Laird erected the Greek Revival building, said to have been the oldest tavern in constant operation west of the Allegheny Mountains. Considered to be the largest inn anywhere in the vicinity, it was the scene of social gatherings, and a center for horsetraders and traveling merchants. It was also used for important town meetings, such as those of the DuPage County Society for Mutual Protection.

Before government surveys were done, land claims lay in a variety of shapes and did not comply with the quarter sections designated by the government. The protection societies settled many land disputes through their arbitration boards. Land feuds and violence accompanied the early efforts of the pioneers, besieged by squatters and land sharks. Well-known early settlers whose names appear among the records as officers of protection societies were Stephen K. Scott, Henry Goodrich, Nathan Allen, Lewis Ellsworth, James Hatch, Pierce Downer, George Martin, William Strong, Morris Sleight, and Isaac Clark.

As the decade of the 1830s progressed, the town became a mixture of Easterners and Hoosiers, both bringing their own flavor to the community. Recalling early days, Judge Robert Murray, son of John Murray, states:

> . . . we were a sort of free people; we believed in doing just about as we pleased. The good brethren of the East Branch Settlement used to come here with their iron bedstead and try to fit us to it, but they found it useless and gave up the people of Naper Settlement as children of the Devil for whom there was no hope.

Despite this description, Naperville's strong religious character was established in the ensuing years. The first church was organized in 1833 by members of the East Branch Settlement. Although Presbyterian when founded, the members changed their affiliation to Congregational one year later. The Evangelical Church, established in 1837, held services in private homes until a church was built later that year. The Baptist Church was organized in 1843. By 1846 Sts. Peter & Paul Parish was started as a mission.

On March 1, 1836, a post office was established at the settlement with Alexander Howard as its first postmaster. It was also a stagecoach stop for the Templeton Line which went to Galena. Named the Pawpaw Post Office, after a grove of paw paw trees nearby, the original building has been restored and today stands in Naperville's museum complex.

DuPage was established as a county in 1839, and Naperville was selected as the county seat. Five thousand dollars were allocated for the erection of a court house, originally located near today's Central Park. Captain Joseph Naper, along with Abraham Lincoln, served in the state legislature during this period.

Naper Settlement doubled its population during the 1840s to approximately 1,300. Land was cheap and, due to the 1841 Land Act, 160 acres of land could be purchased by any head of a family. This brought many new settlers whose descendants still live in Naperville.

In the 1850s Naperville was officially chartered as a village by the State of Illinois. Its first council consisted of Joseph Naper as president, George Martin, Michael Hines, Xavier Egermann, and Hiram Cody as trustees, and Cheney Castle as clerk. Naper took office on February 7, 1857. He swore to perform faithfully the duties of office and not to accept challenges to fight duels during his term of office.

A period of business growth began. Two banks, two nurseries, the Stenger Brewery, and the Martin & King Brick and Tile Works were founded in this decade. In spite of the town's growing importance, villages in the northern section of DuPage County began demanding the removal of the county seat from Naperville. The proposition failed, but the controversy persisted.

As the town grew, a need for more schools resulted in the building of Naper Academy. It opened in 1852, first as a private school, and later as a public school, operating until 1928.

Naperville was still dependent on railroads located in nearby towns. All efforts to obtain one in Naperville failed. A need for better roads was filled, however, when a plank road was built. In 1851 the Southwestern Plank Road from Chicago to Riverside was extended to Naperville where it was linked with one under construction to Oswego. The roads were owned by private corporations which built sections. The Naperville section was owned by Naper, Skinner, Lyman & Co., W. Scott & Co., A Howard & Co., A. Keith, H. L. Peaslee & Co., and George Martin. The road consisted of a single track eight feet wide, made by laying two stringers and covering them with three-inch planks embedded in the earth. The toll charges were: 37½ cents for a four-horse vehicle, 25 cents for a single team, and 25 cents for a horse and rider. Within a very few years the road deteriorated from heavy loads and decay.

The decade of the 1860s was one of expansion, invention and unrest in the country. When the Civil War broke out, a number of Naperville's young men volunteered to go to the front; some enlisted in the 7th, 9th and 13th regiments. In 1861 the 8th Cavalry was formed, claiming more. The name of Charles Beckman stood at the head of the muster roll of Company K, 13th Infantry, the first organization that entered service for DuPage County.

Agitation over the location of the county seat reached fever pitch when an 1867 referendum authorized the change. In 1868 forty daring citizens of neighboring Wheaton appropriated the county records under the cover of darkness, thereby completing the transfer of the DuPage County Seat from Naperville to Wheaton.

The 1870s brought great and lasting improvements to the city. Northwestern College, now called North Central College, was dedicated on October 4, 1870, after its move from Plainfield. Naperville citizens had raised $25,000 and had donated eight acres of land to attract the college to Naperville. The college had a great deal of influence on the cultural and educational life of the town. It is still a growing and active institution. The city also purchased its first fire engine, the Joe Naper Pumper. Naperville's first private telephone, a mechanical type, linked the Beckman Harness Shop and the Beckman residence, over a span of three blocks.

Industrial growth throughout the country characterized the 1880s. Naperville's Lounge Factory was started as Fred Long's Furniture Shop and continued to grow in subsequent decades until it became the Kroehler Manufacturing Company. By 1915 Kroehler's was the country's largest manufacturer of upholstered furniture, and it continued to be the city's major

*Indian Hill West MTS (Members of Technical Staff). Courtesy AT&T Bell Laboratories*

employer for many years. Naperville's quarries brought a wave of German immigrants whose passage was provided because they were skilled in the use of dynamite and cutting limestone. As wealth came with industrialization, elegant homes were built in large cities and small towns alike. Some impressive examples in Naperville are the Martin-Mitchell mansion, the Nichols home, and those in Naperville's Historic District.

Naperville's musical tradition continues even today, as community band concerts capture the flavor of small-town America on summer evenings in Central Park. Friends and neighbors came closer together in the 1880s as the first public telephone and switchboard were put into use. A new city hall was built in this decade. The fire department had to purchase additional fire equipment, such as the "Enterprise" steam engine, to take care of the town's growing needs.

Naperville was organized as a city in 1890. Although agrarian in flavor, the town saw the First National Bank organized in 1891, and the Reuss Bank in 1897. The Von Oven Nurseries shipped plant material nation-wide, the Nichols's Company became known for publishing many business-related books, and the town's breweries thrived.

Thanks to a $10,000 bequest from Professor James Nichols and an appropriation from the city, Nichols Library was dedicated in 1898. By 1900 the population of the city was 2,600. Only ten years later it had reached 3,400.

The first car on the streets of Naperville appeared in 1900, marking a new era in accelerated growth. Within ten years the *Naperville Clarion* published an admonition that "speed maniacs" on newly paved streets of the town would not be tolerated. Two mail carriers were able to handle the city's needs.

The Edward Sanatorium opened on January 15, 1907, under the direction of Dr. Theodore Sachs. This institution of fourteen beds was one of the first hospitals in the Great Lakes region to offer tuberculosis treatment. The Edward Sanatorium served as a model institution for that purpose until the early 1950s when need for a tuberculosis sanatorium diminished. It was converted into a general hospital in 1955. Currently the 163-bed hospital is staffed by 620 employees and offers a complete range of health care.

When the country entered World War I in 1917, Naperville claimed sixteen of the first ninety men to enlist. After the conflict citizens staged a four-day "Homecoming" celebration which they had been planning for two years.

During the decade of the Roaring Twenties, Naperville boasted approximately 5,000 residents. People dined, danced, and listened to the sounds of Orrin Tucker and other big bands at the Spanish Tearoom. Land was purchased for the Naperville Country Club. All this happy activity, however, was interspersed with several major fires, including those of Sts. Peter and Paul Church, North Central's gymnasium, parts of the Grace Evangelical Church, and the grain elevator of Boecker Coal and Grain Co. The decade ended in despair as the stock market crashed in 1929.

The 1930s were difficult years, but with contributions solicited from townspeople, the Centennial Pageant was held and the Centennial Beach was formally dedicated. North Central College started the construction of Merner Fieldhouse, despite a decline in enrollment.

The 1940s saw Naperville with a population of 5,280, including 800 college students. There were twenty churches. Kroehler Manufacturing Company employed 900 residents. Many of the town's young men distinguished themselves in the service of their country as they marched off to fight in the Second World War.

By the 1950s the corporate city limits included slightly over six square miles. Estimates at that time indicate that there were more than 120 organizations active, many of which benefitted the city's development with their fund raising and volunteer work. The oldest among them is the Masonic Order, chartered in 1849. The school population grew significantly. Central High School and Beebe Elementary School were products of this growth.

The year 1960 was to see the single largest geographical expansion in Naperville's history. Over 1,500 acres were annexed. The two school districts had four grade schools, one junior high, and one high school. The *Naperville Sun* and the *Naperville Clarion* were the town's two weekly newspapers. The post office, hospital, and college built additions; but perhaps the most significant mark of things to come in Naperville's future was the construction of the Indian Hill Bell Laboratories. Soon,

*The Riverwalk.*

Northern Illinois Gas built a research center, and in 1967 Standard Oil-Indiana Research Center was welcomed to Naperville.

In 1968 the mayor and councilmen approved a "Fair Housing" ordinance. The Naperville Heritage Society was organized in 1969 to preserve the city tradition; this resulted in today's Naper Settlement, a museum complex. A mayoral-council-managerial form of government was approved.

A setback for Naperville in the early seventies was the annexation of Fox Valley to Aurora instead of to Naperville. This resulted in a major loss in potential sales tax revenue. The downtown, however, began to be revitalized and a major office-research center near the tollway was being developed. Nalco, *The Wall Street Journal* midwest printing facility, and other prestigious businesses located in Naperville. Improvements to Central Park were made during the bicentennial year. The population reached 40,000, and the city's outer boundaries now reached Warrenville, Lisle, Bolingbrook, and Aurora.

The year 1981, Naperville's Sesquicentennial, was typical of the community's activities, which indicate a respect for the past and a concern for the future. An historic pageant, a three-day recreation of Captain Joseph Naper's and the first settlers' trek to Naperville, a parade, concert, and other celebrations were held. Hundreds of volunteers participated and helped in making it an event to remember. Outstanding financial support and volunteer labor were cheerfully provided to the Riverwalk Project, a lasting memorial given by Naperville's citizens to their community. Today the Riverwalk is a show-place park along the banks of the DuPage River, enjoyed by citizens and tourists alike.

As of 1983, the population is 42,601. Almost 80% of employed people are white-collar workers in professional/managerial occupations. Forty-five percent of the city's land is yet undeveloped, but the projected population figure of 97,800 by the year 2,000 promises to utilize almost all existing residential space. City planners and the Naperville Park District took demographic studies into consideration in establishing fifty-nine park sites and Springbrook Golf Course. The police department has eighty-four employees, including civilians, and twenty-five police vehicles. The fire department has fifty-five full-time employees and two fire stations. Naperville has two school districts, Districts 203 and 204, comprising sixteen schools in three divisions — ten elementary, five junior high schools, and two senior high schools.

Naperville's growth has traversed the period from enchanting prairies to that of expanding industrial and residential areas, with appreciation for its pioneer heritage deepening.

**The Author**

Helen Fraser is Associate Director of the Naper Settlement.

# Oak Brook

*Etta Susan Chapek*

The 5,302 acres which now constitute the Village of Oak Brook were in prehistoric times part of the hunting domain of Indians. Artifacts associated with their campsites are idenfied as dating as long as 8,000 years ago.

Among the pioneer families to come to the Oak Brook area after Elisha Fish, who is thought to have been the first settler, were the Atwaters, Fullers, Knapps, Litchfields, Phillips, Plummers, Talmadges, Torodes and Townsends.

The Fullers' story is unusual in that Benjamin Fuller, the oldest of the twelve children of Jacob and Candace Fuller, was the instigator of his father's move from a Broome County, New York farm to what is now known as Ginger Creek and Spring Road. According to George E. Ruchty, Jr., a great-great-grandson of Jacob Fuller, the Fuller family set out for their new home in the spring of 1835. After an arduous journey on horseback and in covered wagon, lasting several weeks, they immediately set about clearing land and cutting logs to build their 25′ × 15′ cabin, with a fireplace and flagstone floor. The cabin ceiling was of rough logs and the sleeping quarters of the children were above it, reached by a ladder through an opening in the ceiling. The roof was of bark and leaked in a heavy rain or snow.

In 1840 Ben Fuller built a Greek Revival house on York Road for his family. This structure has lately been moved onto Fullersburg Forest Preserve land, and is currently being restored by the Ben Fuller Museum Association. The old Fullersburg Settlement that had been platted and recorded in 1851, but never incorporated, has been absorbed and its history shared by the villages of Hinsdale and Oak Brook.

The John Talmadges also were well-known early settlers, arriving in 1836. Their cabin, on the present site of the Hyatt-Oak Brook, was used for school and church services; and Mr.

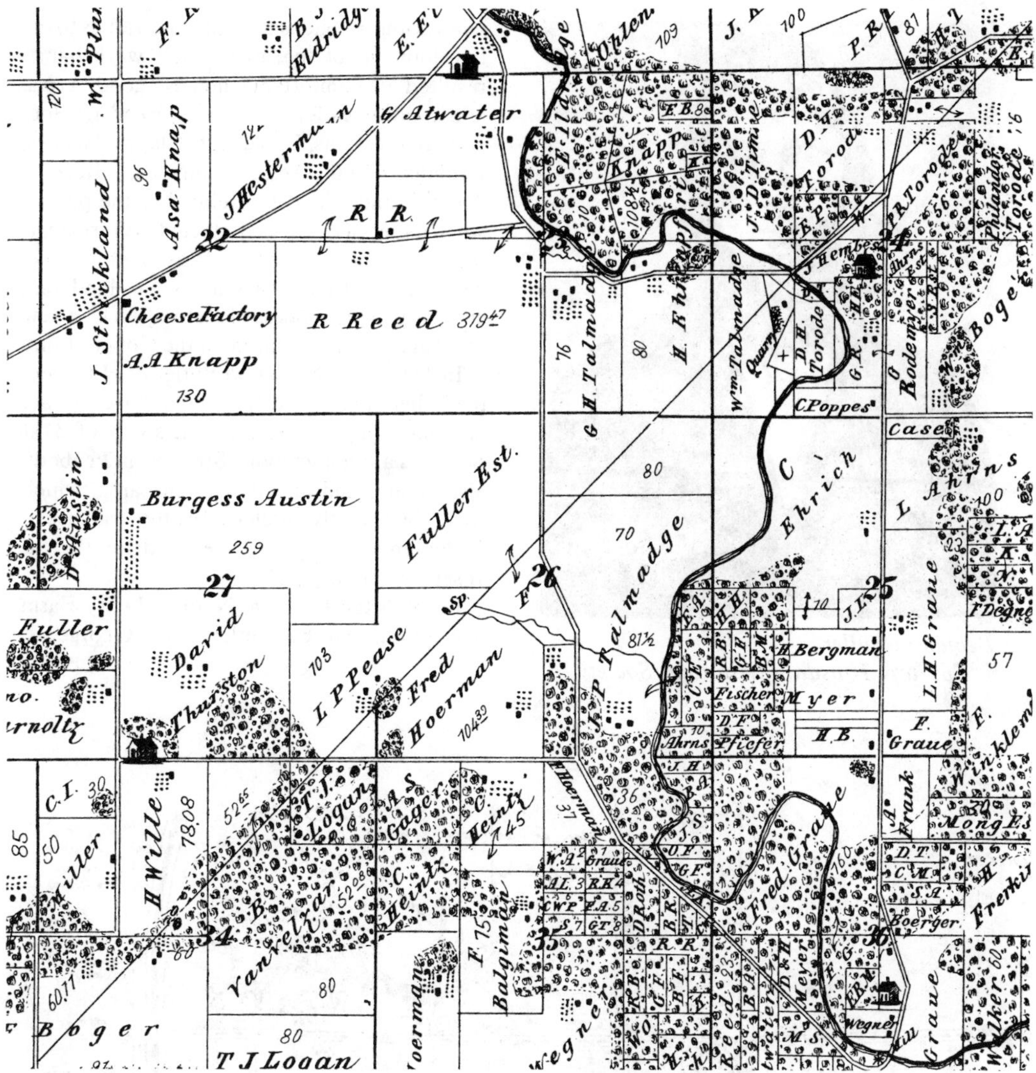


*From the* 1874 Atlas & History of DuPage County, Illinois

Talmadge was instrumental in the establishment, about 1847, of the Rabbit Hill Schoolhouse on the northeast corner of what is now Midwest and Oak Brook Road. It was the Talmadge Family that is said to have been rudely awakened one night by the sudden eruption of a mammoth spring on their farm. The great volume of water was later harnessed and provided many homes in the Oak Brook/ Elmhurst area with running water for almost a generation before its depletion. It also contributed to the success of the Mammoth Spring Ice Company, established on the south bank of Salt Creek at Washington Street by the Ruchty family.

Recruits for the Civil War undoubtedly included young men from the Oak Brook area farms. The first official call, however, took place in 1861 in Fullersburg. The youngest of the twelve Fuller children, Ben's brother Morrell, served in the Illinois Volunteer Infantry, 105th Regiment for three years.

Settlers continued to arrive in great numbers after the Civil War, including many immigrants from Europe, mostly German. These added their industry and skills, their culture

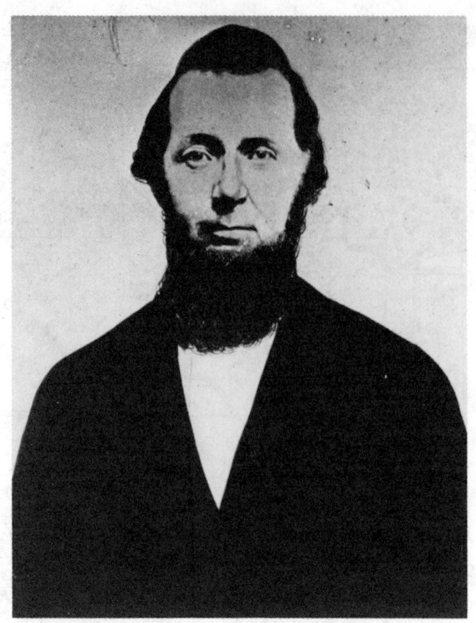

*Benjamin Fuller.*
*Courtesy Hinsdale Historical Society*

and various religious and spiritual values to the development of the area. Their work habits resulted in comfortable homes, good farms, and good times for the Ahrens, Beckers, Boegers, Boergerhofs, Brinkmans, Clapps, Henkes, Rediehs, Reineckes, Reinholds, Retzels, Timkes, and Wendels. Related to the period, when its services were conducted in German, is old St. John's Church on Washington Street near Spring Road, an Oak Brook landmark currently in the process of restoration by a new congregation, the Church on the County Line.

In 1898 Frank Osgood Butler of Hinsdale, the father of Paul and Julius, purchased a tract of land alongside Salt Creek south of 31st Street as a summer home. Stuyvesant Peabody also established an estate in the area, which was subsequently purchased by the Franciscan Order and used for retreats and for the St. Joseph Seminary (1924).

In 1906 the 160-acre Natoma Dairy Farm was purchased by Butler from George B.

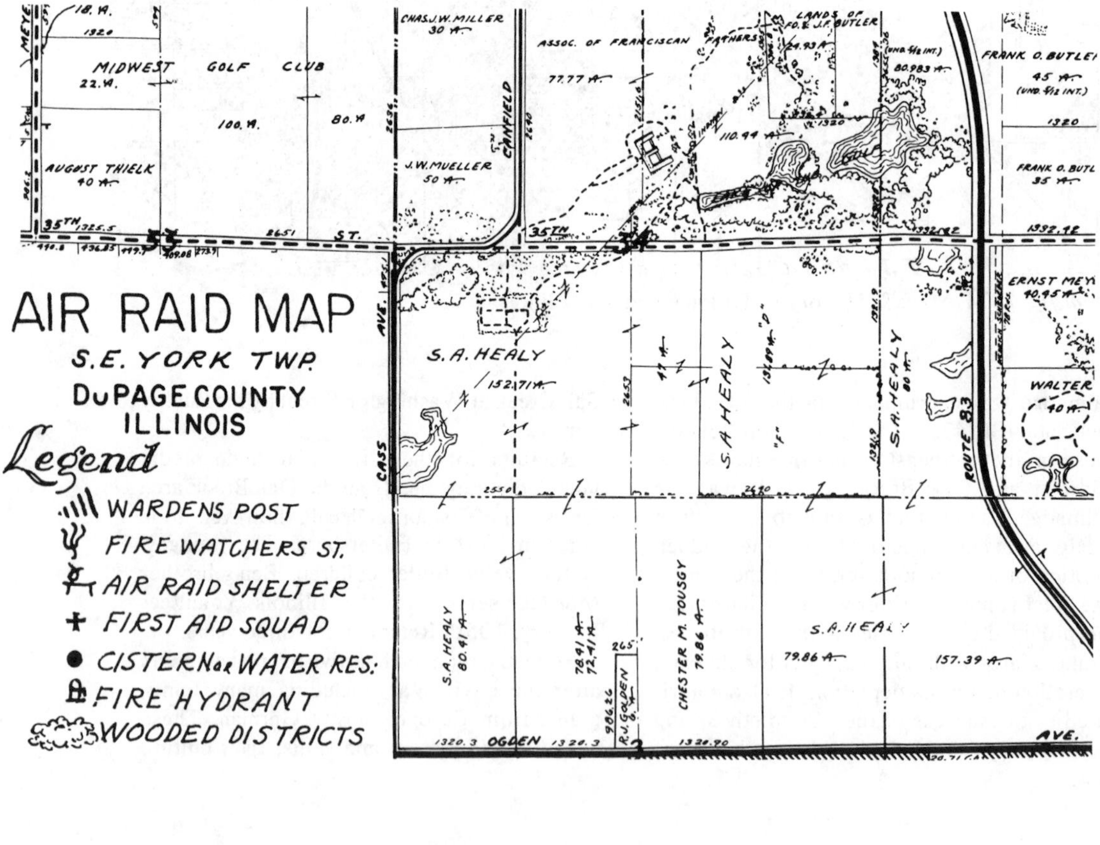
AIR RAID MAP
S.E. YORK TWP.
DuPAGE COUNTY
ILLINOIS
Legend
WARDENS POST
FIRE WATCHERS ST.
AIR RAID SHELTER
FIRST AID SQUAD
CISTERN or WATER RES:
FIRE HYDRANT
WOODED DISTRICTS
MIDWEST GOLF CLUB
AUGUST THIELK
CHAS.J.W.MILLER
J.W.MUELLER
ASSOC. OF FRANCISCAN FATHERS
FRANK O. BUTLER
CANFIELD
CASS AVE.
35TH ST.
S.A. HEALY
CHESTER M. TOUSGY
R.J. GOLDEN
ROUTE 83
WALTER
ERNST MEY
OGDEN AVE.

Robbins, substantially expanded, and for some thirty years was the only commercial enterprise in the rural area. Many of the dairy employees were not themselves local farmers, but came to the area to live near their jobs, thus increasing the population.

The Community Club, formed in Chicago's westward spread after World War I, inspired real estate activity. At least two subdivisions were platted in the Oak Brook area, but collapsed as a result of the 1929 Depression.

During the thirties and forties, however, many small parcels of one, two, five or even ten acres were sold in the Oak Brook area to individuals who proceeded to build the first new homes, with a few exceptions, since the 1880s. These new homeowners, along with the remaining farmers, formed the Community Club in the mid-thirties. This organization established Oak Brook as an entity apart from Hinsdale and Elmhurst more than a quarter of a century before its incorporation. The club combined school, parent-teacher, and recreational functions, which made for a friendly neighborhood (along with the four-to-eight telephone party lines).

By the time of the U. S. entry into World War II, the Oak Brook area had from two to three hundred families, the breadwinners in most cases employed in Chicago. Each home had its own well and septic system.

The Oak Brook Civic Association was formed in early 1942. Initially, it was organized for civil defense and the rationing necessary during the war; but gradually the association came to serve the community as assembly, news center, chamber of commerce (although there was no commercial enterprise in the area after the Natoma Dairy ceased operations in the mid-thirties), and social center. It was duly incorporated in 1945, and was likened to a town meeting, functioning through committees, including those on zoning and taxes, on fire protection, and one on "Equestrian Law

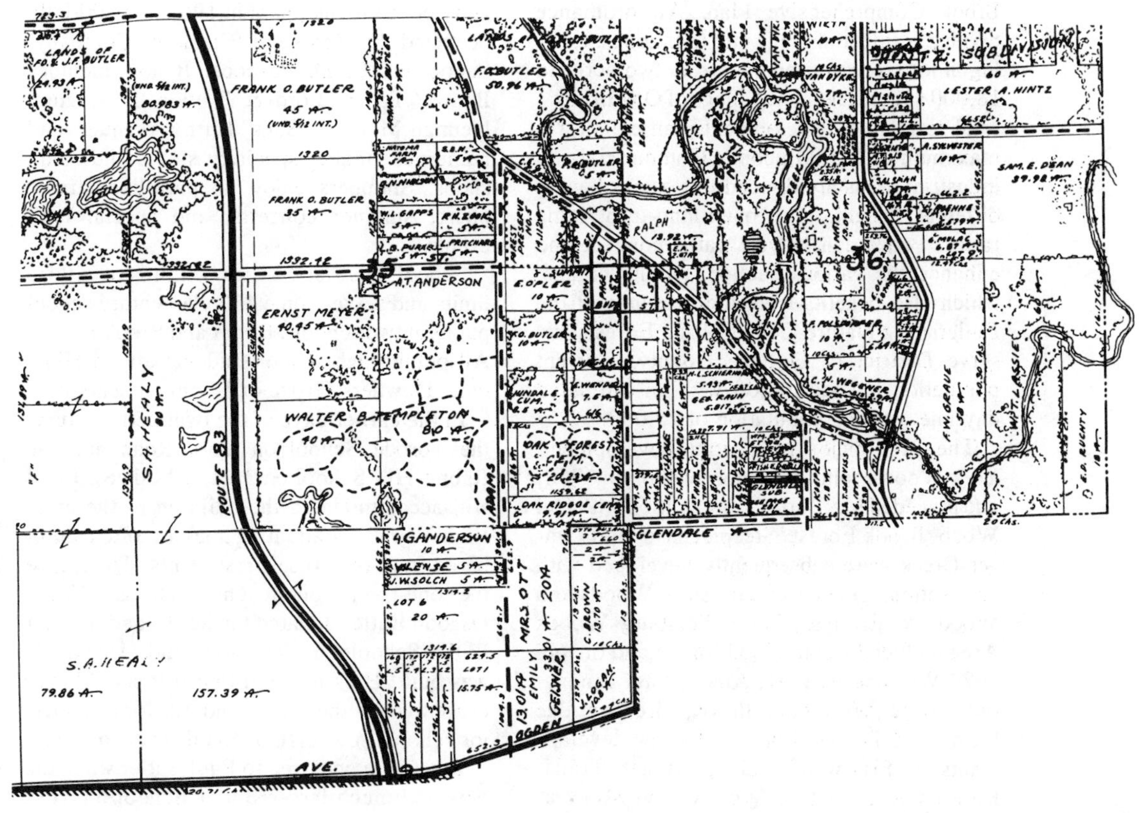

and Order." Many residents owned horses, and several stables in the area rented out or boarded horses.

Incorporation of the village occurred in 1958. The Association continues to monitor and influence developments in the village as a forum for the various homeowners associations. Proceedings of each governmental body are reported in a monthly newsletter issued by The Oak Brook Civic Association to 2,500 members.

The nationally recognized planned village within 8.3 square miles, bounded by the DuPage/Cook County Line on the east, Meyers Road on the west, Butterfield and Roosevelt roads on the north, 39th Street and Glendale Road on the south, celebrated its 25th anniversary in 1983.

It is sometimes referred to as Paul Butler's realized dream. As the largest landholder, he had consulted with such experts as Robert Kingery of the Regional Planning Commission, Carl Gardner Associates, and Garson Rohrback of General Planning & Research. Mr. Rohrbach's studies resulted in the Oak Brook Comprehensive Plan. An ordinance divided residential areas into four zones, ranging in lot size requirements from two acres to 18,000 square feet. The Village of Oak Brook's total residential development plan calls for a maximum of 10,000 people. Commercial and industrial areas are divided into zones having different height and open-land-to-building ratios. Pedestrian/bicycle paths connect and enhance the various sections of the village, which also benefits from the presence of the Fullersburg Nature Center of the Forest Preserve District of DuPage County. Current population is about 6,600 with an estimated daytime working population of 25,000.

The first major residential development, York Woods, followed incorporation in 1958, and preceded Mr. Butler's association with Del Webb. Brook Forest, Steeplechase, and Ginger Creek were subsequently developed with annexations in 1962 of Yorkshire Woods and Woodside Estates. The Fullersburg Woods Area included Robin Hood Ranch and the old 1924 Westchester Park. Among later annexations were West Oak Brook, Breckenridge Farm, and Timber Trails, with new developments in Briarwood Lakes, Hunter Trails, Forest Glen, Chateau Woods, The Midwest Club, and Saddlebrook. Still under construction are Trinity Lakes and Whitehall, with the St. Joseph Seminary property being adapted to apartment dwellings.

A unique feature is the village-owned 270-acre Oak Brook Sports Core, purchased from Paul Butler in 1977 pursuant to a vote by the residents. The Sports Core now boasts an eighteen-hole golf course, bath and tennis club, polo fields, other recreational areas, all supported by user-fees and available primarily to Oak Brook residents. The Sports Core was originally developed by Paul Butler, who was instrumental in bringing polo, the so-called "sport of kings," to the midwest. Mr. Butler, whose accidental death, the day after his 89th birthday in 1982, proved a great loss to the village, had always been an enthusiastic supporter of excellence in all fields of athletics. The Sports Core has over the years been the location of numerous fashionable benefit horse shows, international polo matches, golf tournaments and other events for which Oak Brook was noted long before it developed residentially and commercially.

The Oakbrook Center, dedicated in 1960 and opened to shoppers in 1962, was initially occupied by Marshall Field & Company, Sears, and C. D. Peacock. It now includes Bonwit Teller, Lord & Taylor, I. Magnin, Neiman-Marcus, Saks Fifth Avenue, and numerous smaller specialty stores and chain shops. Shoppers enjoy its park-like atmosphere, summer concerts, and special mall events.

School District 53 lies within the village limits and serves some 450 elementary school pupils at two schools, Butler and Brook Forest. All public high school students attend Hinsdale, Downers Grove or Elmhurst schools.

In the earlier days of the twentieth century, the Torode School on York Road and the Rabbit Hill School on 31st at Midwest Road still accommodated the children of the area. Eighth grade graduating classes often numbered from one to seven students. To replace the one-room, one-teacher schools, Frank Osgood Butler donated ten acres, and the first Butler Schoolhouse at Spring and 31st streets was built. He stipulated that if it should ever cease to meet the state standards for a "superior school," ownership would revert to him.

Reversion occurred to Paul Butler when the new and much larger Butler School on York Road replaced it, opening in September 1961.

*Paul Butler at the celebration of the sixtieth anniversary of the Oak Brook Polo Club. Courtesy The Butler Company*

Paul Butler donated ten acres of land for the new school, while making a gift of the old one to serve as village hall and library.

At that time the library represented a volunteer citizens' effort. In 1975 the village offices vacated the building to move into the adjacent, newly built Village Commons. The library, with its 30,000 volumes, now occupies the entire old Butler School building. The librarian is employed by the Village of Oak Brook.

Scores of Oak Brook residents have served as unpaid members of the board of trustees, on the zoning board of appeals, plan commission, and the school and park district boards. The park district was created in 1962, primarily to prevent any other park district from annexing the area for taxing purposes. The park district provides residents and some of the daytime working population with facilities for indoor and outdoor tennis, racquetball, and fields for baseball, softball, soccer, other outdoor sports, even fishing. A park shelter accommodates year round craft, cultural and physical exercise groups. All of these facilities exist on 141 acres, mostly in Central Park.

Evidence of continuing community involvement is the Oak Brook Volunteer Firemen's Association, survivor of the 1942 Civil Defense organization. After years of discussion and study involving the establishment of a fire district, which would have had taxing power, a volunteer commission and firemen undertook fire protection for the community, with residents making voluntary annual contributions and running benefit horse shows to acquire the necessary funds for equipment and expenses. The whole community participated in the fundraising effort, and the Oak Brook Volunteer Firemen's Association still functions right along with the paid professional and well-equipped fire department now serving the village. This cooperation represents the continuing spirit of civic pride which has characterized Oak Brook from its beginning.

**The Author**

Etta Susan Chapek has served in the Oak Brook Civic Association and Fullersburg Woods Area Association for forty years. Currently president of the Oak Brook Historical Society, she described herself as "definitely not living in the past . . . yet!"

# Roselle

*Charles Southern*

In 1836 Elijah Hough (pronounced Huff) and his family moved into the area from Massachusetts. Others in the family were his wife Electa, his daughter Cornelia, and two sons, Oramel and sixteen-year-old Roselle.

Roselle worked as a butcher and supervisor in the Chicago meat packing business until 1850, when the two brothers opened their own meat packing plant. At the London Exposition of 1852, their beef won first prize for the quality of the imported meat products. He was later a partner in the firm of Hough, Hills and Co., soap and candle manufacturers. This company used the by-products from the meat packing company.

Roselle joined the Union Army on September 10, 1861, with the rank of major. He served in Missouri, where he was wounded. He reenlisted June 13, 1862, with the rank of colonel. In 1864 Colonel Hough was active in recruiting volunteers for the army. With his help 6,000 men were recruited. On May 1, 1865, as chief marshall he led the funeral cortege for slain President Abraham Lincoln down Michigan Avenue. An estimated 37,000 people were in the march, with more than 150,000 lining the streets. This event was the culmination of his public service.

After being elected the first president of the Chicago Chamber of Commerce in 1864, and serving as a founder of the Union Stock Yards in 1865, Roselle retired from the meat packing business.

Meanwhile north Bloomingdale Township had remained rural, with few people and little business. The Civil War had little effect of this region. In 1868, however, when Roselle Hough returned to the area, he found things changing. Cotton production in the South had all but stopped as an aftermath of the war. There was a demand for cloth that could be produced from flax. Roselle began growing this crop on land he had bought from his father, before Elijah's death in 1851. He also formed

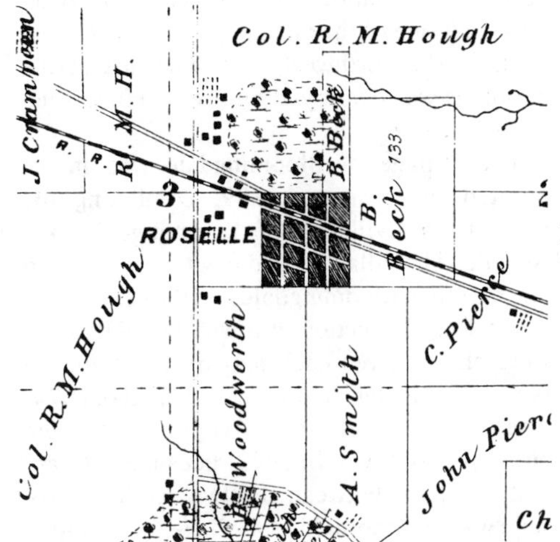


*From the* 1874 Atlas & History of DuPage County, Illinois

the Illinois Linen Company and built a large flax factory to manufacture linen and rope. He found the soil good for growing flax, and so had a profitable business.

When Colonel Hough started this company, he had one major problem; there were no all-weather roads, and travel to Chicago was an all day trip. The Chicago & Pacific Railroad Company, now the Milwaukee Road, solved this problem by building a rail line between Chicago and Elgin. The original plan called for the line to go along Lake Street through Bloomingdale; but because Hough had financial and political clout, he was able, for $10,000, to have the route resurveyed. This took the railroad through the Roselle section of Bloomingdale Township. In 1875 he had his land platted, and called it Roselle.

Because he needed many workers and little housing was available, he erected many buildings. The most famous and the largest, except for the factory, was one to house his workers, called the "Bee Hive," because it was always so busy. But with progress came problems. Because the population of the area was small, and most of its inhabitants were farmers, Hough had to hire men from Chicago, the only place with an adequate labor supply. He hired ruffians and ex-convicts, the only men he could get to do the type of work called for in the flax fields and mill. The men would go to the two saloons in the area after work, start fights, and in a few cases, gunfights. Roselle became comparable to the "wild west," and was often referred to in those days as "Raise Hell."

Colonel Hough stayed in Roselle until 1880, at which time he sold his business interests in this area. Hough then settled in Cheyenne, Wyoming, where he had a cattle company and land holdings. In declining health, the Colonel returned to Chicago in 1890, where he died March 8, 1892.

In 1895 the flax mill was shut down. Cotton was once again king in the South; moreover the Roselle soil had become exhausted after its many years of growing flax. These two reasons rendered the flax mill useless.

The building was converted to a tile and brick company by Chicago businessmen who had purchased the property. By then Roselle had lost all of its wild west flavor, and was once again a middle-American farm town. By 1900 the clay that had been found in the area also gave out, and the brick and tile company was closed. This factory was located on the northwest corner of what is now Roselle and Irving Park roads.

In the year 1898 a few of the business men of Roselle formed an organization called the "Roselle Park Club," in which they sold stock. In a wooded picnic area at the northwest corner of Park and Irving Park, this group built a pavillion with a dance floor, food stands, game rooms and a bowling alley. In 1908 the Milk Dealers Association had their picnic at the grove, with trains bringing over 6,000 people

*Roselle Hough.*
*Courtesy Roselle Historical Society*

from Chicago. Many groups and organizations used these facilities in the years to come, making it one of the most popular recreational spots in the northwest area. The last of the buildings was destroyed by fire on Halloween night in 1939.

The Village of Bloomingdale was incorporated in February 1889, combining the present day villages of Bloomingdale and Roselle. The village board meetings were held one month in Bloomingdale and the next month in the Roselle section of town. Three trustees were chosen from each part of the town, the boundaries being identified by the plat of 1874. The mayor was elected by popular vote from either part of town. In 1922, because of financial problems between the two sections, Roselle was incorporated as a village. At that time the population was 225 on a land area of about one square mile. Roselle still has six trustees, who are elected at large, and a mayor.

In 1902 a charter was granted by the State of Illinois to the Roselle State Bank. It was and is

*The Hattendorf Home, 1890.*
*Courtesy Roselle Historical Society*

*Medinah Country Club.*
*Courtesy Roselle Historical Society*

still located on the corner of Irving Park Road and Prospect Avenue although the original bank building was replaced by the present modern structure in 1959. Because most people who lived in the Roselle area were German, the first bank statement was written in German. The first directors were J. H. Hattendorf, W. Kruse and three brothers H. H., C. A. and W. F. Franzen. This business is still strong after eighty years of operation.

By 1922 Roselle provided electric service for those who could afford it. Illinois Bell built an exchange in 1938 because of the increase in business. A new village hall was built in 1934 to replace the barn that had been in use since 1922. The public library was started in 1941, and in 1982 a new library building opened.

T.V. Channel 5 on June 25, 1972, featured Roselle in one of its specials. When sixty-year-old Trinity Lutheran Church advertised a church for sale, the station noticed the ad. The focus of the show was upon the church and other institutions as stabilizing influences on the community. Interviewed were Reverend Trieglaff, then pastor of Trinity, Mayor R. Frantz, and Mrs. R. Fenz, the oldest resident born in Roselle.

After World War II the population nationally began to shift to the suburbs, and Roselle grew from a small village of 694 in 1940 to a 1983 population of over 17,000. There are currently 3,872 single family homes and 2,677 multiple family dwellings. Current industry includes firms in lithography, in tool & die, and in other light industry.

Roselle is actively working on a new town center, making major improvements on Main Street, and restoring buildings as landmarks as recommended by the Roselle Historical Society. Several have been marked and restored. Roselle looks forward to a bright future.

**The Author**
Charles Southern was elected chairman of the Roselle Historical Society in January, 1978, the year of its establishment. He has continued as an active member ever since.

# Villa Park

*Irene S. Martin*

What is now Villa Park was once open prairie, criss-crossed by Indian trails. By the mid-1800s there were fifteen white families in the present-day Villa Park area. These were mostly German settlers who had come looking for good farm land. A map of the farms in 1862 shows the names of Frederick Graue, Henry Backhaus, Diedrick Meyer, August Strueber, H. F. Goltermann, Frederick Ahrens, and H. Hograue. Some of the old farm houses still stand — the Goltermann home at 27 E. Jackson, the Potter-Finke home at 222 W. Madison, and the Meyer-Domianus home at 618 S. Ardmore. All were built before the Civil War.

In a small handmade book is the first recorded entry for School District 9, dated April 1857. J. Loy, F. Summers, and A. Hatfield were elected directors. The school house was built on two lots on the corner of St. Charles Road and Meyers Road (Westmore). The lots cost $10.00 each. N. N. Johnson was hired to teach and do janitorial work at $33.00 per month.

In 1895 there were twenty-nine families. The district was renumbered District 45, which it remains today. The school was so crowded that when the Walter Olmacht family came to Villa Park in 1911, their son Frank had to delay attending a year until Ardmore School opened in 1912. Most of these same families went to the German United Reformed Lutheran Church in Dunklee's Grove (Bensenville today).

With increasing settlement came the need for better transportation. Farmers first went to Cottage Hill (Elmhurst today) to take the Frink and Walker Stagecoach. By 1849 they traveled on the Galena and Chicago Union Railroad (Chicago & Northwestern). At the close of the 19th century, the vicinity was still sparsely settled farmland. Then came the Aurora, Elgin and Chicago Railway, a double track electric system. Florence Canfield and

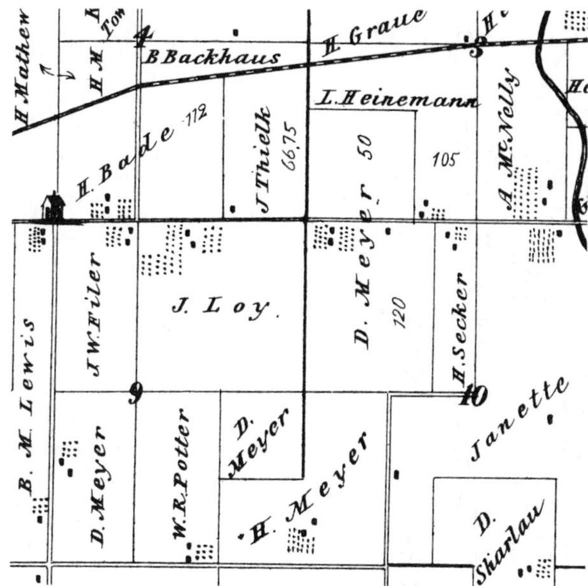


*From the* 1874 Atlas & History of DuPage County, Illinois

Louis Meyer, two farmers, granted it a right-of-way through their land. The farm abstract of the Canfield land showed that it had been granted on April 19, 1900, for a consideration of $1.00. It was not long before Chicago real estate developers, Ballard and Pottinger, spotted the open land and saw an opportunity for opening a town along the new railroad.

What had been rumored to become a new cemetery instead became Villa Park. Its development was unique in that it began as two separate subdivisions. Villa Park was recorded in the DuPage County Recorder's office in 1908, and Ardmore to the west in 1910. To entice buyers of lots Ballard and Pottinger built Ardmore School, a train station, and planted hundreds of poplar trees along the newly laid-out streets. The firm ran free Sunday promotional excursions. Those who bought acre lots had their choice of 200 baby chicks or twenty apple trees.

The new communities attracted Chicago families who wanted country living. Among them were brokers, builders, bankers, and real estate men who built attractive homes. One of these was the Charles C. Heisen home on Villa Avenue, built about 1908. The twenty-one room mansion was constructed for Heisen's second wife, a New York actress. She took one look at muddy little Villa Park and returned to New York. Heisen was the wealthiest man in Villa Park. His office in the Harris Trust Building in Chicago was headquarters for varied business interests. He built many homes in Villa Park and presented a building for the first church, the Community Congregational Church. He also owned the only water system in town.

Another interesting resident was William Calhoun, who preferred to be called "Colonel." His home was also on Villa Avenue. Colonel Calhoun opened the first store in Villa Park. To inform people when the store was open for business, he flew a red flag from a tall pole on top of the store. The building was later moved around the corner to Central Boulevard, and is now an attorney's office.

Near the Heisen home was that of John Montgomery, a Chicago banker. His son Jack became a cowboy stuntman who doubled for Tom Mix and other Hollywood stars in the 1930s. Jack's daughter became a child star at Century Studio where she appeared in 150 two-reel comedies. She was billed as Baby Peggy.

There was much rivalry between Villa Park and Ardmore. However, in order to acquire tax money for community improvements the two subdivisions united in 1914. The Village of Ardmore was incorporated on August 8, 1914.

Subdivision of Villa Park - 1908

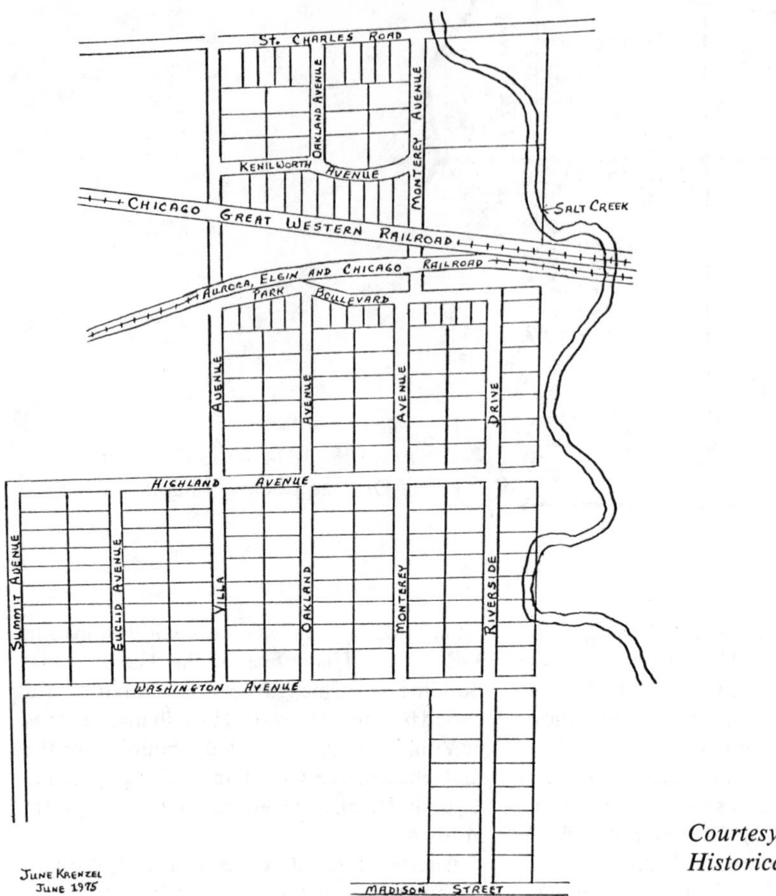


*Courtesy of Villa Park Historical Society*

The name was contested by the Villa Park section, and a vote taken in 1917. Since there were more people living in the Villa Park section, the name was changed to Villa Park on October 15, 1917, leaving many disgruntled citizens on the west side of the village. At that time the population was 300.

Women in Villa Park were interested in politics. Five years before the 19th Amendment gave women the right to vote, Marie Lueck had run for police magistrate, but lost. In 1916 Jeanette Bates was appointed first village attorney. She left office during the next year because she had been appointed assistant attorney general for Illinois, the first woman in an attorney general's office in the United States.

In 1917 Gottlieb Steiner was sent from Bern, Switzerland to set up the American factory for the Wander Company, the maker of Ovaltine. Villa Park had been chosen for the site because of the good water, the availability of farm products used in the manufacturing process, and the excellent transportation. Steiner's temporary assignment lengthened into thirty-seven years. Steiner is remembered for his many civic interests. He was one of the founders of Elmhurst Memorial Hospital and a leader in establishing the Villa Park Trust and Savings Bank.

Since it opened, Ovaltine has been headquartered at Number 1 Ovaltine Court. During both World Wars its product was used in Allied hospitals to aid in the recuperation of soldiers suffering from combat fatigue. Ovaltine has been an official supplier to the Summer and Winter Olympics since 1932. In the 1930s the company sponsored Little Orphan Annie programs on radio; Captain Midnight on radio in the 1940s, and on T.V. in the 1950s. Ovaltine grew to be Villa Park's largest industry and its greatest benefactor, especially during the Depression.

Even though Villa Park was a very small village when World War I began, there were twenty-nine men who enlisted. In 1920 twenty-six of them became charter members of the Villa Park American Legion Post 652. In 1929 the post purchased the old Community Congregational Church for its headquarters.

In the wake of World War I, Villa Park boomed. The population doubled in 1920 and 1925. New homes were going up rapidly. The streets were cinder, and only Ardmore Avenue had street lights, which were paid for by the Ardmore Community Club. There were no sidewalks. A common sight was a row of boots lined up at the train station, awaiting their owners for their muddy walk home. During the 1920s electricity was obtained from Chicago, Aurora & Elgin Railway generators in Lombard.

York High School was opened for Elmhurst and Villa Park students in 1924. Four elementary schools were built and the first full-time school superintendent, H. E. Hinkle, was hired. There were four new churches. Community services included a volunteer fire department organized by the Lions Club. Other developments in that decade were the building of a new village hall in 1929, the paving of Ardmore, Highland and Villa avenues, the publication of a newspaper called the *Villa Park Weekly News,* and house-to-house mail delivery.

Villa Park was acknowledged to be the Chicago, Aurora & Elgin's largest commuting customer; the railway was largely responsible for the community's growth. Villa Parkers no longer had to go to Elmhurst or Lombard to shop, to attend the movies, or to attend a funeral.

*Jeanette Bates, first village attorney. Courtesy Villa Park Historical Society*

Then came the Depression, which hit Villa Park very hard. Many families had bought lots to build homes; instead, they put up garages or only basements. Some lots became gardens, but many were just weed patches. In 1932 there were over 300 destitute families. Stores extended credit; doctors "forgot" to charge; and bartering became common. Kranz Hardware Store exchanged a keg of nails for a woman's diamond ring. Ovaltine (Wander Company) helped the banks remain open, established a relief fund, and took Ovaltine to all the school children. Canning parties were held in the churches. There were many W.P.A. sponsored activities; tennis and basketball courts were installed. The Men's Garden Club was formed, and is known today as the world's largest men's garden club. Free amateur shows were presented at the Community Congregational Church, and a private kindergarten was opened by Mrs. Raymond Sears in her home. In 1931, despite the hard times, Villa Park had the lowest crime rate in DuPage County.

Then came Pearl Harbor. Many young men and women joined the armed services. The Ardmore Community Club raised money for the service men and women. Victory gardens were planted along the Chicago, Aurora & Elgin's right-of-way. Teen-agers collected scrap iron and paper. Red Cross work was done at the V.F.W. Post 2801, and service flags were in windows throughout the town. After World War II young families flocked to Villa Park. Unincorporated areas were annexed and developed along North Avenue on the north and Roosevelt Road on the south. The population increased from 8,000 in 1940 to 25,000 in 1965. In 1950 the Reedy Ranch Homes, with twenty-five-year mortgages at 5½% interest, were rapidly erected. The influx of people brought the need for more schools and churches of other denominations. Elementary schools were enlarged. Jackson Junior High School and Willowbrook High School were built. Harold Reskin's Midland Enterprise opened homes in the northwest section of Villa Park between 1955 and 1960. The library purchased the old Trinity Lutheran Church at 305 South Ardmore for its first permanent home, having been in six different locations previously.

After the opening of Congress Street Expressway (Eisenhower) in the mid-fifties, the Chicago Aurora & Elgin abandoned passenger service in 1957 — a sad event for Villa Park. In the 1960s the track was removed and the roadbed became the Illinois Prairie Path, which extends like a ribbon through the village from east to west.

In the late 1950s Villa Park identified itself as "The Garden Village," incorporating it into the logo which it uses today. In 1954 the Woman's Club was presented with an award by the DuPage County Board of Realtors for extraordinary accomplishment in the improvement and beautification of the community. Also in that year the Easter Seal Center purchased the old Salt Creek School and moved it to 706 E. Park Boulevard. Two years later it became the DuPage Chapter of the Illinois Association for the Crippled.

Progress continued in the 1960s. Tax referenda were passed for enlarging schools and a new wing was added to Willowbrook High School. In 1965 the Park Development Program began with ten parks on forty-five acres. People no longer asked, "Where is the park in Villa Park?" A new library opened in 1969, a far cry from the store front at 317 S. Ardmore in 1928, with its 400 books collected in a little red wagon in a house-to-house drive. There was 90% home ownership. Professional people comprised 15% of the population, which had reached a peak of 25,000. In 1965 Villa Park celebrated its Golden Jubilee.

The last decades have seen many changes. Businesses have sprung up, especially on the north and south boundaries. For years Ovaltine was the only factory of any size. In the 1970s a large industrial tract on North Avenue developed. Today there are seventy-nine manufacturers listed for Villa Park in the 1982 Illinois Manufacturer's Directory, and 846 businesses noted in the Villa Park Chamber of Commerce.

In the early days the two separated business districts on Villa Avenue and Ardmore Avenue flourished. Now two large shopping centers, North Park Mall on North Avenue and Villa Oaks Shopping Center on Roosevelt Road, have again created separate districts in the four-mile long village. The old downtown is suffering. The shopping centers, however, generate revenues which provide capital to meet the need of the village.

The Odeum opened in 1983 and is a multipurpose facility for entertainment, the fourth largest free-span building in the United States. In that same year the first phase of a $12,000,000 project to reduce flooding was completed.

Villa Park is a maturing community, with no room to grow. This fact accounts for the decline of student population from a peak of 6,700 in 1967, to 3,600 in 1983. Eight of the fourteen schools closed are due to declining enrollment. One of the closed school buildings is now a popular senior citizen's center.

There are other changes. In the beginning Villa Park citizens were mostly of German and Swedish origin, and of Lutheran religious practice. Today there are persons of English, Italian, Polish, Spanish, and French descent with 80% of newcomers being of the Roman Catholic faith. According to the 1980 census, there were 22,356 whites, 124 blacks, 22 American Indians, 73 Japanese, 33 Chinese, 107 Filipinos, 79 Koreans, 17 Vietnamese, and 151 Asian Indians.

Thirty years ago there were virtually no apartments in Villa Park. Today there are over

*The Ovaltine Factory.*
*Courtesy Villa Park Historical Society*

1,900 apartments, town houses, and condominium units interspersed with two-story homes, modest bungalows, ranches, and split levels. The population has decreased from 25,000 to 23,185. The village has received a $40,000 state grant for devising a master plan, which will go to the DuPage Regional Planning Commission for an analysis of the community.

This history would not be complete without recognizing the contribution made by a variety of civic minded men and women.

Mrs. Bessie Mabee and her husband bought the first home in Ardmore. She was the first president of the Woman's Club. She is best known for writing in 1936 the first history of Villa Park.

Pete McAleese worked with youths coaching baseball and track for three generations. He worked at R. R. Donnelly Company, and often rode his bicycle to work in the city.

Mrs. Hilda Schulze lived in Villa Park for more than sixty years. She was known for her work as Public Health Nurse for DuPage County.

Dr. L. R. Cortesi started the first emergency medical service in the fire department. He was also the Ovaltine and the Willowbrook sports doctor.

Father Kennedy came to Villa Park in 1924. Under his leadership St. Alexander's Church, fondly called the "Wooden Ark," was built. It was to be only a temporary structure; but due to the Depression it was used until 1953. The St. Alexander's school was built in 1925 because he felt it was needed more than the church building. Father Kennedy lived to see his dream come true. The new church was dedicated in 1954.

Since 1976 Villa Park has become history conscious. During the bicentennial the village purchased the two Chicago, Aurora and Elgin railroad stations. In 1977 the Villa Park Historical Society was incorporated, as was the Historical Commission, an arm of the village government. In 1978 the historical society leased the Villa Avenue station and rededicated it as a museum, exactly fifty years after its construction. In 1980 the Historical Commission was able to obtain listing of the Ardmore station on the National Register of Historical Places, as an example of Prairie School architecture. Restoration of the building is underway. It will be dedicated as a half-way stop on the Prairie Path for hikers and bicyclists.

The 125th year of School District 45 was marked in 1983, with a time capsule buried in Memorial Park. It will be opened in the year 2008.

As viewed in the perspective of this history, it is evident that community spirit, combined with hard work, brought Villa Park through many ups and downs. We trust that the same process will continue to do so in the future.

**The Author**

Irene S. Martin is Young Adult Librarian at the Villa Park Public Library. Previously while teaching in public schools, she developed the concept and served as co-editor of *Illinois Junior Historian Magazine*, presently titled *Illinois History*, now in its 36th year of publication.

# City of Warrenville

*Mary Curtis*

Daniel Warren, accompanied by his son-in-law Frederick Bird, left Westfield New York in April 1833 and claimed land two miles north of the Naper settlement at McDowell Woods. In July his son Julius arrived with his sisters, Sarah Warren and Louisa Bird.

In 1834 Julius took over the land he had claimed the previous year for a lumber business, with holdings on both sides of the DuPage River. At the same time he built a house, which is among the oldest still standing in DuPage County. In 1835 he put up a boarding house for the men who worked in his newly constructed sawmill.

Religion was to play a vital role in the fledgling community. The fact was evident in 1836, with the establishment of the Second Baptist Church, an offshoot of the First Baptist Church in Naperville. The Third Annual Meeting of the Northern Baptist Association of Illinois in 1838 was hosted by the Warrenville church. At that meeting a resolution was passed condemning slavery because Elijah Lovejoy, an Abolitionist newspaper editor, had been recently murdered at Alton, Illinois.

That year also saw Warren's recently built tavern at Warrenville and Winfield roads become a social center, renowned for Friday night dances. A frequent visitor was "Long John" Wentworth, editor of the *Chicago Democrat* and later mayor of Chicago.

Colonel Warren was elected to the state legislature in 1844. The Warrenville Cemetery was incorporated on March 3, 1845.

The Warrenville Seminary, open to persons of all faiths, was incorporated on March 3, 1845. It opened in September 1851 under the leadership of Seraph Warren Holmes. Benjamin F. Taylor, the literary editor of the *Chicago Evening Journal*, briefly taught the men. It attracted many students from Chicago, with as many as 200 enrolled at one time. It was closed during the Civil War.

The Chicago-Southwestern Plank Road was

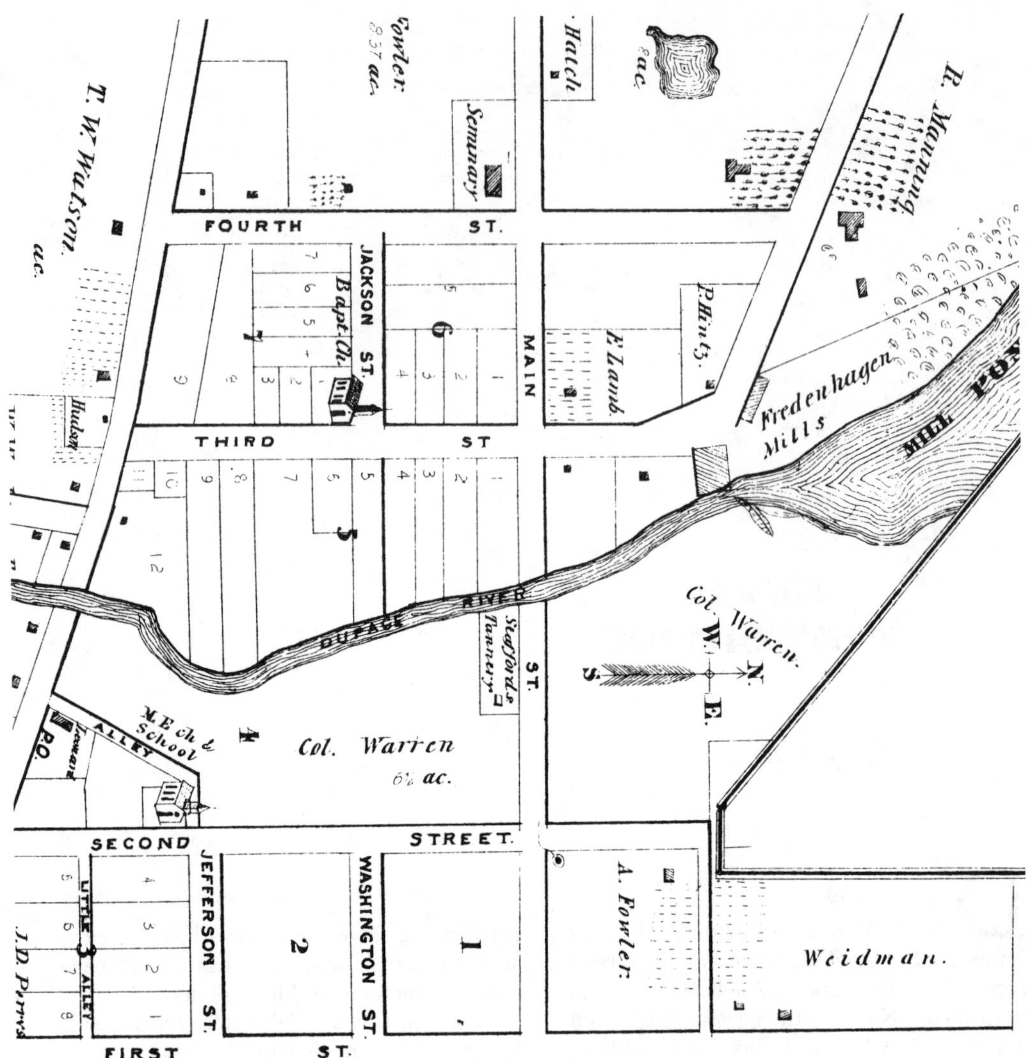


*From the* 1874 Atlas & History of DuPage County, Illinois

approved by the legislature in 1849. Colonel Warren operated a stage between Winfield, Warrenville and Naperville, the true link to the ouside world.

An important part of the business community in 1847 was the newly constructed Warrenville grist mill, operated by Warren and Franklin Smith, and Alvah Fowler. It was later purchased and run by Rockwell Manning and John Grant. In 1857 Victor Fredenhagen and his brother-in-law, William Lambe, acquired the thriving business. The dam by the gristmill also provided a recreational spot for the area. It served as well as a baptismal font for the churches. The gristmill was destroyed by fire in 1879, but was soon rebuilt.

The Methodists, led by Rev. Charles Wesley Gary, were beginning to make their presence known locally, and organized a congregation of seventeen members in 1854. Most of the wood for the new church, which was built on Second Street in 1858, was cut at Gary's Mill, near West Chicago. Since the church had a cement basement, it provided classroom space for the public school until 1883, when a new school was built on Winfield Road. After the Methodist Church discontinued, the building was sold in 1910 to the "Live Wires," a social club which sponsored many dances there. It later housed the studios of Adam Emory Albright and his sons Ivan and Malvin. In recent years it has housed the Footlighters Theatre and the Albright Theatre Company. It is currently being remodeled by the city of Warrenville to provide space for the Centel Cable TV Company, the Warrenville Historical Society and a museum.

From a population of 250 Warrenville sent fifty of its sons to fight in the Civil War. Seventeen of them gave their lives in the Union cause. Ashley Carpenter, at age twenty, was the first casualty to be buried in the Warrenville Cemetery, in 1862.

When the Chicago, Burlington & Quincy completed the tracks to Aurora in 1864, Warrenville was bypassed. The Chicago, Millington and Western Railroad was scheduled to pass through Warrenville in 1873, but the Panic of that year brought the dream to nothing. In 1898 when William Manning had succeeded Colonel Warren as "leading citizen," he pledged $5,000 for the LaGrange, Warrenville & Fox River Electric Railroad; but again this proved wishful thinking. A railroad was finally brought through the area, a year after the first "horseless carriage" had come to Warrenville, in 1901. The Chicago, Aurora and Elgin Electric Railway began service on August 25, 1902, and served the town until declining revenues forced it out of business in 1959. "Growing pains" found the Manning tract becoming the largest sub-division in DuPage County in 1906.

Illinois Bell opened Margaret Mackin Hall as a rest home for telephone operators in 1916. This is now the Warrenville Cenacle, the site of many retreats. The river frontage near the old mill site was sold to the Forest Preserve District. Montgomery Ward established a vacation home for employees in the old Warren mansion.

The Community Building became a reality, thanks to the Men's Club, which eventually became the Warrenville Community Club. In

SOCIAL BALL.

Your company is respectfully requested at a Ball at the Warrenville Assembly Room, on Friday, the 5th instant.

Managers.

| | | |
|---|---|---|
| N. M. Lord, | Charles Clark, | Ralph Haskins. |
| James P. Johnson, | Richard Wilson, | W. V. Plumb. |
| B. T. Hunt, | I. B. Berry, | C. D. Bristol. |
| L. G. Butler, | J. M. Warren, | |

WARRENVILLE, FEB. 1, 1841.

*Invitation to a Warrenville Ball.*
*Courtesy Leone Schmidt*

*Ivan Albright — posing in the model used for his painting provisionally named "The Window." This was one of many works done during the two decades the artist lived in Warrenville.*
*Courtesy Willis Stafford*

1928 it bought land for a town hall, subsequently managing to secure funds for a building from the WPA. This was transferred to the school district as the only taxing body in town. The building was completed in 1938, and a room was set aside for a town library, which was sponsored by the Warrenville Woman's Club. It has also served as a gym and lunchroom for Holmes School, across the street, and storage for District 200. With the latest remodeling, it now houses the Warrenville Public Library and is the center for many community activities. It is also now "home" for the Albright Theatre.

Raoul Lund, the former gardener on the Julius Rosenwald estate, arrived in Warrenville in 1921. Having paid $300 for used buildings, he opened the R. C. Lund Greenhouses on Winfield Road.

Farmers began selling their land to developers after World War I. In 1927 the first addition was made to Warrenville, on the east side of town.

During the days of prohibition, western DuPage County and eastern Kane County had their share of bootlegging activity. The notorious Roger Touhy got his scar from a policeman's bullet in a shootout in the Warrenville area.

As the town grew, incorporation became a matter of debate. The first referendum, on October 29, 1927, was defeated 158–56. The next referendum, in 1954, was followed by five other unsuccessful attempts. Proponents of

*CA&E Station, now Warrenville Municipal Building*

incorporation finally realized their dream when the referendum of May 20, 1967, was approved by a vote of 641–518. In the first city election William Stafford, descendant of one of the early Warrenville families, became the city's first mayor.

It was also in the sixties that the Northern Illinois Gas Company Building on Ferry Road was dedicated. Governor Otto Kerner officiated at this event in 1963.

The Chicago, Aurora and Elgin station was remodeled in 1969–70 to serve as the city hall and police station. Another highlight of the 1970s was the annexation of the Triplett property on Batavia Road, when the town's population was just under 4,000. The Emerald Green and McKeon Development was built on this site later in the decade. The Western Electric Computer Center on River Road became operational in 1972. During the 1970s the Albright Theatre presented plays at the Albright Building. Later it moved to Villa Park; then the theatre returned to Warrenville after the Community Building had been remodeled. Standard Oil of Indiana and The Illinois Department of Corrections exchanged property. Subsequently, Amoco Research Center along Warrenville road and a boys' home on Ferry Road, west of Route 59 were built.

In the 1970s Mount Hoy, nicknamed Mount Trashmore, was built by combining refuse and soil into a hill now popular for tobaggoning and tubing. The construction of Silver Lake has made the Blackwell Forest Preserve a very popular recreational area. During excavations for the lake in 1977, a worker uncovered large bones, which he deemed important. These proved to be the remains of the "Warrenville Mammoth," or sometimes called "Jones Bones," after the discoverer.

Woodland School was closed in 1978, and Bower Junior High became an elementary school. Wheaton-Warrenville High School was closed at the end of the 1982–83 school year, but reopened as a middle school for youngsters in Warrenville and in the southern section of Wheaton.

Warrenville had a 1980 population of 7,800. It marked its sesquicentennial with a 1983–84 celebration. Citizens look forward to a future worthy of its past.

### The Author

Mary Curtis is a thirty year resident of DuPage County, having come as Dean of Women at North Central College in 1955. Since 1967 she has written the "Warrenville News" section of *The Daily Journal.*

# Wayne

*Tannisse T. Blatchford*

Late in July 1832, a contingent of General Winfield Scott's army crossed the Wayne area, on their way to reinforce the Illinois militia which was fighting Chief Black Hawk and his Sauk braves. They camped along the West Branch of the DuPage River, about a mile and a half north of future Wayne Center. The present Army Trail Road commemorates their passage, although this road was not the actual route.

It was May 1834, when permanent white settlers arrived in Wayne Township. John Laughlin, a twenty-seven-year-old bachelor, reached here on May 8th. He was the first to establish a claim in the area. Robert Y. and Nancy Benjamin, with the first four of their eight children, together with Robert's father Daniel and brother John, came from Warren County, Indiana. They chose their land on May 12th, and built a log cabin within three days.

Both companies located in a grove of sheltering trees on a rise of ground that overlooked the newly emerging prairie grasses and flowers. The Benjamins' homestead was located just east of the West Branch of the DuPage River in Section 26, while Laughlin's claim lay four and a half miles to the west, in Section 19.

The following year Edmund Bartlett and Solomon Dunham emigrated from New York State, and "took up land" north and south of the present junction of Dunham and Army Trail Roads. During the next quarter century there was a multiplying of new settlers including: Luther Bartlett, John Glos, Elijah L. Guild, John and Abraham Kershaw, Joseph McMillen, Peter Pratt, Theodore Schramer and John Smith. By 1861 all the land had been claimed, settled, and divided between cultivation and pasture. As DuPage County was divided into nine voting precincts in 1839, the Orange region included Wayne Township, as well as parts of present Bloomingdale and Winfield townships. When Bloomingdale Pre-

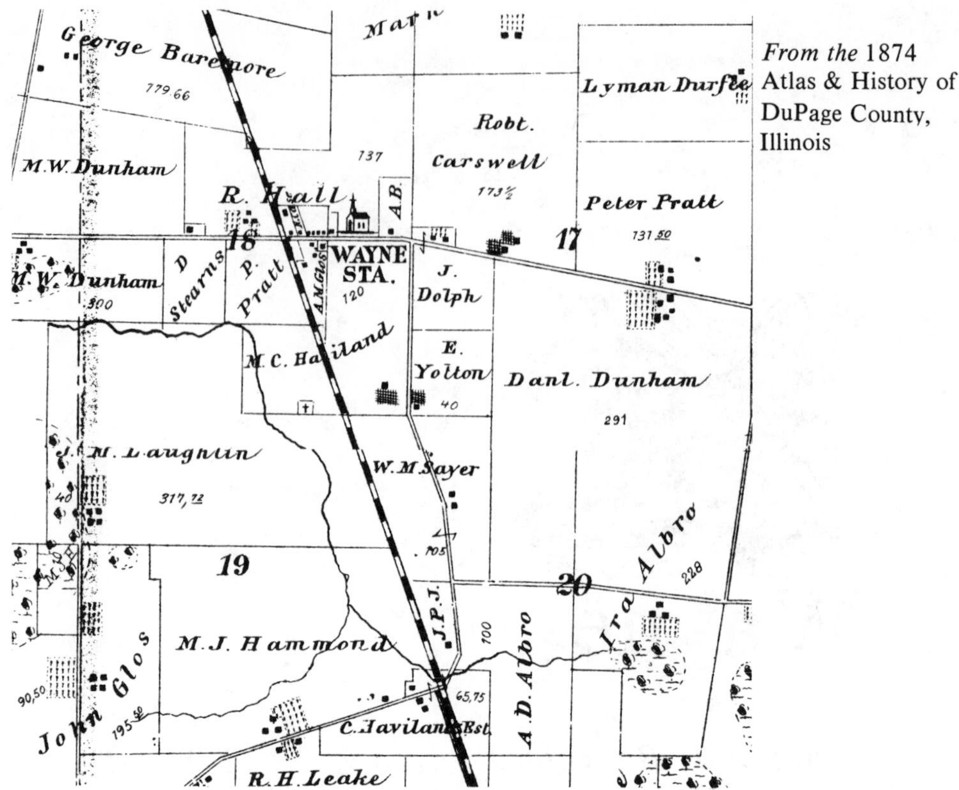


*From the* 1874 Atlas & History of DuPage County, Illinois

cinct was formed in 1841, the original precinct decreased in size. Three years later, the County Commissioners' Court directed that elections be held at Joseph McMillen's farm house, on the northwest corner of present day Route 59 and Army Trail Road.

The first settlement was the small community at Wayne Center, north of the Benjamins' land, straddling the West Branch. Henry B. and Eunice Hemenway and her brother, Elijah Lyman Guild, were the first to stake claims in Wayne Center, about 1836. In 1837 the Reverend William Kimball, a Methodist preacher, arrived in the area with his family and held worship services in his log cabin for the few pioneer settlers. The following year he and his neighbors built a log house which served as a week day school and a Sabbath day church. Abner Guild and James Nind opened a general store in 1844, and people flocked to it in order to exchange their produce and coins for "store boughten" goods. These amenities were the first of their kind in the township.

The Township Organization Law went into effect in January 1850. It is traditionally believed that the Township was named in honor of Major General Anthony Wayne. It was he who had won the Northwest Territory for the United States by defeating a confederation of Indian tribes near Toledo, Ohio, in 1794.

A provision of the law called for the proceeds from land sales in Section 16 of each township to be used for a school fund. A direct result of this specification was the construction of several new school houses. These schools were, most probably, the Benjamin, Dunham's Depot (Wayne), Hammond (near the junction of Smith Road and Route 64), Orangeville, Wayne Center and the Red School (corner of Smith Road and Route 59). The first annual township meeting was held April 2, 1850, at the home of Joseph McMillen, who was also serving as the first postmaster.

Before this meeting took place, high-soaring

hawks along the eastern horizon could have seen movement which foretold the coming of the railroad. Slowly, but steadily, the Galena and Chicago Union's strap rails advanced. From the sixteen-year-old city of Chicago, they made their way across the prairie grasses and bridged their way across the prairie streams and sloughs. By January 1850 "The Pioneer," a small bell funnelled engine, was pulling its log-filled tender and one car over the right-of-way donated by Solomon Dunham, Edward Brewster and other farmers.

Dunham fully appreciated the potential of the railroad, and he took four actions that made him the founder of the second settlement, Wayne Station. The first step was a petition to the road commissioners of St. Charles and Wayne townships to build a road from the door yard of his red brick farmhouse to the state road (Route 59). When this was granted, he proceeded to construct an inn, a general store and a house, all just east of the tracks. He also secured appointments as the community's first station agent and postmaster. Both offices were in the depot.

By 1864 the business district had grown considerably. The *Illinois Gazeteer* for that year listed the following enterprises:

| | |
|---|---|
| Adams, Hiram | Boot and Shoemaker |
| Adams, J. Q. | General Store |
| Arndt, John | Wagonmaker |
| Campbell & Bros. | General Store |
| Carswell, Robert | Carpenter |
| Fren, Lars | Mason |
| Garron, Geo. | Blacksmith |
| Hartz, Michael | Blacksmith |
| Wolcott, Morgan | Carpenter |

Meanwhile, Wayne Center was also thriving. The post office had been moved from the McMillen farm to Abner Guild's store in 1851. Henry Sherman had opened a blacksmith shop. Guild's brother, William K., was operating a broom factory on his farm.

A Congregational Church had been organized in the mid-1840s. By 1851 its parishioners had acquired sufficient funds to buy a third of an acre on the north side of Army Trail Road, between Gerber and Fair Oaks roads, and to build their first house of worship. In 1871 five of its members withdrew to join thirteen others in becoming charter members of the new church at Wayne Station. The older

*Mark Dunham.*

congregation began to decline. Compounding its misfortune was the fact that none of the railroads opted to build through the settlement; thus it slowly ceased to exist. The one reminder of its former presence is the small cemetery on a hill to the west, which was started in the 1840s, and is still in use today.

Another pioneer graveyard is the Little Woods Cemetery, once located on Luther Pierce's farm in the northwest corner of the township. The earliest grave marker is that of a Lucy Hammond born December 1801, died April 1838.

Mark Wentworth Dunham, Solomon's youngest son, inherited his father's 300 acre farm when the senior Dunham died in 1865. Ten years later he bought the Percheron horse "Success" for $3,300 and launched the Oak Lawn Farm Importing and Breeding business. By 1883 he had prospered to such an extent that a west wing was added to the farmhouse to serve as an office, and Dunham Castle was completed as the family residence. It was patterned after the Normandy chateaux he had seen while on stock buying trips in France. During this same period houses were being built along main street by retired farmers, successful merchants, and men who worked in various capacities on the Dunham farm and for the Chicago & North Western Railroad.

Three additional railroads were constructed across the township between 1873 and 1888, the Chicago & Pacific (Milwaukee), the Chicago & Great Western, and the Illinois Central. The hopeful settlements that sprang up in their wake — Ontarioville, Ingalton, Schick, Granger, and Munger — were short lived, with the exception of Ontarioville. Its station has been renamed Hanover Park. The Chicago, Aurora & Elgin Electric Railway was completed in May 1903. It furnished additional train service for the township, and provided a source of electricity for street lights.

Dr. William L. Guild came to Wayne in 1884 and served both the settlement and the township. He had been born at Wayne Center December 5, 1859, a grandson of Massachusetts pioneers Israel and Rachel Guild. William's parents were Dr. Elias and Alice Guild, who had given sanctuary to runaway slaves prior to the Civil War. Among William's first patients was a workman who had caught his foot in machinery. The young doctor performed an amputation by the light of a lantern held by a hired girl. When his father, who had moved to Wheaton, died in 1908, Dr. Guild took over his practice, dividing his time between Wayne and that city, until his death in 1936.

In 1910 Elwood and Louise Powis Brown, she a granddaughter of Solomon Dunham's eldest son, Daniel, were sent to Manila by the Y.M.C.A. While there Mrs. Brown became impressed by the beautiful embroidery done by the native women. As an experiment, she designed a nightgown and commissioned one of the Filipinos to embroider it. The result so pleased her that she sent several samples to her mother, Mrs. Julia Dunham Powis, in Wayne. Eventually, the production of this attire developed into a million dollar business, and moved its headquarters from the family home, "Grove Place," to New York City. The mother-daughter team sold their interest in the company after Mr. Brown's death in 1929. Some years later his widow married Owen D. Young, chairman of General Electric.

The International Harvester Company began testing and improving farm machinery on the 200 acre Daniel Dunham farm in 1916. They completed their experiments in 1921, and Wirth Dunham bought the property. He built a hemp mill and raised this crop for processing. At its peak the plant employed thirty men and produced 350,000 pounds of fiber. The mill was sold and moved to China in 1931.

The Reverend Orlando S. Grinnell accepted a call to the Wayne Congregational Church in the fall of 1918. For that congregation's fiftieth anniversary, in 1921, Grinnell composed a hymn which he entitled "The Little Home Church By the Wayside." This was adopted as its official name in 1940.

Another event of post-war year 1921 was the founding of the Women's Club of Wayne. While its nucleus was comprised of the wives of farmers and merchants in and close to the settlement, several women from the township-at-large were also members. Miss Hattie Glos was the first president. Among the club's many accomplishments was the operation of the street lights, until 1951.

In 1926 Michael J. Bloze established the Illinois Pet Cemetery close to the eastern boundary of the township. In its grounds, located on Jefferson Street, just north of Schick Road, thousands of pets are buried. It continues to be maintained by Bloze's son and grandson.

During the same year Mark Morton of the Morton Salt Company family bought the 400 acre W. S. Lee farm and started the Morton Sand and Gravel Company. It was operated through the 1940s; then it was sold to private owners. The lake, formed by the excavating, is now an important feature of Pratts Wayne Woods, a forest preserve purchased by the county in 1965. Mark Morton's Georgian mansion has stood vacant most of the years since his death in 1951.

About 1927 Wirth Dunham and his sister Bernice Dunham West formed a partnership and began to subdivide the nearly 2,000 acres they had inherited from their father, Mark. The partnership was dissolved after Wirth's death in an automobile accident on July 17, 1931; it was restructured as Dunham's Incorporated. Solomon Dunham's red brick farm house, just two years short of its hundredth birthday, was leased to a group of residents in 1934. They organized the Dunham Woods Riding Club and used the building as their headquarters. On June 30th of that year, a pageant was held celebrating the centennial of John Laughlin's and the Benjamins' arrival in Wayne Township. Jane Dunham, great-granddaughter of Solomon, wrote the script.

*Wayne–DuPage Hunt horse trials, cross country.*

Almost from its beginning, the six mile square area designated "Wayne" has had the smallest population in the county. The census of 1850 lists 856 residents, the vast majority of whom were farmers. Eighty years later there were 1,166, a gain of only 310 people, while the other townships had doubled and tripled their numbers. Growth had been slow because it had remained predominantly agricultural, with only a small part of Ontarioville and the little settlement of Wayne serving as population clusters. There was no major industry until the 1920s, and most of it was confined to North Avenue, and to the south along Powis Road.

Among the first such enterprises was a private airport. A group of aviation enthusiasts bought farmland from Colonel E. J. Baker on the south side of Route 64. They called themselves Air Associates; they had built their first hangar by 1929. George G. Ball purchased the airport in 1939. With the advent of World War II, the flying field became important to the Federal Government, which paid for the first paved runways and lent a large sum of money to have the Howard Aircraft Company plant built. After the war that building was sold; it became the Owens-Illinois Glass Works' Plastic Division in 1947, while the airfield became DuPage Airport.

The prize-winning author Marguerite Henry came in 1940 to Wayne where most of her widely read children's books were written. Among them were *Justin Morgan Had a Horse* (1945), *Misty of Chincoteague* (1947), and *King of the Wind* (1949). She and her husband moved in 1971 to California, where they still reside.

The Wayne Community Association held its first meeting at the school on September 5, 1945. President Corwith Hamill explained that the former Wayne Carnival Committee, whose annual fund-raising event supplemented school funds, had decided to incorporate in order to serve the community more effectively.

As early as 1943 subdivisions began to appear in the township. Hugh M. Cornell developed Waynewood, just east of the angle formed by the junction of routes 64 and 59. Lakewood, to the north, was subdivided in 1946. Noting these basic changes to the landscape, the Community Association appointed a five-person Planning Committee in November 1948 to work with county zoning officials on a long-range area plan. Its purpose was to preserve and protect as much of the remaining open lands as possible.

After a century of service the Chicago & Northwestern passenger train was discontinued in the spring of 1950. The CA&E terminated its service in June, 1958.

When Wayne Township and Wayne Station's first century rolled around, in 1950, 79-year-old Miss Hattie Glos co-authored a little booklet, "Wayne Township: A Commemorative History." In 1953 it was revised and expanded to become the "Wayne Community and Township History," a source which may be found in many local home and public libraries.

In 1955 an immense Spanish-style structure began to rise on the northwest corner of Routes 59 and 64. It was Christ the King Seminary. The land purchased for this endeavor was once part of Theodore Schramer's farm. He had been born in Prussia in 1839, and immigrated to the United States in 1857. He farmed near Wheaton for a number of years. Then Schramer married Mary Lies in 1863, and in the early 1870s bought the land that encompassed the four corners of this intersection. With the single exception of this sale, the remainder of the farm continued to be owned by the family until the early 1970s. The fourth generation of Schramers still farms in the township. Approximately twenty years after purchasing the property, the Franciscan Fathers sold it to a private partnership which converted the building into a convalescent center.

Two years after the seminary had been completed, the Wayne Community Association became alarmed by the expansion of subdivisions. A committee was appointed to study the advisability of incorporating as a village. This option was opposed by those residents who believed it would drastically change the char-

Beautiful Song and Chorus

Words & Music by O.S. Grinnell
author of "BATTLE CRY FOR LIBERTY" ETC.

Harmonized by Bertha Grinnell Fricke

In Memory Of My Friend The DR. WM. S. PITTS
BROOKLYN, N.Y.
Author of "LITTLE BROWN CHUR IN THE VALE."

LITTLE HOME CHURCH BY THE WAYSIDE: WAYNE

50¢

Published by LAKESIDE SUPPLY CO.
416 S. Dearborn St.
CHICAGO

acter of the community. A referendum was held on September 13, 1958, and the proposal passed by the narrow margin of 95 to 87. The first village board was sworn into office that November. Among the earliest measures voted by the board were the adoption of subdivision regulations and a zoning ordinance.

The Community Association continued to serve as the financial unit by collecting voluntary dues of $60 a year from each family. This money supplied funds for street lighting and, in the beginning, a one-man police department.

In the early 1960s William and Theresa Heinz Warner razed their 120-year-old farm house built by Joseph McMillen, the township's first postmaster. A few years later they sold the western ten acres of their farm to the Diocese of Joliet. A new parish, Resurrection Catholic Church, was organized and the first mass was celebrated in their new building on October 4, 1968. In the same year Dunham's Incorporated sold the 1,100 acres which comprised the North and South Farms, on either side of Army Trail Road west of the village, to the Oliver Hoffmann Corporation.

The Pheasant Run resort complex was opened on February 15, 1963. Located just west of DuPage Airport, it was described by *The St. Charles Chronicle* as "The million dollar development of the late Colonel E. J. Baker's 175-acre Airport Farm." In 1979 a fifteen-story tower, the tallest in the township, was completed for offices and other functions.

The Little Home Church by the Wayside celebrated its 100th Anniversary in February 1971. Former parishioners from as far away as California and Oregon returned for the special service and luncheon in June. Descendants of four charter members were present as were the fourth and fifth generations of John Laughlin's family. The planning committee wrote a booklet entitled *The Plow and The Cross,* which traced the church's service to village and township through the years.

The Forest Preserve District's first acquisition in the township was Wayne Grove, purchased in 1923. It was the only local preserve until 1956, when Mallard Lake was acquired. The district's first purchase for what became Pratt's Wayne Woods took place in 1965. George R. Pratt was the guiding hand behind this achievement. In 1974 Pratt elected to sell his Maple Spring Farm, which had been owned by his family for four generations, to the Forest Preserve District, rather than to a developer.

The year 1974 was also when the DuPage Airport was purchased and placed under the management of a Fox Valley Community Airport Authority. The referendum passed by a vote of 4,217 to 1,737 with the communities of Batavia, Geneva, St. Charles, Wayne and West Chicago participating.

Money need, a recurring problem for the Village of Wayne, became acute in 1977. The voluntary dues had been gradually raised to $225 a year. For the first time the concept of taxes was no longer considered an anathema.

The annual township meeting was held on April 5, 1977. There were eight Republican and eight Democratic candidates on the ballots. The Republicans won, as they had in every election since the party was formed in 1854.

Another important event occurred in 1978. A committee was formed in the Village of Wayne to investigate the possibility of its attaining historic district status. The purpose was to protect and preserve the community's 19th-century quality. Founding members were Jesse Burt, Burd Hikes, Nancy Jackson, Isabella Lindsay, Ann Miller and John Walter. The Wayne Village Historic District application was approved and received its official designation as such on December 19, 1978.

In 1984 Wayne celebrated the 150th year of the arrival of John Laughlin and the Robert Benjamins. A gala parade proceeded from the school to the pole barn at Dunham Woods Riding Club, its participants wore period costumes. Appropriately, the site was within half a mile of the Laughlin claim, where the township's history had begun.

**The Author**

Tannisse Twyman Blatchford is the author of *An Honorable Heritage: A Biography of Wayne Township, Illinois, 1834–1984.*

# West Chicago

*Jerry Musich*

West Chicago was the first Illinois community created by the coming of railroads. A few settlers owned property in the area of present-day West Chicago as early as the late 1830s. The town itself, however, did not begin to form until 1849–1850, when the tracks of the new Galena & Chicago Union Railroad reached the vicinity. Because several railroads were the principal cause for the creation of West Chicago, a brief survey of the activities of those companies is in order.

The G&CU (which eventually became the Chicago & North Western) was Chicago's first railroad. The laying of its track west from the city began in 1848, with the intent of reaching the Fox River, Rockford, Freeport, and Galena. The railroad arrived in what is now West Chicago in November 1849, and reached Elgin in February 1850.

The decision to lay tracks directly northwest from the West Chicago area to Elgin upset residents of the Fox River communities of Batavia, Geneva and St. Charles. They realized that the new railroads were going to transform the area. For example, the 40-mile mail run by train in 1850 from Chicago to Elgin took three hours, while the 44-mile mail run by stage from Chicago to Aurora to Sugar Grove over mud roads took 16 hours. Any community without access to this new, speedy means of transportation would be at a serious disadvantage.

Therefore, residents of St. Charles formed the St. Charles Branch Railroad in 1849. This line ran from St. Charles to a junction with the G&CU just north of present-day West Chicago. Another company built a two mile long track from St. Charles to Geneva, thus connecting Geneva, by way of the St. Charles Branch, with the G&CU at West Chicago.

Batavia and Aurora residents were involved in the building of a different railroad, the Aurora Branch. This line (which eventually became the Burlington) laid tracks from the

*From the* 1874 Atlas & History of DuPage County, Illinois

West Chicago area to Batavia, and then Aurora in 1850.

Thus, by late 1850, three railroads joined at what is now West Chicago. Because so many trains met at this juncture, water and fuel facilities for the locomotives were built, as well as an eating house and hotel for travelers. Very quickly a town formed, one that was known as Junction, Illinois.

By 1853, for reasons too complex for this present publication, the G&CU halted the track-laying of its Chicago to Galena line at Freeport. The company decided instead to build a second mainline, running west from Junction to DeKalb and then to Fulton, Illinois. Because its two mainlines met at Junction, the G&CU expanded its facilities, building a three stall roundhouse and a mill for repairing rails. As a result, a number of new employees and their families located in the community.

John B. Turner, president of the G&CU and a resident of Chicago, owned several acres of land in what is now the center of town. As more people settled in Junction, Turner recognized the opportunity to make a profit by platting his land and selling off lots. He, therefore, recorded the community's first plat in 1855 under the name of the Town of Junction. He also donated two lots — one to the Congregational Church, another for an early school.

Turner's plat is the section of town just south of Washington Street. As a railroad executive, he assigned railroad-related names to many of the first streets — Depot Street (now Main Street), as well as Chicago, Galena, and Fulton streets, named after the three projected terminal cities of the G&CU.

In 1857 Dr. Joseph McConnell and his wife Mary platted a second portion of town, those lands lying just north of J. B. Turner's plat. The McConnells were early members of the Congregational Church and were deeply appreciative of Turner's donation of land to the congregation. Therefore, they chose to record their plat as the Town of Turner in honor of the railroad president. There now existed a platted Town of Turner and a platted Town of Junction. As a result, the community took on the name of Turner Junction.

At this time in the mid-1850s, the new community was quite small and undeveloped. John Lakey, who served as master mechanic (superintendent) of the small G&CU shops, wrote the following recollection in 1895:

> It was in the pleasant month of June 1854, that I came to the small railroad town that is now known as Turner, Illinois, then only a Junction station of the Galena and Chicago Union Railroad, with its Dixon Air line and a road running south to Aurora and LaSalle.
>
> The principal buildings belonged to the railroad company. There was a two-story building 30 × 75 feet, used as an eating house. (There was also) the "Store" occupied by the McDonald Brothers and across the road was a small building used by W. I. Mowry as a post office and grocery.
>
> On one side of the highway (then North Street, now Washington Street) there was a brick 3-stall engine house, and adjoining it was a brick blacksmith shop used for repairing T-rails. These were the principal buildings and not one of them are in existence at the present time, they having either been burned or torn down and removed.
>
> The railroad company owned twenty-two acres of land, lying northeast of the main track and south of the highway. This land was vacant at the time. On the north side of North Street lands owned by Dr. Joseph McConnell, and southwest of the main track the lands were the property of the Winslow heirs. None of this land was platted, hence none had land to sell.

Most of the residents, who were chiefly farmers or railroad employees, appear to have been of English or Irish stock. A sizable number came from New York state. Tradition has it that they worked on the new railroads in New York in the 1840s and migrated west as the Illinois' railroad boom began.

Census information of 1860 and 1870 for Turner Junction is imprecise. The community did not draw clearly defined boundaries until it incorporated in 1873. Census takers in 1860

*Heritage Commons — featuring West Chicago's railroad history.*

*Stained glass entry at Congregational Church, serving the "Old Heidelberg" area of West Chicago.*
*Photo by Jim Jarvis*

and in 1870 counted everyone listed in the area of the Turner Post Office. The 1860 figures show 722 residents, while in 1870 there were 1,086 residents.

By the late 1860s, the Chicago & North Western (as the former G&CU was now known) built a substantial brick depot and a major roundhouse here. Several church structures graced the community, including the First United Methodist Church, built in 1855; the Congregational Church, built in 1867; and St. Mary's Catholic Church, built in 1868. In 1871 St. Michael's Evangelical Church was added.

The community had taken on a permanent character, and so the residents incorporated it in 1873 as the Village of Turner. A total of 850 residents lived within the boundaries of the new village, with Lucius B. Church serving as the first village board president.

Population continued to increase, growing from 1,001 in 1880 to 1,506 in 1890. A sizable number of the new residents were German immigrants, who settled in the portion of town near St. Michael's church.

This population growth demanded added services. In 1873 the community built the three-story Turner Public School. Because of the 50% population growth of the 1880s, the community added the Southside School in 1887 (renaming the 1873 building the Northside School). The village board authorized the construction of the three-story town hall in 1884. This multi-purpose building was designed to house the volunteer fire department, a one-man police department, and the village council chambers.

During these early decades, Turner was chiefly a one-industry town. According to census data, nearly 40% of the men employed in non-agricultural occupations worked for the C&NW.

This situation began changing in the late 1880s with the arrival of a new railroad, the Elgin, Joliet & Eastern or Outer Belt Line. This line is a feeder railroad rather than a cross-country one, transferring freight from one outlying Chicago community to another. The prosperity of the EJ&E depended on its having factories located all along its right-of-way, as a means of generating freight traffic for the railroad. The EJ&E offered free factory sites for any industry willing to locate along its right-of-way. Local developers quickly realized that companies that did locate here would create increased demand for housing, stores and services. Much promotional literature was produced including wall maps of 1893 that proclaimed Turner "Chicago's Coming Great Manufacturing Suburb." The advertising copy on the map continues by asserting that

> Turner offers opportunities to manufacturers, mechanics, homeseekers, and investors offered by no other point about Chicago at the present time.
>
> Turner has electric lights, asphalt sidewalks, two wide-awake newspapers, fine schools, prosperous churches, good society, and numerous flourishing factories that are bringing it to the front rank as a manufacturing point.
>
> (It is) located at the junction of the Chicago & North-Western Railway, the Chicago, Burlington & Quincy Railway, and the Outer Belt Line, giving it unequalled shipping facilities with Chicago freight rates.

As part of this effort to attract industry, the community changed its name in 1896 to the Village of West Chicago. The reasoning apparently was that the name helped prospective industrialists to visualize where in the state the town was located, and that "West Chicago" sounded more industrial or metropolitan than did the "Village of Turner."

At the same time that it changed its name, the community also established a public water works. Before 1896 fires were fought by drawing water from individuals wells, which occasionally nearly dried up during summer droughts. Fires were, therefore, a serious problem, one that also hindered the effort to attract new development. As John C. Neltnor, editor of the West Chicago-based *DuPage County Democrat,* editorialized:

> If we expect to induce manufacturers and others to locate in our midst we have got to stir ourselves on the subject of water works. Men cannot be expected to invest their money in a place where there is no fire protection.

In October 1896 a sharply divided community voted for the water works, and the village board authorized the construction of a pumping station, reservoir, and standpipe.

The village's effort to attract industry was hindered by a serious national depression in the 1890s. Nonetheless, several plants did open in West Chicago. Some, such as the Stimmel & Hook Pump Works and Roach & Brandt Millwork (later West Chicago Sash & Door) built plants along the EJ&E. Other plants located along the C&NW tracks, including the Turner Brick Co. and the Turner Cabinet Co.

One of the largest enterprises was a Borden's milk condensing plant, built about 1906. Since the late 1880s, West Chicago had been the site for the formation of one of Chicago's largest milk trains. Each morning the C&NW assembled a fifteen car milk express destined for Chicago. It drew cars from three directions and from as far away as Williams Bay, Wisconsin. Because of the volume of milk passing through West Chicago and because of the dairy farms in the area, Borden's had found this a logical spot for a milk plant. (The plant eventually became a Reid Murdock pickle plant, and later Jel Sert.)

As industry located in West Chicago and new jobs opened up, the population increased. By 1900 it reached 1,877, while 2,378 people resided in town in 1910.

At the same time new subdivisions were springing up in outlying areas. One of the moving forces behind these ex-urban subdivisions was the new electric interurban, the Aurora, Elgin & Chicago (later to be reorganized as the Chicago, Aurora & Elgin). This line began service from Chicago to Wheaton to Elgin in the fall of 1902. In 1909 it added a line from Wheaton through High Lake subdivision to West Chicago, and on to Geneva. Just as the EJ&E earlier had tried to attract industry to its right-of-way, the AE&C promoted residences along its tracks, hoping to generate passenger traffic for itself. High Lake, with its communally owned lake and lodge, was one such street car suburb promoted by the interurban, even to the point of the railroad commissioning the foxtrot "Come Where the Birds Sing," to promote High Lake.

The increased population brought added demands on the community. In 1904 High School District 94 was formed, and in 1908 a new and larger school building replaced the old Northside School. This new building, eventually known as Washington School, housed half of the 1st through 8th grade classes as well as all of the high school classes. In August 1906 the village reincorporated itself as the

*The Chauncey Reed Home.*
*Photo by Jim Jarvis*

City of West Chicago, with banker Grant A. Dayton serving as first mayor.

The city's population grew by only 9% after 1910, reaching 2,594 in 1920, but then grew a dramatic 30%, to 3,477, by 1930. Industry continued to expand although a major foundry, Union Tool Co., relocated to Ohio.

Several changes occurred during these decades. In 1912 the C&NW built a new passenger depot (now the West Chicago Community Center) and an underpass, as well as the Wilson Street bridge over its mainline as a means of reaching its roundhouse area. At the same time the railroad moved its 1869 depot to the north side of what is now Washington Street, converting it into a freight depot. This new location for the old depot was adjacent to the coach yards, where the suburban commuter coaches were stored overnight, and where as many as four coal-burning steam engines fired up at a time each morning.

Two important changes relating to schools also took place. After the Southside School had been destroyed by fire in 1919, Lincoln School was built in 1921. By the mid-1920s the Northside School had become so overcrowded that two rooms for high school classes were rented at the back of the nearby Buick salesroom. In 1926 the new high school was built on Joliet Street.

Between 1923–25, the city government under Mayor Edward J. McCabe embarked on a major street improvement program, building nine miles of concrete streets and installing an ornamental street lighting system. Starting in 1930, the city renamed several streets and instituted a new numbering system for building addresses.

The decade of the 1930s saw the town's development slow dramatically. The population actually decreased by 122 residents to a total of 3,355 in 1940. The CA&E interurban abandoned its West Chicago branch in 1937, and the city government opened the City Hall at night as a sleeping place for the homeless.

World War II brought new economic vitality, which was dramatically increased in the post-war years of suburban growth. The population grew 17% during the 1940s to a 1950 total of 3,973; a whopping 80% during the 1950s, to 10,100 in 1970. Part of this growth reflected annexations of existing developments; but much of it resulted from new building, including the construction of a number of apartment complexes. By 1980 the population reached 12,500.

Significant changes in the face and structure of West Chicago occurred throughout the postwar period. The newly formed Rotary Club of West Chicago created the Swimming Pool Association in 1954-5, which in turn sold $100,000 in bonds and built an outdoor pool in the city-owned Reed-Keppler Park. Through local volunteer effort a scout cabin was also built in that park. The West Chicago Railroad and Historical Society was formed in the 1960s, and attempted to save one of the town's most famous houses, the Neltnor or Anthony Home, as a museum. This effort failed and the building eventually was destroyed by fire, although the Society remained in existence until it was absorbed in 1975 by the new West Chicago Historical Society.

There were, of course, several notable exceptions to the general pattern of civic groups, rather than governmental agencies, trying to carry out community projects. In 1954 the new public library building was built with tax monies. In 1964 the city government assumed the operation of Oakwood Cemetery established in 1858 by the McConnells.

While civic groups remained active in community efforts during the 1970s and '80s, governmental bodies assumed more of a leadership role. In 1972 the park district was formed. It signed a long-term lease with the city to assume operation of Reed-Keppler Park; for several years it operated the outdoor swimming pool for the Swimming Pool Association, until the city began operating it in 1981; and it acquired Easton Park, Pioneer Park, and Manville-Oaks Park.

The city government, in the meantime, found it had outgrown the 1884 Town Hall building. Fire fighting equipment had already been moved out when the separate fire district was formed. The district replaced the volunteer company. A fire station was built in 1969 on the former site of Washington School, while the police department relocated to McConnell Street. In 1975, under Mayor Richard Truitt, the city bought and renovated a former Jewel Food Store, and moved its offices and council chambers there.

In 1976 the city created the West Chicago Historical Commission and the West Chicago Historical Museum in the old city hall. As its bicentennial project, the city established Heritage Commons next to the new city hall. This park, honoring the community's railroad heritage, is part of the West Chicago Historical Museum.

Under the leadership of Mayor A. Eugene Rennels, the city worked with Nature Conservancy to purchase a 150 acre tract of virgin prairie on the western edge of town. The operation of this land, possibly the largest remaining tract of virgin prairie in Illinois, has been turned over to the Forest Preserve District of DuPage County.

Civic groups, of course, continued to play an important role. Starting in 1974, the West Chicago Railroad Days Committee sponsored an annual summer festival. In 1975 the West Chicago Historical Society was formed. Initially intended in part as the volunteer arm of the West Chicago Historical Museum, it added its own museum facility in 1979 when Celia Kruse willed the society her 1916 family home.

In 1981 the new West Chicago Community Center, Inc., a not-for-profit group that had its genesis in the West Chicago Coordinating Council of the late 1970s, acquired the 1912 C&NW depot for use as a community center. Raising tens of thousands of dollars and receiving much volunteer labor, the Center renovated the old depot, dedicating it in July 1983. The Chamber of Commerce, another active organization of the time, moved its offices to the depot that summer.

In one small sense, West Chicago's history was brought full circle in 1981 when the C&NW located its Illinois Division headquarters in West Chicago, on the former site of the old roundhouse. This move by the C&NW appears to guarantee that West Chicago, the first Illinois community created as a result of the coming of the railroads, will remain a significant railroad town for the foreseeable future.

The Author

Jerry Musich is Curator of the West Chicago Historical Museum.

# Westmont

*Sharon Heiden*

Westmont is 740 feet above sea level, 23 feet above Downers Grove and 59 feet higher than Hinsdale. From Chicago to the Mississippi, Westmont is the highest point on the Burlington Railroad line. As excavators know, this "west mound" consists largely of clay; and as geologists explain, it was heaped up as a terminal moraine by the last of the ice sheets.

Westmont was mainly prairie, rather than woodland. The first farm owner mentioned in local histories was Henry Faul, from Bavaria, who staked out a 160-acre homestead a mile and a half east of Downers Grove, on virgin prairie.

Nothing was more important in paving the way for the future Westmont than the building of the Chicago-Aurora branch of the Chicago, Burlington & Quincy Railroad, completed in 1864. Shortly afterward, a large share of the future Westmont was bought up by the Phipps Industrial Land Trust. Some of this land, after the Chicago Fire of 1871, was sold to a number of brick manufacturers who were eager to supply bricks for the rebuilding of Chicago.

The most notable of the brick manufacturers was William L. Gregg, who chose the highest point of land along the CB&Q for his company so that shipping by steam locomotive, with a full load of brick, would be downhill. In the spring of 1872 Gregg began manufacturing bricks under the name of the Excelsior Brick Company. His company started with a capital investment of $250,000, employed 120 people, and produced 70,000 bricks per day. While in the area Mr. Gregg invented and patented a triple pressure brick machine which revolutionized the brick industry. His bricks could withstand one hundred thousand pounds of pressure without cracking or other disturbance.

Early in the 1890s, the various brick companies laid out streets and planted trees along them, expecting that the Columbian Exposi-

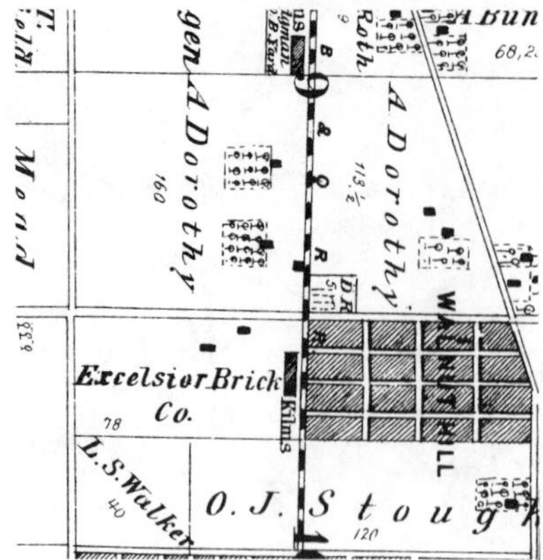


*From the* 1874 Atlas & History of DuPage County, Illinois

tion of 1893 would bring a surge of settlement. Nothing came of these hopes. A truer sign of growth was the establishment of a flag-stop on the "Q" known as "Gregg's Milk Station," later shorted to Gregg. By 1900 brick-making ceased.

It was during World War I that settlers began to come in great numbers. In 1917 Mr. and Mrs. Joseph Haller and family came from Chicago and made initial purchases of land from the Branigar Brothers, who owned much of the land now in Westmont. Haller, in turn, sold to Arthur T. McIntosh in 1919. Immediately following the war, McIntosh began an aggressive campaign to sell houses and lots. In the spring of 1920 he started laying out streets and sidewalks. Cottages sold from $2,500 to $3,500. Lots of an acre or more could be bought for as little as $5.00 down and the balance in monthly payments.

Families whose breadwinners worked for Western Electric, Harvester, the "Q" and other Chicago industries were attracted by the opportunity to move to the country. They sought the space to raise livestock and garden. Many of these settlers were either directly from Bohemia, Austria, Poland or Germany, or else not more than one generation removed from their roots in the soil of their mother countries. Their fingers belonged in the loam. As late as 1939 the population of Westmont was 35% foreign-born; this set it apart from neighboring towns.

These people lived like pioneers. Their bungalows and shacks were dotted over a terrain that had no paved streets, sidewalks, electricity, gas, sewers, or water mains. A few families sunk wells. Children of other families, carrying a pair of empty buckets, met their fathers at the evening train. They would then take their place in line at the public pump, with the tired breadwinner pumping the buckets full and carrying them home. It was not until 1925 that the village water system was completed.

Local transportation, other than "hoofing it," was at a premium. It was long before a "flivver" or "tin lizzie" appeared in town in any numbers; and if such autos had been affordable, they would have made little progress, with muddy, rutted Burlington the only "improved" street. Traveling to Downers Grove to see Lillian Gish or Tom Mix in a flicker involved the same hardships. Courting couples might splurge and take the train. Sometimes the projectionist would hold up the show a bit on a Friday or Saturday evening, if the train from Westmont was a little overdue. But often the Westmost crowd had to leave before the last reel had clicked through in order to catch the last train home.

The year 1921, when dance bands were playing *Barney Google* and *Stumbling All Around,* witnessed the incorporation of Gregg's Milk Station as Westmont, "The Progressive Village." From that time its growth rate increased.

Father Eneas B. Goodwin, first resident pastor of Saint Joseph's Church in Downers Grove, wanted permission to say Mass at the public school building in Westmont. There had been no previous Roman Catholic Church in that village. On December 1, 1923, he wrote his superior, Archbishop George W. Mundelein of Chicago: "Nearly all of my flock are about one month's wages ahead of poverty... About a year and a half ago I began working among them and can assure you they have kept me busy, especially in sick calls and straightening out difficulties resulting from 'moonshine'."

The liquor traffic, illegal under the 18th Amendment, continued to be a problem of the community. This is not to imply that the majority of patrons were drawn mainly from Westmont. Thirsty residents of neighboring dry communities would converge on the newer, less-organized Westmont, where entrepreneurs in spirituous beverages had set up the contraband trade. Westmont was sometimes taunted with the appellation "Wet Mont" or "Whiskey Hill."

This stereotype, plus the larger number of first-generation Americans, created a noticeable "looking down" on Westmont among longer-established towns. This attitude was especially hard on boys and girls of high school age because Westmont did not have its own secondary schools. Until the 1970s Westmont youth attended either Downers Grove or Hinsdale high schools.

The expansion of Westmont came to a virtual halt with the Great Depression. The 1930 census showed a population of 2,733; the 1940 census registered a gain of only 311 individuals. Westmont men were out of work through layoffs at Western Electric and other plants. Many families were on relief. The WPA eventually helped those who could not get private employment, and a number of the younger men went to CCC Camps.

World War II, however, brought new residents to Westmont. Western Electric and

*Szalkowski Home, 1924.*
*Courtesy Westmont Historical Society*

*Theatre Building.*
*Courtesy Westmont Historical Society*

*South School, third grade, 1933.*
*Courtesy Westmont Historical Society*

Electro-Motive hired extra workers for completion of defense contracts. Homes to rent were difficult to find. Labor and construction materials were also hard to come by; but somehow there were families who managed to erect houses in the area at that time.

Following World War II, the building boom resumed. One of the largest developments was Blackhawk Heights, immediately to the east of the village. There scores of brick houses for middle and upper-income families were built on a large tract, formerly the site of Bassett and Washburn's Greenhouse and Nursery. By 1959 the town of Westmont had so filled up that there were very few vacant spaces left for building.

Many tradesmen and blue collar workers remain; but inhabitants are generally more skilled and better paid than those of the early years of settlement. The community now includes many businesses and professional residents. Gone are the days of setting up housekeeping in a tent or garage, working all day in the city, then working half the night by automobile light or lantern on one's house.

Today Westmont provides the full range of public facilities and services. A large community center, with many activities for senior citizens, was built in 1975. One of the most important additions to the town in recent years has been the Westmont High School, built in 1976. One of many local activities each year is Westmont's Pow Wow Days — held in late summer. This is a week-long affair of picnics, a carnival, a parade and many other family-oriented activities.

At a 1976 picnic life-long resident Marge Smejkal spoke with 84-year-old Mary Peters about what to do with the memorabilia, pictures, and school histories that the teacher had collected since 1925. In looking for a place to display the materials properly, Ms. Smejkal remembered the oldest building in town, the 104-year-old former residence of brickyard owner William L. Gregg. This structure was scheduled for demolition by its owner at that time, Holy Trinity Church.

A meeting was held of local residents, who decided to form the Westmont Historical Society for the purpose of procuring and maintaining the history and artifacts of the village. On December 14, 1976, Holy Trinity Parish was approached about "Gregg House." The church donated the building, providing the society would move it. A site was then acquired from the park district. Memberships were sold; rummage and bake sales held. With money from these projects, along with the help of the village, businesses and area residents, it was possible to make the move.

The above ground foundation walls are constructed with the original brick salvaged from the old location. Many of the bricks are clearly marked "EXCELSIOR" (with the backward "S"), the name of the Gregg's brick company.

The restored eight-room building currently serves as Westmont's Historical Society Museum. Many programs are conducted during the year, aimed primarily at children, with a particular emphasis on Westmont's rich ethnic heritage. Puppet shows are presented at Christmas. Food and customs from Bohemia, Austria, Poland and Germany are featured. President Smejkal sums up the museum's purpose when she says, "We want our children to know their history — the story of Westmont — so they can be proud!"

**The Author**

Sharon Heiden is publicity director of the Westmont Historical Society.

# Wheaton

*Edith E. Back*

The story of Wheaton began in Pomfret, Connecticut, the birthplace of Erastus, Jude, Orinda and Charles Gary, and the Wheaton brothers, Warren and Jesse. It was due largely to the generosity of these New England settlers, who gave of their land, funds and time that Wheaton became the leading city it is today.

By 1837 the early pioneers and their families had claimed large stretches of land in the area. DuPage County was organized in 1839, the year that Jesse Wheaton and Orinda Gary were married. The settlers built their homes of lumber cut to size at Gary's Mill on the West Branch of the DuPage River.

In 1848 the tracks of the Galena and Chicago Union Railroad were laid on the three mile right-of-way donated by Jesse and Warren Wheaton and Erastus Gary, who now owned adjacent land. In 1849 the first train left Wheaton for Turner Junction, now West Chicago. Fast rail connections with the markets in Chicago replaced the tiresome journey by wagon or on foot over dirt roads.

In 1850 Milton Township was organized in the home of Jesse Wheaton, with Warren L. Wheaton as supervisor and Erastus Gary as justice of the peace. The village of Wheaton, surveyed in 1853 by Jonathan Vallette and platted by the Wheaton brothers, included a number of businesses clustered around its depot. A public school was built for the growing families with children.

In 1853 the Wesleyan Methodists opened the doors of the Illinois Institute in a hilltop building that later became the central portion of Blanchard Hall, Wheaton College. A good portion of the land and funds were contributions from the Wheaton and Gary families. The first principal, the Rev. John Cross, served on the site committee with Jesse Wheaton, who also hauled the stones for the building from a Batavia quarry. The same year the DuPage County Agricultural and Mechan-

*From the* 1874 Atlas & History of DuPage County, Illinois

ical Society was formed, and the first call in Wheaton for a new Republican Party occurred. In 1857 Jesse Wheaton donated land for the first fairgrounds and also for the first church building for the Wesleyan Methodist congregation, organized earlier in 1843. In 1859 Wheaton was incorporated as a village comprising about twelve square blocks, now the downtown business district.

The 1860s brought Jonathan Blanchard, former head of Knox College in Galesburg, to be president of the newly-founded Wheaton College, successor to the Illinois Institute. He was a New Englander, born in Vermont, an Abolitionist, a temperance supporter, and an opponent of secret societies. Many young men in the community served in the Union Army during the Civil War. The *Northern Illinoisan,* a newspaper started in 1861 by Henry Clay Childs, kept the people of Wheaton informed of events in the war zones and in the state capitol. When the war ended in 1865, Wheaton College had survived, partly because of the Ladies' School and the preparatory school. Free tuition was offered to returning veterans.

In 1867 Warren Wheaton successfully led the fight in the state legislature to move the county seat from Naperville to the more centrally-located Wheaton. The first courthouse, built on a barren block of land donated by the Wheatons, was soon surrounded by newly planted trees. In 1869 the village was organized as a town.

As the county seat of a prosperous farming

*The Jesse Wheaton Home.*
*From the* 1874 Atlas & History of DuPage County, Illinois

community, with a college, a railroad, churches, schools and a business district at its center, Wheaton entered the 1870s with the second generation of the pioneers taking on leadership. The *Northern Illinoisan* became the *Wheaton Illinoisan* in 1870. Ownership changed from time to time in the years that followed. That same year the Wheaton branch of the National Bank of Chicago was established.

In the dry Fall of 1871, a fire nearly wiped out the business block on Front Street. After the Chicago Fire that same autumn, many families moved to the suburbs, including Wheaton. The Gary-Wheaton Bank was founded on October 1, 1874, with the resources of Jesse Wheaton, Erastus and Elbert Gary providing the capital. Central School, later Longfellow School, was built in 1874. In 1876 John Quincy Adams, a distant relative of the Adams Presidents, came to Wheaton with his son and daughter, and built a large home on the square block which is now Adams Park.

The town of Wheaton progressed slowly but steadily in the 1880s as a residential, commuter community. The "Wheaton Look" in homes — Victorian, Italianate, New England Federal, Farmhouse, Queen Anne, and occasionally Colonial or combined styles — included many large, ornate, comfortable residences on extensive grounds. Smaller, more utilitarian houses were sprinkled in between. Many of the homes are still in use today.

Rufus Blanchard, a mapmaker and historian, published a *History of DuPage County* in 1882. The same year Dr. Charles Blanchard (no relation to Rufus) succeeded his father, Jonathan Blanchard, as the second president of Wheaton College, serving until 1925. Also in that year, telephone lines were extended from Chicago through Wheaton to Aurora and beyond. Three years later, when a fire proved too much for the bucket brigade of the Volunteer Fire Department fighters, a phone call to Chicago brought equipment on the next crack train to put out the fire after twenty homes and businesses had been destroyed. The need for a central water system was apparent. In 1887 alcoholic and intoxicating beverages were banned through the influence of Warren Wheaton, who had been a member of the first temperance society in Massachusetts in 1826.

In 1891 John Q. Adams built the Adams Memorial Library, across the street from his home, in memory of his wife, Marilla Phipps Adams. His daughter, Katherine Adams Wells, was deeply involved in library affairs until her death.

The Chicago Golf Club, the first eighteen-hole course in the United States, was located in Wheaton in 1893 in the south part of town, where the Chadwicks and Hadleys had settled in the early 1840s. The club was soon surrounded by summer homes of the elite from Chicago; Robert Todd Lincoln served as an early president.

Paved streets, sidewalks, a water system and sewers followed in 1894. Forty phones were in use by 1895, and a new courthouse was erected the next year. By the last year of the century, the police department had been organized, and an electric light plant had been built.

Growth continued as the twentieth century began. Front Street was paved with bricks, and sidewalks were made of brick or gravel. The Chicago, Aurora, and Elgin electric railroad made transportation easier and more comfortable, with its diners and even a funeral car, when service began in 1902. J. S. Peironnet owned the first auto, a Pierce-Arrow, in 1903. Mercury vapor street lights were installed. A new railroad station was built in 1911 and used until 1973, when it was renovated for commer-

*The DuPage County Courthouse.*

cial use. In the same year the city government was moved to more permanent headquarters on Wesley Street, continuing in this location until 1966.

As early as 1904/05 basketball was being played at Wheaton High School. Formal football was offered in 1912. When the United States entered World War I, the Woman's Department Club was formed, and its members became active in Red Cross work. William A. Gamon was elected mayor, with the help of women voters. City government changed from alderman/mayor to commission/mayor in 1917. That year there were 1,336 school age children, six to twenty-one years of age.

The end of World War I was followed by the disastrous world-wide flu epidemic. Undaunted, the community sponsored the YMCA, and the newly organized park district purchased the "Gary Block," the former residence of Judge Elbert Gary, for a memorial park dedicated to the men who had served in the war. Harold (Red) Grange entered high school in 1919; he became a renowned football player in high school, at the University of Illinois, and with the Chicago Bears. His father served on the city's police force.

A spurt in growth occurred in the next decade, before the Great Depression set in. Adams Library was taken over by the city. Dr. J. Oliver Buswell, Jr. became the third president of Wheaton College in 1926. Home construction increased; 135 homes were built north of Harrison and west of President. A new YMCA structure was built on Roosevelt Road.

A new post office was built in 1933. Culligan's water softening plant opened in 1937. Despite the slow progress in these Depression years, a low-key celebration in 1939 marked the one hundred years that DuPage had been organized.

At the beginning of the 1940s, Wheaton Chamber of Commerce replaced the earlier Wheaton Business Men's Association, and Dr. V. Raymond Edman became the fourth president of Wheaton College. When war was declared at the end of 1941, many male students left to serve their country; coeds predominated at the college as they had during the Civil War and World War I. Billy Graham and his future wife Ruth Bell, graduated from the college in 1943. William Gamon retired from banking to become mayor for the second time. When the war ended, there was a community celebration in the Gary Memorial Church.

The post-war years were marked by the population explosion and resulting growth of the city. By 1950 there were 11,638 residents, and seven miles of streets, including one mile of business frontage. The bandshell was built in Memorial Park in 1952 for summer concerts by the Wheaton Municipal Band. Radio personality Everett Mitchell moved to Beautiful Day Farm in 1954.

Wheaton celebrated the centennial year of its incorporation as a village in 1959 with a historical pageant and a parade. A Billy Graham Crusade followed in 1960.

Following a study by the League of Women Voters, the citizens approved a council/manager form of government in 1961 aimed at greater efficiency. Serious renewal of the business area began in 1963 under the leadership of Rosemary Ziska, executive director of the Greater Wheaton Chamber of Commerce. The establishment of Central DuPage Hospital in 1964 was sparked by the Wheaton Kiwanis Club.

An Olympic-size pool was opened in 1965 in Northside Park. That same year the Friends of the Library backed a bond issue to replace the Adams Library facilities with a new building, with space for 80,000 volumes. The vacated building was then purchased and given to the DuPage Historical Society by Edwin F. Deicke, a local insurance executive. This same benefactor made available his colonial style building on West Wesley Street for an expanded city hall in 1966.

The Illinois Prairie Path for bicycling, hiking and horseback riding was extended in 1967 through Wheaton, with branches to Aurora and Elgin on the right-of-way of the defunct CA&E. The B. R. Ryall YMCA facility was built at the Wheaton–Glen Ellyn border, to serve both communities. Margaret Hamilton became the first woman mayor in 1969.

Rapid growth in the 1960s culminated in the selection of Wheaton as an All-American City in 1968 by *Look* magazine and the National Conference on Governments. The award was based on citizen initiative, leadership, and support of programs designed to improve city living. Plans of the city for future development, large scale beautification, and passage of

*Topping of the Billy Graham Center, via helicopter, 1980.*
*Courtesy Wheaton College*

a fair housing ordinance in July 1967 were specific criteria.

During Mayor Ralph Barger's administration (1971–82), the Wheaton Center complex, with its twin high-rise towers, low-rise apartments and new depot, was completed. The Senior Citizens Center in the Memorial Park building was developed under Mary Lubko and the V.I.P. Council

Two new county buildings were occupied in 1973 on the western edge of Wheaton – the DuPage Center/Administration Building and Health Department. The Convalescent Center across County Farm Road was enlarged and renovated.

In November 1973 the Sister City connection was announced with Karlskoga, Sweden, a town comparable to Wheaton in size and political makeup, with similar problems and projects. Communication and visits were designed to bring international understanding and friendship between the two communities. A one block street south of the Memorial Park bandshell was renamed Karlskoga. Over 400 Wheaton residents at the time were of Swedish descent.

In 1974 the Cosley Animal Farm and Museum was established on Gary Avenue. One half of Wheaton's second railroad station, built in 1856 and used during the Civil War, had been moved to this location in 1887 as a residence. The oldest barn in the Wheaton area, as well as a variety of wild and domestic animals, are on display for visitors of all ages.

The DuPage Heritage Gallery was begun in 1975, honoring national celebrities from the county. In 1979 the Wheaton Historic Preservation Council was organized to preserve the heritage and landmarks of Wheaton. By midsummer of 1982 eleven homes and three public buildings had been designated as historic landmarks. The oldest buildings selected were the Tower of Blanchard Hall, Doenges Stationery Store (formerly Kampp's Furniture Store and Funeral Home), and the Bricker Apparel Store on Front Street (formerly the CNW depot).

The Billy Graham Center was opened in Wheaton in 1980 on land given by Wheaton College, opposite Blanchard Hall. The initial cost of $13,500,000 was a gift from the Billy Graham Evangelism Association to the college. The five-story building contains archives, a library and displays on evangelism, mission and revivalism. It also houses the Billy Graham School of Communications, and the major part of the correspondence and memorabilia of the Billy Graham Crusades.

Wheaton is world famous as a center of other religious activity, with more than fifty Christian organizations headquartered in the community and in neighboring Carol Stream.

The growing population of Wheaton, which in 1980 exceeded 44,000, has necessitated an increase in public services. Wheaton-Warrenville Unit School District 200 is composed of two high schools, three middle schools, and thirteen elementary schools (two of which are in Warrenville). Private schools include Wheaton Christian Grammar School, St. Michael's (Roman Catholic) and St. John's (Lutheran) elementary schools, and St. Francis High School (Roman Catholic). The Youth Outreach Program, supported by churches and individuals, serves troubled teenagers with counseling and lodging in two homes.

Cultural interests are served by a Wheaton College Artist Series, a municipal band, Youth and DuPage Symphonies, Wheaton Drama Club, Wheaton Art League, and one hundred forty other clubs and organizations.

Beautification of Adams Park by horticulturalist Yvonne Burt, and the cultivation of the garden plot, called the Liberty Square Garden, south of the depot by Green Gardeners of the Woman's Department Club are typical of paid and volunteer efforts.

Challenges for the future include development of outlying areas, such as the Wheaton Park Manor on the southwest, and the Rice Estate property, near Naperville and Butterfield Roads. Improvement of the water supply, expansion of light industry to broaden the tax base, and resolution of the controversy growing out of school closings and reorganization are other issues or concerns.

This quote comes from Dick Noble's speech in favor of granting All-American City status to Wheaton in 1967: "We accept and meet the challenge of changing times. But the character of the town has not been lost. It retains the influence of the founding fathers who sought responsible and responsive local government, educational excellence and moral order. Wheaton is still church-going, conservative and dry — a good place to bring up a family. But most important, Wheaton is people who care."

**The Author**

Edith E. Back is active in the local branch of the American Association of University Women, and did research for that organization's bicentennial project.

THE VILLAGE OF WINFIELD

# Winfield

*Adrienne Rose*

Winfield is a small village situated between West Chicago and Wheaton in DuPage County. The village was recorded in February 1853 as the "Plat of the Town of Fredericksburg" by James P. Doe, a former New Hampshire resident. He had received a land grant in 1845, but did not have the town platted until January 25, 1853. The importance of this early settlement lay in its position on the Galena and Chicago Union Railroad, which was completed to West Chicago (Turner Junction) in November, 1849.

Reference is made to one building in the town, put up by John Hedges and used as the railroad depot. Earlier histories of Winfield spelled the name "Hodges." Further investigation into the official document, which legalized the sale of the property from Doe, has revealed the correct name to be Hedges. He was the first stationmaster.

The name given to the station on tickets from Chicago was initially "Warren," after neighboring landowner Colonel Julius Warren. The name of Winfield came into early use, however. The post office was established on July 12, 1852, with Hedges its first postmaster. In 1854 Winfield was the name which appeared on the railroad's maps.

Today the station building used by Hedges is referred to locally as the "Besch House" because the Besch family was the last resident prior to the sale of the house to the Village of Winfield in 1977. The Winfield Historical Society is restoring the structure under the name of Hedges Station, in honor of its first stationmaster.

The station provided a shipping point for the residents of Naperville and surrounding farmlands. The town itself began to grow so rapidly that by 1857 it boasted three stores, several factories and a brewery. Freight tonnage from Winfield was topped only by that shipped from Wheaton, Turner Junction, and Cottage Hill (Elmhurst). A stagecoach line ran between

*From the* 1874 Atlas & History of DuPage County, Illinois

Winfield and Naperville, operated by J. C. Vallette and H. H. Fuller. It began the spring of 1854, with records indicating that George Streubler operated it after 1858. When the Chicago, Burlington & Quincy Railroad laid its line through Naperville in 1864, the bulk of the freight business at Winfield was lost and the town's growth stunted. Colonel Warren continued to operate a mail and passenger service to Naperville, however, well into the 1870s.

The composition of the town by resident clearly shows German immigration to have had a marked impact. While the 1850 census listed settlers from New England as the predominant land holders, the 1860 census showed half the residents to be from Germany. Many of the town's immigrants came from southern Germany. Among other lands from which immigrants hailed were Holland (Caspar Kline) and the Alsace-Lorraine area of France (Nicholas Enders). Many of these early immigrants have descendants residing in the village today. Among these are the family names of Enders, Schmitt, Schramer, Besch, Kline, Berkes, Dieter, Mueller, and Klein.

The German immigrants who resided in the town were, for the most part, Catholics. They attended worship at the German mission church of St. Stephen at Gretna. The long traveling distance, however, and rumors that a new church would be forming in Wheaton, caused a delegation to petition the Rt. Rev. James Duggan, Bishop of Chicago, to establish a church in Winfield. His approval brought prompt action. A one-acre plot was deeded to Bishop Duggan on February 21, 1867, by Julius Warren. Payment of $1.00 was made. The deed stipulated that a church building 30′ by 50′ be built, along with a dwelling for the priest and a school house. Father Corbinian, a Benedictine priest, was delegated to serve the new mission.

By 1869 a permanent pastor, Father John Wiederhold, was assigned. He remained the pastor until his death on February 6, 1921, never serving another parish during these 52 years. The parish retained use of the German language until World War I; then it became an English language church. This trend has continued, and today the practice of the parishioners has become increasingly Americanized. There is no longer the German traditional practice of a Corpus Christi celebration. To accommodate the projected figures of an increased congregation and facing a shortage of priests in coming years, a new building was undertaken in 1982 to accommodate a thousand persons. This was dedicated on October 1, 1983, by Bishop Imesch of Joliet.

St. John's parish school opened in 1882. Its original structure still stands as the Piekarski home, across from St. John's. In 1940 a new classroom building was completed, and it continues to serve students from the neighboring towns of Carol Stream and Warrenville, as well as those in Winfield.

Public school had commenced in the locality in 1856. At a special meeting of the villagers in December 1869 to elect school directors, a motion was also made to employ a teacher who could speak both English and German; this action reflected the community's ethnic change. A public school building was built in 1871 at the corner of Winfield and Beecher. With the opening of St. John's school in 1882, most of the students left the public school, which remained a one-teacher school until 1939.

With the growth of Winfield after World War II, public school officials were hard-pressed to keep up with the expanding enrollment. The eighth grade was sent to the West Chicago Junior High School in 1946, and the seventh grade followed in 1950. Four classrooms were added in 1956; three classrooms and a gymnasium, in 1960; and five more classrooms, in 1964. The old school building was almost surrounded by that time. With the class rolls still swelling, five relocatable classrooms were added to the complex during the latter half of the sixties. The enrollment then began to decline after 1970.

Overall, enrollment had increased from 80 to 520 between 1955 and 1966. After this trend reversed itself, the figure stood at 350 in January 1984. The many classrooms built to accommodate an increased student load are now being leased to a Day Care Center, a Montessori School, and the Western Regional offices of SASED, a special educational service unit. The five relocatables have been removed. The middle school, built in 1972 to accommodate grades 6–8, is being utilized by grades 4–8. The superintendent since July 1977 has been Robert T. Cobb.

A change in the town was also evident in the first church for Protestant families; this had its beginning in 1925 when Albert Hopkins, Willard Allanson and Ralph Brumbaugh started the Winfield Community Church. The cornerstone for the first church building was laid in 1939, at the southeast corner of Beecher and Summit streets. On January 1, 1959, the Winfield Community Church became a member of the Illinois Conference of Evangelical United Brethren Church, with 165 members listed. A new building was erected on Jefferson Street, south of Sunnyside, in 1964. The denomination merged with the Methodists in 1968, and the congregation is now known as the Winfield Community United Methodist church. Since 1960 pastors have included Rev. Lew Albee, Pastor Paul Beghard, Rev. James Cox, Rev. George Woosnam, Jr. and Rev. Edward Heyer.

*Besch House.*
*Photo by Janis Baumanis*

# St. John The Baptist Parish

*Winfield's Oldest Church.*

It was not until the 1960s that interest became apparent in another Protestant congregation in Winfield. By the end of 1970 the community had three new churches — Winfield Christian Reformed, Winfield Lutheran, and Faith Baptist. Both the Lutheran and Faith Baptist congregations used the facilities of the first Winfield Community church building on Beecher Street prior to the construction of new churches. The current resident of the old corner church is the Shrine of the Tridentine Latin Mass.

Since the publication of *Winfield's Good Old Days: a History* in 1978, other changes have taken place which reflect the rapid growth of the town. The census of 1954 recorded a population of 862. The 1984 figure stands at 4,442.

The diversity of residents has given Winfield a cosmopolitan flavor in recent years. Descendants of many nationalities now call Winfield home. These, and other new inhabitants live in such developments as Winfield Heights, Winfield Knolls and, most recently, the Hemphill Development. Condominiums, townhouses and single family homes appear in the last mentioned housing cluster.

The progress of modern health facilities is documented in Winfield's history. On the site of Jessie P. Forsythe's 1897 rest home, which became the Chicago-Winfield Tuberculosis Sanitarium in 1909, Central DuPage Hospital now stands. Since 1962 Central DuPage Hospital has drawn skilled physicians and technologists into the area. As of January 1984, CDH had 373 beds and a medical staff of 213 physicians, with an additional 36 consulting physicians. Dr. Richard Dominguez is president of the medical staff, and the administrative head is George G. Holzhauer. The hospital is noted for several specialities, notably eye surgery and orthopedics.

During the past few years the town has acquired two modern fire houses, the second established in 1979. The Winfield Library Association which originated in 1964, saw its

*Central DuPage Hospital.*

efforts fulfilled during the summer of 1981, when the library moved into its own building on the corner of Sunnyside and Winfield Road. Meeting rooms in the basement area provide the town with space for group meetings, such as 4-H, Ladybugs, the Winfield Historical Society, and the Lions. The current librarian is Rosemary Kelly.

The village offices were remodeled in 1983, and re-opened in February 1984. The current mayor of the town is James L. Collins. Patricia Stuart is the village clerk, and Michael Allison, the village manager.

The local newspapers, which provide news to Winfield residents, are the *Winfield Examiner* and the *Winfield Press.* Randall Petrik is the editor and publisher of the former, and Wayne Woltman serves in those capacities for the latter.

Another recent development highlights the connection between the old and the new in Winfield; this pertains to the moving of the Besch House. After the village had announced intention to demolish the house and to put a parking lot in its place, evidence was uncovered that the structure was the original station, the oldest building on the town plat of Fredericksburg, as filed by James Doe. A group of interested citizens met at the home of Martha Ingram to determine how the structure might be saved. As a result of this meeting, the Winfield Historical Society was organized and received its charter from the state in July 1978. The primary objective of the society was to lobby for the preservation of the building on its original site, and to gain recognition for it as an historic landmark.

These efforts, however, did not dissuade village officials. They gave the society the option of purchasing the building at a nominal fee and moving it, or seeing it demolished. Thereupon the WHS began a program of fund-raising, and sought interested parties in the town to provide a new location. An agreement was reached between the Winfield Park District and the society to lease one-third of an acre of the district property for $1.00 per year for a period of 99 years. The building was moved to the site at 555 Winfield Road in August 1981, at a cost of over $24,000. The members of the society are convinced that this preservation effort will well serve Winfield's future.

**The Author**

Adrienne Rose has served as president of the Winfield Historical Society.

# Wood Dale

*Mary Lou Mittel*

The historic Indian tribes who inhabited Illinois have been classified into several groups: the Illinois, Miami, Kickapoo, Potawatomie, Sac, Fox, Winnebago, and the Shawnee. The Winnebago were part of the Sioux nation, which originally lived along the central and north Atlantic coast. For many years they were pushed further west, until they reached the Wisconsin River, beyond which the tribe refused to go.

The Winnebago claimed the area called Wood Dale for their hunting grounds. Their range was extensive. Their signal hill was at Army Trail Road, Lake Street and Addison Road. Their main camp was in Beloit, Wisconsin. It was their custom to build a camp near Salt Creek at Thorndale Road and burn the prairie; thus they chased the game into the woods where hunters were waiting. Their continued use of the hunting grounds caused alarm to the first settlers. When Illinois became a state in 1818, the Winnebago signed a treaty giving up these hunting grounds.

The first white settler came to Addison Township in 1833. A native of Hillsborough, New Hampshire, Hezekiah Dunklee met a fellow traveler named Mason Smith. They traveled to Fort Dearborn. Here they purchased supplies and sought information. They followed the path made by General Winfield Scott's army on its way west during the Blackhawk War. This trail is called Grand Avenue and Army Trail Road in DuPage County. They followed it to a creek where they made their camp.

At first light they continued west to the Meacham trading post. The Meacham brothers shared their knowledge of wilderness living, and advised the two men to go back along the trail to the large stand of trees by the Salt Creek, and to make their claim on both prairie and timber.

Dunklee and Smith made their claims on the north end of the forest. Because it was September they decided to share one cabin, which they built on the site of the juncture of Hem-

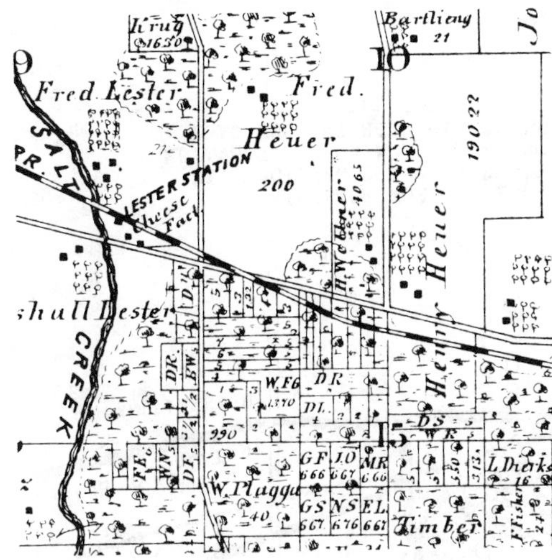


*From the* 1874 Atlas & History of DuPage County, Illinois

lock and Irving Park Road. They attempted to prepare ground for spring planting, but found their tools could not penetrate the vast network of roots that supported the prairie grass, which they described as "shoulder high to a man on horseback." They then cut trees and prepared the soft forest soil. The forest, which is the largest of three natural stands of trees in Addison Township, became known as Dunklee's Grove.

Early in 1834 Ebenezer Dunklee, brother of Hezekiah, arrived at the grove with his wife Amy and three children. A friend, Mr. Perrin, had accompanied them. Mr. Perrin died soon after their arrival. His is the first recorded death in Addison Township. On January 8, 1835, a daughter Julia Amanda was born to Amy and Ebenezer. She was the first white child born in Addison Township.

Thirteen years after his long trek from New Hampshire to the Illinois area which would bear his name, Hezekiah Dunklee was dead, leaving a widow, Eliza, and a one-year-old son, Horace. The 1850 census shows that Eliza, age 39, and son Horace, age 5, were still in the adjacent area called Sagone, living with friends, Nathan and Lucy Packert (Packard).

More is known of Ebenezer Dunklee because three generations of his family remained in the area. He was a member of the Congregational Church, a Whig, and the first Abolitionist in Addison Township. He took an active interest in community activities with his name appearing repeatedly in early township records. His wife Amy died in 1852, when a tornado blew their barn on her. Ebenezer married again in 1853, taking Ruth L. Hanson, a forty-two year old widow as his wife. He died on July 22, 1863.

Another young man arrived in the Grove in 1834. His name was John Lester. He liked the potential of the area and returned to New York to persuade his father to move with him to Dunklee's Grove. Trusting his son's judgement, Edward Lester brought his wife and other five sons. They made their claim on an Indian trail, Irving Park Road, at the Salt Creek. Having arrived in November 1835, they quickly built a 14′ × 16′ board shanty, to shelter them through the winter.

The following spring each son staked his claim, which spread the name Lester throughout the vicinity. That summer the Lesters built a home. A daughter, Julia, also requested a small building in which to teach school. She thereby became the first teacher in Addison Township. The building was located at the present site of the Water Treatment Plant.

A town named Sagone (sa-go-na) developed north of Dunklee's Grove, between Thorndale and Wood Dale roads to Devon Avenue. It was built on another Indian trail, which became a stagecoach line. It boasted several homes, a blacksmith, inn, general store, post office, jail, a German Lutheran school (at Wood Dale Road near Devon), and a public

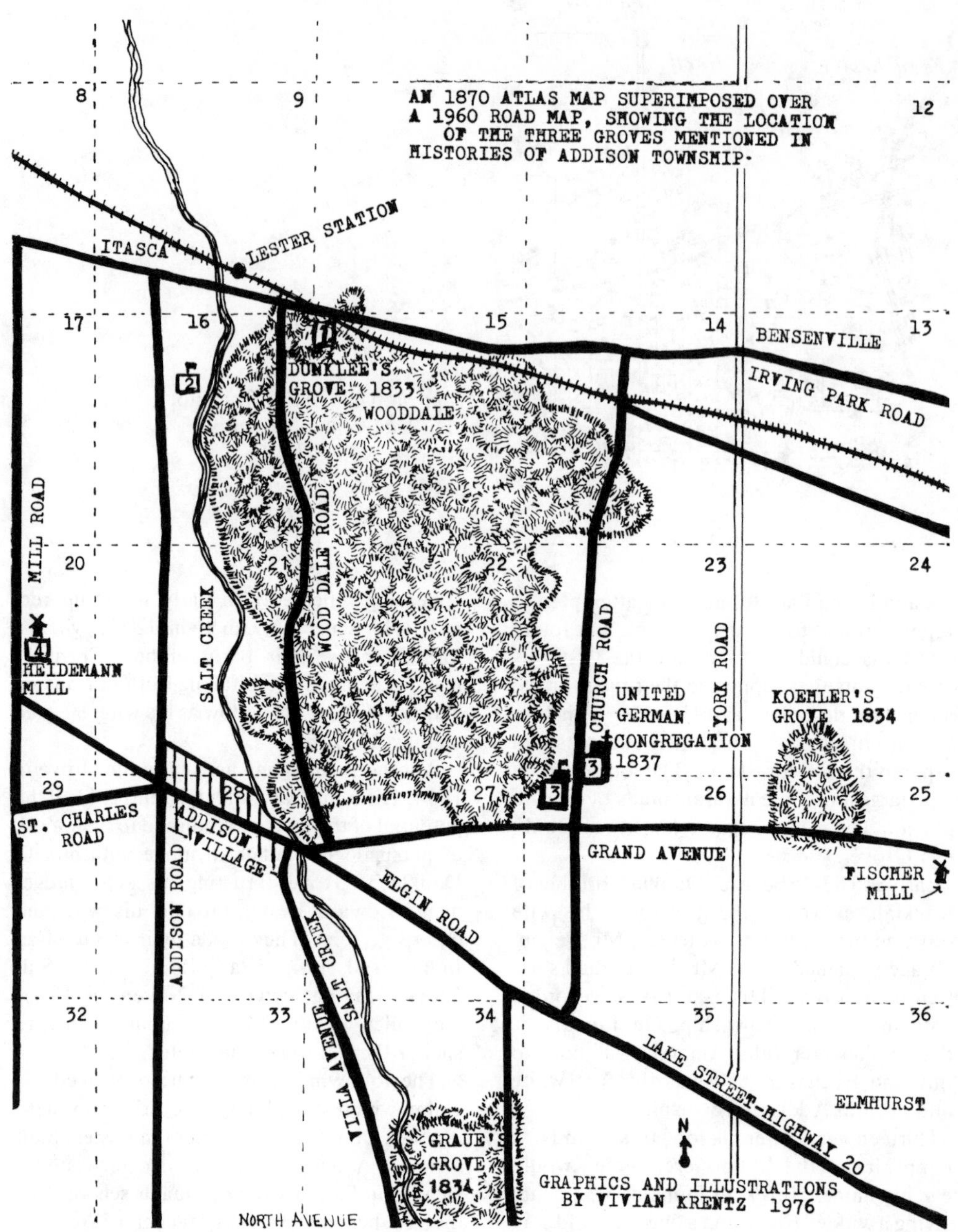


*Art by Vivian Krentz*

school for English speaking children (at Central and Thorndale roads).

Among the early settlers in Sagone was Smith D. Pierce. He became the first supervisor when Addison Township was formed in 1850. He also served as postmaster, justice of the peace and constable. The post office and jail were in his home. While he had held many offices during those formative years, the most important gift he left the area is his diary from 1836 through 1859. In it are the details of his life and that of his neighbors. There are also lists of the plants of the area and home remedies for humans and animals.

The 1850 census conducted, following the organization of Addison Township, showed a population of 818. This was also the first record of family names. Some of the names of the first settlers are not listed because they had moved from the area or had died. A cholera epidemic in 1848 claimed several lives, including that of P. T. Barnum's cousin, Cyrus Barnum, who had settled near Addison Road and Irving Park.

On May 31, 1852, Frederick Lester married Julia A. Dunklee. He built a home for his bride facing Salt Creek at Irving Park Road, the oldest remaining house. Here they raised the four survivors of their eight children. Frederick was the youngest of Edward Lester's sons. Although he had his leg amputated following a threshing machine accident at 18, he went on to become a respected businessman, farmer, and dairyman.

In the two decades before 1860, a large influx of German immigrants came to the area around Dunklee's Grove. These new residents were fleeing a nation in which conscription was mandatory and where parents often saw their sons sent to fight as mercenaries in foreign wars. Those parents who could afford to do so sent their sons and their families to the United States. Another reason for their emigration was that in Europe only the oldest son was the family heir. This new group also produced merchants, doctors, lawyers and teachers. They built churches, schools, hospitals, stores, and banks; thus they brought culture and prosperity to the area. Germans claimed the remaining land in the township and created a bilingual community.

In June 1847 a hail storm swept across northern DuPage, stripping the fruit from the trees in Dunklee's orchard, uprooting or leveling half of the crops. In 1854 another hail storm struck the area causing much destruction. This storm led to the formation of the Addison Farmers Mutual Insurance Company in 1855, which continued as Mutual Fire Insurance Company.

The Civil War was declared in 1861. Not every man could leave his farm, but many did sponsor young men who fought in their names. They rewarded them with a team of horses, a wagon, a cow, and a cash bonus with which to start a new life.

The first enlistee from Addison Township was Frederick Fischer, whose family had settled on the south end of Dunklee's Grove at Church Road and Grand Avenue. Frederick's brother, August, lost his life in the war.

After memorial services and the return of the soldiers, the work of establishing the township continued with only a few differences of opinion, usually over the placement of roads. The deep prairie loam, which made the area a farmer's dream, was a road builder's nightmare. Many methods of road maintenance were tried, such as towing a huge log over the rutted road to "smooth" it. Corduroy roads, made by laying logs across the road, were tried. They were a dismal failure.

What the area needed was a railroad. Frederick Lester joined a syndicate, comprised of businessmen from each community, along a proposed line. This group met with the owners of the Chicago and Pacific Railroad and persuaded them to build the track through their properties. Lester gave the right-of-way across his land and donated the site for a depot next to his home on Salt Creek. He then contributed toward its construction. The line was completed in 1873, a single track from Chicago to Elgin.

Despite the fact that the nation was again in financial trouble, Mr. Lester and Frederick Heuer built a cheese factory next to the depot. This was the first industry in the area.

In February 1874 a postal franchise was granted in the name Salt Creek, and President U. S. Grant appointed Frederick E. Lester postmaster. The area at the north end of Dunklee's Grove became known as Lester's Station or simply Lester. Frederick Lester deserves the title of "founder," because his actions made commercial growth in the area possible. In the spring of 1874 the Lester land east of Salt Creek and north of the railroad was subdivided as residential lots. In 1878 a mercantile store was opened on the second floor of the cheese factory. On July 13, 1886, Newton Lester, Frederick's son, became postmaster of Salt Creek.

The year 1890 brought a change which turned Lester's Station into a business "corner." A request was made of Frederick Lester for property next to the station on which to build an inn. Mr. Lester, a teetotaler, refused to have such an establishment on his property. Because he had done so much for the com-

*Wood Dale Station on the Milwaukee Line. Courtesy Wood Dale Historical Society*

munity through the years, the town's people did not want to upset him. However, they were not dissuaded from their desire for an inn. They simply waited for the ice storms of early January to glaze the ground, and then moved the station building east along the tracks to the northeast corner of the junction of the present Wood Dale Road and Irving Park Road.

Although Mr. Lester was a man of principles, he was not a vindictive person. After the station had been moved, he arranged for a small house to be moved to the northwest corner, across from the depot, for use by the stationmaster. It was only a few days after the moving took place that Frederick Lester died on January 21, 1891, at age 63.

Also in 1891, Mr. and Mrs. Henry (Hy) Timm had a barn moved from the Lester farm to the southeast corner, next to the inn. It was remodeled into a general store with family living quarters above. The store had a post office section, and Mr. Timm became postmaster in 1895. Mrs. Timm was the widow of August Hoppensteadt. Fred Hoppensteadt, her son, married Adele Mess on December 16, 1893, in Zion Lutheran Church in Churchville. They had four children — Edwin, Fred, Alvinia, (Mrs. Alfred Rosenwinkel) and Edna (Mrs. Monroe Fischer of Wood Dale).

Mr. Hoppensteadt became storekeeper in 1898. It has been said that he had the three best jobs in town. He was a storekeeper, a carpenter contractor, and the owner of a beer franchise in a German community. He left much of the store tending to his family. Among the buildings he erected were the original school on north Wood Dale Road in 1922, and the Adolph Rosenwinkel house in 1921, now Yesterday's Farm Museum.

Before the turn of the century, land speculators named a proposed subdivision in the forest, south of the tracks and east of Wood Dale Road, Wooddale. The area residents liked the name, and in 1899 the station name was changed from Lester to Wooddale. The post office remained Salt Creek.

The area around Wooddale Station changed slowly. Although Frederick Lester had subdivided a small portion of his land, hoping to attract new residents and businesses, the Depression of 1892 slowed the development.

The railroad was responsible for what development had occurred and it very thoroughly regulated the people's lives. At 9:15 a.m. the "mail" train stopped to pick up dairy products, and each evening the "can" train returned the empty milk containers. The owners of the railroad were aware of the dependence of the people on their service. In 1916 a special "Theater Train" ran each Saturday from Elgin to downtown Chicago, where the passengers could attend a stage-show at the McVicker's Theater. They would then return to the train for the "late run" home.

A few homes were moved from Sagone, as the Wooddale station became the shipping point for the surrounding farms. The children still attended school in Sagone, both Lutheran and public.

An enterprising man named William O'Beirne came to Wood Dale in 1915. He was employed by a real estate company in Elgin to sell land in the area. His enthusiasm was sparked by the promise of a large bonus if he sold a given number of lots. The view from the station did little to encourage a prospective buyer. The original corner buildings stood facing an ill-kept Irving Park Road. The streets were muddy, or had just received their first coat of gravel. Often a potential customer could not leave the station because of the mud. Mr. O'Beirne attached strips of white cloth to trees on land parcels, and then expounded on the obvious desirability of any lot within sight of the station.

He was successful! Between the lots he sold and those he claimed for himself, he qualified for the bonus which, in turn, paid for his property. He purchased the Blieze farm for his home. The house was west of Grove at Commercial. He promptly subdivided the remainder of the land and advertised it as "suitable for chicken farms."

The Ernest Julius Heinrich family were the first residents in the new subdivision. Ernest was originally from Michigan. His wife, Elizabeth Marie, was from England. The Heinrich purchase was on Commercial Street west of Wood Dale Road. They put their own battery operated electric plant in the basement, the first in the area.

In 1916 Wood Dale Road was stoned from Lake Street to Irving Park Road. This provided better access to the Village of Addison and the south DuPage area. The need for rapid improvement was made imperative because of the many automobiles in the area.

The years following World War I brought more land speculators to Wood Dale. The huge William Heuer farm was divided. The farm stretched from Wood Dale Road east along Irving Park Road to encompass the present site of Fenton High School and Plentywood Farm.

In 1923 a citizens' committee requested electric service for the area. Upon hearing the number of homes and the population, the company denied the request. The committee returned home and made plans to purchase the poles and wire, and to prepare the area from their homes to the nearest company owned connection site. Their determination so impressed the company that they assured the homeowners it would not be necessary to carry out their plans. Electricity came to Wood Dale in April. Mrs. Monroe Fischer recalls the first time the electric lights were turned on as the most exciting memory of her childhood.

Telephone service came at about the same time. The exchange office was located on the top floor of the Green Street School in Bensenville. In 1923 Joseph Culec purchased the Frederick Lester home, and soon became the first police marshall of Wood Dale.

Another resident of the period was Joseph Kleppner, who operated a basket company. The work was done in a building behind his home on north Wood Dale Road. Mr. Kleppner raised his own crop of reeds from seeds shipped from his native Pennsylvania. The reed farm was on School Street near River Road. In 1928 the Village of Itasca announced that it would build a sewage disposal plant on the

west bank of Salt Creek to accommodate an anticipated population increase.

The crash of the stock market in October 1929 plunged the nation into the Depression. Owners of the farms which had been incorporated into the Village of Wood Dale sought relief from the state. They were permitted to withdraw from the village, which shrank to a few blocks around the original "corner."

The fire department was organized in 1937 after obtaining a unique charter from the State of Illinois which permits them to "fight fires wherever needed." The charter was so written following a fire in which two children had perished. The neighboring Bensenville Fire Department, village owned, was not permitted to leave the village limits, which ended at that time on the south side of Irving Park Road, without receiving council permission. The burning building was on the north side of Irving Park Road in a section then called Georgetown. When the men proposing the formation of a Wood Dale fire department learned of this tragedy, they determined that such an experience must never happen to them; this accounts for the unique wording of their charter.

Pearl Harbor was a shock to the nation, just starting to emerge from the Depression. Once again Wood Dale residents tightened their belts. They collected radios, metal, fat and paper for reprocessing. They hung service flags in the windows, while husbands and sons went to war.

Wood Dale's post-war population growth was so slow until the sixties that chief of police Adolph Sofka could still operate with messages taken at his home. His wife Helen would then relay them to him in his car by means of a walkie-talkie.

But major changes were in store as the population almost tripled in a decade from 3,071 in 1960 to 8,831 in 1970. The 1980 census showed a total of 11,262 people residing in the village.

Housing construction expanded rapidly to accommodate the newly arrived. Among the notable buildings are the Brookwood Green high-rise condominiums, 190 W. Wood Dale Road. It is the consensus of fire inspectors, architects and such specialists from other parts of the nation and world, who toured the complex during construction, that it ranks among the safest anywhere. Very much like a submarine, in which flood and fire damage can be contained in one section, Brookwood is compartmentalized. Developer Richard Fencl was willing to construct a model in high-rise safety for the nation. He also donated $125,000 for the purchase of special equipment for the Wood Dale Fire Protection District.

From the Winnebago's burning of the prairie to the fire protection of the present, Wood Dale's history has been long and varied. A representative of its achievement, Jim Spivey, a world-class miler, aspired to the 1984 Olympics, and thus symbolized the high expectations of Wood Dale, his hometown, for the future.

### The Author

Mary Lou Mittel is Curator of the Yesterday's Farm Museum, and served as first president of the Wood Dale Historical Society when it was formed in 1971.

# Woodridge

*Joel and Laurie Kagann*

The early settlers of the southwest section of Lisle Township, DuPage County — Nadelhoffer, Greene, Goodrich, Kohley, Pfaff and Faulhaber — had no idea that the land they farmed in the late 1800s would some day become the community known as Woodridge.

In the late 1950s Albert Kaufmann, president of Surety Builders, started a development south of 75th Street and east of Illinois Route 53. He called this development Woodridge. Like the neighboring Woodridge Golf Course and an earlier settlement located on Route 53, the name was chosen from a description of the land itself, a wooded ridge overlooking the East Branch of the DuPage River. Kaufman started the Woodridge Sewer & Water Company to provide service to this subdivision. In 1971 this Woodridge Company was purchased by the Village of Woodridge.

By mid-1959 the population of the area had grown to 459, and the residents petitioned the county court for permission to incorporate as a village. A referendum was held and the Village of Woodridge was incorporated on August 24, 1959. The residents elected the first president (mayor), Leon Werch, and a board of trustees. With incorporation came the need for other municipal services. An all volunteer police department was established in 1960 with the assistance of Elmer Messer, a security office at International Harvester's Burr Ridge plant. Also in 1960 a volunteer fire company was organized, which later merged with the Lisle Fire Protection District. Today the village is served by three fire protection districts: Lisle/Woodridge, Belmont and Downers Grove Estates.

By early 1963 many of the farms east of Route 53, between 71st Street and 63rd Street, were purchased by the Winston-Muss Corporation (presently, Centex Winston) to build a community of over 2,000 homes. This area became known as Winston Hills, and the first section of homes was opened in early 1964.

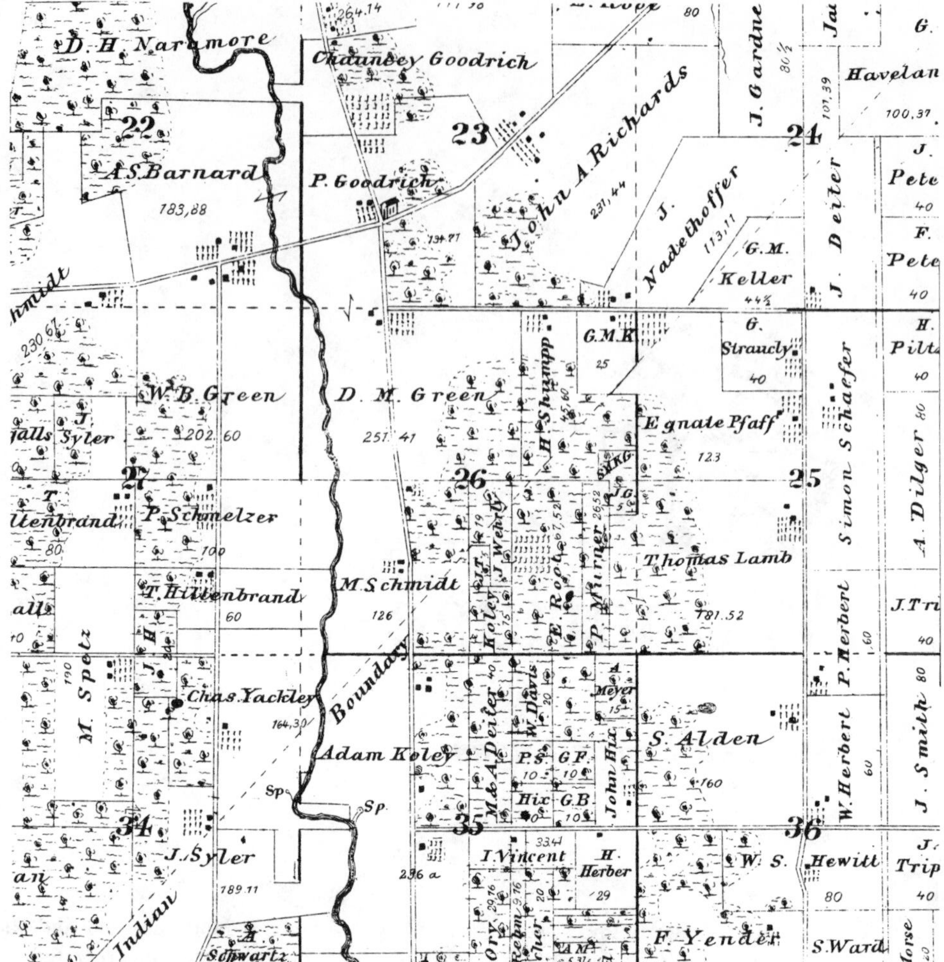


*From the* 1874 Atlas & History of DuPage County, Illinois

Immediately, a division within the community became apparent between the north and south. Because there was no direct access between the two sections of the village, several similar social and community organizations were formed, each reflecting its individual section name, Woodridge or Winston Hills. In 1974 a roadway, Woodridge Drive, connecting both sections of the village, was dedicated and opened to the public. The sectionalism of the Woodridge community has disappeared.

A highpoint in the development of Winston Hills was a publicity promotion sponsored by the Winston-Muss Corporation, together with a Hollywood film studio. In the summer of 1967, film actress Debbie Reynolds appeared in Woodridge at a picnic given for the entire community. Later, residents were taken by bus to the Chicago Theatre where they attended a special preview of "Divorce American Style," a film about family life in suburbia, starring Miss Reynolds.

Another expansion in the land area of Woodridge occurred in 1972, when several large farms centered around the Nadelhoffer property along 71st Street were annexed to Woodridge and developed as "Woodridge Center." A combination of single family, duplex and town houses with provisions for a commercial center for the community was to be provided. However, this latter aspect of the development never materialized. A site was also provided for the establishment of a community government. This expansion doubled the square miles of Woodridge.

Prior to 1966 the very basic needs of the new community were provided by itinerant merchants (dairy and bakery products). For other shopping needs Woodridge residents had to travel either to Downers Grove or to Lisle. The long-awaited shopping center opened at 75th Street and Janes Avenue in 1965, when other neighborhood shopping areas opened. A large shopping center is currently under development on the southwest corner of 75th Street and Lemont Road.

During the mid-seventies, in spite of recession, Woodridge continued to grow and expand as a fully developed community. Today many community residents continue to work in downtown Chicago. A local commuter bus service to the Burlington Northern railroad stations in Lisle and Belmont was established in the mid-1970s and today this route is operated by the Regional Transportation Authority.

In 1977 a major industrial company, Wilton Industries, a division of Pillsbury, located its international corporate offices and distribution center in Woodridge. This company will eventually provide over 500 jobs for the residents in the area.

Woodridge continues to move slowly away from simply being a "bedroom" community. Land which has been set aside for light industry and research will be developed.

After incorporation in 1959 and the opening of a permanent school, Surety Builders rented a small house, located at 2909 Forest Glen Parkway, to the village for the sum of $1.00 per year. Over the years this facility housed the police department, village clerk, a courtroom, building department and even the public library. These quarters were soon outgrown and a temporary village hall and police station were constructed at the south end of the area in 1971. In 1980 the village purchased and remodeled the bank building at 75th Street and Woodward Avenue, and the general offices were moved to that location. The "temporary" building on 83rd Street continues to house the public works and police departments.

The history of School District 68 dates back to the mid-19th century. On April 6, 1858 a warrantee deed was recorded, deeding the land now at the northeast corner of Hobson Road and Route 53 from the Pomeroy Goodrich family to the board of school trustees. The present school on that site, Goodrich, was built in the 1920s, with an addition added in the 1950s. Even with the expansion of the school in the late 1950s, it was not able to accommodate the increased enrollment that was being generated from the area known as Woodridge.

*Greene Home, Oak Cottage, ala Currier & Ives.*

In 1961 Woodridge School, located on Larchwood Lane, was opened. The land adjacent to the Woodridge School property was sold by Mr. Kaufman to the Diocese of Joliet. This became the site of St. Scholastica School and Church.

Additional schools were opened over the years to serve the educational needs of the Woodridge young people: Meadowview School in 1968; Edgewood School in 1969; Sipley School in 1973; Thomas Jefferson Junior High School in 1973; and Willowcreek in 1976. The majority of young people attending public schools in Woodridge go to one of six schools and the junior high school operated by School District 68. High school youth needs are served by Community High School District 99. The district operates two high schools, North and South, both of which are located in Downers Grove. Graduates from Woodridge's Jefferson Junior High School can choose which high school to attend, and there are Woodridge students in attendance at both campuses.

In 1967 the residents of Woodridge went to the polls to provide another service in the community, a public library. In 1969 the fledgling library hired its first full-time employee. Its collection of books numbered 553 in 1969. Now the library has over 43,000 volumes and a staff of twenty two. During its short history the library has moved three times, each time into a larger "model home." Finally, in 1977, the voters approved a bond issue to build the current 23,000 square foot facility at 2525 Center Drive.

The recreational needs of the community were met in 1969 when village residents passed a referendum establishing the Woodridge Park District. The part district today operates over 250 acres of land. The majority of the prime park land owned by the district was deeded to it by the village between 1973 and 1977. Approximately sixty four of the acres are used exclusively for park sites. The other acreage is shared with the school district and maintained by the park district. Two swimming pools and several tennis courts are also available to residents.

Additional open area was acquired by the village in 1973 when voters approved a referendum to purchase the Maplecrest Golf Course. This 130 acre site has open space available for future recreational land use. The municipality continues to operate it under the name of Village Greens of Woodridge, as a golf course during the summer and as an outdoor recreational center during the winter.

As the community grew, its spiritual needs were met by the establishment of the first church in 1960, when the Village Baptist church was formed. Shortly thereafter, the

*Actress Deborah Reynolds with Woodridge Mayor Joel Kagaan and Sgt. Keith Porter, 1967.*

Prince of Peace Lutheran (LCA), Saint Scholastica Roman Catholic and the Woodridge Methodist Churches were founded. For a period of time, three of the four churches in Woodridge had their rectories or parsonages on the same street and in the same block. Village residents referred to the area as "church row." By 1984 several additional churches were established in the community: Good Shepherd Community Church, Lumen Christi Presbyterian Church, Trinity Lutheran Church (Missouri Synod), and the Church of Latter Day Saints of Jesus Christ (Woodridge Ward).

The 459 people who gave birth to the village have been succeeded by 23,000 residents today. The early names are mostly memories and that first school is preserved only in the core of a much larger facility of the growing school system. The part-time volunteer firemen and police officers have given way to large, paid, professional departments. There is not much plowing, lumbering, milking or barn-dancing on the ridge overlooking the East Branch of the DuPage River. But Woodridge, with its motto "Pride in Progress," is indeed proud of the progress it has made during its first quarter century.

The Authors

Joel and Laurie Kagann serve as officers of Woodridge Special Events Committee. He has also been chief of police, mayor and village clerk, while she is currently Woodridge's Public Library Administrator.

# DUPAGE MUSEUMS AND HISTORICAL SOCIETIES

The Historical Museum of Addison
130 West Lake St. (Municipal Bldg.)
Addison, IL 60101
628–1433

Bensenville Historical Society
c/o Bensenville Community Public Library
200 S. Church
Bensenville, IL 60106
766–4642

Bloomingdale Park District Museum
172 S. Circle
Bloomingdale, IL 60108
529–3650

Cantigny Gardens & Museums
1 S 151 Winfield Road
Wheaton, IL 60187
668–5161

(Carol Stream) Gretna Museum
391 Illini Drive
Carol Stream, IL 60187

Churchville Historical Society
4 N 030 Church Rd.
Bensenville, IL 60106
766–4841

Clarendon Hills Historical Committee
Clarendon Hills Public Library
7 N. Prospect
Clarendon Hills, IL 60514
323–8188

Darien Historical Museum
7422 Cass Avenue
Darien, IL 60559

Downers Grove Historical Museum
831 Maple Avenue
Downers Grove, IL 60515
963–1309

DuPage Heritage Gallery
Red Grange Archives
The DuPage Center Atrium
421 N. County Farm Rd.
Mailing address: P.O. Box 77
Wheaton, IL 60189

DuPage County Historical Museum
102 E. Wesley Street
Wheaton, IL 60187
682–7343

Elmhurst Historical Museum
120 E. Park Avenue
Elmhurst, IL 60126
833–1457

Glen Ellyn Historical Society –
Stacy's Tavern
557 Geneva Rd.
Glen Ellyn, IL 60137
858–8696

Graue Mill Museum
York and Spring Roads
Oak Brook, IL 60521
655–2090

Hanover Park–Ontarioville
Historical Society
Chamberlain House
Jefferson & Greenbrook Boulevard
Hanover Park, IL 60103
837–3800

Hinsdale Historical Society
1 S. Clay
Mailing address: P.O. Box 336
Hinsdale, IL 60521

Itasca Area Historical Society
P.O. Box 112
Itasca, IL 60143

Lisle Heritage Society of the Old Indian Treaty
Boundary Line
P.O. Box 623
Lisle, IL 60532

Lombard Historical Museum
23 W. Maple
Lombard, IL 60148
629–1885

Lizzardo Museum of Lapidary Art
220 Cottage Hill Avenue
Elmhurst, IL 60126
833–1616

Morton Arboretum
Rte. 53
Lisle, IL 60532
968–0074

Naperville Heritage Society
Naper Settlement
201 W. Porter
Naperville, IL 60540
420–6010

Oak Brook Historical Society
c/o Oak Brook Village Hall
1200 Oak Brook Rd.
Oak Brook, IL 60521
654–2220

Roselle Historical Society
Roselle Village Hall
31 S. Prospect
Roselle, IL 60172
980–2000

Villa Park Historical Museum
220 S. Villa Avenue
Villa Park, IL 60181
833–1123

Warrenville Historical Society
P.O. Box 311
Warrenville, IL 60555

West Chicago Museum
132 Main Street
West Chicago, IL 60185
231–3376

Westmont Area Historical Society
Gregg House Museum
15 S. Linden
Westmont, IL 60559
963–5252

Winfield Historical Society
c/o Winfield Public Library
0 S 291 Winfield Road
Winfield, IL 60190
653–7599

(Wood Dale) Yesterday's Farm Museum
7 N 040 Wood Dale Road
Wood Dale, IL 60191

# Bibliography

## DUPAGE GENERAL

### Bibliography

Bateman, Newton and Selby, Paul (eds.) *Historical Encyclopedia of Illinois and History of DuPage County.* 2 vols. Munsell Publishing Co., Chicago, 1882.

Blanchard, Rufus. *History of DuPage County, Illinois.* O. L. Baskin & Co., Chicago, 1882.

*DuPage County Historical Society Portfolio.* No. One-Four, 1956–1959.

*DuPage Historical Review.* 3 vols.

1950 Titles

"An Eventful Year (Relating to 1850)." p. 22.
"Another DuPage Book: Hinsdale." (short) p. 2.
"Beginning of a DuPage Institution. The Winfield Sanitarium." p. 55.
"Century-old Naperville Doings." p. 19.
"Concerning Local History." p. 43.
"The County Seat Tug-of-War." p. 49.
"Downers Grove in its Infancy." p. 9.
"DuPage Bibliography Cumulative for 1949." p. 16.
"DuPage Commentary." pp. 48, 56.
"The DuPage County Court House in Retrospect." p. 17.
"The DuPage County Historical Society News." (short) p. 19.
"DuPage's Dateless Lincoln Legends." p. 7.
"DuPage's Lost Name Bearer." p. 12.
"Early Times Around About Glen Ellyn." (short) p. 7.
"Echoes of the Mexican War." p. 41.
"Editorial contributions solicited." (short) p. 5.
"Has DuPage's Historical Theme Run Its Course?" p. 8.
" 'Michigan': A Proposed and Rejected County Name." p. 8.
"More Light on Proposed 'Michigan County'." p. 10.
"Our Salutatory." p. 1.
"Page of Post Office History, A."
"Cloverdale Post Office Discontinued." p. 6.
"Medinah Post Office Changes Hands." p. 6.
" 'Prairie Farmer' Editor Chronicles An 1854 DuPage Visit." p. 4.
"Some Editorial Observations." (short) p. 15.
"Some Facts About Illinois County 'Histories'." p. 3.
"Wayne Township (Commemorative Edition)." p. 25.
"The Warren Women on a Pioneer Trek." p. 23.
"Your Home Town in Review – "
"Elmhurst." pp. 20, 44.
"Wheaton." p. 51.

1951 Titles

" 'A Light Shining on a Hill' (Naperville Academy)." September 1.
"An 1847 Letter Revives Pioneer Times." September 8.
"Century-old Map Defines DuPage County." September 11.
"DuPage Commentary." March 4, June 11, Dec. 11.
"DuPage County Historical Society–News and Notices." All issues 12.
"A DuPage Pioneer's Name Perpetuated Elsewhere." March 9.
"DuPage's 'Little Black Book' (1857 History)." December 8.
"Historical Matters Are Important." December 9.
"John Warne, the Big Woods Pioneer." June 4.
"Lombard: 'The Lilac Town' in Review." March 5.
"Oft-Chronicled Pioneer Beginning." December 1.
"Old Graue Mill to be Historical Exhibit." March 3.
"Old Landmarks Tell a Story." March 11.

"Our County Historical Society." by H. A. Berens. March 1.
"Pioneer Reminiscences (John Warne's)." June 1.
"So Close and Now So Far Away." September 5.
"Some Projected Railroads Through DuPage County." June 8.
"Warrenville Pioneered for Higher Learning." December 4.
"Your Home Town in Review – "
"Downers Grove." June 6.
"Itasca." September 6.
"Lombard." March 5.
"Wood Dale." December 6.

1952 Titles

"Bloomingdale Pioneers Pen Their Story." p. 19.
"Carl Sandburg's 75th Birthday." p. 46.
"Caroline Martin Mitchell Historical Museum." p. 22.
"DuPage Commentary." pp. 16, 35, 49.
"DuPage County Historical Society — News and Notices." pp. 12, 24, 36, 50.
"Ebenezer Duncklee." by Mrs. Mabel Lester Goreham. p. 42.
"Extracts From a Pioneer's Journal." p. 40.
"Genealogical Section." Edited by Laura K. Thomas. p. 21, 33, 47.
"Granddaughter's Recollections of Judge Cody." p. 27.
"Hobson Mill Site Rededication." p. 25.
"Joy Morton: A Man of Affairs." p. 2.
"The Last of Bonaparte." p. 6.
"The Lost Records of DuPage County." p. 37.
"Mason Brayman, Lincoln's Friend, Once a Warrenville Resident." p. 39.
"The Morton Arboretum: A Brief History." p. 4.
"Morton Commemorative Arbor Day." p. 1.
" 'Review' Publications For Sale." p. 48.
"Stacy's Tavern." by Dorothy I. Vandercook. p. 13.
"Subject: Bailey Hobson." p. 26.
"Three Volume Index of 'Review' Contents." p. 51.
"Yackley's Recollections as Told to Joy Morton." p. 8.
"Your Home Town in Review – "
"Naperville." p. 17.
"Villa Park." p. 44.

*1874 Atlas & History of DuPage County, Illinois.* Republished by the DuPage Historical Society, 1974.

Knoblauch, Marion (ed.) *DuPage County Guide, A Descriptive and Historical Guide.* DuPage Title Company, Wheaton, 1951.

"Looking Back" Series. *Suburban Trib* (In chronological order)

| *Article* | *Date* | *Author* |
|---|---|---|
| History of the Name "DuPage" | 2/17/81 | Louise Spanke |
| Plank Roads | 2/14/81 | Louise Spanke |
| Joseph Naper | 3/3/81 | Pat Miller |
| Railroads | 3/10/81 | Alice Purnell |
| Windmills | 3/17/81 | Amy Crisler |
| Fredenhagens/Lambe's | 3/24/81 | Amy Crisler |
| James Breasted | 3/31/81 | Marjorie Wyman |
| Bailey Hobson | 4/7/81 | Mattie Choice |
| Sheldon Peck | 4/14/81 | Pat Wallace |
| Colonel Warren | 4/21/81 | Leone Schmidt |
| Churchville School | 4/28/81 | Martha Jones |
| Hiram Leonard's Journal (Warrenville) | 5/5/81 | Bernice Smith |
| Lake Ellyn | 5/12/81 | Amy Crisler |
| Underground Railroad | 5/19/81 | Glenette Turner |
| Warrenville Seminary | 5/16/81 | Leone Schmidt |
| Thomas Hill | 6/2/81 | Lois Sicher |
| Bonaparte Area | 6/9/81 | Richard Thompson |
| Gypsies in DuPage | 6/16/81 | Alice Purnell |
| Change in DuPage County Boundaries | 6/23/81 | Marjorie Peters |
| Downers Grove Canon in 1860s | 6/30/81 | Pauline Wandschneider |
| Charles Heisin – Villa Park | 7/7/81 | Irene Martin |
| Anning Ransom – Carol Stream area | 7/14/81 | Jean Moore |
| Israel Blodgett | 7/21/81 | Pauline Wandschneider |
| Itasca Post Office | 7/28/81 | Joyce Usher |
| Carl Sandburg | 8/4/81 | Margaret Pruter |
| German Catholics in Gretna Area | 8/11/81 | Jean Moore |
| Westchester Park Subdivision in Oakbrook | 8/18/81 | Etta Chapet |
| Glen Ellyn High School | 8/25/81 | Susan Molin |
| Elijah McKinney's Fanning Mill and DuPage Tannery | 9/1/81 | Leone Schmidt |
| Early DuPage Teachers | 9/8/81 | Alice Purnell |
| How Hinsdale Got Its Name | 9/15/81 | John Poynton |
| Cross County Club | 9/22/81 | Carol Ortman |
| Franzen Millstones | 9/29/81 | Martha Jones |

| | | |
|---|---|---|
| Charles Gary and Gary's Mill | 10/2/81 | Don Rayno |
| Effect of Chicago Fire on Danby | 10/6/81 | Amy Crisler |
| Jack Travers Montgomery, actor and his daughter Peggy Jean, actress | 10/9/81 | Irene Martin |
| Benjamin Franklin Taylor, literary editor of *Chicago Daily Journal* | 10/13/81 | Leone Schmidt |
| West Branch of DuPage River (Naperville) | 10/16/81 | Don Rayno |
| Elfring's Store in Bensenville | 10/20/81 | Martha Jones |
| Stagecoaches and Drivers | 10/17/81 | Margaret Pruter |
| Geil's Funeral Home in Bensenville | 11/6/81 | Martha Jones |
| Daniel Benjamin Family | 11/3/81 | Alice Purnell |
| DuPage County Courthouse History | 11/10/81 | Barbara Henk |
| Old Water Tower on York Road, Mammouth Springs | 11/13/81 | Nancy Wilson |
| Effect of Chicago on Elmhurst Residents | 11/24/81 | Amy Crisler |
| Elmhurst Harness Shop (Strauschild) | 11/27/81 | Nancy Wilson |
| John Wesley Powell | 12/1/81 | Bernice Smith |
| Big Woods Church | 12/4/81 | Amy Crisler |
| Murder of Clarence Curtis, Gravel Pit Owner | 12/8/81 | Virginia Spears |
| Fred Grote, Horses | 12/11/81 | Genevieve Ackerman |
| Pfaff School, Woodridge | 12/15/81 | Genevieve Doletowske |
| DuPage County Fair, 1863 | 12/22/81 | Bernice Smith |
| Senn House, Bensenville, Dr. Bartels | 12/25/81 | Martha Jones |
| Interscholastic Sports | 12/29/81 | Robert Pruter |
| Dr. Elijah Smith | 1/5/82 | Joyce Usher |
| Churchill Log Cabin | 1/1/82 | Dorothy Vandercook |
| Gary and U.S. Steel | 1/8/82 | Jean Moore |
| "Out On The Farm" Radio Show | 1/12/82 | Jean Moore |
| Pioneer Buildings in Glen Ellyn Area | 1/19/82 | Alice Purnell |
| Occult in DuPage, Early 1900's | 1/26/82 | Bernice Smith |
| Zion Lutheran Church | 2/2/82 | Martha Jones |
| Adam Glos Weather Journal | 2/5/82 | Dorothy Vandercook |
| DuPage Residents Killed in Iroquois Fire | 2/7/82 | Elma Hadley |
| Pleasant Hill Cemetery | 2/16/82 | Alice Purnell |
| Potowatomi Indians | 2/23/82 | Don Rayno |
| Itasca and Railroad | 3/2/82 | Joyce Usher |
| 1918 Blizzard | 3/2/82 | Nancy Studt |
| "Home Bureau" | 3/23/82 | Alice Purnell |

Maas, David E. and Weber, Charles W. (eds.) *DuPage Discovery, 1776–1976, A Bicentennial View.* DuPage County Bicentennial Commission, 1976.

Moore, Jean and Crabb, Richard. *Young People's Story of DuPage County.* DuPage Heritage Gallery, Wheaton, 1981.

*Portrait & Biographical Record of DuPage & Cook Counties, Illinois.* Lake City Publishing Co., Chicago, 1894.

Richmond, C. W. (comp.) *History of DuPage County, Illinois.*

Richmond, C. W. and Vallette, H. F. *A History of the County of DuPage, Illinois.* Scripps, Bross & Spears, Chicago, 1857. (Republished, The Naperville Heritage Society, 1974.)

Thompson, Richard A. *Around the Arboretum.* DuPage Historical Society, 1981.

*20th Century Atlas of DuPage County, Illinois.* Middle-West Publishing Co., Chicago, 1904.

White, Marian A. *Book of the Western Suburbs.* J. Harrison White, Chicago, 1912.

## Audio-Visual

*Bicentennial Focus: Women of DuPage,* Wheaton-Glen Ellyn Branch American Association of Univeristy Women, 1975.

Level One "Women of Yesterday" – taped interviews.

June Wanless
Elizabeth Huested
Mrs. George Goodrich
Lillian Budd

Level Two "Women of Today" – taped interviews.

Mae Watts
Katherine K. Moore

Level Three "A Future for All – Images . . . Women of Today" – slide/script.

*The Evidence Around Us. The Daily Journal* and Gary Wheaton Bank, slide/cassette on Central DuPage, 1974.

*Have You Ever Met a Building?* DuPage Historical Museum, slides/tape on county architecture.

Thompson, Richard A., *DuPage Discovery, An Historical Survey,* DuPage Historical Museum, slides/tape, 1982.

## CHAPTER ONE

### Bibliography

Claus, Marilyn. "In Search of an Erratic Erratic."

*Illinois Magazine,* January–February 1984.

*The DuPage Conservationist,* published by the Forest Preserve District of DuPage County, Glen Ellyn, provides the most systematic treatment of the natural history of this vicinity. Issues, according to publication chronology, include:

a) "The Natural History of DuPage County." Wayne Lampa.
Part I, 'Nature's Part' Autumn/Winter, 1973.
Part II, 'Man Steps In' Spring, 1974.
Part III, 'What's Left for the Future?' Summer, 1974.

b) "A Glimpse of Prehistory." Wayne Lampa. Fall, 1977.

c) "A Find of Mammoth Proportions." Gail Legner Wetta. Fall, 1977.

d) "Glacial Stew." Jim Walser. Spring, 1980.

e) "Just Do-in Our Thing." Wayne Lampa. Winter, 1980-81.

**Audio-Visual**

"What Has Happened to Our County?", Forest Preserve District of DuPage County, slides.

## CHAPTER TWO

Beggs, Stephen R. *Pages from the Early History of the West and Northwest.* Methodist Book Concern, Cincinnati, 1868.

Blodgett, Henry. "Autobiography." Unpublished, 1906.

Early, Ann. *1971 Salvage Excavations.* Fermi National Accelerator Laboratory, Batavia, 1971.

Gates, Standford. "Archaeological Survey of the DuPage River Drainage." *Illinois Archaeological Survey.* Bulletin No. 3, University of Illinois, Urbana, 1961.

Hatch, Luther A. *The Indian Chief Shabona.* Author published, 1915.

Hoglund, Kenneth G. *The Excavations at Du-33: A Preliminary Report.* Forest Preserve District of DuPage County, Glen Ellyn, 1978.

Kutter, Elizabeth. "DuPage Presbyterian Celebrates 150 Years." *The Naperville Sun,* June 17, 1983.

Lee, George R. *The Beaubiens of Chicago.* Culver-Stockton College, Canton, Mo., 1973.

Peters, Marjorie Herlache. *DuPage County, Illinois, Churches and Their Records, 1833–1920.* Lombard Suburban Genealogical Society, 1981.

Quaife, M. M. *Chicago's Highways Old & New.* D. F. Keller & Co., Chicago, 1923.

Robb, Ruth Flesher. *1840 DuPage County, Ill. Federal Census.* Author published, 131 West North Ave., Lombard, 1978.

Santeford, Lawrence Gene. "Prehistoric Populations of DuPage County." *DuPage Conservationist,* Forest Preserve District of DuPage County, Spring, 1979.

Santeford, Lawrence Gene. "Prehistoric Populations Archaic Indians – DuPage County, Autumn, 1979.

Schmidt, Royal J. *The Potawatomie Indians of DuPage County.* DuPage County Historical Society, Wheaton, 1974.

## CHAPTER THREE

"Clues Link Historic Home to Underground Railroad." *West Chicago Press,* November 5, 1981.

Dieter, Raymond. *A Dieter Family Tree.* Author published, Glen Ellyn, 1981.

Robb, Ruth Flesher. *1850 DuPage County, Ill., Federal Census.* Author published, Lombard, 1983.

Robb, Ruth Flesher. *1860 DuPage County, Ill., Federal Census.* Author published, Lombard, 1983.

Schmidt, Royal J. *Bugles in a Dream, DuPage County in the Civil War.* DuPage Historical Society, 1962.

Turner, Glennette Tilley. *The Underground Railroad in Dupage County, Illinois.* Newman Educational Publishers, Wheaton, 1978.

*Zion Lutheran Parish,* 1838–1963, Anniversary booklet.

## CHAPTER FOUR

Andrews, Wayne. *Battle for Chicago.* Harcourt, Brace & Company, New York, 1946.

Feely, Ralph. *From Camelot to Metropolis.* (Ontarioville – Hanover Park.) 1916.

Fegelman, Andrew. " 'Progress' Scores Another Casualty in Old Food Mart." *Chicago Tribune,* December 19, 1983.

Fuller, Loie. *Fifteen Years of a Dancer's Life.* Small, Maynard & Co., Boston, 1913.

Harris, Margaret Haile. *Loie Fuller, Magician of Light.* The Virginia Museum, Richmond, 1979.

Herrick, Bartle C. *What You Didn't Know About Downers Grove and Didn't Know Who to Ask.* Author published, 1982.

"Hunt Designed Home for Summer Residence." *The Daily Journal,* July 18, 1982.

Ibata, David. "Rahabbing Suburb Estate Reveals 70 Years of Surprises." *Chicago Tribune,* July 2, 1983.

Moore, Jean. "Ontarioville, a Community Surrounded," *Daily Journal,* November 22, 1973 and June 22, 1983.

Norris, James D. and Livingston, James. "Joy Morton and the Conduct of Modern Business Enterprise." *Chicago History,* The Chicago Historical Society, Spring 1981.

"100 Anniversary Issue." *Downers Grove Reporter,* May 23, 1973.

## CHAPTER FIVE

"A. T. McIntosh Offers Prizes to Home Owners." *Chicago Tribune,* April 16, 1933.

Croydon, Michael. *Ivan Albright.* Abbeville Press, New York.

"Francis S. Peabody Drops Dead After Watching Hunt." *Chicago Daily Tribune,* August 18, 1922.

Herrick, Frank Earl. *Poems of DuPage County.* Wheaton Journal, 1936.

"Knoch of Naperville." *The Chicago American,* August 18, 1958.

Lewis, Charles. "The Arboretum as a Museum." *The Morton Arboretum Quarterly.* Winter 1981.

Martinez, James. "Artist Albright, the 'Master of Decay' is Dead." *Chicago Sun-Times,* November 19, 1983.

McShane, Stephen. "Danada: An Historical Report on the Rice Farm in DuPage County." Forest Preserve District of DuPage County, 1981.

McShane, Stephen and Harvey, Miles. "A Salute to the History of McDowell Grove." *The DuPage Conservationist,* Winter 1981–82.

Nash, Jay Robert. *Bloodletters and Badmen.* Warner, New York, 1975.

Wood, Doris. *A Small Town Weathers the Depression, Naperville, Illinois. 1930–40.* Unpublished thesis.

## CHAPTER SIX

"The Arts in DuPage." Century III and College of DuPage booklet, 1979.

Bartlett, Alyce. "Industry Plays Key Role in Communities." *Daily Journal,* February 18, 1982.

Bennett, Jay C. (comp.) *1983–84 Reference & Yearbook of DuPage County, Illinois.* DuPage County Clerk, Wheaton, 1983.

Bingle, James D. *Bolingbrook.* Bolingbrook Historical Society, 1979–80.

Buursma, Bruce. "Catholics in DuPage Burgeoning "*Chicago Tribune,* September 28, 1983.

Crabb, Richard. "Gallery Begins Historic Campaign." *The Daily Journal,* June 29, 1980.

Dold, R. Bruce and Sullivan, Barbara. "Suburb Irony: Poor Surrounded by Plenty." *Chicago Tribune.* February 13, 1983.

Draeger, Harlan and Ingersoll, Bruce. "Oak Brook Waste Company Mired in EPA 'Sewergate'." *Chicago Sun-Times,* March 6, 1983.

*DuPage County Water Supply Public Information Resource Manual.* DuPage County Development Department – Planning Division. 1982.

"DuPage Minorities Making Impact." *Suburban Life Graphic,* September 7, 1983.

"Existing Land Use Analysis and Trends." DuPage County Regional Planning Commission, 1980.

*Fermilab Highlights.* The Public Information Office, Fermi National Accelerator Laboratory, 1982.

Freedman, Sam. "A Need to Belong." *Suburban Trib,* August 15, 1979.

Freedman, Sam. "The Hidden Poor." *Suburban Trib,* series, November 21, 22, 23, 26, 28, 29, 30, 1979.

Freedman, Sam. "The Other Machine." *Suburban Trib,* series, October 22, 23, 24, 1980.

Goldstein, Neil. "DuPage Latinos Unite." *Chicaco Sun-Times, Suburban Week.* April 30/May 1, 1975.

Hafferkamp, Jack. "The Quark Hunters." *Chicago,* June 1979.

Hansen, Arlene. *25th Silver Anniversary City of Oakbrook Terrace.*

Kirkpatrick, Truman. "History of York Center Community Cooperative, Inc." Unpublished, 1976.

Kleina, Bernard. "HOPE for the Suburbs." H.O.P.E. Inc., 1975.

Little, Anne. "Founders' Visions Take Root." *Suburban Trib,* March 23, 1982.

McCaron, John. "Unincorporated Areas – They're Doing Just Fine." *Chicago Tribune,* June 29, 1978.

McCullough, Purdie. "A Very Special Place, The Village of Burr Ridge." Burr Ridge Bicentennial Committee, 1976.

McNamee, Tom. "Waste Issue Splits West Chicago." *Chicago Sun-Times,* July 17, 1983.

"Naper Settlement: Holding the Fort." *The DuPage Magazine,* Lombard, October/November 1980.

Nelson, Eleanor. "Naperville Shoots Past Elmhurst in Population." *Suburban Trib,* October 21, 1983.

O'Conner, Phillip J. "DuPage Housing Ruling Criticized." *Chicago Sun-Times,* October 28, 1983.

O'Hara, Delia. "Westward Home – DuPage County Rivals the Sun Belt for Boom." *Chicago Sun-Times,* July 15, 1983.

*Profile DuPage County Statistical Handbook.* Development Department – Planning Division, 1983.

Reardon, Patrick and Fegelman, Andrew. "DuPage Housing Crusader Stirs Conflict in Fairness Fight." *Suburban Trib,* July 12, 1983.

Sabine, Mike. "Chronicle of C/D Past Runs Gamut of Environmental Changes." *Courier,* March 11, 1982.

Sargeant, Winthrop. "Profiles: Singing With the Big Dads." *The New Yorker,* March 29, 1976.

Schonauer, David. "Water Wars." *Chicago,* July 1983.

"Village of Willowbrook." Pamphlet, 1982.

## ADDISON

Krentz, Vivian and Morris, Pearl. *Addison, Village of Friendship.* 1984.

Morris, Pearl and Hinkle, Elvera. *Addison, 1833–1976.* Bicentennial booklet, 1976.

## BENSENVILLE

### Bibliography

"Bensenville." Chamber of Commerce pamphlet, 1976.

"Bensenville Comprehensive Plan Report." DuPage County Regional Planning Commission, 1981.

Doherty, Richard P. "The Origin and Development of Chicago–O'Hare International Airport." Unpublished doctoral dissertation, 1970.

Eckert, Allan W. *Gateway to Empire.* Little Brown, Boston, 1983.

Edmunds, R. David. *The Potawatomies: Keepers of the Fire.* University of Oklahoma Press, Norman, 1978.

"Historical Sketch of Immanuel Evangelical Church." Unpublished, 1959.

Jones, Martha Kirker. *Bensenville.* Village of Bensenville, 1976.

Pooley, William V. *The Settlement of Illinois from 1830 to 1850.* Madison, 1908.

Ritzert, Kenneth. *The Bensenville Story.* Pageant Script, 1962.

"A Review of the History of Zion Church." Pamphlet, Bensenville, Ill.

*Two Worlds.* Flick-Reedy Corporation, 1966.
Village Board Statistics, Village of Bensenville, 1980.
Wooley, Gertrude, "Story of Bensenville." Unpublished.

### Oral

(Oral History Transcripts from Bensenville Public Library)
George Adis
Mrs. Luella Barth
Mrs. Fred Boeske
Esther Burianek
Mrs. Alvar A. Eklov
Monroe Fischer
Chester Franzen
Leonard Geils
Mrs. Erna Ehlers Hackmeister
Katherine Howell
Wesley A. Johnson
Armin Korthauer
Mrs. Lillie Lange
Martin and Lydia Luessenhop
Mrs. Erwin Luebking
John Pangiotaros
William Redmond
John Reher
Alvina Rittmueller
Martin Romme
Mrs. Adolph Rosenwinkle
Marvin and Grace Rusteberg

### (Interviews)

Charles Earhart
James Gau
Kenneth Kaufman

## BLOOMINGDALE

### Bibliography (published)

*Bloomingdale Voice.* October 4, 1978; March 9, 1983.
*Decennial United States Census,* from 1840–1880, including material from:

Schedule One, Individual; Schedule Two, Productions of Agriculture: Schedule Three, Products of Industry; Schedule Five, Mortality; Special Schedule of Manufacturing Number One, Agricultural, Implements; Special Schedule of Manufacturing Numbers Seven and Eight, Flour and Grist Mills.

*History of St. Paul's Church.* Centennial Edition, Bloomingdale, 1978.
*Village Almanac, Village of Bloomingdale,* September, 1975 – October, 1983.
*Village News.* Bloomingdale, June 6, 1973.

### (Manuscripts and Records)

Bloomingdale Township Offices
Miscellaneous records on file dating from April 2, 1850.
Town Auditor's Meeting Records, May 31, 1880 - March 28, 1916.
DuPage County Recorder's Office
Plat of the Sixteenth Section Township 40 North, Range 10 East of the Third Principal Meridian, July 1, 1842.
Plat of the Town of Bloomingdale, January 4, 1845.
Genealogical and Historical Records of Bloomingdale Township, Vol. I. Wheaton Public Library.
Records of the Village of Bloomingdale, 1889–1960.

### (Correspondence)

Cathee Neilson, Olathe, Colorado (A Meacham descendant, providing information from the Meacham family bible, and sharing 1820-30 census material on the family in New York.)
Rutland County Historical Society, Rutland, Vermont.
Vermont Historical Society, Montpielier, Vermont.

### Oral

Bob Bender
Mr. and Mrs. Gus Fessler
Lowrey Hedstrom
Ruth Hillmann
Louise Olson
Becky Wilhelmi
Shirley Williams
Ethel Williamson

## CAROL STREAM

William L. Guild, interview.
Kelley-Kohli family records.
Moore, Jean. *Build Your Own Town.* 1984.

## CLARENDON HILLS

Evans, Helena. *History of Clarendon Hills.* 1954.
Leipper, Lois. *The Village of Volunteers.* 1974.
Richert, Paul and Mann, Roberts. *History of Clarendon Hills, DuPage County, Illinois, 1929–1930.* Unpublished manuscript.

## DARIEN

Argonne National Laboratory 1982–83, booklet.
Elbe, Anita. *A Community Called Cass – A Portion of Darien's Heritage.* Unpublished, 1978.
Clara Anderman, interview.
Melinda Weirmeister, interview.

## DOWNERS GROVE

"The Downers Grove Historical Trail." Pamphlet, 1980.
*The Downers Grove Village Book.* Downers Grove Chamber of Commerce, 1983.
Dunham, Montrew and Wandschneider, Pauline. *Downers Grove 1832–1982.* The Heritage Festival Task Force, Downers Grove, 1982.

### Audio-Visual

*The History of Downers Grove.* Video cassettes, available through High School District #79 CA TV.

#1 Pierce Downer
#2 Israel Blodgett
#3 The Downers Grove Cemeteries
#4 Prince Pond and The Blacksmith Shop
#5 The Railroad
#6 Avery Coonley School
#7 The Historical Museum Part I
#8 The Historical Museum Part II
#9 The Fire Department

#10 The Movie Theatres
#11 The Schools
#12 The Library
#13 Potpourri

## ELMHURST

### Bibliography

Armstrong, Ann. *Story of a Parish.* Elmhurst, 1966.

Bates, Dr. Frederick H. *"'Old Elmhurst." Being the Personal Recollections of a Native.* Elmhurst Historical Commission, second printing, 1973.

Berens, Helmut Alan. *Elmhurst: Prairie to Tree Town.* Elmhurst Historical Commission, 1968.

*Elmhurst-Chicago Stone Company: 75 Years of Progress, 1883–1958.* Company published, Elmhurst, 1958.

*Elmhurst Historical Map.* Elmhurst Historical Society.

*Elmhurst: Origin of Names, Streets, Schools, Parks, and Landmarks.* Elmhurst Branch, American Association of University Women, 1976.

*The Elmhurst Story . . . Biography of Progress, 1910–1960.* The Elmhurst Story Steering Committee, 1960.

Fischer, Howard C. (ed.) *100 Years of Elmhurst News, 1836–1936.* Elmhurst Centennial Historical Committee, 1936.

Immanuel Lutheran School. *A Century of Grace and Growth, 1879–1979.* Elmhurst, 1979.

Russell, Don. *Elmhurst: Trails from Yesterday.* Heritage Committee of the Elmhurst Bicentenial Commission, 1977.

*Self-Guided Tours of Historic Elmhurst.* Elmhurst Historical Museum, 1983.

Stanger, Robert C. "Elmhurst College, 1871–1971, The First One Hundred Years." *Elmhurst College Magazine.* Vol. IV, No. 3, 1971.

*St. Peter's United Church of Christ, Elmhurst, Centennial.* Elmhurst, 1976.

*The Story of a Bank, 60th Anniversary, Elmhurst National Bank.* Elmhurst, 1954.

### Audio-Visual

(Slide programs available at the Elmhurst Historical Museum)

"Decade of Development, Elmhurst 1919–1936."

"Doorways to History." Architectural and social history of Glos Mansion (now Elmhurst Historical Museum), 1892–1983.

"Germantown on the Prairie." German-American history and heritage in Elmhurst.

"Prairie Village." Elmhurst history, 1836–1910.

"Walter Burley Griffin in Elmhurst." Architectural history of Griffin buildings and Griffin's life in Elmhurst.

"Women on the Move." Women's history in Elmhurst, 19th and 20th centuries.

## GLENDALE HEIGHTS

Blanchard, Rufus. *Discovery and Conquests of the Northwest with the History of Chicago.* R. Blanchard & Co., Chicago, 1898–1900, Vol. 2.

*Community Profile and Industrial Site Inventory.* Village of Glendale Heights, 1983.

Comprehensive Plan. Village of Glendale Heights, 1983.

Davis, Marion. *Glendale Heights.* The Dale Company, Glendale Heights, 1972.

Harmon, Ada Douglas. *Story of An Old Town.* Glen News Printing Co., 1928.

Patrick, Ruth. *Story of a Pioneer Farm.* Unpublished manuscript, 1939.

## GLEN ELLYN

### Bibliography

*The Glen Ellyn News,* selected articles.

Harmon, Ada Douglas. *The Story of An Old Town.* Glen News Printing Co., 1928.

Kaiser, Blythe P. and Vandercook, Dorothy I. *Glen Ellyn's Story and Her Neighbors in DuPage County.* Author published, 1980.

Perkins, Gerald A. "Stacy's Tavern Restoration Log." Unpublished.

### Audio-Visual

"Pictures of an Old Town" – slide presentation by Lee Hestermann.

"Stacy's Tavern" – a slide presentation. The Glen Ellyn Historical Society.

## HINSDALE

Bakken, Timothy H. *Hinsdale. Hinsdale Doings,* 1976.

Dugan, Hugh G. *Village on the County Line.* The Lakeside Press, 1949.

McElhone, Fred. *Early Hinsdale.* A manuscript, 1940.

Manuscript accompanying *Historical Slides of Hinsdale.*

## ITASCA

Greenblatt, Mirian. *The History of Itasca.* Itasca State Bank, 1976.

"Itasca, Illinois." American National Publications pamphlet, 1977.

*Itasca, Scenes of the Past,* 1979.

Usher, Joyce. *This is Itasca.* 1965.

## LISLE

*Courant* clippings from the 1930's.

1895 letter written by Alois Schwartz.

Hatch family records, lent by the late Harry Hatch and June Frey Hatch.

*Lisle Advertiser.* Various articles.

Lisle Cemetery Association first record book.

*Lisle Sun.* Various articles.

No. 1 Lisle Township School Record Book.

Riedy family records, including family history by Leona Riedy.

St. Joan of Arc parish records.

## LOMBARD

Budd, Lillian. *Footsteps on the Tall Grass Prairie.* Lombard Historical Society, 1977.

Dunning, Mildred Robinson. *History of the Methodist Church.* Unpublished, 1957.

Dunning, Mildred Robinson. *The Story of Lombard 1833–1955.*

First Church of Lombard, United Church of Christ, Original Record Books, 1850–1976.

Gray, Harold. *"Arf" The Life and Hard Times of*

*Little Orphan Annie.* Arlington House, New Rochelle, N.Y., 1935–1945.

*The House on Maple Street.* Film by Lombard Historical Museum.

Lombard Historical Society, Interviews on Tapes at Lombard Historical Museum.

Mons, Ardyce G. *Through Years of Grace.* Memorials Committee of First Church, Lombard, 1979.

Peck, Frank. Undated, unpublished, and unedited collection of historical narratives.

Sacred Heart Parish of Lombard, *Sacred Heart Golden Anniversary Book.*

Taylor, Henry Copeland. *Historical Sketches of the First Church of Lombard, Illinois.* Written for 85th anniversary, 1936.

Thompson, Edna L. *Plums & Lilacs.* Undated and unpublished collection of narrative poems and photographs.

Trinity Lutheran Church, *One Hundred Years of Growth Through Grace,* 1968.

## NAPERVILLE

City of Naperville Annexation file.

City of Naperville history files.

City of Naperville Profile Sheet, 1983.

Edward Hospital 1983 Fact Sheet.

Fraser, Helen. *Footsteps Through Old Naperville.* 1982.

Givler, James H. *Naperville Review – "Our Town."* September, 1959.

League of Women Voters. *Naperville – Your Town.* 1960, 1966.

Naperville Centennial 1831–1931. 1931 Fort Payne Chapter of the Daughters of the American Revolution.

"Naperville – Today, Tomorrow." City of Naperville.

"Portrait of Naperville." *Naperville Sun.* Monday, October 7, 1974.

"Progress Report." *Naperville Sun.* 1958, 1965, 1967.

Souvenir of Naperville Homecoming, 1917.

Special Sesquicentennial Section, The Naperville *Sun,* June 5, 1981.

Towsley, Genevieve. *Historic Naperville.* 1975, 1976, 1979.

Wehrli, Jean and Mary Lou. *The Naperville Sesquicentennial Photo Album, 1931–1981.*

## OAK BROOK

Archaeological Surface Survey contracted for in 1974 by the Village of Oak Brook with Dr. Stuart Struever of Northwestern University; and archaeological test excavations of two sites contracted for by the Oak Brook Historical Society in 1978 with the Foundation for Illinois Archaeology; Dr. Struever, Director and Summary Report by Michael D. Wiant, of the Department of Anthropology at NWU.

Abstracts of Title to land in the NW¼ and also in the NE¼ of Section 36, Twp. 39 North of Range 11 and East of the 3rd Meridian in DuPage County, Illinois.

The Oak Brook Civic Association Minutes.

Ruchty, George E. *The Fullers of Fullersburg 1834–1923.* The Hinsdale Historical Society, Hinsdale, 1978.

## ROSELLE

### Bibliography

Andreas, A. T. *History of Chicago.* Vol. 2 & 3.

Crandall, Earl. *The Roselle Story,* 1972.

*History of Roselle.* Illinois Sesquicentennial, 1968.

Loeper, R. V. *History of Roselle.* National College of Education, 1959.

*Medinah/Meachem 1874–1976.* 1976.

Newman, Ralph G. *Lincoln Funeral.*

*Roselle Record.* Newspaper, various dates.

Sanborn, D. *History of Roselle, 1818–1968.*

### Oral
### (tapes)

William Sauerman
Herman Scholdt

## VILLA PARK

### Bibliography

Brochure from Villa Park Chamber of Commerce, 1977.

"Fifty Years Anniversary Book of St. Alexander's Parish." 1974.

"50th Anniversary – Community Congregational Church." 1962.

*A Glimpse of Villa Park.* Villa Park Plan Commission, 1920.

Local History Files at Villa Park Public Library.

Mabee, Bessie. *History of Villa Park.* Villa Park Woman's Club, 1936.

Post history, Villa Park American Legion Post 652.

*Recollections: Story of Villa Park.* Committee for the Bicentennial, Village of Villa Park, 1976.

*Villa Park Argus.* Various articles.

Villa Park Public Library History Committee File.

### Oral
### (Tapes)

Mrs. Howard Buck and Mrs. Eunice Plass
Mrs. Clara Lawson, granddaughter of Peter Case
Mrs. Bessie Mabee
Mr. and Mrs. Raymond Sears
Villa Park Chamber of Commerce dinner honoring Villa Park's long-time residents 9/10/75.
Villa Park History Interview at WKDC with June Krenzel and Sandi Toika 2/6/75.

### (Interviews)

Mrs. George Featherstone
Mr. and Mrs. Charles Karnstedt
Mr. Karl Pearson
Mr. John Sinibaldi
Mrs. Esther Wallen
Mr. and Mrs. George Williams

## WARRENVILLE

### Bibliography

Moore, Jean. *From Tower to Tower.* Wayside Press, Mendota, 1974.

Natzke, Barbara. *The Living Past of Warrenville.* 1964.

Schmidt, Leone. *Come Fly to the Prairie.* Wayside Press, Mendota, 1968.

Schmidt, Leone. *The Life and Times of Warrenville.* City Council of Warrenville, 1975.

Schmidt, Leone. *In and Around Warrenville.* Warrenville Historical Society, 1982.

*Warrenville Heritage Cookbook.* Warrenville Homemaker's Extension Unit. 1983.

*Warrenville Digest,* 1964–1983.

*Warrenville News,* issues from 1962–April, 1964.

### Audio-Visual

Porter, Doris. *Come Fly to the Prairie.* An historical musical video tape, 1983.

### Oral

Verna Anderson

Paul and Lillian Behr, John Behr and Eleanor Seymour

Lydelle Bentz

## WAYNE

Blatchford, Tannisse. *An Honorable Heritage: A Biography of Wayne Township, Illinois, 1834–1984.* Wayne Community Association, 1984.

Glos, Hattie G. and Weiser, Frederick S. *Wayne Community and Township History.* Privately printed July, 1953.

*The Plow and the Cross* – Biography of a Parish Church – Wayne, Illinois 1871–1971. *The Naperville Sun,* 1971.

The Woman's Club of Wayne scrapbooks, 1945–1983.

## WEST CHICAGO

Hardy, Beverly B. *The Heritage Homes of West Chicago.* Hardy Publications, 1976.

Scobey, Frank F. *A Random Review of West Chicago History.* West Chicago Historical Commission. West Chicago, 1976.

Walking Map of Historic West Chicago – brochure.

## WESTMONT

### Bibliography

Mahoney, John. *Holy Trinity Church School and Convent – the 20th Year.*

Van Koughnett, Scott. "Westmont – from Prairie to Condo." *The Challenger,* June 18, 1976.

Westmost Chamber of Commerce. *Westmont, Illinois Golden Jubilee.*

Westmont Park District, records.

### Oral

Eunice Grimm

Clifford and Joyce Feltz

Marge Smejkal

## WHEATON

*Annual Report, 1982.* City of Wheaton, Illinois, 1983.

*City of Wheaton, Handbook of the Chamber of Commerce.*

*Daily Journal* special sections and clippings:
The Spirit of '76, June 30, 1974.
It's a Woman's World, 1975, 1979.
The DuPage Heritage Notebook, June 27, 1982 and June 26, 1983.

*Milton Township Citizens' Handbook.*

Moore, Jean. *From Tower to Tower.* Wayside Press, Mendota, 1974.

Noble, Dick. *New Stirrings in Old Wheaton.* Files of Chamber of Commerce.

*Wheaton and Its Homes.* Wheaton Historic Preservation Council, Graham Burnham Press of Cramer, Atkenes & Cramer, Milwaukee, 1982 (reissued 1983.)

Willard, W. Wyeth. *Fire on the Prairie, Story of Wheaton College.* Van Kampen Press, Wheaton, 1950.

Vestuto, Frances. "The Town of Wheaton." Unpublished paper, 1981.

## WINFIELD

Spanke, Louise. *Winfield's Good Old Days: A History.* Winfield Public Library Board, 1978.

### Oral (Interviews)

Carol Anderton

Williams Enders

Rosemary Kelly

Patricia Stuart

## WOOD DALE

Mittle, Mary Lou. "Yesterday's Brides." Manuscript, February 14, 1983.

## WOODRIDGE

Greene, William Bertram. *The Greenes on the East Branch of the DuPage.* Author published, 1966.

Griffen, Kitty. "Woodridge Seeks Roots in Farm Past." *Suburban Life Graphic,* February 2, 1984.

Hogrewe, Doll Carlson. "Woodridge . . . from Farm Land to Growing Community." *Suburban Life Graphic,* September 3, 1977.

Williams, Dorothy A. *A History of Woodridge School District 68.* Published by the district, 1978.

"Woodridge Grows Rapidly in 17 Years." *Suburban Life Graphic,* July 3, 1976.

*Woodridge Progress,* 20th Anniversary special section, September 6, 1979.

Woodridge Sesquicentennial Committee, special newspaper, 1968.

# Index

# PATRONS

DuPage Bank and Trust (Glen Ellyn)
Elmhurst National Bank
Edwin & Lois Deicke
Brooks McCormick
Mr. & Mrs. George Pratt
Stephens Plumbing & Heating, Inc.
Harold A. Reskin
Mr. & Mrs. J. Robert Stockner
Dr. & Mrs. William Stroner
Amy E. Crisler
William and Corrine Weigt
Wheaton Pharmacy
Harold and Eva White
Trammel-Crow Co., Itasca

# DONORS

Terry and Jane Allen
Mr. & Mrs. Robert Baker
Mrs. Howard Boysen
Claire Brown
DuPage Society of Model Engineers
George F. Hammersmith, Sr.
Itasca Bank & Trust Company
Lee Jens
Jensen-Souders & Associates, Inc.
Dr. & Mrs. Mark J. Mayeau
Dr. & Mrs. Keith McHenry
Agnes M. Perrow
Charles P. Royer
Mr. & Mrs. Albert N. Schmidt
Mr. & Mrs. Emil Shebik
Mr. & Mrs. Jack Wallace
Mr. & Mrs. Eugene C. Wilson
York Furriers
Mr. & Mrs. C.W. Youker

## THE BOOK MANUFACTURE

Composition of *DuPage Roots* was by Professional Graphics of Itasca. Printing and binding was by Braun Brumfield, Inc., of Ann Arbor, Michigan. Production management was by Joyce Usher. The cover and text design was by John Goetz. The typeface is Times Roman.

# WESTERN TOUR

C.O.D. - 22nd & Lambert ______ 0.0
(S to Butterfield; E to Park; S to Rte. 53; right to:

MORTON ARBORETUM ______
(S to Warrenville Rd; W to Yackley, S to Ogden; W to:

BEAUBIEN TAVERN ______ 6.8
(SW on Plank Rd. to Columbia, S to School, W to Brainard, S to Franklin to:

NORTH CENTRAL COLLEGE ______ 9.2
(W to Washington, S to Hobson, E to:

BAILEY HOBSON HOME ______ 11.0
(W to Washington, N to Hillside, W to Webster and:

NAPER SETTLEMENT ______ 13.1
(N to Aurora Rd., W to Eagle, N to Jackson, W to Mill, N to Warrenville Rd., W to Winfield Rd., and NW corner to:

WARREN HOTEL ______ 17.3
(W to Second, N one block to:

OLD ALBRIGHT STUDIO ______ 17.5
(E to Winfield Rd., N past Butterfield to:

ST. JAMES FARM ______ 18.5
(S to Butterfield, W to Batavia Rd., SE to Main St. and NW corner to:

WARREN HOME ______ 20.0
(W to Fourth, S to Aurora Rd., W to:

WARRENVILLE CEMETERY ______ 20.4
(NW to Butterfield Rd., W to Eola Rd., S to:

BIG WOODS CONGREGATIONAL CHURCH ______ 23.4
(N to Butterfield, W to Kirk Rd., N to Wilson, E to Batavia Rd., to A Road, SW to:

FERMI LAB ______ 29.5
(NE to Wilson Rd., E on D (Batavia Rd) to Rte. 59, N to Gary's Mill Rd., E to:

GARY'S MILL SCHOOL ______ 33.0
(W to Rte. 59, N to Main St., W to 132 Main and:

WEST CHICAGO HISTORICAL MUSEUM ______ 35.6
(NW to Washington, SW to 185 and:

BOLLES OPERA HOUSE ______ 38.3
(E to Prince Crossing Rd., N to North Ave., W to Klein Rd, N to Smith, W to:

WAYNE CEMETERY ______ 43.7
(W to Petersdorf, N to Army Trail Rd., W to:

LITTLE HOME CHURCH BY THE WAYSIDE ______ 47.0
(E to Rte. 59, N (one block) to Schick, E to Morton, N to Lawrence, E to Jefferson, N to:

## BYWAYS

Sts. Peter & Paul Catholic Church at 26 N. Ellsworth
Willard Scott home, NW corner Franklin & Washington
Hobson School, opposite home
Hobson Mill grinding stones at Pioneer Park
Naperville Cemetery at Hillside

Centennial Beach at 500 W. Jackson

Cantigny Gardens & Museums at 1S151 Winfield Rd.
Site of Warrenville gristmill at Batavia & Fourth

Gates Home, NW corner of Rte. 59 and Forest
Heritage Commons at 475 Main

Chauncey Reed house 38.7
Campbell Soup Research Depot at 40.3
Old Wayne Golf Club at 41.7

Samuel Dunham 1852 home at 32 W 215 Army Trail Rd.; Dunham Riding Club & Mark Dunham "Castle" at SE & NW corners of Army Trail & Dunham Road